A Communion of Love

A Communion of Love

The Christ-Centered Spirituality of
Robert Murray M'Cheyne

JORDAN STONE

Foreword by J. Stephen Yuille

WIPF & STOCK · Eugene, Oregon

A COMMUNION OF LOVE
The Christ-Centered Spirituality of Robert Murray M'Cheyne

Copyright © 2019 Jordan Mark Stone. All rights reserved. Except for brief quotations in critical publications or reviews, no part of this book may be reproduced in any manner without prior written permission from the publisher. Write: Permissions, Wipf and Stock Publishers, 199 W. 8th Ave., Suite 3, Eugene, OR 97401.

Wipf & Stock
An Imprint of Wipf and Stock Publishers
199 W. 8th Ave., Suite 3
Eugene, OR 97401

www.wipfandstock.com

PAPERBACK ISBN: 978-1-5326-7206-4
HARDCOVER ISBN: 978-1-5326-7207-1
EBOOK ISBN: 978-1-5326-7208-8

Manufactured in the U.S.A.   JANUARY 24, 2019

For Matt Boswell, David Rea,
Dr. R. Carlton Wynne, and Afshin Ziafat—
champions of Christ.

Contents

Foreword by J. Stephen Yuille | xi
Preface | xv
Abbreviations | xvii

1. Introduction | 1
    Thesis | 3
    History of Research | 4
    Methodology | 9

2. Trusting Christ: M'Cheyne's Story | 13
    Formative Years (1813–1831) | 13
    Training (1831–1835) | 21
    Ministry (1835–1843) | 27
    Conclusion | 42

3. Learning Christ: M'Cheyne's Context | 43
    Ecclesiastical Context | 44
    Philosophical Context | 52
    Cultural Context | 56
    Pastoral Influences | 60
    Historical Influences | 67
    Conclusion | 72

4. Knowing Christ: M'Cheyne's Theology | 74
    The Westminster Confession of Faith | 75
    The Free Offer of the Gospel | 93
    Conclusion | 97

5. Loving Christ: M'Cheyne's Devotion | 99
    The Expression of Love | 100
    The Demonstration of Love | 107
    The Manifestation of Love | 116
    Conclusion | 119

6. Communing With Christ: M'Cheyne's Sacramentalism | 121
    The Word of God | 122
    The Sacraments | 126
    Prayer | 135
    Conclusion | 144

7. Proclaiming Christ: M'Cheyne's Preaching | 146
    M'Cheyne's Method | 146
    M'Cheyne's Manner | 149
    M'Cheyne's Message | 153
    Conclusion | 165

8. Offering Christ: M'Cheyne's Evangelism | 168
    Evangelism and Visitation | 171
    Evangelism and Children | 175
    Evangelism and Revival | 178
    Evangelism and Church Extension | 184
    Conclusion | 187

9. Delighting in Christ: M'Cheyne's Sabbatarianism | 189
    The Sabbath Railway Controversy | 191
    Defense of Sabbath-Keeping | 194
    Personal Devotion to Sabbath-Keeping | 200
    Congregational Exhortation to Sabbath-Keeping | 203
    Conclusion | 206

10. Looking For Christ: M'Cheyne's Millenialism | 208
    Influences | 209
    Expectations | 214
    Implications | 217
    The Christ of Eternity | 220
    Conclusion | 224

11. Conclusion | 225

Appendix | 229
    Notebooks | 229
    Letters | 230

Bibliography | 231

Index | 251

Foreword

THE APOSTLE PAUL DESCRIBES the saints at Ephesus as "being rooted and grounded in love" (Eph 3:17). The term "rooted" suggests a tree while the term "grounded" suggests a building; therefore, Paul's point seems to be that just as the earth sustains a tree, and the foundation supports a building, so too God's love sustains and supports his people. Convinced of this, Paul asks God to enable the Ephesian believers "to comprehend with all the saints what is the breadth and length and height and depth, and to know the love of Christ that surpasses knowledge" (v. 18). Interestingly, he makes two requests in this verse. First, he prays that they would "comprehend" God's love—that is, know it *conceptually*. He wants them to understand that it is boundless: its breadth is without border; its length is without end; its height is without limit; and its depth is without measure. Second, he prays that they would "know" God's love—that is, know it *experientially*. In the context, he wants them to grasp the dimensions of God's love (which surpass conceptual knowledge) in their daily experience. When they do, they will be "filled with all the fullness of God" (v. 19).

Throughout its history the church has struggled to maintain the balance between this *conceptual* and *experiential* knowledge, often emphasizing the head (the speculative) at the expense of the heart (the affective) or vice versa. Avoiding these extremes is a tall order, and this is one of the reasons why those individuals who exemplify a religion of both the head and the heart capture our special interest and merit our careful attention. In *A Communion of Love*, Dr. Jordan Stone introduces us to one such individual: Robert Murray M'Cheyne.

It has been my pleasure to read Dr. Stone's work in its various stages of development, and I have gleaned a great deal from his insights and conclusions. It is now my privilege to recommend it to you in its final form. What can you expect as you read this weighty monograph?

First, we have a superb introduction into the field of M'Cheyne studies. Dr. Stone demonstrates his extensive knowledge of all previous studies of M'Cheyne's theology and spirituality as well as his familiarity with the broader literature that deals with M'Cheyne's social, intellectual, theological, and ecclesiastical setting. Sorting through this material is a sizeable task in itself, and Dr. Stone has done an admirable job at engaging with it while ultimately providing a fresh analysis of M'Cheyne based on his own letters, sermons, and diaries.

Second, we have an insightful analysis of the various portraits of M'Cheyne that have been presented over the past two centuries. These have tended to depict him as an archetype of personal holiness without ever considering the doctrinal loci that serve as the foundation for his practice of holiness—namely, the person and work of Christ. Dr. Stone rectifies this oversight by moving the discussion away from the *how* of M'Cheyne's spirituality to the *why*. While acknowledging (among other things) M'Cheyne's ardent pursuit of holiness, fervent devotion to the means of grace, and uncompromising observation of the Lord's Day, Dr. Stone shows that the common driving force behind all these things is love. In a word, M'Cheyne was consumed with Christ's love for him and compelled by his love for Christ.

Third, we have a poignant example of what it means to wed sound theology and deep piety. M'Cheyne preached doctrine with warmth and simplicity, and he lived out that doctrine with conviction and sincerity. While he stood at a unique cultural, philosophical, and ecclesiastical moment in Scottish history, he was unwavering in his commitment to a doctrinal tradition encapsulated in the Westminster standards. It was within the framework of this tradition that he emphasized a theology centered on knowing God's love in Christ, and a spirituality focused on returning love to Christ. In this way, M'Cheyne illustrates the inseparable relationship that exists between faith and love, doctrine and practice, creed and conduct.

Fourth, we have an important glimpse into what true devotion to Christ looks like. M'Cheyne pursued holiness because he viewed it as a profound expression of love for Christ. He was so diligent in his use of the means of grace because he believed these were special occasions when he communed with Christ. He preached the gospel with such fervency, and exalted Christ with such regularity, because he was convinced that

Christ was altogether lovely. He observed the Sabbath with such singular devotion because he was certain that it was the day on which Christ delighted to visit his people. From start to finish, therefore, M'Cheyne's spirituality was shaped by Christ's love for him and his love for Christ—a communion of love indeed.

That is but a sampling of what awaits the reader in the pages that follow. For his painstaking research, discerning analysis, and compelling presentation of Robert Murray M'Cheyne, Dr. Stone is to be commended. My sincere prayer is that his work will receive the attention and appreciation it deserves.

J. STEPHEN YUILLE
Associate Professor of Biblical Spirituality
The Southern Baptist Theological Seminary, Louisville, KY

Preface

In 2007, I first encountered Robert Murray M'Cheyne when reading D. Martyn Lloyd-Jones's *Preaching and Preachers*. In these lectures given at Westminster Seminary in Philadelphia, Lloyd-Jones reminded,

> You remember what was said of the saintly Robert Murray McCheyne of Scotland in the last century. It is said that when he appeared in the pulpit, even before he had uttered a single word, people would begin to weep silently. Why? Because of this very element of seriousness. The very sight of the man gave the impression that he had come from the presence of God and that he was to deliver a message from God to them. That is what had such an effect upon people even before he had opened his mouth.

Lloyd-Jones's comments sent me on a quest to know more about "the saintly" M'Cheyne. What I learned captivated me.

So it was, in 2015, that I began PhD studies at The Southern Baptist Theological Seminary knowing I wanted to study M'Cheyne. I initially planned to examine M'Cheyne's vast ministerial network and its subsequent influence in the Free Church of Scotland. As I studied the sources, I saw a need to think more foundationally about the theology that drove M'Cheyne's famous piety. I am grateful for such a shift in my study's focus. The redirection let me ask questions that every young pastor should consider: How is Christ central in the Christian ministry? What is the relationship between ministerial piety and a Spirit-blessed congregation? What kind of preaching does God bless? What prerequisites fuel revival in churches, cities, and countries?

M'Cheyne's legacy has encouraged my pastoral soul countless times ever since in answering such questions. His love for Christ convicts me, his preaching inspires me, and his ministry instructs me.

PREFACE

What you now hold in your hands is the fruit of my doctoral studies. I am thankful for those who helped bring this project come to completion. Enormous credit goes to Dr. J. Stephen Yuille, who stewarded this work from start to finish. He is a charter member of the modern-day M'Cheyne School. I am grateful for Mark Belonga's initial reading and feedback. Dr. Sinclair B. Ferguson read the dissertation and offered many needed corrections and insights. I am also indebted to those family members and friends who supported me with constant prayer. Of course, this study would never have happened without my wife, Emily. She is my beloved rose of Sharon. Our six little children provided an endless stream of joyful distractions from my research. It is now my delight to tell them, "I finally finished 'the Mr. M'Cheyne book.'"

JORDAN MARK STONE
McKinney, Texas
October 2018

Abbreviations

BOF	*Basket of Fragments*
CIS	*Comfort in Sorrow*
FL	*Familiar Letters*
HTD	*Helps to Devotion*
MACCH	Manuscripts of Robert Murray M'Cheyne, New College Library, Edinburgh
MAR	*Memoir and Remains of Robert Murray M'Cheyne*
NTS	*New Testament Sermons*
OTS	*Old Testament Sermons*
SC	*The Seven Churches of Asia*
SOH	*Sermons on Hebrews*
TBJ	*The Believer's Joy*
TPH	*From the Preacher's Heart*
TPP	*The Passionate Preacher*
WCF	*Westminster Confession of Faith*
WLC	*Westminster Larger Catechism*
WSC	*Westminster Shorter Catechism*

1

Introduction

THE CHRISTIAN LIFE IS a spiritual life. We praise the God who is Spirit (John 4:24). We trust in Christ who has redeemed us and poured out the Holy Spirit upon us, so that we might grow in the holiness required to see God (Heb 12:14). Our walk of union and communion with Christ involves keeping in step with the Holy Spirit (Gal 5:25), as we seek to mortify sin and live to righteousness. As such, historic Christianity has always concerned itself with the nature of spirituality.[1] All Christian traditions have unique emphases in their view of the Christian life.[2] Some Christian traditions accentuate ritual sacramentalism, others, a second blessing or baptism of the Holy Spirit, others, a crisis experience in sanctification, and yet others, the practice of the spiritual disciplines. One missing note in the growing discussions related to spirituality is how a truly biblical view of Christian spirituality must focus on God's revelation in Christ.[3] He is our life and our all (Col 3:4–5). Michael Haykin summarizes the biblical basis for a Christ-centered spirituality as follows:

---

1. Alistair McGrath defines spirituality as "the outworking in real life of a person's religious faith." McGrath, *Christian Spirituality*, 2. Hughes Oliphant Old notes, "Calvinists have usually preferred the term *piety* to the term *spirituality*." Old, "What is Reformed Spirituality?," 8 (emphasis original). See also, Old, "Rescuing Spirituality from the Cloister," 27–29. The present volume uses the terms "spirituality" and "piety" interchangeably.

2. For overviews of the various Protestant understandings of spirituality, see Gundry, *Five Views of Sanctification*; Alexander, *Christian Spirituality*.

3. Joel Beeke asserts, "The problem with most spirituality today is that it is not closely moored in Scripture and too often degenerates into unbiblical mysticism."

The New Testament is filled from start to finish with ardent devotion to Jesus Christ. He is declared to be the fountain of knowledge and wisdom (Col. 2:3), the One who sustains every particle of the universe and every fibre of our being (Col. 1:16–17; Heb. 1:3). He is set forth as the supreme reason for living (2 Cor. 5:9). Gazing into his face one can see perfectly and without the slightest distortion the very glory of God (Heb. 1:3). He owns the angels (Matt. 24:31), and they know well their Master and are not afraid to bow in worship before him (Heb. 1:6). To him belongs the incredible privilege of bestowing the Spirit of God upon whom he wishes (Acts 2:33). And his name is supremely precious because by no other name can sinners be saved (Acts 4:12).[4]

One notable example of such Christ-centered spirituality is Robert Murray M'Cheyne (1813–1843).[5] He fixed his eyes on Christ with uncommon passion. His life's ambition was to encourage every man, woman, boy, and girl to look upon Christ. To that end, he proclaimed,

> When you gaze upon the sun, it makes everything else tasteless; so when you taste honey, it makes everything else tasteless; so when your soul feeds on Jesus, it takes away the sweetness of all earthly things—praise, pleasure, fleshly lusts, all lose their sweetness. Keep a continued gaze. Run, looking unto Jesus. Look, till the way of salvation by Jesus fills up the whole horizon, so glorious and peace-speaking. So will the world be crucified to you, and you unto the world.[6]

M'Cheyne offers a model of Christ-centered spirituality that merits attention.

Beeke, *Puritan Reformed Spirituality*, vii. Other recent studies dealing with Christ-centered spirituality include Matthews, *Anxious Souls Will Ask*; Kelly, "Freedom and Discipline"; Yuille, *Looking Unto Jesus*; Ferguson, *In Christ Alone*; Goodwin, *A Habitual Sight*; Willard, "Christ-Centered Piety"; Burns, *A Supreme Desire*.

4. Haykin, *The God Who Draws Near*, 23–24.

5. A brief survey of the sources reveals no agreement on the spelling of his last name. John Ross writes, "Andrew Bonar in his *Memoirs and Remains of Robert Murray M'Cheyne* abbreviated the Mac or Mc to M', thus M'Cheyne." Ross, "Man About Town," 29. Following Ian Hamilton, the present work employs "M'Cheyne" unless an original quotation contains an alternate spelling. See Cameron et al., *Dictionary of Scottish Church*, 504–5.

6. *MAR*, 380. M'Cheyne longed for a generation of Christians who would be "witnesses for Christ, who saw the king's face and testified of his beauty." *MAR*, 166.

THESIS

The primary objective of this dissertation is to demonstrate the crucial place that love for Christ occupies in M'Cheyne's spirituality. His theology centered on knowing God's love in Christ, and his spirituality was essentially his return of love to Christ. For M'Cheyne, the pursuit of holiness was the mature expression of what it means to know the love of Christ and return love to Christ. Previous studies on M'Cheyne have noted the centrality of Christ in his ministry,[7] but they have not demonstrated how a communion of love forms the animating principle behind his Christocentric spirituality.

This dissertation will also give some attention to M'Cheyne's historical context. His spirituality did not develop in a vacuum. A number of factors influenced and encouraged his view of the Christian life. (1) Theologically, M'Cheyne held to the Westminster Standards. In short, he was unoriginal in his theological formulations. (2) Culturally, M'Cheyne lived in a milieu affected deeply by romanticism and burgeoning Victorian values. Crawford Gribben observes that M'Cheyne, after his death, became known as "the patron saint of Victorian evangelicals."[8] William Blaikie notes the element of pathos in M'Cheyne's ministry, saying that M'Cheyne brought "winsomeness" to the pulpit—"an almost feminine quality."[9] (3) Philosophically, M'Cheyne ministered in a context that offered new contours and challenges to enlightenment thinking. Scottish common sense realism "enabled Evangelicals to express in a fresh way their belief in the accessibility of God."[10]

These elements combined with such powerful pastoral and personal influences as Henry Duncan, Thomas Chalmers, John Bonar, and Robert Smith Candlish. Collectively, they provided the context for the formulation and expression of M'Cheyne's communion of love with Christ.

---

7. For example, David Robertson writes, "McCheyne's theology was a key part of his success. It is not that the theology was incidental, nor that it was something that he had to overcome by experience or character. Rather it was the theology that shaped his experience and his character. Theology is the study of God. McCheyne was absorbed by Jesus Christ and he desired to know him better." Robertson, *Awakening*, 217. David Yeaworth is more succinct: "The core of McCheyne's message was the person and work of Jesus Christ, and His relation to God and man." Yeaworth, "Robert Murray M'Cheyne," 231.

8. Gribben and Stunt, *Prisoners of Hope?*, 191.

9. Blaikie, *Preachers of Scotland*, 294–95.

10. Bebbington, *Evangelicalism in Modern Britain*, 59.

HISTORY OF RESEARCH

The most notable works published on M'Cheyne are biographies. Andrew Bonar set the standard with his 1844 book, *The Life of Robert Murray M'Cheyne*.[11] His appreciative volume fits within the biographical tenor of the time.[12] J. C. Smith's *Robert Murray M'Cheyne: A Good Minister of Jesus Christ* followed in 1870.[13] It contains several points of interest but is too diffuse to be of much value. In 1896, Kirkwood Hewat arranged and published excerpts related to M'Cheyne from William Lamb's diary as *M'Cheyne from the Pew*.[14] The diary proves to be an attractive source of firsthand material. Alexander Smellie's *Robert Murray McCheyne* was the first major biography on M'Cheyne published in the twentieth century. Smellie does not offer any new insights into M'Cheyne, which is a disappointment given his access to previously unavailable manuscripts.[15] James A. Stewart's *Robert Murray M'Cheyne: Scholar, Saint, Seer, and Soul-Winner* was published in 1964, and is little more than a collection of highlights from M'Cheyne's letters and sermons.[16] Handsel Publications produced a small book entitled, *Let the Fire Burn*, in 1978, and devoted one of its three chapters to M'Cheyne.[17] No new biographical works were forthcoming until 2002 when Christian Focus translated into English L. J. Van Valen's *Constrained by Love: A New Biography on Robert Murray McCheyne*.[18] His research is vast, and makes a substantial contribution to the field. Not long after this, David Robertson's *Awakening: The Life and Ministry of Robert Murray McCheyne* appeared. Robertson's book is of interest for two reasons. First, he is the current pastor at M'Cheyne's church in Dundee—St. Peter's. Second, Robertson began his research skeptical of

---

11. Bonar, *Life of Robert Murray M'Cheyne*.

12. Marcus Loane comments, "The *Memoir* . . . has all the hallmarks of fine Victorian spiritual biography." Loane, *They Were Pilgrims*, 144.

13. Smith, *Robert Murray M'Cheyne*.

14. Lamb, *M'Cheyne from the Pew*. Lamb served first as a Sabbath school teacher at St. Peter's, and then as its superintendent. He was subsequently ordained as a ruling elder and served as session clerk.

15. Smellie, *Biography of R. M. McCheyne*, 1995.

16. Stewart, *Robert Murray McCheyne*.

17. Hudson, Jarvie, and Stein, *Let Fire Burn*, 4–23. For other twentieth century volumes that also include chapters devoted to M'Cheyne, see Loane, *They Were Pilgrims*, 139–83; Miller, *Ten Famous Evangelists*, later published as a stand-alone booklet, Miller, *Robert Murray M'Cheyne*; Gordon, *Evangelical Spirituality*, 111–47.

18. Van Valen, *Constrained by His Love*.

M'Cheyne's "saintly" legacy. He thus writes with an objectivity not always found in the M'Cheyne lore. Two years later, Peter Jeffrey committed a chapter to M'Cheyne in his *Preachers Who Made a Difference*.[19] Derek Prime's biographical tour, *Robert Murray McCheyne: In the Footsteps of a Godly Pastor*, is an excellent introduction to M'Cheyne's life and times.[20] The most recent popular work on M'Cheyne is Bruce McLennan's *M'Cheyne's Dundee*.[21] McLennan focuses on M'Cheyne's years at St. Peter's, giving much attention to its effect on the city of Dundee.

Although M'Cheyne's life and ministry continue to generate discussion,[22] he has received little academic attention. In 1954, Virginia Robinson's master's thesis at Biblical Seminary examined M'Cheyne's ministry to young people.[23] Three years later, David Victor Yeaworth completed the only PhD dissertation to date on M'Cheyne, titled "Robert Murray M'Cheyne (1813–1843): A Study of an Early Nineteenth-Century Scottish Evangelical." The project situates M'Cheyne in his wider cultural and ecclesiastical context. Yeaworth believes that M'Cheyne "typified the Evangelical spirit of the early nineteenth century."[24] His stated purpose "is to portray McCheyne as a typical Evangelical minister—not merely a 'saint' but a man—whose spark was an intense spirituality, and yet

---

19. Jeffrey, *Preachers Who Made a Difference*, 64–72.
20. Prime, *Robert Murray McCheyne*.
21. McLennan, *McCheyne's Dundee*.
22. In the twenty-first century alone, a wide array of authors use M'Cheyne to bolster their arguments. A sampling includes, Beeke, *Puritan Reformed Spirituality*, 163–64; Beeke, *Living for God's Glory*, 271; Begg and Ferguson, *Name Above All Names*, 37; Bloom, *Things Not Seen*, 13; Murison, "'Old Favourites' or 'New Styles,'" 76; Carson, *Praying with Paul*, xii, 3; Carson, *For the Love of God*; Coleman, *Heart of the Gospel*, 196; Fernando, *Acts*, 184, 492; Fernando, *Call to Joy*, 134, 169, 183–84; Helopoulos, *New Pastor's Handbook*, 76; Hildebrand, *Praying the Psalms*; Hughes, *Disciplines of a Godly Woman*, 223; Kea, *Amazed by Grace*, 42–43; Keller, *Walking with God*, 150–51; Keller, *Encounters with Jesus*, 164; Kyle, *An Uncommon Christian*, 51; MacIntosh and Graham, *Falling in Love*, 9; McCraw, *Victorian Dundee*, 56; Morgan and Peterson, *Hell Under Fire*, 223–24; Packer and Nystrom, *Praying*, 145; Lewis, *Future Shape*, 105; Palau, Sorenson, and Sorenson, *Stop Pretending*, 152; Begg and Prime, *On Being a Pastor*, 35; Reid, *Light the Fire*, 17, 40, 64; Sarkissian, *Before God*, 215–25; Carson, *Telling the Truth*, 179; Sloan and Wray, *A Life That Matters*, 121; Stewart, *British and Irish Poets*, 249; Wiersbe, *Be Equipped*, 103; Wilkinson, *For Zion's Sake*, 204; Wolffe, *Expansion of Evangelicalism*, 86.
23. Cheney, "Approaches to Spiritual Problem."
24. Yeaworth, "Robert Murray McCheyne," xi.

whose human involvements were sane and well balanced."[25] Yeaworth's work functions as something like a contextual biography, arguing that M'Cheyne was not a saint pursuing piety in isolation, but as "a man of the time." The most recent academic work on M'Cheyne arrived in 2014 when David Beaty published his Gordon-Conwell D.Min. project as *An All-Encompassing Fellowship: Learning from Robert Murray M'Cheyne's Communion with God*.[26] Beaty's work is clear and pastoral, if not academically rigorous. He presents the basic spiritual and devotional lessons M'Cheyne offers to Christians today.

M'Cheyne's sermons continue to be printed. In 1975, Christian Focus republished a collection of M'Cheyne's sermons entitled, *A Basket of Fragments*. In 1987, Free Presbyterian Publications republished an 1858 collection of eight sermons and two communion addresses from M'Cheyne under the title, *The Believer's Joy*. Then, in 1993, Christian Focus reprinted an 1846 volume of sixty-four sermons and fifteen lectures, retitled as, *From the Preacher's Heart*. Six years later, Christian Focus put out yet another M'Cheyne anthology, *The Passionate Preacher*, which totals fifty-eight previously unpublished sermons. Editor Michael McMullen writes in the preface, "This present volume is an addition to [M'Cheyne's] corpus, but a very special addition, for it contains, to the best knowledge of the editor, sermons taken directly from the manuscripts of McCheyne and sermons, therefore, which have never before been published."[27] McMullen, Professor of Church History at Midwestern Baptist Theological Seminary, edited more unpublished sermons a few years later. Banner of Truth published them as a three-volume set in 2004, respectively titled, *Old Testament Sermons, New Testament Sermons*, and *Sermons on Hebrews*. McMullen provides some background to the recently released sermons:

> The vast majority of the sermons in this set of three volumes are taken directly from M'Cheyne's original handwritten sermon manuscripts. A few were published in the nineteenth century but never reprinted, some in *Revival Truth: Being Sermons Hitherto Unpublished*. This was a small volume published in 1860 and edited by William Reid. In Alexander Smellie's biography of M'Cheyne, published in 1913, we read of Smellie receiving an unexpected parcel from James Macdonald of Edinburgh.

---

25. Yeaworth, "Robert Murray McCheyne," xii.
26. Beaty, *An All-Surpassing Fellowship*.
27. *TPP*, 9.

> The parcel was, says Smellie, altogether priceless, containing as it did, numerous M'Cheyne manuscripts, including letters to and from his family and friends; notebooks (several of which have been used in these volumes); sermons (some appear here); and documents of different kinds. Smellie was lent this material in preparation for a volume that later became his biography of M'Cheyne. Macdonald had purchased the box and contents from William Scott of Thornhill, at that time one of the few surviving relatives of the M'Cheynes. Macdonald proposed to give the content to the Jewish Committee of the United Free Church of Scotland, to be preserved in the Library of New College, Edinburgh, and this is where they are today.[28]

As biographies on M'Cheyne and sermons from M'Cheyne remain in print, it is not surprising to find his legacy is alive and well. What kind of legacy is it?

On October 2, 1840, Robert Murray M'Cheyne wrote a few words of counsel to Dan Edwards: "In great measure, according to the purity and perfections of the instrument, will be the success. It is not great talents God blesses so much as great likeness to Jesus. A holy minister is an awful weapon in the hand of God."[29] The last two sentences are among the most quoted statements from M'Cheyne.[30] They also summarize, for most people, the heartbeat of M'Cheyne. L. J. Van Valen, for example, affirms that "the great secret of M'Cheyne's proclamation is holiness."[31] Likewise, David Yeaworth says, "The key to McCheyne's ministerial success lay in his personal holiness and its manifestation to those around him."[32] A few years after M'Cheyne's death, John Angell James referred to him "that seraphic man."[33] J. W. Alexander, the great pastor-theologian of Princeton

---

28. *NTS*, xii.

29. *MAR*, 282.

30. The quote most commonly attributed to M'Cheyne is, "The greatest need of my people is my personal holiness." The statement appears apocryphal. This epigram is heralded far and wide by men like J. I. Packer as quoted in Lewis, *Future Shape*, 105; Fernando, *Acts*, 184, 492; Coleman, *Heart of the Gospel*, 196; Carson, *Telling the Truth*, 179; Helopoulos, *New Pastor's Handbook*, 76; Piper, "He Kissed the Rose," lines 355–56; Sargent, *Sacred Anointing*, 128; Olford and Olford, *Anointed Expository Preaching*, 221; Boice, *Renewing Your Mind*, 44. If any of the works cite the quotation, they reference Bonar's *Memoir and Works* without a page number. The quote is not found in any edition of *Memoir*.

31. Van Valen, *Constrained by His Love*, 477.

32. Yeaworth, "Robert Murray M'Cheyne," 96.

33. James, *An Earnest Ministry*, 120.

Seminary, wrote to a friend, "The [holy] life of M'Cheyne humbles me. What zeal and faith! What a proof that Old Calvinism is not insusceptible of being used as an arousing instrument!"[34] According to *The Methodist Review*, M'Cheyne was "a marvel . . . of holiness."[35] In the words of *The Christian Review*, he was a man "eminently devoted to God."[36] He was, to Martyn-Lloyd Jones, the "saintly Robert Murray M'Cheyne."[37] A. T. B. McGowan called him the "godly preacher."[38] Derek Prime and Alistair Begg echo this sentiment in their work on pastoral ministry, saying that M'Cheyne was "the godly Dundee minister."[39] David Robertson, the current pastor of St. Peter's Dundee and M'Cheyne biographer, humorously recounts his exasperation at how many people were interested in seeing "the godly Robert Murray M'Cheyne's church."[40] After earnest study, Robertson concluded that M'Cheyne was in fact peculiarly holy, and that this holiness was the key to his success.[41] David Beaty introduces his valuable study by asserting that M'Cheyne's "enduring influence flows from the depth and vibrancy of his walk with God."[42]

The consensus is widespread: M'Cheyne's personal holiness was his ministry's enlivening power. Modern studies on M'Cheyne are correct in highlighting his unwavering pursuit of holiness, yet they fall short in their assertion that it lies at the center of his spirituality. What tends to go unnoticed is that M'Cheyne's pursuit of holiness is the direct result of his

---

34. Quoted in Garretson, *Thoughts on Preaching*, 210.

35. Whedon, *Methodist Review*, 172.

36. Smith, *Christian Review*, 581.

37. Lloyd-Jones, *Preaching and Preachers*, 231. See also, Carson, *For the Love*, 11.

38. McKim and Wright, *Encyclopedia*, 230.

39. Begg and Prime, *On Being a Pastor*, 35.

40. Robertson, *Awakening*, 9. Derek Prime recounts similar initial sentiments regarding M'Cheyne: "'Too good to be true' was my reaction when I first heard people speak of McCheyne. Gifted as a student, pastor, teacher, poet, hymn-writer, and artist—so much was complimentary. This meant that I read biographies of him with a degree of skepticism. However, the more I read, the more I was convinced of the value of his godly influence and the enriching qualities of his example." Prime, *Robert Murray McCheyne*, 5.

41. He adds, "I became amazed, angry, and awakened. Amazed at the relevance of McCheyne for today, angry that the hagiography and ignorance about him has largely obscured that relevance, and awakened to the wonder of the gospel." Robertson, *Awakening*, 10.

42. Beaty, *An All-Surpassing Fellowship*, 2.

love for Christ. James Hamilton expressed something of this in a letter to M'Cheyne's father upon hearing of Robert's death:

> I never knew one so instant in season and out of season, so impressed with the invisible realities, and so faithful in reproving sin and witnessing for Christ . . . *Love to Christ was the great secret of all his devotion and consistency*, and since the days of Samuel Rutherford, I question if the Church of Scotland has contained a more seraphic mind, one that was in such constant flame of love and adoration toward Him that liveth and was dead.[43]

METHODOLOGY

Andrew Bonar mentions that M'Cheyne's preaching "was little else than a giving out of his own inward life."[44] What is noticeable in M'Cheyne's sermons is how Christ, in all his beauty and glory, occupies the center, while the pursuit of holiness flows from the center like rays from the sun. "This is the chief object of the Bible," he announced, "to show you the work, the beauty, the glory, the excellency of [Christ]."[45] Based on Revelation 2:1–7 he declared,

> Ministers only shine as long as they are in the hand of Christ. People now look too much to ministers; they expect to get wisdom from them; but we are not put up to be between you and Christ. As I have told you before, the only use of the pole was to hold up the brazen serpent. No one thought of looking at the pole: so are we here to hold up Christ in the sight of you all; we are to give testimony to the truth; we are witness for Christ; we are to hold up Jesus before you, and before ourselves too: so that we shall disappear, and nothing shall be seen but Christ.[46]

---

43. James Hamilton, quoted in Smellie, *Biography of R. M. McCheyne*, 173 (emphasis added).

44. *MAR*, 28.

45. *SOH*, 87.

46. See also, *TPH*, 75. "The saved soul longs to give glory to Christ," M'Cheyne said in a sermon entitled "The Song to Jesus." *TBJ*, 68. "He looks back over all the way by which he has been led, and says from the bottom of his heart, *to him be the glory*. He looks to the love of Jesus—to his awakening, drawing, washing, renewing, making him a king and a priest. Ministers may have been used as instruments, but he looks far beyond these and says, *to him be the glory*. A true Christian will cast his crown nowhere but at the feet of Jesus." M'Cheyne warned his congregation of the danger of

A study of M'Cheyne's spirituality that concentrates on the minister at the expense of his exaltation of Christ, misses the point. For, in M'Cheyne's ministry, Christ undeniably held the center. Bonar says of M'Cheyne's preaching, "It was not *doctrine* alone that he preached; it was *Christ*, from whom all doctrine shoots forth as rays from a centre."[47] M'Cheyne noted this emphasis in his diary, writing, "It is strange how sweet and precious it is to preach directly about Christ, compared with all other subjects of preaching."[48]

This christological emphasis is the key to understanding M'Cheyne. James Gordon correctly notes, "M'Cheyne seemed to have a heightened awareness of the reality and near presence of Christ, and sensed in him a fragrance and loveliness that was breathtaking in power and attraction. The suffering of the crucified Jesus kindled an ardor and devotion he could sometimes barely contain."[49] He labored to point people to the love *of* Christ, and to lead them to show love *to* Christ in return. Love to Christ is the pulsating power of his piety. In his exposition of 2 Corinthians 5:14, M'Cheyne expounded Christ's love and what his love compels in his people's lives. God knows that our desire for sin regularly outweighs our desire for holiness, therefore, "He hath invented a way of *drawing us* to holiness. By showing us the love of his Son, he calleth forth our love."[50] The love of Christ, according to M'Cheyne, "is the secret spring of all the holiness of the saints." The cause of holiness is clear: "We are constrained to holiness by the love of Christ."[51]

---

making a savior out of sanctification. He said, "Study sanctification to the uttermost but see thou make not a Christ of it, else it will come down one way or another." TPP, 196. At the close of a communion service, M'Cheyne similarly declared, "Study sanctification to the utmost, but make not a Christ of it. God hates this idol more than all others, because it comes in the place of Christ; it sits on Christ's throne." *MAR*, 462. Such sentiment reflects a common seventeenth-century concern in Puritan piety, as demonstrated by the following words from Thomas Wilcox: "In every prayer, in every ordinance, labor after sanctification to your utmost, but make not a Christ of it to save you. If so, it must come down one way or another." Quoted in Yuille, *Looking unto Jesus*, 10. The importance of magnifying Christ, not the minister, was vital because M'Cheyne himself struggled with it: "*I see a man cannot be a faithful minister, until he preaches Christ for Christ's sake*—until he gives up striving to attract people to himself, and seeks only to attract them to Christ. Lord, give me this!" *MAR*, 45 (emphasis original).

47. *MAR*, 65.
48. *MAR*, 65.
49. Gordon, *Evangelical Spirituality*, 128–29.
50. *TPH*, 52 (emphasis original).
51. *TPH*, 53.

Most studies on M'Cheyne's spirituality concentrate on how he used the means of grace in his personal pursuit of holiness. However, a right focus on M'Cheyne's spirituality starts with why, not how, he used the means of grace. He believed it is through these means that Christ's love descends while the church's love ascends. Nothing demonstrates this better than his preference for speaking of the means of grace as "trysts"—meetings between lovers:

> In the daily reading of the Word, Christ pays daily visits to the soul. In the daily prayer, Christ reveals himself to his own in that other way than he doth to the world. In the house of God Christ comes to his own, and says: 'Peace be unto you!' And in the sacrament he makes himself known to them in the breaking of bread, and they cry out: "It is the Lord!" These are all trysting times, when the Savior comes to visit his own.[52]

> The Sabbath is Christ's trysting time with his church. If you love him, you will count every moment of it precious. You will rise early and sit up late, to have a long day with Christ.[53]

> The hour of daily devotion is a trysting house with Christ.... The Lord's Table is the most famous trysting place with Christ.[54]

> [Gathered worship] is a trysting place with Christ. It is the audience chamber where he comes to commune with us from the mercy-seat.[55]

> We love everything that is Christ's (word, prayer, sacrament, fellowship).... We love his House. It is our trysting-place with Christ, where he meets with us and communes with us from off the mercy-seat.[56]

For M'Cheyne, the means of grace were pathways for loving communion with Christ. Why, then, did he famously pray, "Lord, make me as holy as a pardoned sinner can be made?"[57] He did so because he viewed holi-

---

52. *TPH*, 232–33.
53. *TPP*, 330. See also, *SOH*, 32–33.
54. *TPH*, 234.
55. *TPP*, 28.
56. *TPP*, 33.
57. *MAR*, 160.

ness as the mature and indeed highest experience of love for Christ. He said the ordinary desires of a redeemed heart are "communion with God; the delighting in Him; loving, adoring, admiring Him."[58] These were the consistent expressions of M'Cheyne's life in Christ.

M'Cheyne's name will be linked forever with Andrew Bonar's biographical work. According to Charles Spurgeon, "[Bonar's *Memoir and Remains of Robert Murray M'Cheyne*] is one of the best and most profitable volumes ever published. The memoir of such a man ought surely to be in the hands of every Christian and certainly every preacher of the Gospel."[59] Countless people have read Bonar's work, and the book remains in print. Any current study must interact with Bonar's valuable contribution. Most of M'Cheyne's substantial letters and sermons are available in print today. There remain a large number of manuscripts in the New College archives that have never been published. This volume incorporates the entire catalog of M'Cheyne's writings. It also interacts with the various secondary sources—biographies, histories, and monographs—related to nineteenth-century Scottish presbyterianism. Of special interest to the ensuing study are several doctoral theses that contribute to the field of M'Cheyne studies.[60]

---

58. *NTS*, 41.

59. *MAR*, dust jacket.

60. Palmer, "Andrew A. Bonar"; Oliphant, "Horatius Bonar"; Currie, "Growth of Evangelicalism"; Enright, "Preaching and Theology."

2

Trusting Christ
M'Cheyne's Story

THE YEAR 1813 SAW evangelical interest surging in Scotland. Andrew Bonar writes, "Eminent men of God appeared to plead the cause of Christ. The cross was being lifted up boldly in the midst of church courts which had long been ashamed of the gospel of Christ. More spirituality and deeper seriousness began . . . to prevail among the youth of our divinity halls. In the midst of such events . . . [M'Cheyne] was born."[1] This chapter surveys the essential contours of M'Cheyne's life. Grasping the broad sweeps of his biography provides needed context for subsequent chapters that examine the intersection of his theology and spirituality.

FORMATIVE YEARS (1813-1831)

M'Cheyne was born in Edinburgh on May 21, 1813 to Adam and Lockhart M'Cheyne.[2] At the time, Adam (1781-1854) was an ordinary lawyer,

---

1. *MAR*, 1.

2. For a concise biographical overview, see McMullen, "McCheyne, Robert Murray," 122-23, and Thomson, *A Biographical Dictionary*, 389-93. The most extensive biographical work to date is Yeaworth, "Robert Murray McCheyne." Modern biographies lean heavily Yeaworth's work. Notable popular biographies include Beaty, *An All-Surpassing Fellowship*, 7-54; Loane, *They Were Pilgrims*, 139-182; Prime, *Robert Murray McCheyne*; Robertson, *Awakening*; Smellie, *Biography of R. M. McCheyne*; Smith, *Robert Murray M'Cheyne*; Stewart, *Robert Murray McCheyne*; Van Valen, *Constrained by His Love*. The most heralded biographical work is still Bonar's volume,

but the next year he became a member of the Society of Writers to His Majesty's Signet—that "ancient society of law agents who conduct cases before the Court of Session and have the exclusive privilege of preparing crown writs, charters, precepts, etc."[3] This position brought Adam increased wealth and social advancement from the working class of his youth. He became, in the words of Alexander Smellie, "a man of social importance, who had more than an average share of the world's wealth and goods."[4] Adam was a firm disciplinarian, later recalling, "It was no part of my character to spare the rod."[5] He was attentive to the political movements of his time, and friendly with several influential figures in Scotland.[6]

Like her husband, Lockhart M'Cheyne (1772–1854) was the youngest in her family. Unlike her husband, she came from society's upper echelon. Her father "was the proprietor of Nether Locharwood estate, the most prosperous in Ruthwell parish," and she was thus accustomed to the comfortable lifestyle that Adam's position as writer would bring.[7]

---

found in *MAR*, 1–170. Charles Spurgeon called it "one of the best and most profitable volumes ever published. Every minister should read it often." Spurgeon, *Lectures to My Students*, 70.

3. *Signet History*, quoted in Yeaworth, "Robert Murray McCheyne," 4.

4. Smellie, *Biography of R. M. McCheyne*, 23. For a more thorough account of Adam M'Cheyne's life and career, see Yeaworth, "Robert Murray McCheyne," 1–7.

5. Smellie, *Biography of R. M. McCheyne*, 24. Van Valen notes that in spite of Adam's stern rule, he could never remember using the rod on Robert. Van Valen, *Constrained by His Love*, 16.

6. Adam wrote to his son William in India: "Have you any vermin called Whigs and Radicals or Radical-Whigs in Hindustan? If you have, I pray you to keep clear of them. They are very venomous creatures." Quoted in Yeaworth, "Robert Murray McCheyne," 6–7. See also, Smellie, *Biography of R. M. McCheyne*, 24. Yeaworth lists such influential figures as Henry Cockburn, Francis Jeffrey, Adam Gillies, David Wilsone, and John Hunter. Yeaworth, "Robert Murray McCheyne," 5–6.

7. Yeaworth, "Robert Murray McCheyne," 7. Ruthwell is a small village close to the Solway Firth and lies between the towns of Dumfries and Annan. Yeaworth further comments on Lockhart's family, writing, "A certain snobbishness existed in the Dickson family." Yeaworth, "Robert Murray McCheyne," 7. Apparently, such snobbery did not mark Lockhart. Smellie writes that she was of a nature more "light-hearted, at times more gay than that of the vigorous Writer to the Signet." Smellie, *Biography of R. M. McCheyne*, 25. Loane describes her as "a woman of great charm and sweetness, with gifts of mind to match her warm heart." Loane, *They Were Pilgrims*, 139. Biographers differ on how M'Cheyne responded to his parents. Smellie believes he viewed his father as "approachable." Smellie, *Biography of R. M. McCheyne*, 24. Robertson, however, writes, "Although there was affection and respect between McCheyne and his father it is also clear that he felt closer to his mother whose character he evidently

Adam and Lockhart wed in 1802.[8] They had five children, with Robert being the youngest. David Thomas (1804–1831) was the eldest. He followed his father into the legal profession and was "the pride of his home."[9] Next came Elizabeth Mary (1806–1888), Robert's constant companion and helper in his years at St. Peter's. Because she lived with Robert in adulthood and took care of his domestic affairs, Robert called her "my own Deaconess and helpmeet."[10] Adam and Lockhart's third child was William Oswald (1809–1892). After studying medicine at Edinburgh, he went to India with the Bengal Medical Service in 1831. William eventually retired as a surgeon in the honorable East India Company. Isabella was born in 1811 and died four months later.[11] None of the M'Cheyne children married.[12]

Education

The home of Robert's youth was a pleasant one. "The McCheyne children," Yeaworth reports, "were closely knit together, the elder ones patiently helping the younger and contributing to their happiness."[13] Further, Adam's occupation provided relaxed living quarters and an atmosphere for intellectual growth. The M'Cheynes prized and pursued education.[14] From the start, Robert displayed a keen aptitude for learning. Adam recounted how, at the age of four, Robert memorized the Greek alphabet "as an amusement" while recovering from an illness.[15]

---

shared." Robertson, *Awakening*, 22. Robertson bases his assessment on how many more letters Robert wrote to his mother than to his father. There does appear to be a special connection between mother and son. It was based on similar temperament and deportment. Yeaworth argues that M'Cheyne's father excelled in his societal relations, but lacked vibrancy in his familial relations and became detached from his extended family "in later life." Yeaworth, "Robert Murray McCheyne," 8.

8. Smellie, *Biography of R. M. McCheyne*, 35.
9. Smellie, *Biography of R. M. McCheyne*, 35.
10. Smellie, *Biography of R. M. McCheyne*, 22.
11. No biographer mentions the cause of death.
12. Yeaworth, "Robert Murray McCheyne," 9.
13. Yeaworth, "Robert Murray McCheyne," 12.
14. Robertson, *Awakening*, 26.
15. Van Valen, *Constrained by His Love*, 16. See also, *MAR*, 1; Beaty, *An All-Surpassing Fellowship*, 8; Prime, *Robert Murray McCheyne*, 10; Robertson, *Awakening*, 26; Smellie, *Biography of R. M. McCheyne*, 26; Yeaworth, "Robert Murray M'Cheyne," 35. The incident is notable because it not only shows M'Cheyne's intellectual commitment,

Marcus Loane describes young Robert as "quick and alert, readily teachable, a natural and attractive boyish figure."[16] He cut so striking a figure that Charles Dent Bell could write in 1889, "My recollections are of a tall slender lad with a sweet pleasant face, bright yet grave, fond of play, and of a blameless life."[17] From the first, he displayed interest in friends, athletics (particularly gymnastics), poetry, sketching, and achievement. These characteristics combined to make Robert a leader among his peers.[18]

M'Cheyne's ability to influence peers instead came from his winsome personality combined with disciplined ambition.[19] His earliest let-

---

but also his frail disposition. Bouts with illness were constant from an early age.

16. Loane, *They Were Pilgrims*, 139. Bonar says, "From his infancy his sweet and affectionate temper was remarked by all who knew him." *MAR*, 1. M'Cheyne himself agreed with the assessment, for he recorded in a diary entry on May 6, 1832, "[I am] naturally of a feeling and sentimental disposition." *MAR*, 16.

17. Bell, *Reminiscences of Boyhood*, 165. See also, Loane, *They Were Pilgrims*, 140; Smellie, *Biography of R. M. McCheyne*, 29; Van Valen, *Constrained by His Love*, 22; Yeaworth, "Robert Murray McCheyne," 14. Recollections of M'Cheyne abound with similar statements. Bonar says, "His companions speak of him as one who had even then (in the High School) peculiarities that drew attention: of a light, tall form—full of elasticity and vigor—ambitious, yet noble in his dispositions, disdaining everything like meanness or deceit." *MAR*, 2. His father later wrote, "He was always a boy of the most amiable, I may even say noble, disposition. I never found him guilty of a lie, or of any mean or unworthy action; and he had a great contempt for such things in others. I hardly recollect an instance of my having to inflict personal chastisement upon him." Quoted in Smellie, *Biography of R. M. McCheyne*, 33. See also, Van Valen, *Constrained by Love*, 16. Smellie remarks, "His outward presence satisfied the eye. He was tall, slender, of fair complexion, regular and handsome in feature, pleasant to look upon as young David coming from the sheepfold to be anointed king." Smellie, *Biography of R. M. McCheyne*, 59.

18. Adam M'Cheyne recalled meekly that his youngest son's "proficiency was above mediocrity." Quoted in Robertson, *Awakening*, 30; Smellie, *Biography of R. M. McCheyne*, 31. For additional comments on M'Cheyne's intellectual ability, see Loane, *They Were Pilgrims*, 140; Robertson, *Awakening*, 30; Van Valen, *Constrained by His Love*, 16. Adam M'Cheyne believed his son's social interactions impeded his academic proficiency: "Robert, though perfectly correct in his conduct, was of a more lively turn than David and during the first three years of his attendance at the University turned his attentions to elocution and poetry and the pleasures of society rather more, perhaps, than was altogether consistent with prudence. His powers of singing and reciting were at that time very great and his company was courted on that account more than was favourable to graver pursuits." Quoted in Yeaworth, "Robert Murray McCheyne," 35–36.

19. M'Cheyne left the English school with second prize, which "was a little disappointing in that his brother and sister had left with first prize before him." Robertson,

ters and notebooks demonstrate care, organization, and neatness. As a sixteen-year-old, he wrote an essay entitled, "On Early Rising." Yeaworth says of M'Cheyne's argument, "While sleep was necessary for babies and children, [Robert believed] there came a time when it was more profitable to curtail the hours in which man wastes 'the best and most useful part of his life in drowsiness and lying in bed.'"[20] The earliest portrait, then, of M'Cheyne is a lively one. The traits that would serve him so well in ministry—winsomeness and attractiveness—were present from the start.

M'Cheyne attended the English School from 1818–1821 under the tutorship of George Knight,[21] proving most adept in recitation and singing.[22] In 1821, M'Cheyne moved to the High School, where he enrolled in Rector Aglionby Ross Carson's class. Carson was an excellent teacher. George Smith writes, "He sent out from his classes a succession of remarkable Scotsmen all over the world, who traced to his character and learning all that made them honourable and prosperous."[23] Under Carson's tutelage, M'Cheyne actively studied the classics and history. Yeaworth comments, "Virgil, Horace, Ovid, and Tibullus enthralled him; and he did more than the required translations."[24]

After high school, M'Cheyne entered the University of Edinburgh in November 1827, "when it was basking in the glory of many outstanding professors, and when science and letters were at their zenith."[25] He continued his study of the classics, relishing his Latin and Greek classes. He

---

Awakening, 26. See also, Yeaworth, "Robert Murray McCheyne," 24. Adam M'Cheyne remarked, "He gained several prizes, though I cannot now condescend upon any of them, except one from Professor Wilson for the best poem on the Covenanters." Quoted in Smellie, *Biography of R. M. McCheyne*, 31. Bonar remarks on M'Cheyne's high school career: "He maintained a high place in his classes, and in the Rector's class distinguished himself by eminence in geography and recitation." *MAR*, 2.

20. Yeaworth, "Robert Murray M'Cheyne," 15.

21. According to Robertson, Knight was considered to be one of the "finest" tutors: "He certainly took an interest in his pupils and encouraged them to develop their gifts." Robertson, *Awakening*, 26.

22. *MAR*, 2.

23. Smith, *A Modern Apostle*, 6. For additional context on the High School, see Prime, *Robert Murray McCheyne*, 12–13.

24. Yeaworth, "Robert Murray McCheyne," 25.

25. Yeaworth, "Robert Murray McCheyne," 27. For an overview of these "outstanding professors," see Yeaworth, "Robert Murray McCheyne," 27–32; Robertson, *Awakening*, 27–28.

earned honors in every class, and left the university with a well-formed mind and broad array of interests.

Conversion

M'Cheyne lived an outwardly religious life during his first eighteen years. His family attended the Tron Church in Edinburgh, where Alexander Brunton and William Simpson served as ministers. Brunton moderated the 1832 General Assembly and later served as professor of Hebrew and Oriental languages at the University of Edinburgh.[26] M'Cheyne attended the catechism class between services and friends remembered "his correct and sweet recitation" of various Scripture passages or answers to the Shorter Catechism.[27]

The M'Cheynes moved to the newly erected St. Stephen's in 1829, which, providentially, saw the family exchange a moderate ministry for one with pronounced evangelical leanings, under the ministry of William Muir.[28] M'Cheyne committed himself to serve in the Church, engaging in its various ministries. During the winters of 1829–1830 and 1830–1831, he attended Thursday night meetings in Muir's vestry, becoming close with his minister. Muir was taken with his young parishioner's religious devotion. He recommended M'Cheyne for his "sound" principles and "exemplary" conduct.[29] However, M'Cheyne later reckoned this outward piety as nothing more than a "lifeless morality."[30] According to Andrew Bonar, M'Cheyne "regarded these as days of ungodliness—days wherein he cherished a pure morality, but lived in heart a Pharisee."[31]

26. Yeaworth, "Robert Murray M'Cheyne," 21.

27. *MAR*, 2.

28. Yeaworth writes, "Muir was a man of definite Evangelical sympathies, but he could not assent to the ecclesiastical policy of the Evangelical party. At the same time, he disagreed with the older moderates as to the part the people should have in the selection of ministers. In 1839, when forced to state his position, he became famous for his 'middle course,' trying to reconcile the two opposing views regarding the settlement of ministers." Yeaworth, "Robert Murray McCheyne," 22. Van Valen asserts that the move to St. Stephen's was because "Moderatism no longer had any appeal." Van Valen, *Constrained by His Love*, 34. Prime disagrees, saying the move was more likely due to St. Stephen's "reasonable proximity and newness." Prime, *Robert Murray McCheyne*, 26.

29. Quoted in Yeaworth, "Robert Murray McCheyne," 22.

30. Quoted in Robertson, *Awakening*, 34.

31. *MAR*, 2.

M'Cheyne described his first eighteen years as a time of joy and peace: "When the tears that we shed were tears of joy, and the pleasures of home were unmixed with alloy."[32] Yet, as he concluded his collegiate work, sudden change struck the M'Cheyne family. To begin with, his brother William went to India under the Bengal Medical Service in April 1831. Until this point, the entire M'Cheyne family had lived near each other. William's departure disrupted the family's harmony and brought cause for much anxiety, given the prevailing conditions in far off India. The second change was one of profound loss. When William left England, the oldest M'Cheyne child, David, was suffering from a serious fever. He never recovered, dying on July 8, 1831. His death struck a blow from which Robert never recovered.

M'Cheyne was close with all his siblings, but he "regarded [David] as a youthful idol" and closely watched "his every action."[33] David's sense of "eternal realities" especially affected Robert, and challenged his own spiritual laxity.[34] Bonar describes David's piety as exuding divine grace "with rare and solemn loveliness."[35] David took an interest in each family member's spiritual condition, counseling them to close with Christ. Not long into his ministry, M'Cheyne described his brother's influence in a letter to young boy in his congregation:

> I had a kind brother as you have, who taught me many things. He gave me a Bible, and persuaded me to read it; he tried to train me as a gardener trains the apple-tree upon the wall; but all in vain. I thought myself far wiser than he, and would always take my own way; and many a time, I well remember, I have seen him reading his Bible, or shutting his closet door to pray, when I have been dressing to go to some frolic, or some dance of folly.[36]

---

32. M'Cheyne, "Birthday Ode," quoted in Yeaworth, "Robert Murray McCheyne," 41.

33. Yeaworth, "Robert Murray McCheyne," 42. Loane writes, "Robert M'Cheyne had long looked up to [David] as the ideal of all that a true man should be, and his death touched him more deeply than words could well express." Loane, *They Were Pilgrims*, 141.

34. Adam M'Cheyne said that "during the last years of his life [David's] mind became deeply impressed with eternal realties." Quoted in Yeaworth, "Robert Murray McCheyne," 42.

35. *MAR*, 4.

36. *MAR*, 46.

M'Cheyne memorialized David's influence in a poem entitled, "On Painting the Miniature Likeness of One Departed":

> Ah! how oft that eye
> Would turn on me, with pity's tenderest look,
> And only half-upbraiding, bid me flee
> From the vain idols of my boyish heart—![37]

The exact details of M'Cheyne's conversion remain a mystery, but the catalyst is clear. "There can be no doubt," writes Bonar, that M'Cheyne "looked upon the death of his eldest brother, David, as the event which awoke him from the sleep of nature, and brought in the first beam of light to his soul."[38] George Smith, biographer of M'Cheyne's close friend Alexander Somerville, writes, "Somerville [found] . . . that Robert M'Cheyne also had become a new man since the death of a brother."[39] M'Cheyne himself understood the role Robert's death played in his salvation. In a letter to a church member, on the anniversary of David's death, he wrote, "This day eleven years ago, I lost my loved and loving brother, and began to seek a Brother who cannot die."[40]

At his moment of spiritual crisis, M'Cheyne found no one to whom he could turn for counsel. He wrote to a young parishioner:

> This dear friend and brother died; and though his death made a greater impression upon me than ever his life had done, still I found the misery of being *friendless*. I do not mean that I had no relations and worldly friends, for I had many; but I had no friend *who cared for my soul*. I had none to direct me to the Saviour—none to awaken my slumbering conscience—none to tell me about the blood of Jesus washing away all my sin—to change the heart, and give the victory over passions. I had no minister to take me by the hand, and say, "Come with me, and we will do thee good."[41]

---

37. MACCH 1.13.

38. *MAR*, 4. Adam M'Cheyne commented, "The holy example and the happy death of his brother David seem by the blessing of God to have given a new impulse to his mind in the right direction." Quoted in Yeaworth, "Robert Murray McCheyne," 46. One year after David's death, M'Cheyne records, "On this morning last year came the first overwhelming blow to my worldliness, how blessed to me, Thou, O God, only knowest who has made it so." *MAR*, 10.

39. Smith, *A Modern Apostle*, 10.

40. *MAR*, 9.

41. *MAR*, 47 (emphasis original).

With no living counselor available, M'Cheyne turned to books. He began with *The Sum of Saving Knowledge*, a short theological work generally appended to the *Westminster Confession of Faith*. The book, Bonar says, "brought him to a clear understanding of the way of acceptance with God."[42] M'Cheyne penned in his diary years later, "Read in the *Sum of Saving Knowledge*, the work which I think first of all wrought a saving change in me."[43]

Assured of his salvation, M'Cheyne devoted himself to Christ's service. Bonar notes, "His poetry was pervaded with serious thought, and all his pursuits began to be followed out in another spirit. He engaged in the labours of a Sabbath school, and began to seek God to his soul, in the diligent reading of the Word, and attendance on a faithful ministry."[44] M'Cheyne's subsequent diary entries reflect his newfound zeal: "I hope never to play cards again"; "Never visit on a Sunday evening again"; "Absented myself from the dance; upbraidings ill to bear. But I must try to bear the cross."[45]

TRAINING (1831–1835)

M'Cheyne decided to enter the ministry soon after his conversion. Two men in particular fueled his desire to be a minister. The first was Henry Duncan, who exhibited an all-encompassing zeal for Christ and made the ministry attractive to M'Cheyne. The second was his brother David, who "used to speak of the ministry as the most blessed work on earth, and often expressed the greatest delight in the hope that his younger brother might one day become a minister of Christ."[46] Noticing M'Cheyne's natural gift of leadership, David encouraged him to use it in the most profitable way possible: the gospel ministry. Thus, on September 28, 1831, M'Cheyne appeared before the Presbytery of Edinburgh to indicate his desire to enroll in the Divinity Hall at the University of Edinburgh. The

---

42. *MAR*, 11. The *British and Foreign Evangelical Review* commented, "The Holy Spirit, no doubt, is sovereign in the use of the means which He blesses for conversion; but it is difficult to imagine anything more unlike the style of McCheyne's preaching than the cold and stiff dialectics of that *summa theologiae*." Quoted in Yeaworth, "Robert Murray M'Cheyne," 47.

43. *MAR*, 11.

44. *MAR*, 8.

45. *MAR*, 10.

46. *MAR*, 11.

presbytery found him to be proficient in all the required areas and encouraged him to proceed.[47]

M'Cheyne matriculated into the thriving Divinity Hall in November 1831. "Thomas Chalmers," Marcus Loane writes, "was at the height of his amazing influence; no one since the days of John Knox had been held in such deep veneration."[48] Chalmers taught the divinity courses and endorsed a ministerial pattern which M'Cheyne came to personify. Alexander Brunton, M'Cheyne's former minister, was professor of Hebrew. M'Cheyne relished his Hebrew lessons and instructions on ancient Eastern customs. In a diary entry for March 6, 1834, he recorded, "Hebrew class—Psalms. New beauty in the original every time I read."[49] David Welsh, professor of church history, was the third faculty member. Welsh's exacting historical lectures appealed to M'Cheyne, but it was Welsh's piety that most intrigued the young student.[50] "[Welsh] influenced his students not only by his lectures but by his personal spiritual devotion to Christ and his obvious care and concern for them shone out," Prime writes.[51] Welsh wrote out a series of private resolutions, several of which related to training students. For example, he resolved "to set apart one hour *every* Saturday for prayer for my students," and, "in looking at a student, ask, how can I do him good, or have I ever done him good?"[52]

---

47. Yeaworth, "Robert Murray McCheyne," 52.

48. Loane, *They Were Pilgrims*, 142. According to Loane, Chalmers enthralled his students: "He cast the spell of his cosmic thought and solar sweep round all his students: they could hardly resist the force of his massive intellect and rugged character and dynamic energy. Andrew Bonar always spoke of him with unbounded enthusiasm as one to whom they all owed a debt which they could never repay." Loane, *They Were Pilgrims*, 143. Yeaworth agrees, "The predominant attraction at the Divinity Hall was Thomas Chalmers, whose prelections and personality energized generations of students." Yeaworth, "Robert Murray McCheyne," 61. Derek Prime calls Chalmers "the outstanding member of the Divinity Faculty" and "the icing on the cake." Prime, *Robert Murray McCheyne*, 34.

49. MAR, 13. Bonar says that M'Cheyne had already taken a private class in Hebrew before entering the Divinity Hall. He thus had a unique ability in the Old Testament language: "He could consult the Hebrew original of the Old Testament with as much ease as most of our ministers are able to consult the Greek of the New." MAR, 28.

50. Robertson, *Awakening*, 45. M'Cheyne's interest in historical studies was strong enough that he told Alexander Somerville he hoped to write a popular history of the German Reformation. Yeaworth, "Robert Murray McCheyne," 61.

51. Prime, *Robert Murray McCheyne*, 35.

52. Dunlop, *Sermons*, 56–57 (emphasis original).

The faculty animated and shaped M'Cheyne's pursuit of holiness and passion for Scripture. They presented a Savior who was lovely and compelling. M'Cheyne grew enormously under their training and derived additional spiritual support from his like-minded peers.

M'Cheyne deepened existing friendships and forged new ones at the Divinity Hall, each one proving significant for his future in gospel ministry.[53] He entered his ministerial studies at the same time as Alexander Somerville—a particularly close friend since high school.[54] George Smith recalls how "the two boys passed from school to college in November 1827, and through the Arts classes, foremost in athletic sports, in dancing, and in youthful frolic. Both were handsome and accomplished in the social graces, were great favourites with their fellows, and were inseparable companions."[55] The pair soon joined the visiting society at the Divinity Hall, which purposed "to set apart an hour or two every week for visiting the careless and needy in the most neglected portions of the town."[56] M'Cheyne and Somerville concentrated on a district in the Canongate, teaching a Sunday School class and distributing the *Monthly Visitor*.[57] The friends exchanged letters throughout M'Cheyne's life, and often assisted one another at communion seasons.[58]

During his first year of study, M'Cheyne also joined "The Exegetical Society"—Thomas Chalmers's creation.[59] Yeaworth recounts how the society was "select in point of membership," because Chalmers wanted

---

53. M'Cheyne had a gift for making and keeping friends. Smellie says, "A book might be dedicated to the subject of McCheyne's friendships." Smellie, *Biography of R. M. McCheyne*, 53. Van Valen adds, "One of McCheyne's characteristics was that he so quickly became attached to people." Van Valen, *Constrained by His Love*, 127.

54. For biographies of Alexander Somerville, see Smith, *A Modern Apostle*, and his son's memoir in Somerville, *Precious Seed Sown*, ix–xlvii.

55. Smith, *A Modern Apostle*, 6. James Dodds remembered that M'Cheyne and Somerville "seemed literally inseparable; along with many others I was often amused at the closeness of their companionship. They sat beside each other in the classroom; they came and went together; they were usually seen walking side by side in the street; or if one of them turned round a corner, the other was sure to come a minute after. The one seemed to haunt the other like a shadow, and nothing, apparently, could separate the two friends." Quoted in Smith, *A Modern Apostle*, 12. See also, Robertson, *Awakening*, 139; Van Valen, *Constrained by His Love*, 88.

56. MAR, 22.

57. MAR, 22.

58. For examples, see MACCH 2.1.59, 2.4.1.

59. Smellie wrongly attributes the Society's founding to M'Cheyne. Smellie, *Biography of R. M. McCheyne*, 40.

"none but the very *elite* of the Hall for taste and skill in the languages."[60] The society met each Saturday at 6:30 a.m., at which time members presented papers and interacted on their interpretations. The meetings served to sharpen the participants' theological and biblical insight. The society was so popular and beneficial that those students who remained during the summer holiday still met once a week.[61] The summer meetings included an element of personal accountability as each member shared the "amount and result" of their private Bible reading.[62]

The society's roll was numbered some sixteen students, and no member became more precious to M'Cheyne than Andrew Bonar.[63] Throughout their time at the Divinity Hall, M'Cheyne, Bonar, and Somerville could be found studying together and caring for each other's spiritual well-being. Bonar wrote in his diary on May 30, 1835: "In a walk round Duddingston Loch with Robert M'Cheyne and Alexander Somerville this afternoon, we had much conversation upon the leading

---

60. Yeaworth, "Robert Murray McCheyne," 71 (emphasis original).

61. Bonar writes, "During the summer vacations,—that we might redeem the time,—some of us who remained in town, when most of our fellow-students were gone to the country, used to meet once every week in the forenoon, for the purpose of investigating some point of *Systematic Divinity* . . . At another time we met in a similar way, till we had overtaken the chief points of the *Popish Controversy*. Advancement in our acquaintance with the Greek and Hebrew Scriptures also brought us together; and one summer the study of *Unfulfilled Prophecy* assembled a few of us once a week, at an early morning hour." *MAR*, 28 (emphasis original).

62. *MAR*, 27.

63. Bonar lists the society's members as "*William Laughton*, now minister of St. Thomas's, Greenock, in connection with the Free Church; *Thomas Brown*, Free Church, Kinneff; *William Wilson*, Free Church, Carmyle; *Horatius Bonar*, Free Church, Kelso; *Andrew A. Bonar*, Free Church, Collace; *Robert M. M'Cheyne*; *Alexander Somerville*, Free Church, Anderston, Glasgow; *John Thomson*, Mariners' Free Church, Leith; *Patrick Borrowman*, Free Church, Glencairn; *Walter Wood*, Free Church, Westruther; *Henry Moncrieff*, Free Church, Kilbride; *James Cochrane*, Established Church, Cupar; *John Miller*, Secretary to Free Church Special Commission; *G. Smeaton*, Free Church, Auchterarder; *Robert Kinnear*, Free Church, Moffat; and *W. B. Clarke*, Free Church, Half-Morton." *MAR*, 30 (emphasis original). It is striking to see that each member of the society, save James Cochrane, left the established church. Chalmers thus sowed the seed for the Disruption of 1843 not merely in his teaching but through selecting students for more intimate mentoring—such as the formation of "The Exegetical Society." Yeaworth singles out several society members as eminent lights in the church: "Further distinctions, aside from Somerville and the Bonars: Thomas Brown was the author of *Annals of the Disruption*, Wilson was the biographer of R. S. Candlish, George Smeaton was Professor of Theology at Aberdeen and Edinburgh, and Moncrieff was Clerk of the Free Church." Yeaworth, "Robert Murray McCheyne," 71.

of Providence and future days. We sang together, sitting upon a fallen oak-tree, one of the Psalms."[64]

Spiritual and Pastoral Developments

M'Cheyne's years at the Divinity Hall were indeed marked by growth in the grace and knowledge of Christ. Increased piety matched his ever-increasing theological ability.[65] His diary reveals a consistent longing for greater conformity to Christ:

> What right have I to steal and abuse my Master's time? "Redeem it," He is crying to me.[66]

> Not a trait worth remembering! And yet these four-and-twenty hours must be accounted for.[67]

> Oh that heart and understanding may grow together, like brother and sister, leaning on one another![68]

> Oh for true, unfeigned humility![69]

> More abundant longings for the work of the ministry. Oh that Christ would but count me faithful, that a dispensation of the gospel might be committed to me![70]

Such a "dispensation" came in due course. On February 16, 1835, one month before completing his studies, M'Cheyne completed the mandatory examinations for licensure to preach the gospel. He recorded the

---

64. Bonar, *Andrew A. Bonar*, 27.

65. Bonar remarks on M'Cheyne's intellect at this time: "His intellectual powers were of a high order: clear and distinct apprehension of his subject, and felicitous illustration, characterised him among all his companions. To an eager desire for wide acquaintance with truth in all its departments, and a memory strong and accurate in retaining what he found, there was added remarkable candour in examining what claimed to be the truth. He had also an ingenious and enterprising mind—a mind that could carry out what was suggested, when it did not strike out new light for itself. He possessed great powers of analysis; often his judgment discovered singular discrimination... He might have risen to high eminence in the circles of taste and literature, but denied himself all such hopes, that he might win souls." *MAR*, 30.

66. *MAR*, 12.
67. *MAR*, 12.
68. *MAR*, 16.
69. *MAR*, 17.
70. *MAR*, 17.

previous night: "To-morrow I undergo my trials before the Presbytery. May God give me courage in the hour of need. What should I fear? If God see meet to put me into the ministry, who shall keep me back? If I be not meet, why should I be thrust forward? To thy service I desire to dedicate myself over and over again."[71]

M'Cheyne was uncertain as to his performance during the exams in New Testament Greek, church history, and systematic theology. He told his brother, William, that the examiners "all heckled me, like so many terriers on a rat."[72] Yet his concern was unfounded, for "Dr. Chalmers was highly pleased, and all the other ministers."[73] Yeaworth describes what followed in the subsequent weeks:

> Before he completed his public trials, several ministers invited McCheyne to assist them. Particularly attractive was the offer of John Bonar, minister of Larbert and Dunipace, whose assistant, William Hanna, had just been called elsewhere. The assistantship was considered to be a favorable opening for a young probationer, and Robert was advised by his friends to accept it. But since it appeared that it might be a year before his license would be obtained from Edinburgh Presbytery, he applied to Annan Presbytery to complete his trials sooner.[74]

On July 1, 1835, M'Cheyne submitted five linguistic and homiletic assignments: (1) a Hebrew translation and analysis from Psalm 109; (2) a lecture on Matthew 11:1-15; (3) a homily on Matthew 7:13-14; (4) a concise commentary on Romans 3:27-28; and (5) a sermon on Romans 5:11.[75] M'Cheyne wrote in his diary:

> Preached three probationary discourses in Annan Church, and, after an examination in Hebrew, was solemnly licensed to preach the gospel by Mr. Monylaws, the moderator . . . What I have so long desired as the highest honour of man, Thou at length givest me—me who dare scarcely use the words of Paul: "Unto me who

---

71. *MAR*, 26.

72. Quoted in Smellie, *Biography of R. M. McCheyne*, 43.

73. Quoted in Smellie, *Biography of R. M. McCheyne*, 43. See also, Yeaworth, "Robert Murray McCheyne," 77.

74. Yeaworth, "Robert Murray McCheyne," 77-78. William Hanna, M'Cheyne's predecessor, married Thomas Chalmers's daughter in 1836. In 1847, upon Chalmers's death, he was commissioned to write the authorized biography of Thomas Chalmers, later published as *Memoirs of the Life and Writings of Thomas Chalmer*.

75. Yeaworth, "Robert Murray McCheyne," 79.

am less than the least of all the saints is this grace given, that I should preach the unsearchable riches of Christ." Felt somewhat solemnized, though unable to feel my unworthiness as I ought. Be clothed with humility.[76]

M'Cheyne did not officially begin his labors in Larbert and Dunipace until November 7, 1835. In July, he preached his first sermons as a licensed minister in Henry Duncan's Ruthwell church. The great solemnity which he felt was missing upon licensure came when he ascended to the sacred desk for the first time. He recorded in his diary: "Found it a more awfully solemn thing than I had imagined to announce Christ authoritatively; yet a glorious privilege!"[77]

MINISTRY (1835-1843)

In accepting the call to assist John Bonar, M'Cheyne confessed, "It has always been my aim, and it is my prayer, to have *no plans* with regard to myself, well assured as I am, that the place where the Saviour sees meet to place me must ever be the best place for me."[78] Serving with Bonar at Larbert and Dunipace established a ministerial pattern that shaped M'Cheyne for his eventual ministry at Dundee. As Loane observes, "Here the groundwork was laid for his future greatness in the pastoral ministry."[79]

Larbert and Dunipace

The united parish of Larbert and Dunipace consisted of close to 6,000 souls.[80] Smellie summarizes the differences between the two stations as follows: "Larbert was noisy, grim, industrial, with villages clustering round where the coal-miners and iron-moulders lived; Dunipace, three miles distant, was rural and secluded, the home of shepherds and small

---

76. *MAR*, 31.
77. *MAR*, 32.
78. *MAR*, 32 (emphasis original).
79. Loane, *They Were Pilgrims*, 147. See also, Prime, *Robert Murray McCheyne*, 49; Robertson, *Awakening*, 57.
80. For a useful historical and ecclesiastical survey of the parish, see Yeaworth, "Robert Murray McCheyne," 81-83.

farmers."[81] Both M'Cheyne and Bonar preached on the Sabbath; one ministered at Larbert and the other at Dunipace. They also visited the parish throughout the week. M'Cheyne told his mother that, during this time, he enjoyed visitation more than any other aspect of ministry.[82]

M'Cheyne's early sermons were simple and evangelistic.[83] While earnest, they do not reflect the depth of winsomeness that brought eventual acclaim. Congregants listened appreciatively, if not expectantly. Ministry in the united parish gave M'Cheyne many opportunities to hone his homiletical ability. There were five preaching stations[84] around Larbert and "so McCheyne preached three times on Sunday and several times during the week at Bible classes and meetings."[85]

Sickness, a constant companion until his death, disrupted M'Cheyne's ministry in Larbert and Dunipace. In December of 1835, "a doctor diagnosed the beginnings of tuberculosis and determined that his right lung hardly functioned."[86] He was later laid up for an extended time, unable to minister in his regular way. He believed that the illness was God's chastisement for being "too anxious to do great things,"[87] and that God was using it to teach him the importance of intercessory prayer. He wrote to John Bonar: "I feel distinctly that the whole of my labour during this season of sickness and pain should be in the way of prayer and *intercession*."[88] Illness again set M'Cheyne aside several months later. He remarked, "Set by once more for a season to feel my unprofitableness and cure my pride."[89] M'Cheyne believed that God meant for the illness

---

81. Smellie, *Biography of R. M. McCheyne*, 43–44. See also, Loane, *They Were Pilgrims*, 147.

82. Quoted in Yeaworth, "Robert Murray McCheyne," 84.

83. Yeaworth argues the simplicity was intentional, saying, "[McCheyne] felt it to be necessary for his industrial and agricultural audiences to know and believe." Yeaworth, "Robert Murray McCheyne," 87.

84. Henry Moncreiff describes preaching stations as follows: "A congregation for the regular worship of God, and the preaching of the gospel, may be formed and kept up under the superintendence of the Presbytery, without its having been constituted as a pastoral charge. It may be maintained under the name of a Preaching Station until its condition shall appear sufficient for enabling it to call a Pastor." Moncreiff, *Practice of Free Church*, 54.

85. Robertson, *Awakening*, 61.

86. Beaty, *An All-Surpassing Fellowship*, 17. See also, MAR, 37.

87. *MAR*, 36.

88. *MAR*, 36 (emphasis original).

89. *MAR*, 43.

to humble his ministerial ambitions: "The Lord saw I would have spoken as much for my own honour as His, and therefore shut my mouth. *I see a man cannot be a faithful minister, until he preaches Christ for Christ's sake*—until he gives up striving to attract people to himself, and seeks only to attract them to Christ. Lord, give me this!"[90]

M'Cheyne enjoyed his ministry at Larbert and Dunipace but longed for increased opportunity. In the spring of 1836, he confided to his father, "My own inclination is to sit still until God see fit to call me somewhere. If not I am well employed here—and indeed have as much to do as I have strength for. At the same time I sometimes feel the lack of not having the full powers of a minister of God, for that reason alone I would desire an exchange."[91] The opportunity to exercise those full powers arrived speedily, for in the spring of 1836 the leaders of St. Peter's Church, in Dundee, invited M'Cheyne to preach as a candidate to become their first minister.[92]

The kirk session of St. John's—St. Peter's mother church—had asked Thomas Chalmers, David Welsh, and Robert Candlish to provide six names worthy of consideration—men who were "pious, active and . . . efficient preacher[s]."[93] Their recommendations included M'Cheyne, Andrew Bonar, Thomas Dymock, James Gibson, Alexander Somerville, and

---

90. *MAR*, 43 (emphasis original).

91. MACCH 2.6.27.

92. Although Dundee's population in the years between 1780 and 1835 had doubled to 51,000, the number of established churches remained at seven, with three Chapels of Ease. The combined seating capacity of all the churches—including dissenting churches—was 18,000. Due to the work of John Roxburgh, minister of St. John's Dundee, efforts were made to erect "a chapel in the northwest end of Hawkhill: the building to be plain and substantial, so as to secure at one quantity and cheapness of accommodation." *History of St. Peter's Free Church, Dundee*, quoted in Yeaworth, "Robert Murray M'Cheyne," 91. St. Peter's was built on Perth Road and constitutionally approved by the Assembly of 1836, with the kirk session of St. John's serving as the provisional session for the new work. See Yeaworth, "Robert Murray M'Cheyne," 91–92. Bonar's diary entry for Wednesday, June 29, 1836, records, "I have got a letter telling me that I am one of those nominated for Dundee, and am to preach there soon, along with Somerville and M'Cheyne." Bonar, *Andrew A. Bonar*, 44.

93. The selection of St. Peter's minister went against the norm to such a degree that the *Dundee, Perth and Cupar Advertiser* grumbled about "evangelical patronage." Robertson, *Awakening*, 97. A St. John's circular published in 1835 mentioned the need for a "pious, active, and efficient preacher" who would "*excavate* a congregation for himself from the surrounding district." Quoted in McLennan, *McCheyne's Dundee*, 42 (emphasis original).

a Mr. White.[94] Robert Candlish, the eminent minister of St. George's in Edinburgh, "particularly favored McCheyne" for the St. Peter's position and even tried to secure the most opportune preaching date.[95] M'Cheyne displayed modesty throughout the process, remarking, "My two greatest intimates [are] made my rivals. I have no doubt we will be content with all humility in honour preferring one another."[96] He then tipped his hand as to what he thought best: "If the people have any sense, they will choose Andrew Bonar who, for learning, experimental knowledge, and all the valuable qualities of a minister, outstrips all the students I ever knew."[97] While M'Cheyne's humility surely contributed to his assessment, his longing for a rural parish was also a reason. He told his family, "If I were to choose the scene of my labours, I would wish to be away from a town—as riding and country air seem almost essential to my existence."[98] Yet, if called, he was willing to go St. Peter's. After each candidate had preached, a meeting was convened in August to reduce the list. However, as Yeaworth notes, "there was so decided a preference for McCheyne that

---

94. Yeaworth, "Robert Murray McCheyne," 92. There is no record of Mr. White's first name.

95. Yeaworth, "Robert Murray McCheyne," 92.

96. Yeaworth, "Robert Murray McCheyne," 92.

97. Smellie, *Biography of R. M. McCheyne*, 53.

98. Yeaworth, "Robert Murray McCheyne," 92. See also, *MAR*, 51. In July of 1837, Sir Thomas Carmichael offered M'Cheyne the Skirling parish. He refused but told his parents: "You cannot imagine—unless you know how rural my tastes are—how suitable to my nature this change would have been. And yet God has seen fit to place me here—among the bustling artisans and political manufacturers of Dundee . . . Perhaps He will make this wilderness of chimney tops to be green and beautiful as the garden of the Lord." Quoted in Yeaworth, "Robert Murray McCheyne," 188. M'Cheyne wrote to Lady Carmichael as to why he declined the call: "I am here (in Dundee), I did not bring myself here. I did not ask to be made a candidate for this place. I was hardly willing to be a candidate . . . I was as happy at Larbert as the day was long . . . And yet God has turned the hearts of this whole people towards me like the heart of one man." MACCH 2.1.6. M'Cheyne's mother, in particular, was in anguish about her son's refusal to go to Skirling. M'Cheyne wrote, "Dear Mamma you must just make up your mind to let me be murdered among the lanes of Dundee—instead of seeing me fattening in the green plebe of Skirling. Perhaps it would have been very good for my frail body Dear Mamma—but then I fear my soul would have turned sickly . . . I would have felt myself a renegade . . . I never had a shade of doubt that I would refuse . . . Dear Mamma be content and be happy, we are only pilgrims—we shall soon be in the land of plenty." MACCH 2.1.8.

a motion was made to dispense with any further hearings. This was carried by a large majority, and the minority agreed to make it unanimous."[99]

M'Cheyne proceeded to preach his final sermons in Larbert and Dunipace,[100] and he was delighted to discover that Alexander Somerville would succeed him as John Bonar's assistant. Thus his first pastorate came to an end.[101]

> During these ten months the Lord had done much for him, but it was chiefly in the way of discipline for a future ministry. He had been taught a minister's heart; he had been tried in the furnace; he had tasted deep personal sorrow, little of which has been recorded; he had felt the fiery darts of temptation; he had been exercised in self-examination and in much prayer; he had proved how flinty is the rock, and had learnt that in lifting the rod by which it was to be smitten, success lay in Him alone who enabled him to lift it up. And thus prepared of God for the peculiar work that awaited him, he had turned his face towards Dundee.[102]

99. Yeaworth, "Robert Murray McCheyne," 93. John Roxburgh was pleased with M'Cheyne's election to St. Peter's. George Cameron mentions the happy relationship between Roxburgh and M'Cheyne: "Mr. Roxburgh welcomed this young brother as a fellow-worker with most cordial affection, and mutual friendship." Cameron, *Memorials of John Roxburgh*, 13. A. W. Milne also comments, "From [the day of M'Cheyne's ordination] they wrought and labored together as brothers, encouraging each other's hearts, and strengthening each other's hands in the work of the Lord, in their adjoining parishes." Quoted in Cameron, *Memorials of John Roxburgh*, 21.

100. M'Cheyne's reckoning of his ministry in Larbert and Dunipace comes in a letter written to his family in September of 1836: "I preached my farewell sermon at Dunipace last Sabbath day . . . I never saw the church so full before . . . It is very sad to leave them now and to leave them thus. What multitudes of houses I have never entered. So many I have only stood once on their hearthstone—and prayed. In some few I have found my way so far into their affections—but not so far as to lead them to Jesus. My classes are a little more anxious and awakened than they were—especially some of the young men; but permanent fruit—none is visible. Yet I leave them just as the farmer leaves the seed he has sown. It is not the farmer that can make it grow—he can only pray and wait for the . . . latter rain." Quoted in Yeaworth, "Robert Murray McCheyne," 93–94.

101. *MAR*, 51. M'Cheyne was confident in Somerville's ability, writing to John Bonar, "I see plainly that my poor attempts at labour in your dear parish will soon be eclipsed." *MAR*, 51. M'Cheyne exhorted his friend to "take more heed to the saints than I ever did . . . Speak boldly, what matters in eternity the slight awkwardnesses of time?" Quoted in Smith, *A Modern Apostle*, 20.

102. *MAR*, 51. The rest of M'Cheyne's life was spent as the minister of St. Peter's. Marcus Loane says, "His full career as a preacher was to divide into two three-year terms, with his journey to the Holy Land in between. The first three years were the

Dundee

In 1836, Dundee was a bustling industrialized city.[103] Approximately 3,400 people resided within the parish boundaries of St. Peter's, "many of whom never crossed the threshold of any sanctuary."[104] M'Cheyne looked upon Dundee as "a city given to idolatry and hardness of heart. I fear there is much of what Isaiah speaks of: 'The prophets prophesy lies, and the people love to have it so.'"[105]

M'Cheyne was ordained to the gospel ministry on November 24, 1836. The following Sunday morning he preached his first sermon as minister of St. Peter's on Isaiah 61:1–3,[106] a text he used in following years to commemorate the anniversary of his first Sabbath as pastor. He sought to minister in common and creative ways. He continued the practice of diligent visitation learned in Larbert and Dunipace, not stopping even when influenza swept through the district for several months.[107] He preached three times each Lord's Day, and the gallery of 1,100 seats was full from the start.[108] He installed ten elders to the session.[109] With the kirk session's support, he introduced a Thursday night prayer meeting

---

seed-time; the last three saw the harvest: and the golden glow which those years were to cast over the people of Dundee was long to brood above the grey city on the banks of the Tay." Loane, *They Were Pilgrims*, 149.

103. For analyses of Dundee's history and culture, see Robertson, *Awakening*, 77–96, and Bates, "Sociological and Demographic Analysis," 30–47.

104. MAR, 56–57.

105. MAR, 57.

106. "The Spirit of the Lord God is upon me; because the Lord hath anointed me to preach good tidings unto the meek; he hath sent me to bind up the brokenhearted, to proclaim liberty to the captives, and the opening of the prison to them that are bound; to proclaim the acceptable year of the Lord, and the day of vengeance of our God; to comfort all that mourn; to appoint unto them that mourn in Zion, to give unto them beauty for ashes, the oil of joy for mourning, the garment of praise for the spirit of heaviness; that they might be called trees of righteousness, the planting of the Lord, that he might be glorified." All Scripture quotations taken from the authorized (King James) version.

107. MAR, 57.

108. Robertson says, "[M'Cheyne] saw the prime need of the area as evangelism and he acted accordingly. Although the seat rents were cheap (so much so that of 1,100 sittings, 700 people had never held seats before), he opposed the practice of letting seats and sought to minimize their cost and ultimately do away with them altogether." Robertson, *Awakening*, 102. For more on seat rentals, see McLennan, *McCheyne's Dundee*, 29–30.

109. Yeaworth, "Robert Murray McCheyne," 170.

that soon overflowed with eight hundred participants. During the summer months, he held weekly "meetings for singing," intended to improve the congregation's ability in song. Other innovative practices included increasing the number of communion seasons from two to four times per year. In 1837, M'Cheyne started a Sabbath school to reach young children. Recognizing that older children required specific instruction, he began a Tuesday evening class attended by some two hundred and fifty young people.[110] The class examined various Bible passages as well as the Shorter Catechism.

M'Cheyne also participated in the Church's various courts, becoming secretary to the Association for Church Extension in 1837.[111] The 1838 General Assembly appointed a committee "to ascertain the numbers, condition and character of the Jewish people in Palestine and Europe; to discover what means had been previously employed for their spiritual good, and the success of such enterprises; and to seek possible locations for mission stations."[112] M'Cheyne was appointed to the committee, engaging zealously in the work because he believed God still had a plan for "his peculiar people."

The Holy Land

When M'Cheyne sat on the Church of Scotland's committee of Jewish inquiry, he did not expect to join the actual mission. In late 1838, heart palpitations struck him, requiring him to leave Dundee for his parent's home in Edinburgh. It was Dr. Candlish who suggested that M'Cheyne should join the deputation to Palestine, believing the change in climate would aid the young pastor's health.[113] After prayer and consultation, M'Cheyne agreed. He was joined on the mission by Alexander Black, professor of divinity at Marischal College, Aberdeen; Alexander Keith,

---

110. Van Valen, *Constrained by His Love*, 150. See also, Prime, *Robert Murray McCheyne*, 70.

111. *MAR*, 69. See also, Cameron, *Memorials of John Roxburgh*, 14.

112. Yeaworth, "Robert Murray McCheyne," 263.

113. Andrew Bonar later recalled, "In those days [Candlish's] love for Robert McCheyne was very interesting . . . it was his anxiety for McCheyne's health that led to the idea of the mission to the Jews and visit to Palestine." Quoted in Wilson, *Memorials of Robert Smith Candlish*, 68. M'Cheyne's sixth pastoral letter confirms a medicinal aim: "My medical men are agreed that it is the likeliest method of restoring my broken health." *MAR*, 202. See also Bonar's comments in *MAR*, 86.

minister at St. Cyrus; Robert Wodrow, a ruling elder in Glasgow (illness ultimately prevented him from going); and Andrew Bonar.[114]

M'Cheyne traveled to London on March 27, 1839 to make preparations for the deputation's other members. He spent two weeks soliciting English support for the mission, and the team departed on April 12. They proceeded to France, then to Egypt by steam ship, and then to Palestine by camel.[115] On June 7, they arrived in Jerusalem. M'Cheyne described the day as "one of the most privileged" of his life.[116] He recorded, "Soon, all of us were on the spot, buried in thought, and wistfully gazing on the wondrous scene where the Redeemer died. The nearer we came to the city, the more we felt it a solemn thing to be where 'God manifest in the flesh' had walked. The feelings of that hour could not even be spoken. We all moved forward in silence, or interchanging feelings only by a word."[117]

114. Andrew Bonar was appointed only after great deliberation. Somerville described the committee's debate to M'Cheyne: "The sentiment seemed to prevail in the meeting that it was highly important that a Mission should take place, as proposed. The difficult lies with the choice. They seem to feel the youth of the individuals a good deal—but all agreed that *you* should go. As to Andrew, I feel his millenarianism will knock the prospect of his going upon the head." Quoted in Yeaworth, "Robert Murray McCheyne," 266. Yeaworth comments, "Bonar was greatly disappointed and asked McCheyne to intercede on his behalf, which he and others did (stressing Bonar's value as a linguist), and permission was granted eventually." Yeaworth, "Robert Murray McCheyne," 266-67. Robert Palmer, however, reads Bonar in a more favorable light: "When the opportunity of going to Palestine was presented to Bonar, he hesitated to accept. He was uncertain as to his own duty. He had been in Collace only six months. Would it be right to leave his people?" Palmer, "Andrew A. Bonar," 94-95. Palmer proceeds to quote from a letter (dated March 8, 1839) which Bonar sent to M'Cheyne. It lists various difficulties Bonar faced in joining the deputation. Palmer selectively dismisses Bonar's plea for assistance, choosing instead to reference a letter (dated March 8, 1839) from Candlish that informed Bonar "that the General Assembly's Committee on Jewish Missions considered his participation as 'indispensable to the carrying on of the plan.'" Palmer interprets Candlish's letter as proof that the committee did not deliberate over Bonar's involvement. Yet, such warmth from Candlish was characteristic of his political ability, and one need not expect Candlish would have felt obligated to tell Bonar that his ardent millenarianism nearly cost him a place on the commission.

115. M'Cheyne wrote with youthful wonder to Eliza on May 24: "When you find yourself exalted on the hunch of a camel, it is somewhat of the feeling of an aeronaut, as if you were bidding farewell to sublunary things; but when he begins to move with solemn pace and slow, you are reminded of your terrestrial origin, and that a wrong balance or turn to the side will soon bring you down from your giddy height." *FL*, 92-93.

116. *FL*, 98.

117. Quoted in Prime, *Robert Murray McCheyne*, 82-83. Bonar felt that in Palestine "every spot is just a page of scripture spread out and addressed to the soul."

After several days, the deputation decided to split into two groups (because of Black's ill health). Black and Keith returned home via Constantinople,[118] while M'Cheyne and Bonar traveled throughout Palestine, recording their observations. They returned home by way of Bosphorus, Moldavia, Wallachia, and Poland. Their passage home was not without difficulty, especially in Poland. Yeaworth says, "Being contrary to Roman Catholic doctrine, their books were confiscated, and every movement was followed with 'inquisitorial suspicion.' McCheyne was also attacked bodily by two shepherds as he read in an open field, being left only as he lay helpless on the ground after a bitter struggle."[119]

The deputies arrived back in London on November 6 to great acclaim. They proceeded to preach in churches throughout the United Kingdom, recounting their journey and soliciting support for additional missions to the Jews. At the 1840 General Assembly, Keith assisted M'Cheyne in submitting the final report.[120] That same year, M'Cheyne and Bonar set to work on publishing their *Narrative of a Mission of Inquiry to the Jews from the Church of Scotland in 1839*.[121] It received extensive praise. Chalmers said, "I have the greatest value for it."[122] The Church encouraged ministers to read the book at prayer meetings, offer it as prizes to children, and include it in parish libraries.[123]

While M'Cheyne was away in Palestine, the Holy Spirit had awakened St. Peter's—a movement he had prayerfully anticipated. Before leaving for Palestine, he wrote, "I sometimes think that a great blessing may come to my people in their absence. Often God does not bless us in the midst of our labours, lest we shall say, 'My hand and eloquence have done it.' He removes us into silence, and then pours 'down a blessing so there

---

Quoted in Palmer, "Andrew A. Bonar," 98.

118. Black's and Keith's journey home ultimately paved the way for a Jewish mission in Budapest.

119. Yeaworth, "Robert Murray McCheyne," 271–72.

120. Yeaworth, "Robert Murray McCheyne," 273.

121. Bonar and M'Cheyne, *Narrative of a Mission of Inquiry*. There is some debate as to who was the primary author for *Narrative*. Yeaworth portrays the work as a joint effort, whereas Palmer concludes, "It may be said that the volume is largely the work of Bonar, with many passages added, and several corrections and alterations made, by M'Cheyne." Palmer, "Andrew A. Bonar," 301.

122. Smellie, *Biography of R. M. McCheyne*, 83.

123. Yeaworth, "Robert Murray McCheyne," 279.

is no room to receive it; so that all that see it cry out, 'It is the Lord!'"[124] M'Cheyne's words proved prophetic, for he returned to a congregation in the midst of revival.

Revival Labors

In February 1839, M'Cheyne asked Alexander Somerville to approach William Chalmers Burns (1815–1868) about the possibility of filling St. Peter's pulpit while he served on the deputation to Palestine.[125] Burns had already committed himself to missionary service in India, but the colonial committee permitted him to minister at St. Peter's as no missionary openings were available. Burns agreed to M'Cheyne's request and commenced preaching at St. Peter's. From April to late July, Burns's preaching had little unusual effect.[126] At the end of July, Burns went to Paisley to attend his brother-in-law's funeral. The service made a deep impression. Burns then assisted his father in the communion season at Kilsyth, and "he brought . . . that hidden fire which at Paisley was roused into a flame."[127] He preached several times in the communion services, and the congregation's response gave reason to believe the Holy Spirit was about to move in a mighty way. The following Tuesday, Burns preached from Psalm 110:3: "Thy people shall be willing in the day of thy power." The sermon elicited throbbing emotional outbursts. The Kilsyth Revival continued for three months.[128] One observer recounted the breadth of spiritual awakening:

---

124. *MAR*, 86.

125. For biographies of Burns, see Burns, *Memoir of the Rev.*; McMullen, *God's Polished Arrow*; Stewart, *William Chalmers Burns*. M'Cheyne's early appreciation of Burns focused on his Christ-centered piety. M'Cheyne told Mrs. Collier, before Burns agreed to fill the pulpit: "He is one truly taught of God—young, but Christ lives in him." *MAR*, 215. For a useful overview of Burns' seven months labor in Dundee, see McLennan, *McCheyne's Dundee*, 72–87.

126. Burns later attributed this lack to holding back: "I never came, as it were, to throw down the gauntlet to the enemy by the unreserved declaration and urgent application of the divine testimony regarding the state of fallen man and the necessity of an unreserved surrender to the Lord Jesus in all his offices that he may be saved." Quoted in McMullen, *God's Polished Arrows*, 32.

127. Quoted in Yeaworth, "Robert Murray McCheyne," 290.

128. For nineteenth-century accounts of the Kilsyth Revival, see Anton, *Kilsyth*, 209–22; Burns, *Memoir of the Rev.*, 83–107; Holland, *Kilsyth Revival*.

The web became nothing to the weaver, nor the forge to the blacksmith, nor his bench to the carpenter, nor his furrow to the ploughman. They forsook all to crowd the churches and the prayer-meetings. There were nightly sermons in every church, household meetings for prayer in every street, twos and threes in earnest conversation on every road, and single wrestlers with God in the solitary places of the field and glen.[129]

Burns returned to Dundee on August 8—"one of the days when [M'Cheyne] was stretched on his bed, praying for his people under all his own suffering."[130] Burns led the Thursday prayer meeting as usual, recounting God's work at Kilsyth, and then invited those to remain "who felt the need of an outpouring of the Spirit to convert them."[131] Roughly one hundred anxious souls remained. At the end of Burns's address, "suddenly the power of God seemed to descend, and all were bathed in tears."[132] A similar service was held the following night with comparable results. From then on, meetings were held nightly, and it was as if God woke the whole city.[133]

M'Cheyne first heard of God's work while in Hamburg. On November 15, he posted a note to Burns: "You remember it was the prayer of my heart when we parted, that you might be a thousandfold more blessed to the people than ever my ministry had been. How it will gladden my heart, if you can really tell me it has been so!"[134] Upon his return to Dundee, M'Cheyne found that it was indeed so. At the prayer meeting on Thursday, November 21, an enormous crowd filled St. Peter's. The congregation was eager to hear of the mission to Palestine. Sensing a new spirit, M'Cheyne preached from 1 Corinthians 2:1-4. The response was unlike anything he had experienced before. He told his parents, "I never preached to such an audience, so many weeping, so many waiting for the words of eternal life. I never heard such sweet singing anywhere, so

---

129. Quoted in Prime, *Robert Murray McCheyne*, 96.
130. *MAR*, 109.
131. *MAR*, 114.
132. *MAR*, 114.
133. McMullen, *God's Polished Arrow*, 36.
134. *MAR*, 234. Burns reciprocated such humble prayer, when he wrote of M'Cheyne: "O, Lord I would praise thee with all my heart . . . and would entreat that when [M'Cheyne] is restored to [St. Peter's], he may be a hundredfold more in winning souls to Christ than I have been in thine infinite and sovereign mercy." Quoted in Burns, *Memoir of the Rev.*, 128.

tender and affecting, as if the people felt that they were praising a present God."[135] Congregants were unable to restrain their emotions as the Holy Spirit moved. Bonar recalled, "On one occasion, for instance, when [M'Cheyne] was speaking tenderly on the words, 'He is altogether lovely,' almost every sentence was responded to by cries of the bitterest agony."[136]

M'Cheyne and Burns co-labored at St. Peter's for several weeks. "During the autumn of 1839, not fewer than 600 to 700 came to converse with the ministers about their souls."[137] The Dundee revival continued through the spring of 1840, even spreading to surrounding areas as M'Cheyne and Burns itinerated. By July 1840, however, M'Cheyne noted that a few were crying out in "extreme" agony, but that such cases were increasingly rare. He lamented that many people had allowed the revival "to slip past them without being saved," yet he rejoiced that he could only count two people who had "openly given the lie to their profession."[138]

Final Years

Many of the features common in M'Cheyne's early ministry marked his last years in Dundee. He continued preaching, praying, and visiting. One marked difference, however, was the amount of time he gave to itinerant preaching. He traveled extensively throughout Scotland, visited Belfast on two occasions, and, in 1842, contributed to what he called "a preaching raid into England."[139] He was so successful as an evangelist that William Burns urged him to consider full-time itinerant ministry:

> Oh! that you and a few more of our brethren were cast forth by the Lord to the field in which I am favoured to be. The people

---

135. Smellie, *Biography of R. M. McCheyne*, 139.

136. *MAR*, 501.

137. *MAR*, 497.

138. *MAR*, 497. For a survey of the revival's aftermath in Dundee, see McLennan, *McCheyne's Dundee*, 149–56.

139. Quoted in Yeaworth, "Robert Murray McCheyne," 300. M'Cheyne's regular absences were not met with St. Peter's full support. Robertson writes, "Many of his congregation understood and appreciated his passion for and need to be involved in other work—but many were also unhappy and could not understand how a minister who was so often ill could manage to go to Israel, England, Ireland and all over Scotland." Robertson, *Awakening*, 187. See also, Yeaworth, "Robert Murray McCheyne," 301. Even Bonar criticized his friend's itinerant work: "Many of us thought that he afterwards erred in the abundant frequency of his evangelistic labours at a time when he was still bound to a particular flock." *MAR*, 60.

are waiting in the market place until someone call them in the name of Jesus . . . I often wish I were laboring along with you from place to place . . . Why should St. Peter's or any other parish have shower upon shower when many districts have not a drop! The time is short. Come away to the help of the Lord.[140]

M'Cheyne's personal preference was indeed to "come away" into the fields of itinerate preaching. He admitted to his sister Eliza, "I think God will yet make me a wandering minister. My nature inclines thereto."[141] Alexander Smellie describes M'Cheyne's leaning as follows: "Had McCheyne's life been spared through a few weeks longer, he would have resigned his pastorate in St. Peter's, and gone out over broad Scotland to publish and commend the love of God in Christ Jesus our Lord."[142]

M'Cheyne lived in the light of eternity, even expecting to die young. According to Bonar, M'Cheyne's "incessant activity was the decided impression on his mind that his career would be short. From the very first days of his ministry he had a strong feeling of this nature."[143] M'Cheyne's

---

140. Quoted in Yeaworth, "Robert Murray McCheyne," 300. See Burns' letter to M'Cheyne on the same subject, quoted in Smellie, *Biography of R. M. McCheyne*, 145–46.

141. Quoted in Yeaworth, "Robert Murray M'Cheyne," 301.

142. Smellie, *Biography of R. M. McCheyne*, 147.

143. *MAR*, 84. David Beaty ponders, "It may have been M'Cheyne's belief that his life would be short that prevented him from ever marrying." Beaty, *An All-Surpassing Fellowship*, 50. The question of M'Cheyne having been engaged to marry is one that has vexed biographers ever since Alexander Smellie posited, "the fact appears to be indisputable." Smellie, *Biography of R. M. McCheyne*, 152. First, Smellie argues, M'Cheyne was engaged to a Miss Maxwell, the daughter of a Dundee physician. However, "her relatives, as some of their descendants believe, interposed to prevent it. They feared for that frail body of his, and judged it wiser that there should not be any wedding-bond." Smellie, *Biography of R. M. McCheyne*, 153. Second, Smellie refers to a letter from Somerville to M'Cheyne that he takes as an allusion to M'Cheyne's engagement to Jessie Thain, the daughter of an elder at St. Peter's. Smellie, *Biography of R. M. McCheyne*, 153–57. Murdoch Campbell, the editor of Jessie Thain's diary, believes Jessie's words upon Robert's death are "strongly suggestive of a relationship nearer than that of a pastor to his flock." Campbell, *Diary of Jessie Thain*, 8. However, Smellie's evidence for M'Cheyne's purported engagements is anecdotal at best. See Yeaworth, "Robert Murray M'Cheyne," 137. Van Valen agrees, "There was talk of an association between him and Jessie Thain, but no evidence for this has ever appeared." Van Valen, *Constrained by His Love*, 250, 445. Robertson adds, "There is no evidence of an engagement. McCheyne does not mention this, nor for that matter does he hint at any relationship with Miss Maxwell in any of his papers and diaries. There is no doubt that Jessie Thain did have an affection for McCheyne, but there were good reasons for that and it is by no means clear that this affection extended into what we might call 'being in love.'"

"activity" continued until the spring of 1843. In February, he traveled on his final evangelistic tour in the districts of Deer and Ellon, preaching twenty-four times over three weeks.[144] He returned to Dundee on March 1 and was soon exposed to the typhus fever raging through his parish.[145] He preached his final sermon at St. Peter's on March 12. According to Bonar, he preached on Hebrews 9:15 in the morning "with uncommon solemnity," and on Romans 9:22–23 in the afternoon "with peculiar strength upon the sovereignty of God."[146] God blessed M'Cheyne's preaching until the end. A note from a visitor, present at these sermons, was found unopened in M'Cheyne's study days after his death: "I heard you preach last Sabbath evening, and it pleased God to bless that sermon to my soul. It was not so much what you said, as your manner of speaking that struck me. I saw in you a beauty in holiness I never saw before."[147]

By Tuesday, M'Cheyne was in the typhus fever's grip.[148] He was confined to his bed as his health continued to deteriorate. On the morning

---

Robertson, *Awakening*, 143. Smellie also does not recognize that M'Cheyne's closest friends did not marry early (Andrew Bonar married at age 38, Horatius Bonar at 35, James Hamilton at 32, and Alexander Somerville at 28). Thus, M'Cheyne's lack of a formal engagement before entering his fourth decade was not unusual.

144. *MAR*, 160.
145. *MAR*, 161.
146. *MAR*, 162.
147. *MAR*, 163.
148. David Robertson (*Awakening*, 144) and Derek Prime (*Robert Murray McCheyne*, 107) erroneously believe, following Thomas Guthrie, that a gymnastic collapse was the catalyst for M'Cheyne's early death. See also, Van Valen, *Constrained by His Love*, 252–53. Guthrie recounts the story in his autobiography: "On behalf of Church Extension I visited a considerable portion of Forfarshire, to stir up to zeal in that cause both the ministers and people. It was then that Robert McCheyne met with an accident which began the illness that terminated in his death. He accompanied me on my tour to Errol, full of buoyant spirits and heavenly conversation. After breakfast we strolled into the garden where there stood some gymnastic poles and apparatus set up for the use of Mr. Grierson's family. No ascetic, no stiff and formal man, but ready for any innocent and healthful amusement, these no sooner caught McCheyne's eye than, challenging me to do the like, he rushed at a horizontal pole resting on the forks of two upright ones, and went through a lot of athletic maneuvers. I was buttoning up to succeed, and try if I could not outdo him, when, as he hung by his heels and hands some five or six feet above the ground, all of a sudden the pole snapped asunder, and he came down with his back on the ground with a tremendous *thud*. He sickened, was borne into the manse, lay there for days, and was never the same man again." Guthrie, *Autobiography of Thomas Guthrie*, 174–75 (emphasis original). Smellie correctly concludes that Guthrie "perhaps magnified overmuch." Smellie, *Biography of R. M. McCheyne*, 76. He then supplies Dr. Grierson's account of the injury, in which the

of March 25, "he lifted up his hands as if in the attitude of pronouncing a blessing, and then sank down. Not a groan or a sigh, but only a quiver of the lip, and his soul was at rest."[149]

Bonar hurried to Dundee to serve at St. Peter's. He arrived at 9:00 p.m. to find hundreds of people weeping in the church. He recorded, "During prayer, the cries and lamentations of the people resounded through the church, as if their hearts were bursting . . . O, it was truly solemn, and when I gazed upon Robert's face, I cannot tell what agony it was to think he was away."[150] Bonar preached at St. Peter's twice the next morning from Romans 8:38 and 8:28–30.

M'Cheyne was buried in the St. Peter's cemetery on Thursday, March 30. Bonar, Burns, and Somerville led the services. John Roxburgh captured the prevailing sentiment regarding M'Cheyne's life and legacy by saying:

> The grave was dug in the pathway, near the south-west corner of the church, and within a few yards from the pulpit from which he has so often and so faithfully proclaimed the word of life; and in this his lowly resting-place all that is mortal of him was

---

medical man determines, "The utmost that can be said as to the fall is, that it was justly regarded as an additional reason for his obtaining rest from hard study, pulpit, and other professional labor." Quoted in Smellie, *Biography of R. M. McCheyne*, 76. For an account of M'Cheyne's typhus fever in relation to the overall epidemic in Dundee, see McLennan, *McCheyne's Dundee*, 13–16.

149. *MAR*, 165. Bonar records in his diary: "This afternoon about five o'clock, a message has just come to tell me of Robert M'Cheyne's death. Never, never yet in all my life have I felt anything like this. It is a blow to myself, to his people, to the Church of Christ in Scotland . . . My heart is sore. It makes me feel death near myself now. Life has lost half its joys, were it not the hope of saving souls. There was no friend whom I loved like him." Bonar, *Diary and Letters*, 101. March 25 also marked the death of Bonar's father, and so, in subsequent years, he remembered and reflected on this solemn date. See Bonar, *Diary and Letters*, 116, 119, 139, 166, 194–95, 207, 213, 225, 232, 235, 244, 256, 269, 274, 288, 298. Somerville said of M'Cheyne's death: "I am praying not merely to be comforted under this stroke, but, what is of infinitely greater importance, that the death of Robert may be sanctified to me. I have great need of quickening in private and in my ministerial work . . . His death I do not think could ever have made a deeper impression." Quoted in Smith, *A Modern Apostle*, 69. James Hamilton notes in a letter to Andrew Bonar: "When the post brought two letters this afternoon from Dundee, giving an account of the funeral, and I felt that the grave had really closed upon him, I cannot tell the feelings of desolation that came over my mind." Quoted in Arnot, *Life of James Hamilton*, 213–14. William Cunningham heard of M'Cheyne's death between Sunday services and exclaimed, "Help, Lord, for the godly man ceaseth." Quoted in Yeaworth, "Robert Murray McCheyne," 349.

150. Bonar, *Diary and Letters*, 70.

deposited, amid the tears and sobs of the crowd. There his flesh rests in that assured hope of a blessed resurrection, of the elevating and purifying influences of which *his life and his ministry were so beauteous an example. His memory will never perish.*[151]

CONCLUSION

What is noteworthy from the foregoing account of M'Cheyne's life and ministry is the all-encompassing nature of his commitment to Christ. Christ captivated M'Cheyne's heart, occupied his thoughts, and governed his life. M'Cheyne's spent his brief life seeking Christ in private and public. He wrote to an inquirer, "I do trust you are seeking hard after him whom your soul loveth ... He is a powerful and precious Saviour, and happy are they who put their trust in him. He is the Rose of Sharon, lovely to look upon, having all divine and human excellencies meeting in himself."[152] M'Cheyne sought earnestly after the one whom his soul loved, and it is this ardent affection that shaped his Christocentric spirituality.

---

151. *MAR*, 603 (emphasis added). Yeaworth says the funeral crowd was estimated 6,000–7,000. See, Yeaworth, "Robert Murray McCheyne," 350.

152. *MAR*, 282.

3

Learning Christ
M'Cheyne's Context

M'Cheyne's ministry took place "against a backdrop of astonishing change, profound and many-faceted, which left few areas of Scottish life untouched."[1] The present chapter surveys M'Cheyne's historical moment by concentrating on three key contexts. The first is ecclesiastical. M'Cheyne ministered during the Ten Years' Conflict when upstart evangelicals wrestled with long-tenured moderates for power in the Church of Scotland. The battle ultimately ended with the Disruption of 1843, which occurred less than two months after M'Cheyne's death. The second is philosophical. Scottish common sense realism saturated much of the kirk and provided a sensible outlook on both theology and spirituality. The third context is cultural. The values of a nascent Victorian culture were altering Scottish life. Additionally, the influence of romanticism cultivated emotional subjectivism and provided fertile soil for evangelical piety.

After the contextual survey, the chapter considers M'Cheyne's influences under two categories. The first category is pastoral. Men such as Henry Duncan, John Bonar, Thomas Chalmers, and Robert Smith Candlish recognized M'Cheyne's potential. Here was a minister who promised to perpetuate their respective ideals of an evangelical ministry. They granted M'Cheyne unusual prominence and influence in the Church's courts. The second category is historical. M'Cheyne's theology and spirituality did not develop in a vacuum, but emerged from a rich heritage

1. Cheyne, *Studies in Scottish Church*, 107.

provided by the Reformers and Puritans. His soul especially resonated with the writings of Jonathan Edwards and David Brainerd.

ECCLESIASTICAL CONTEXT

The changes sweeping through Scotland in the early nineteenth century were vast, as the country moved from a rural to an urban society, from an agricultural to an industrial economy, from an oligarchic to a more democratic form of government, and from a religious to a secular worldview. David Currie concludes that "many people caught up in the midst of those transitions embraced Evangelicalism as a social and intellectual movement which, through its commitment to actively spreading vital Christianity throughout the Kirk, the nation, and the world, had the best potential to transcend the growing divisions within Scotland."[2]

By 1834, the evangelicals had assumed "a majority in the General Assembly for the first time in approximately one hundred years."[3] The moderates, who had dominated the Church for over a century, stood against the evangelicals. Scholars debate the origin of moderatism, but agree that it had flooded the established church by the 1750s.[4] Scholars also differ on the precise meaning of moderatism.[5] Broadly speaking, moderates were those in the Church who "were so satisfied with the ecclesiastical settlement secured by the Revolution of 1690 that they were prepared to endure hardships such as the presentation of ministers to parishes by patrons and the necessity of subscribing to the Westminster Confession of Faith."[6] Moderates valued culture, education, and the core principles of

---

2. Currie, "Growth of Evangelicalism," 141.

3. Cameron et al., *Dicitionary of Scottish Church*, 246.

4. According to C. H. Sefton, part of the difficulty is explained by a failure to distinguish "between moderate 'trends' in the C of S and the moderates perceived as a party by nineteenth-century opponents." Cameron et al., *Dictionary of Scottish Church*, 596. For competing views on the origins of the moderate party, see Stanley, *Lectures on History*, 97–139; Rainy, *Three Lectures*; Brown, "Dean Stanley," 145–72; Tulloch, "Dean Stanley," 698–717. See also Drummond and Bulloch, *Scottish Church*; Voges, "Moderate and Evangelical Thinking," 141–57.

5. See Miller, *Two Parties*.

6. Cameron et al., *Dictionary of Scottish Church*, 596. G. D. Henderson says, "[Moderates] loved the ancient classics and modern literature more than works of Dogma." Henderson, *Church of Scotland*, 15. Edwin Sydney expresses typical evangelical sentiment regarding moderates as follows: "A moderate divine is one who has a very moderate share of zeal for God. Consequently, a moderate divine contents

the Enlightenment.[7] They tended to downplay the proclamation of God's grace toward sinners in Christ in favor of moralistic rationalism.[8]

The shift in ecclesiastical power began, in part, as a result of the democratic idealism sweeping through Europe in the early decades of the nineteenth century. Democratic fervor caused many in Scotland to see moderatism "as one step toward the infidelity of the free-thinking revolutionaries. [Thus,] a return to orthodoxy in the early decades broke Moderatism's long-held grip on the Church, with long-suppressed Evangelicalism ready to fill the vacuum."[9] Who were the evangelicals? Their core tenets were found in the flourishing missionary and Bible societies, both of which thrived on a blossoming prayer movement in the Church. Additionally, a fresh evangelical piety was replacing the old and cold

---

himself with a moderate degree of labour in his Master's vineyard. A moderate divine is too polite and rational to give any credit to the antiquated divinity of our articles, homilies and liturgy. And, therefore, he seldom quotes them except it be to show his contempt for them, or to torture their meaning; nevertheless, a moderate divine is ready enough to subscribe to them, if by so doing he can get an immoderate share of church preferment. A moderate divine is always very cool and calm in his pulpit; he never argues, except when he is preaching, against such fathers of Israel as the pious and lowly Mr. Hallward; and then a moderate divine loses all his moderation. And so, I daresay, do the moderates of the kirk of Scotland, when denouncing the principles and conduct of the evangelical and zealous servants of Christ, who seek to do away with abuses which are favourable to moderatism. A moderate divine is usually an advocate for card-parties, and for all assemblies except religious ones; but thinks no name too hard for those who assemble to spend an hour or two in prayer, and hearing God's word." Quoted in Buchanan, *Ten Years' Conflict*, 176–77.

7. Voges, "Moderate and Evangelical Thinking," 142.

8. Macleod, *Scottish Theology*, 199. See also, Cunningham, *Church History of Scotland*, 413. Cunningham goes so far as to call moderatism nothing less than "Pelagian Unitarianism." Quoted in Rainy and Mackenzie, *Life of William Cunningham*, 63.

9. Yeaworth, "Robert Murray McCheyne," 226. Currie demonstrates that one key to evangelicalism's increasing influence was university appointments. "First generation Evangelicals had largely been unable to tap the potential of the professoriate, mainly because Moderates were so firmly in control of the university appointment system." Currie, "Growth of Evangelicalism," 335.

intellectualism.¹⁰ Yet, an unresolved conflict continued into the 1830s: the matter of patronage.¹¹

Erastianism in the Church of Scotland

K. R. Ross provides the following description of patronage: "The landowners, who supplied church accommodation and ministerial stipends, retained, as a right of property, their positions as patrons. Often the patron, through informal consultation, presented a candidate acceptable to the people, but difficulties arose when the patron was out of sympathy with parochial opinion."¹² Patronage had been a divisive issue in the Church since the early seventeenth century. It caused the first secession from the established church when, in 1733, Ebenezer Erskine's opposition led him and three others to form the associate presbytery.¹³ By the mid-eighteenth century, moderates had come to terms with patronage, in part "because they believed the system produced a ministry of higher caliber than could be expected from the operation of popular call."¹⁴ Evangelicals viewed patronage as nothing less than Erastianism, according to which the state is superior to the church in ecclesiastical

---

10. Currie argues that four factors contributed to evangelicalism's rise: (1) the growth of evangelical periodicals; (2) the formation of missionary and Bible societies; (3) the concentration on lay education; and (4) the commitment to personal and corporate prayer. Currie, "Growth of Evangelicalism," 1–9. See also, Yeaworth, "Robert Murray McCheyne," 226. Bruce McLennan says, "In the days of Burns and McCheyne . . . the church in Scotland was still slowly emerging from the age of the Moderates." McLennan, *McCheyne's Dundee*, 32.

11. According to Voges, the simplest definition of moderates and evangelicals is that the former stood "for" and the latter "against" patronage. Voges, "Moderate and Evangelical Thinking," 142.

12. Cameron et al., *Dictionary of Scottish Church*, 649. For studies of the Church of Scotland's relationship with the state, see Brown, *Church and State in Scotland*; Lyall, *Church and State in Scotland*, 1–68. See also, Brown, *Thomas Chalmers*.

13. For the background to this controversy, see M'Kerrow, *History of the Secession Church*. For concise treatments, see M'Crie, *Story of Scottish Church*, 465–75, and Henderson, *Church of Scotland*, 105–7.

14. Cameron et al., *Dictionary of Scottish Church*, 649.

matters.[15] They believed that Christ is the church's true head.[16] Therefore, they strongly opposed the prevailing moderate opinion. It was not until evangelicals gained a majority at the 1834 General Assembly, however, that the conflict overtook the Church's courts.

Ten Years' Conflict

M'Cheyne was licensed to the gospel ministry in 1835. Thus his ministerial labors took place "within the controversial and prosperous period of the history of the Church of Scotland known as the 'Ten Years' Conflict' which culminated in the Disruption of 1843."[17] The struggle began when an evangelical majority at the 1834 Assembly led to the passing of the Veto Act.[18] The Act asserted that patrons could not "intrude" unacceptable ministers on unwilling congregations. Instead, if most male communicant heads of families objected to the candidate, for any reason, the presbytery was bound to reject him for the position. The Assembly also passed the Chapel Act, granting "chapels of ease"[19] equal status to parish churches in matters *quoad sacra*. It also permitted chapel ministers to occupy seats in Church courts.[20] Alan Rodger explains why this

---

15. David Little defines Erastianism as follows: "The doctrine that the civil state has final earthly authority over expression and practice of religious beliefs and over ecclesiastical organizations. It found its most characteristic form in the middle of the seventeenth century during and after the Westminster Assembly debates concerning the shape and organization of English religious life." McKim, *Encyclopedia*, 122.

16. See also, WCF 25.1. Stewart J. Brown writes, "Patronage became a symbol of the subordination of the Church to the upper social orders, especially the landed interest." Brown and Fry, *Scotland in the Age*, 6. For a representative defense of Christ's headship over the church as the animating principle in the formation of the free church, see Wilson, *Free Church Principles*, 33–66.

17. Yeaworth, "Robert Murray McCheyne," 336. For a concise history, see Cheyne, *Ten Years' Conflict*. The best extensive history is Buchanan, *Ten Years' Conflict*. The most useful overview from a judicial perspective is Rodger, *The Courts*, 1–55.

18. Thomas Chalmers first proposed the Act at the 1833 Assembly, and it was narrowly defeated. It passed at the 1834 Assembly by a vote of 184 to 139. Watt, *Thomas Chalmers*, 129–34.

19. Such chapels had only a preaching function and stood in contrast to the *quoad omnia* (literally "with respect to all things") parishes, which signified a constituted governmental unit for ecclesiastical and civil purposes. Cameron et al., *Dictionary of Scottish Church*, 162.

20. Buchanan, *Ten Years' Conflict*, 317–48. The expression *Quoad sacra* ("in respect to sacred things") refers "to a parish constituted for ecclesiastical purposes only,

move threatened moderatism: "The Evangelicals tended to favour, and the Moderates oppose, giving full rights to the ministers of the Chapels of Ease because so many were evangelicals who would reinforce that strength of that party in the church courts, especially in the General Assembly."[21]

The Court of Session checked the evangelicals's ascendancy four years later when, by a vote of eight judges to five, it ruled that the patron alone could nominate a minister to a vacant charge. They also declared it illegal for the Church to create new parishes independent of the State. Legal battles ensued, and ultimately reached the House of Lords, which upheld the Court's ruling.

The evangelicals's response led to the 1842 Assembly passing the "Claim of Right," which declared, "The Acts of Parliament dealing with the government, etc. of the Church which Parliament had passed after the Act of Union, without the consent of 'the Church and nation,' are 'void and null, and of no legal force or effect.'"[22] Essentially, the legislation insisted on Christ's headship over the Church and the Church's exclusive power over ecclesiastical affairs. In November 1842, four hundred and sixty-five evangelical ministers gathered for a convocation in Edinburgh, to discuss the Church's present problems and possible remedies. The Convocation ultimately decided to withdraw from the Church if their Claim of Right was rejected.[23] The government's stance on ecclesiastical sovereignty stood unchanged, and so, on May 18, 1843, the Disruption occurred—what Michael Fry has called "the most important event in the whole of Scotland's nineteenth-century history."[24] Some 450 ministers,

---

and without civil responsibilities, jurisdiction or significance." Cameron et al., *Dictionary of Scottish Church*, 688.

21. Rodger, *The Courts*, 10. Evangelicals and moderates disagreed not only on patronage but also on church extension. Chapels of Ease were something close to modern day church plants, and evangelicals, not moderates, filled the rolls of chapel ministers.

22. Quoted in Rodger, *The Courts*, 27. The Act of Union refers to the 1707 union of Scotland and England. While Scotland remained independent in its legal and religious systems, the two became one in coinage, taxation, trade, and parliament.

23. For a defense of the Claim of Right, see Moncreiff, *Vindication*. For the sermon M'Cheyne preached on Thursday, November 24, 1842, after returning from the convocation, see *BOF*, 112–16.

24. Fry, *Patronage and Principle*, 52. For histories of the Disruption, see especially Henderson, *Heritage*; Brown, *Annals of Disruption*; Cameron et al., *Dictionary of Scottish Church*; Brown and Fry, *Scotland in Age*; Withrington, "Disruption," 118–53. Yeaworth, reflecting a standard view, argues that the Disruption was due in large part to the democratic values increasingly prevalent throughout Scotland after the Reform

along with at least one-half of the members, left the established church to found the Free Church.[25] The consequences of the Disruption were far reaching. To begin with, the Church of Scotland lost an astonishing number of ministers of high caliber. Thomas Guthrie states, "Within their ranks was contained beyond controversy a very large proportion of the talent and piety of the Scottish Ministry."[26] While Sir Owen Chadwick regrets that Chalmers and his constituents could not wait for the requisite changes, his valuation of the Ten Years' Conflict is positive: "The headship of Christ is that without which churches may as well be swept aside into heaps of rubble or converted into gymnasia. In all the span of Christian history one can find no clearer demonstration of the sacred appeal to that headship . . . than in the events of 1842–43."[27]

M'Cheyne's Place in the Conflict

The evangelical movement in Scotland found many ministers ready to champion the cause. Few young pastors embodied the conflict's spirit so thoroughly as M'Cheyne. Fleming refers to M'Cheyne as "the brightest spirit" of the evangelical movement that continued in the Free Church.[28] A. J. Campbell goes even further, choosing M'Cheyne over Chalmers and Candlish as the "characteristic Evangelical of the period. . . . The sacrifices and venturesomeness of the Disruption would have been impossible save in an atmosphere such as he created."[29] The conflict provided a perfect

---

Bill of 1832. Yeaworth, "Robert Murray McCheyne," 336. See also, Coleman, *Remembering the Past*, 24. Ian Hamilton disagrees, saying, "The Ten Years' Conflict was not about the democratization of the Church. It was about the desire of the Church to be the Church, sovereign within its own domain. Although it was part of a European-wide movement of thought that sought to give new degrees of power to the ordinary people, the Disruption was essentially a spiritual phenomenon." Cameron et al., *Dictionary of Scottish Church*, 247.

25. Brown and Fry, *Scotland in the Age*, 1.

26. Guthrie, *Autobiography of Thomas Guthrie*, 394. Lord Henry Cockburn similarly recalls, "It may be doubted if there be a dozen ministers in Scotland who are, or deserve to be, popular either with the lower or the higher ones, who are not among these. This band contains the whole chivalry of the Church." Cockburn, *Journal of Henry Cockburn*, 337.

27. Cheyne, *Practical and Pious*, 82.

28. Quoted in Yeaworth, "Robert Murray M'Cheyne," 356.

29. Quoted in Yeaworth, "Robert Murray M'Cheyne," 357.

ecclesiastical atmosphere for M'Cheyne's stated views on the church. Bonar assures us of M'Cheyne's evangelical and ecclesiastical *bona fides*, writing,

> Regarding the great public questions that were then shaking the Church of Scotland, his views were decided and unhesitating. No policy, in his view, could be more ruinous to true Christianity, or more fitted to blight vital godliness, than that of Moderatism. He wrote once to a friend in Ireland—"You don't know what Moderatism is. It is a plant that our Heavenly Father never planted, and I trust is now to be rooted up."[30]

The *Dundee Courier* described M'Cheyne as "famous for his non-intrusion violence."[31] He was a recognized leader among young evangelicals, often asked to stir up support for the cause throughout Britain, believing it to be "a righteous struggle."[32] He wrote letters, made speeches, organized meetings, and collected finances.[33] He reasoned in print that Christ's headship is as significant as Christ's divinity.[34] At the evangelical convocation of 1842, M'Cheyne offered a proposal for "united prayer which was widely circulated throughout the country," and he led the meeting in prayer "after a particularly tense and crucial debate."[35] Chalmers's biographer recounted that "the spirit of prayer . . . from the lips of Mr. M'Cheyne . . . conveyed a profounder sense of the divine presence than we ever felt before or since in the most hallowed of our Christian

---

30. *MAR*, 70. In a speech (dated October 13, 1841) on the state of the Church of Scotland, M'Cheyne spoke of the "unholy lives, desolate parishes, and Christless sermons" of the moderates. Quoted in Yeaworth, "Robert Murray McCheyne," 339.

31. Quoted in Yeaworth, "Robert Murray M'Cheyne," 345. Earlier in 1841, the *Courier* attacked M'Cheyne for his evangelical views, stating, "This gentleman is quite superterrestrial and looks down evidently with sublime piety, not only on the minority of Presbytery, but on very many of the majority. He cannot express himself like any other body. Common language is too profane a vehicle for his thoughts." Yeaworth, "Robert Murray M'Cheyne," 345. For an overview of the non-intrusion cause in the Dundee press, the town council, and presbytery, see McLennan, *McCheyne's Dundee*, 35–38.

32. *TPP*, 259.

33. Yeaworth, "Robert Murray McCheyne," 341–43.

34. *Dundee Courier*, April 13, 1841.

35. Yeaworth, "Robert Murray McCheyne," 342. For M'Cheyne's personal notes on the convocation, see MACCH 1.16.

assemblies."[36] Stewart Brown credits M'Cheyne's influence for leading fifteen of the twenty-nine ministers in Dundee to join the free church.[37]

M'Cheyne pastored St. Peter's through the Ten Years' Conflict, often referencing it in his sermons. On June 7, 1840, he declared, "Be not discouraged at the clouds that threaten the Church of Scotland. It may be that an evil day is near, but I believe it will be short."[38] A month earlier, he encouraged his congregation:

> You know the danger with which our church is threatened. We have declared that it is a fundamental law of our church that no pastor be intended on any Christian parish contrary to the Christian people. For since 1834 the civil courts have commended us to ordain in the face of this resolution. They have even forbidden us to preach the gospel within a certain district of our country . . . The government may declare that it shall be the law of the land that pastors be dismissed. In this case there may be, as there was over in England, multitudes of the best ministers set adrift. You may lose your pastor in a single day. In Edinburgh, out of her thirty-four ministers, I suppose not more than six would remain. In Glasgow out of forty, I suppose not so many as six. In your own town, I suppose no more than three. To many I know this appears no calamity, but in the light of eternity it would be a heavy stroke on Scotland. I know that the sensual and political ministers and lovers of this world would like to see the clear riddance of our faithful ministers.[39]

The kirk session at St. Peter's threw their support behind the evangelical cause, publishing a declaration in December 1842 on Christ's supreme headship over the church:

> We are enabled also to assure [our pastor] of the unshaken attachment of his Congregation; and if for the reasons above stated he shall be forced to quit his position as Minister of the Established Church, we have no doubt that, true to the principles of the Reformation Church of Scotland the great majority of his people as well as of the Elders of this congregation will feel themselves called upon to leave the Established Church along with him.[40]

36. Quoted in Yeaworth, "Robert Murray McCheyne," 342.
37. Brown, *Thomas Chalmers*, 335.
38. *OTS*, 81. See also, *BOF*, 76; *TPP*, 259; Lamb, *M'Cheyne from the Pew*, 98–99.
39. *TPP*, 47. See also, *TPH*, 512, 516–17.
40. MACCH 2.7.14.

That M'Cheyne rose to prominence at such a time as the Ten Years' Conflict should not be overlooked. The conflict was a period in which evangelical convictions occupied much of the day's attention and even shaped legislative concerns in the country. In every way, from doctrinal matters to revival impulses, it was an ecclesiastical era suited perfectly for M'Cheyne's personality and gifts.

PHILOSOPHICAL CONTEXT

M'Cheyne lived in a philosophical milieu profoundly affected by what was later called the Enlightenment. Enlightenment philosophy governed intellectual expression throughout the eighteenth century into the early nineteenth century. It also affected religious life. As David Bebbington notes, "Nowhere was the Enlightenment more fully assimilated by an established church than in Scotland."[41] The country housed many Enlightenment thinkers,[42] and soon developed its own distinct emphases.[43]

Divergent Views

When it comes to Scottish philosophy, George Davie notes the difference between the Berkeleian and Hutchesonian systems. The former, in the interest of reconciling progress with traditional standards, affirms that thinkers are to set aside the instincts of the farmer in favor of the sophistication of the philosopher, and to think with the learned while talking with the vulgar. The Hutchesonian system shares the same aim

---

41. Cameron et al., *Dictionary of Scottish Church*, 294. Bebbington has argued that evangelicalism is itself an Enlightenment creation. Bebbington, *Evangelicalism in Modern Britain*. See also, Bebbington, "Evangelical Christianity," 36. For a critique of Bebbington's thesis, see Haykin, and Stewart, *The Advent*, 39–59.

42. While many focus on the French Enlightenment philosophers, Arthur Herman argues, "The Scottish Enlightenment may have been less glamorous, but it was in many ways more robust and original. More important, it was at least as influential. In fact, if one were to draw up a list of the books that dominated the thinking of Europeans in the last quarter of the eighteenth century, the Scottish names stand out"—Adam Smith, David Hume, William Robertson, Adam Ferguson, Thomas Reid, Francis Hutcheson, and Lord Kames. Herman, *How Scots Invented*, 54.

43. For accounts of the Enlightenment in Scotland, see Porter and Teich, *The Enlightenment*; Sher, *Church and University*; Campbell and Skinner, *Origins and Nature*; George, *A Passion for Ideas*; Broadie, *Cambridge Companion*; Stewart, *Studies in Philosophy*.

of reconciling material advanced with the intellectual principle; however, it affirms that thinkers are to respect the instincts of the farmer against the sophistication of the philosopher, and initiate a dialogue between the vulgar and the learned, instead of talking down to the farmer from the standpoint of the philosopher.[44]

Graham Gordon concludes, "Cast in these terms it is easy to place the two most famous philosophers of the Scottish Enlightenment on either side of the divide."[45] On one side, stemming from Berkeleian presuppositions, stands the skepticism of David Hume (1711–1776). On the other side stands Thomas Reid (1778–1820).[46] Hume held that knowledge is based on human perception—we learn through experience. Therefore, we cannot know the world directly; rather, our experienced ideas represent the world to us. While other philosophers taught that the world consists entirely in ideas of the mind, Hume believed the mind too was suspect. As John Frame notes, "If there was no material substance (just experiences and perceptions), there is no mental substance either, just a bundle of perceptions."[47]

While profoundly influential, Hume's skepticism did not make the same inroads in the Church of Scotland as did the thinking of Thomas Reid.[48] Reid rejected Hume's premise that all we understand are personal perceptions.[49] What we know is indeed the real world. We possess innate abilities that lead to concepts of qualities and sensed objects. Against Hume, Reid taught that these concepts are not mere sensations, but

---

44. Davie, *A Passion for Ideas*, 41–42.

45. Graham, "Scottish Philosophy."

46. James McCosh (1811–1894), president of Princeton University, consolidated nineteenth-century Scottish philosophy into a self-conscious identity, teaching "a unity . . . in its methods, its doctrines, and its spirit." Quoted in Graham, *Scottish Philosophy*, 1. McCosh attributed this unity largely to Thomas Reid (1710–1796), who, if not the founder, was at least the archetype of Scottish common sense philosophy. Lowber, *Thought and Religion*, 77.

47. Frame, *History of Western Philosophy*, 242.

48. The church's antagonism toward Hume is evident in the 1755 and 1756 General Assembly's recommendation that ministers be vigilant against philosophical skepticism. See Drummond and Bulloch, *The Scottish Church*, 98. Jack Whytock says, "It would appear that both parties (Moderates and Evangelicals) were united against the skepticism of a Hume but could work well with Common Sense Realism." Whytock, "An Educated Clergy," 133.

49. Reid, *An Inquiry*, 16.

are indeed concepts of something. Frame helpfully summarizes Reid's position:

> [According to Reid, there] are principles accepted by people in everyday conversation and business. They cannot be justified by Cartesian arguments or reduced to sensations as in empiricism. But they do not need that kind of justification. They are *first* principles, the principles that we assume when we seek to gain additional knowledge. We have the right to believe these principles even if we cannot justify them, even if we cannot demonstrate that they belong to common sense. The fact is that common-sense principles are better known than any of the claims that people might use to refute them.[50]

Reid's common sense ideas soon infiltrated the departments of art, science, and religion. According to Paul Helm, Scottish common sense realism "cohered with theism, since God is both the source of the common-sense principles, for he has implanted them in our nature, and, on some accounts at least, is himself one of those principles."[51] The wedding of common sense philosophy to religion was inescapable as many of its earliest proponents—including Reid—were presbyterian pastors.[52] One of Reid's protégés was Thomas Brown (1778–1820), who took up the chair of moral philosophy at Edinburgh University and further developed common sense philosophy.[53] Brown was a significant influence on Thomas Chalmers (1780–1847),[54] who proved to be the greatest influence on M'Cheyne.

M'Cheyne's Common Sense

Before his conversion, Chalmers "became acquainted with Common Sense philosophy,"[55] and soon was a "most enthusiastic follower" of Brown.[56] When evangelicals assumed ecclesiastical power, Chalmers

---

50. Frame, *History of Western Philosophy*, 243.
51. Cameron et al., *Dictionary of Scottish Church*, 760.
52. Rogers, *Presbyterian Creeds*, 143.
53. See Brown, *Selected Writings*.
54. Redekop, "Reid's Influence," 316. See also, Hart et al., *Rationality*, 71.
55. Cheyne, *Practical and Pious*, 158.
56. Graham, *Scottish Philosophy*, 26. See also, Fergusson, *Scottish Philosophical Theology*, 56–66, 122–29. For Chalmers's appreciative interactions with Reid's rebuttal of Hume, see Chalmers, *Works of Thomas Chalmers*, 91, 154–56; Chalmers, *Butler's*

was teaching his own version of common sense principles at the Divinity Hall.[57] David Bebbington writes, "Chalmers built on a class of writing increasingly regarded as the foundation of Evangelical thinking, the works of the Scottish common-sense school of philosophers."[58] Michael Gavreau believes Chalmers reshaped common sense philosophy into "a weapon in the arsenal of Christian apologetic."[59] Chalmers's "reshaping" of common sense philosophy is better understood as his submitting reason to God's revelation in Christ, which is received by faith. He taught that man's reason alone is incapable of grasping ultimate truth, yet reason is a necessary servant when it comes to inquiry.[60] Gavreau concludes, "The Common Sense epistemology . . . accorded perfectly with the Presbyterians' need for religious truth to appeal to the mind."[61]

Currie argues that evangelicals possessed a notable "commitment to common sense philosophy."[62] The philosophical system played something of a shaping role in the evangelical pulpit. Paul Helm says it "enabled busy preachers to maintain a largely non-theoretical stance in the pulpit, while at the same time vindicating certain metaphysical positions widely believed to be endorsed by Scripture."[63] Common sense realism's permeation meant that evangelical preaching, which often rested on sensible arguments regarding eternity and godliness, became increasingly popular and desirable. In such a philosophical milieu, M'Cheyne found audiences prepared for his logical and rational preaching. He understood certain universal truths (e.g., God's authority, man's sinfulness, hell's punishment, and heaven's blessedness) to be clear to every hearer, and so he preached accordingly. For example, when speaking of Christ's tears in

---

Analogy, 180–82; Chalmers, *Posthumous Works*, 172–74.

57. For an overview of the Scottish Enlightenment's relationship to theological education, see Whytock, *An Educated Clergy*, 115–17.

58. Bebbington, *Evangelicalism in Modern Britain*," 59. Although A. T. B. McGowan believes Bebbington's argument for the Enlightenment as a beneficial movement for evangelicalism is misguided, he states, "The work of Thomas Reid was a significant influence for good." Haykin and Stewart, *The Advent*, 79.

59. Gavreau, *Evangelical Century*, 28. Gavreau argues that while common sense philosophy was attractive to Chalmers, he demoted it to a position well below God's revelation in Christ, which can be only received by faith. Such demotion, however, does not remove the utility of reason in religious inquiry.

60. Gavreau, *Evangelical Century*, 29.

61. Gavreau, *Evangelical Century*, 28.

62. Currie, "Growth of Evangelicalism," 281.

63. Cameron et al., *Dictionary of Scottish Church*, 760.

Gethsemane and his cry to the Father to take away the cup of suffering, M'Cheyne declared, "This shows us the amazing stupidity and sottish insensitivity of you who are *unconverted* and *unconcerned*."[64] His reasoning is sensible and realistic: if Christ trembled before God's wrath, how can sinners not live in fear before God? M'Cheyne also understood God's love in Christ to be obvious. In a sermon on Hebrews 9:6–8, he preached, "The moment that Christ died the way into the holiest of all was made completely manifest; and this is the glory of the gospel above the Jewish dispensation. The freeness, the completeness, the all-sufficiency of it, is made manifest. It is made so plain a child can understand it."[65]

M'Cheyne's common-sense preaching was hardly unique in his time—or even in Scottish history.[66] Nonetheless, noticing his philosophical context shows how he was "in harmony with the spirit of the age,"[67] and helps explain why his ministry was so readily received.

CULTURAL CONTEXT

In Tim Blanning's estimation, one of the most significant eighteenth-century revolutions was the "romantic."[68] It was a new way of looking at the world that "deeply affected the evangelical movement."[69] David Bebbington goes so far as to say that "the chief explanation for the transformation of Evangelicalism in the years around 1830 is the spread of Romanticism."[70]

---

64. *SOH*, 76 (emphasis original). Thomas Chalmers, in a sermon on Isaiah 7:3–5, reveals something of a similar realistic approach when he exhorts his hearers to examine if "you are in a state that will do for you to die in." After a series of appeals to show that the unbeliever lives in a dreadful state in relation to death, Chalmers declares, "Now, all this, you know, must and will happen—your common sense and common experience serve to convince you of it." Chalmers, *Sermons*, 430.

65. *SOH*, 154. See also, *SOH*, 35, 75, 109, 126, 140; *TPH*, 21, 33, 125, 182, 222, 312; *BOF*, 85, 106, 114, 163; *OTS*, 50; *TPP*, 133, 155; *NTS*, 92, 169.

66. Enright, "Preaching and Theology," 263.

67. Bebbington, *Evangelicalism in Modern Britain*, 60.

68. Blanning, *Romantic Revolution*, x. For an in-depth analysis of romanticism in Britain, see Dabundo, *Encyclopedia of Romanticism*.

69. Bebbington, *Dominance of Evangelicalism*, 150–51.

70. Bebbington, *Evangelicalism in Modern Britain*, 103. Bebbington argues that romanticism's "influence was felt not only on particular doctrines . . . but also in due course on the whole temper of theology." Bebbington, *Evangelicalism in Modern Britain*, 144. See also, Hopkins, *Nonconformity's Romantic Generation*, 3–4. For arguments

Romanticism

The term "romanticism" refers to a mood that permeated society throughout the nineteenth century, and even into the twentieth century.[71] According to some scholars, it defies precise definition.[72] For example, Arthur Lovejoy, former professor of philosophy at Johns Hopkins, writes, "Any attempt at a *general* appraisal even of a single chronologically determinate Romanticism—still more, of 'Romanticism' as a whole—is a fatuity."[73] Other scholars are more confident in defining romanticism. H. R. Mackintosh calls the movement "an impassioned return to natural instincts, to life, to freedom, to individual predilection, to the spontaneity of the creative fancy."[74] Most scholars agree that romanticism was, at minimum, a movement that emphasized feeling in contrast to Enlightenment rationalism.[75]

Although romanticism was in many ways a literary movement, it also "caught the imagination of the day's greatest philosophical minds, and theologians were numbered among its most seminal thinkers."[76] These theologians cultivated a romantic taste that, according to Bebbington, caused evangelicals to expect "ideas to be conveyed in a way that evoked powerful emotion."[77] Mark Smith argues that this romantic spirit led British evangelicals to develop a heightened supernaturalism, articulate more robust views on the inspiration of Scripture, emphasize revivalism, insist on the pursuit of holiness, and place greater stress on the second advent of Christ.[78] The romantic spirit also allowed Scottish evangelicals to express their long-tenured Calvinism with more palatability. Currie

---

against Bebbington's evaluation of romanticism's influence, see Haykin and Stewart, *The Advent*, 33–34.

71. Bebbington, *Evangelicalism in Modern Britain*, 80.

72. Reardon, *Religion in the Age*, 1. F. R. de Toreinx, the first French historian of romanticism, says his field is "just that which cannot be defined." Quoted in Blanning, *Romantic Revolution*, xiv.

73. Lovejoy, *Essays in History*, 252 (emphasis original).

74. Mackintosh, *Types of Modern Theology*, 33.

75. Brown, *Romanticism*, 8.

76. Edwards, *A History of Preaching*, 592.

77. Bebbington, *Dominance of Evangelicalism*, 162.

78. Smith, "Religion," 342–43. For more on romanticism and the church in Scotland, see Pittock, *Edinburgh Companion*, 112–23. See also, Stubenrauch, *Evangelical Age*, 58–99. For relevant primary source material, see Parsons and Wolffe, *Religion in Victorian Britain*.

suggests that romanticism created a "progressive and practical version of Calvinism," that toned down "the preoccupations of high Calvinism with God's eternal decrees."[79] Additionally, romanticism's appreciation for an emotional approach to religion fueled a revival of prayer meetings and societies throughout the country. Participants at these meetings looked to prayer as the soul's "contact" with God.[80] George Kitson Clark says the marriage between romanticism and evangelicalism is undeniable: "Evangelical Christianity seems to satisfy all the categories of Romanticism, except the love of fancy dress."[81]

Bernard Reardon has shown that while literary critics distinguish between the romantic and Victorian periods, from a religious perspective, "the whole of the nineteenth century exudes an aura of Romanticism to a greater or lesser degree."[82] Therefore, an account of M'Cheyne's cultural context must situate him within the burgeoning Victorian culture of the 1830s. Victorian Scotland came to birth as the evangelicals grew to prominence in the 1830s.[83] The Victorian Era (1837–1901) saw transformation in science, education, politics, communications, medicine, mass culture, the physical fabric of life, as well as the legal status of workers and women.[84] It was an age that valued learning, morality, and expansion. Ian Bradley has demonstrated that evangelicals and Victorians had a symbiotic relationship—with each benefitting the other.[85] The Victorian context provided the cultural soil in which evangelicalism could grow with relative freedom, and the evangelicals fueled the Victorians's seriousness and high-mindedness. T. M. Devine argues, "The Victorian Age saw a quite remarkable and hitherto unprecedented fusion between Christian ethos and civic policy. Many of the great issues of the day, such as poor housing, sanitation, crime and the provision of public utilities, were dealt with from an overtly religious perspective."[86]

---

79. Currie, "Growth of Evangelicalism," 71.

80. Currie, "Growth of Evangelicalism," 386.

81. Clark, "Romantic Element," 230. Robert Palmer calls evangelicalism and romanticism "kindred mode[s] of thought." Palmer, "Andrew E. Bonar," 357.

82. Reardon, *Religion in the Age*, 2.

83. Drummond and Bulloch, *Church in Victorian Scotland*, 1.

84. Michael, *Victorian Britain*, ix. For more on Victorian religion, see Clark, *The Making*, 147–205.

85. Bradley, *The Call*.

86. Devine, *Scottish Nation*, 365.

The Victorian spirit affected the Scottish church in two notable areas. The first was in its esteem of preaching. "It was not worship, as normally understood, that drew the crowds in Victorian Scotland, but oratory. Even the prayers were rhetorical."[87] In his magisterial work on the history of preaching, Hughes Oliphant Old says, "[In the Victorian Era] there was enormous interest in heroic preachers. That was one of the contributions of romanticism. The virtuosity of individual preachers was cherished, as were the talents of extraordinary singers or instrumentalists. In this respect preaching was a popular art."[88] Lord's Day sermons were valued entertainment in Victorian Scotland, with unconverted people regularly flocking to the buildings of celebrated preachers. M'Cheyne acknowledged and lamented as much, telling his St. Peter's congregation, "This is an age for hearing sermons; but there is little hearing the Word for all that."[89]

Secondly, the Victorian age emphasized a devotional and individual approach to spirituality. There was a time when the objectivity and intellectualism of the Westminster Confession influenced public thinking, but since the growth of the evangelical party, beginning in the late eighteenth century, there had been a spontaneous increase in the emotional content of Scottish devotion, a subjectivism, and an awareness of the personal and inward consequences of belief.[90]

Such hallmarks were congruent with M'Cheyne's temperament. In his valuable study of nineteen century evangelical preaching, William Enright argues that M'Cheyne was a model of romantic evangelical preaching.[91] Regarding religious matters, M'Cheyne was indeed a careful thinker and a deep feeler. In a diary entry dated May 6, 1832, he provides the following self-assessment: "Naturally of a feeling and sentimental disposition, how much of my religion has been, and to this day is, tinged with these colours of earth."[92] Significantly, M'Cheyne's preaching was an expression of his affections—a fact best observed in noting the emotive language that permeates his sermons. He declared, "O it is sweet to have

---

87. Drummond and Bulloch, *Church in Victorian Scotland*, 48.
88. Old, *Reading and Preaching*, 348.
89. *TPH*, 89.
90. Drummond and Bulloch, *Church in Victorian Scotland*, 184.
91. Enright, "Preaching and Theology," 281.
92. *MAR*, 14.

the smile of Christ! It is sweet to get the love of Christ!"[93] Or again, "There is nothing so lovely to the eyes of a believer as the features of Christ."[94] The following section from a sermon on 2 Corinthians 5:21 entitled, "A New Creature in Affections," is typical of M'Cheyne's preaching:

> [When the Spirit converts a sinner] then it is that flame of love to God who hath so loved him is kindled into a blaze in the believing bosom. This is the first love of the believer. Like the woman in the gospels, forgiven much, he cannot but love much. Nor is this a fitful affection, a mere blaze of romantic attachment; it settles down into an ever-growing, ever-increasing affection. Indeed, if we were left to ourselves this grace would all vanish away; the flame so happily kindled would flicker and die as a lamp would. But God is faithful and has declared that when He begins a good work He will finish it! He reveals to us more and more of the love of Jesus, and this adds new fuel to the flame of our love to Him. The more we gaze the more we love. The more we look upon that Sun, the more our faces shine with the refulgence. Beholding as in a glass this love of his, which is indeed the glory of God, we are changed![95]

M'Cheyne possessed requisite qualities for sermonic appeal to a cultural context characterized by romantic and Victorian values. His spirituality wedded deep devotion and emotion to evangelical doctrine. As such, Crawford Gribben is right to recognize M'Cheyne "as the patron saint of Victorian evangelicals."[96]

PASTORAL INFLUENCES

While M'Cheyne's early ministerial network was extensive, formative, and positive, four relationships stand out as especially significant for his life and ministry.

---

93. *BOF*, 42.
94. *TPP*, 304.
95. *NTS*, 175.
96. Gribben and Stunt, *Prisoners of Hope?*, 191. Gribben maintains that Andrew Bonar's theology and piety were "very much part and parcel of the Romantic tenor of his age." Gribben and Stunt, *Prisoners of Hope?*, 184.

Henry Duncan (1774–1846)

In his youth, M'Cheyne and his siblings often vacationed with a maternal aunt in Ruthwell. He relished the rural scenery, sketching the panoramas in his notebooks. Henry Duncan served as minister at Ruthwell, and he was a giant in the community. M'Cheyne, along with the other parish children, loved to visit the manse. A kinship formed quickly between the boy and the minister, with M'Cheyne often referring to Duncan as "Uncle Henry."[97] L. J. Van Valen says the relationship had much compatibility: "[Duncan's] qualities and interests differed little from Robert's. The minister loved nature, was proficient in geography, and was familiar with literature."[98] For close to fifty years, Duncan's broad abilities and interests shaped the parish. He pursued schemes for assisting the poor and increasing the educational standards of his parishioners. He instituted a system of non-charitable savings banks in 1810.[99] Duncan began his ministry with moderate leanings but later turned evangelical, publicly opposing patronage in 1827. He was elected moderator of the General Assembly in 1839 during the evangelical ascendancy.[100] Duncan was also a close friend of the popular Edward Irving,[101] but he later participated in the Assembly's defrocking of Irving for his heretical views on Christology.[102] Duncan guided M'Cheyne through licensure in the Presbytery of

---

97. The best biography of Duncan is Duncan, *Memoir*. Also useful, especially for its account of his social work, is Hall, *Dr. Duncan*.

98. Van Valen, *Constrained by His Love*, 28.

99. Yeaworth, "Robert Murray M'Cheyne," 55. See also, Dinwiddie, *Ruthwell Cross*, 130.

100. Yeaworth, "Robert Murray M'Cheyne," 55.

101. On hearing of Irving's death in 1834, M'Cheyne wrote, "Heard of Edward Irving's death. I look back on him with awe, as on the saints and martyrs of old. A holy man in spite of all his delusions and errors. He is now with his God and Saviour, whom he wronged so much, yet, I am persuaded, loved so sincerely." *MAR*, 25. Irving represented romantic evangelicalism in all its strengths and weaknesses. He was among the most celebrated preachers of the day, outshining even Chalmers in oratory skill. He was close friends with Thomas Carlyle, a towering romantic figure in Scotland. His intense millenarianism was a catalyst for the rise of premillennial theology within English-speaking evangelicalism. His disregard for the Westminster Confession anticipated later nineteenth-century views regarding confessional subscription in the Scottish presbyterian churches. For biographies on Irving, see Wilks, *Edward Irving*; Bennett, *Edward Irving Reconsidered*; Dallimore, *Life of Edward Irving*; Grass, *Edward Irving*; Grass, *Lord's Watchman*. Also useful is Bebbington's overview in Bebbington, *Evangelicalism in Modern Britain*, 75–104.

102. For a study on Irving's Christology, see Dorries, "Edward Irving," 183–85;

Annan, and gave the young licentiate his first opportunity to preach. As a minister, M'Cheyne returned to Ruthwell to assist Duncan with communion seasons.[103]

David Robertson argues that in "some sense" Duncan became a model for M'Cheyne, as the Ruthwell minister exemplified a rare combination of "scholarship, pastoral care and evangelical zeal."[104] Duncan's main influence on M'Cheyne was aspirational and ministerial. M'Cheyne saw that literary proclivities (which Duncan also possessed) and broader cultural instincts need not compete with a minister's love for souls. A lover of the arts could indeed pastor faithfully. Duncan's ministerial model shaped M'Cheyne's desire to do good to the entire parish. Although M'Cheyne never pursued expansive social reform to the extent that Duncan did, he sought to reach every soul. Another facet of Duncan's ministry that shaped M'Cheyne was his vibrant ministry to children.[105] At Dundee, M'Cheyne's youthful charm combined with Duncan's ministerial model led to noticeable efforts to reach young souls with the gospel.

Macleod, "Doctrine of Incarnation," 40–50; McFarlane, "Edward Irving," 217–29; McFarlane, *Christ and Spirit*; Lee, "*Christ's Sinful Flesh*," 51–82.

103. One interesting interaction between Bonar and M'Cheyne was when Bonar called M'Cheyne for counsel and assistance in a case involving James Roddick. See Yeaworth, "Robert Murray McCheyne," 57. Apparently, James Roddick was M'Cheyne's cousin. Little is known about him other than the following entry in Dumfries Presbytery's documents of 1840: "Petitions to the Presbytery of Annan and Synod of Dumfries by Sir Patrick Maxwell and others concerning the Revd James Roddick, Minister of Graitney. The petition to the Presbytery of Annan alledges that he 'has, on many occasions, since he was inducted to his living, been guilty of conduct altogether unbecoming a minister of the Gospel.' That he '. . . has, on many occasions, since he was inducted to his living, been guilty of striking, beating and abusing, not only his servants but even Mrs Roddick his wife, to the extent, on one occasion at least, of causing her to leave her home and to take the advice of friends whether she ought to return to it or not . . . That he has further been guilty in the houses of others, of allowing himself to be overcome by guilt of passion. That he refused to visit the sick and dying when requested . . . when an infirm female travelling pauper was carried to his house, on her passage into England, he, in a perfect fury of rage, broke up the barrow on which she was carried, threw the fragments of it . . . over his gate . . . and violently assaulted struck and abused one of the persons by whom she had been brought . . .' Plus, lists of witnesses and petitioners, detailed charges etc. Several counter-claims were made." Dumfries-Galloway-L Archives, accessed August 6, 2017, http://archiver.rootsweb.ancestry.com/th/read/DUMFRIES-GALLOWAY/2002-06/1024927854.

104. Robertson, *Awakening*, 19.

105. Prime, *Robert Murray McCheyne*, 11. See also, Van Valen, *Constrained by His Love*, 28.

Thomas Chalmers (1780-1847)

When M'Cheyne arrived at the Divinity Hall in 1831, he came within the orbit of Thomas Chalmers—"the greatest spiritual force Scotland saw in the nineteenth century."[106] According to Iain Murray, Chalmers "was at the centre of a recovery which brought the churches in Scotland from mediocrity, indifference, and unbelief to new conditions of spiritual vitality."[107] Chalmers was arguably the most popular British preacher of his time,[108] a brilliant mathematician who theorized on everything from astronomy to politics to economics to social reform,[109] and an evangelical who longed to see Christ proclaimed in the slums of Scotland as well as faraway nations.[110] As professor of divinity, Chalmers's lectures and "conversational classes" enthralled students to such an extent that the school added an extensive gallery to his auditorium.

Chalmers stamped his seal on every facet of M'Cheyne's thought and life. The young student's class notebooks reveal how captivating he found Chalmers's theological and ecclesiastical vision—his annotations on Chalmers's class outlines abound.[111] Yeaworth says these "analyses, to-

---

106. Murray, *Scottish Christian Heritage*, 75. Chalmers was so powerful that Andrew Fuller exclaimed, "If that man would but throw away his papers in the pulpit, he might be king of Scotland!" Quoted in Murray, *Scottish Christian Heritage*, 85. Marcus Loane adds, "[M'Cheyne] took his place in the Divinity classrooms at a time when Thomas Chalmers was at the height of his amazing influence; no one since the days of John Knox had been held in such deep veneration." Loane, *They Were Pilgrims*, 142. William Beveridge, writing in 1908, says, "Thomas Chalmers, *as all the world knows*, was born in the Fifeshire town of Anstruther in 1780." Beveridge, *Makers*, 185 (emphasis added). For biographies of Chalmers, see Hanna, *Memoirs of the Life and Writings*; Oliphant, *Thomas Chalmers*; Fraser, *Thomas Chalmers*; Brown, *Thomas Chalmers*; Finlayson, *Thomas Chalmers*.

107. Murray, *Scottish Christian Heritage*, 78. For an analysis of Chalmers's expansive agenda, see Cheyne, *Practical and Pious*; Murray, "Thomas Chalmers," 1–32; Kaczmarek, "Thomas Chalmers," 19–35; Walker, "Thomas Chalmers," 29–36.

108. See Henderson, "Thomas Chalmers as Preacher," 346–56; Dargan, *A History of Preaching*, 2:490-95. Biographer Stewart Brown recounts a time when Chalmers, preaching in London, had to walk on a plank through an open window to reach the pulpit due to the eager mob surrounding the church. Brown, *Thomas Chalmers and the Godly Commonwealth*, 109.

109. Perkins, "Thomas Chalmers," 25–36; Steven C. Adamson, "The Apologetic Distinctives," 63–74; Harper, *The Social Ideal*. See also Cheyne, *Practical and Pious*..

110. Roxborogh, "Legacy of Thomas Chalmers," 173–76. See also, Roxborogh, *Thomas Chalmers*, and Ian J. Shaw, "Thomas Chalmers," 31–46.

111. For example, see MACCH 1.7.

gether with Chalmers's remarks in the class sessions, contributed greatly to the formulation of M'Cheyne's own ideas."[112] Further, it was Chalmers's guidance that led to M'Cheyne's involvement in the exegetical and visiting societies. Chalmers also imparted a passion for church extension to M'Cheyne, commissioning him and other students "to ascertain the state of the church's facilities and attendance all over Scotland."[113] Near the end of his ministry, and under Chalmers's gaze, M'Cheyne took an active part in the events leading up to the Disruption.[114] M'Cheyne understood the debt he owed to Chalmers and wondered at how such a figure would consider him a friend. Writing to his father, he described his relationship with Chalmers as "quite moving."[115]

Chalmers came to the Divinity Hall with the stated aim of shaping "the clergy of the next generation."[116] And shape it he did. Almost 90 percent of his students joined him in the Disruption of 1843, and fostered a new ecclesiastical communion that caused J. W. Alexander—son of the celebrated Princeton professor Archibald Alexander—to write, "[The Free Church] seems to me all in one great revival . . . I should like to spend three months in the Free Church, to try and find out the secret of their ardour."[117] Chalmers focused his theology on the person and work of Christ, and so fueled M'Cheyne's fervor for Christ. Yeaworth thus concludes, "In Chalmers, more than any other person, McCheyne found the mould for his ecclesiastical and religious thought, and a worthy pattern for his own ministerial life."[118]

---

112. Yeaworth, "Robert Murray M'Cheyne," 62–63.

113. Yeaworth, "Robert Murray M'Cheyne," 68.

114. Yeaworth, "Robert Murray M'Cheyne," 330.

115. Quoted in Yeaworth, "Robert Murray M'Cheyne," 90.

116. Quoted in Murray, *Scottish Christian Heritage*, 88. Palmer says, "Chalmers was more distinguished for the influence he had on his students than for any original contribution to the study of theology." Palmer, "Andrew Bonar," 56.

117. Quoted in Murray, *Scottish Christian Heritage*, 78.

118. Yeaworth, "Robert Murray M'Cheyne," 79. M'Cheyne's other biographers agree. L. J. Van Valen says, "Thomas Chalmers exercised the greatest influence on M'Cheyne." Valen, *Constrained by His Love*, 80. See also, Beaty, *An All-Surpassing Fellowship*, 13. "It is almost impossible to exaggerate the importance of Chalmers to McCheyne and his future ministry," writes Robertson. "Chalmers was his pattern for thought, life and ministry." Robertson, *Awakening*, 46.

John Bonar (1801–1861)

M'Cheyne assisted John Bonar[119] at Larbert and Dunipace for only ten months, yet the short season made a lasting impression. Though M'Cheyne found Bonar reserved at first, he was soon referring to him as "my good bishop."[120] Bonar's most exemplary quality was industry. He was responsible for over seven hundred families,[121] and labored zealously to shepherd each one. He pursued his shepherding agenda primarily through home visitation. After she stayed in Larbert and hearing that Bonar had returned from visiting twenty-eight different homes in a single day, Eliza wrote home, "[Bonar] seems a very active pushing man—very peculiar, very zealous—quite wrapped up in himself and his parish."[122] Bonar's visitation strategy was a real-life example of Chalmers's vision for parish ministry. M'Cheyne participated eagerly, saying that he enjoyed visiting more than any other aspect of ministry.[123] In Bonar's example, he saw faithfulness worthy of emulation and examination. He wished "church commissioners would make a trial of a day's visiting and see how they cast a burden of so many souls on one set of shoulders."[124]

Duncan's ministry cemented M'Cheyne's interest in ministering to young people, but it was Bonar's example that provided a deeper model for successful interaction with parish youth. While in Larbert, M'Cheyne wrote to his mother: "I heard Mr. Bonar teach his children . . . in his inimitable way. He possesses a wonderful power of interesting children."[125]

Under Bonar's influence, M'Cheyne grew in his ability to preach. He observed that Bonar preached "with great effect and plain common-sense power," yet his sermons (which often exceeded ninety minutes) were too long. M'Cheyne reacted by preaching sermons less than thirty-five

---

119. Alexander Smellie says John was a cousin to Horatius and Andrew. Smellie, *Biography of R. M. McCheyne*, 55. Van Valen states that Bonar was "a nephew of both [Horatius and Andrew]." Van Valen, *Constrained by His Love*, 109. Presumably, Van Valen is referencing Smellie in his comment, and the English translators of *Constrained by His Love* are wrong. The Dutch word "*neef*" can be translated "nephew" or "cousin."

120. MACCH 2.6.16.

121. Commission of Religious Instruction, *Report of the Commissioners of Religious Instruction, Scotland*.Edinburgh: W. & A. K. Johnston, 1838, 6:364.

122. Quoted in Yeaworth, "Robert Murray M'Cheyne," 84.

123. Quoted in Yeaworth, "Robert Murray M'Cheyne," 84.

124. Quoted in Yeaworth, "Robert Murray M'Cheyne," 86.

125. MACCH 2.6.20.

minutes, a length that brought "universal satisfaction."[126] It was also at Larbert and Dunipace that M'Cheyne learned the value of preaching Christ clearly, applying the Savior to industrial and agricultural workers alike. He improved on these experiences in his future evangelistic labors, preaching to everyone everywhere he went.

One final lesson emerges from M'Cheyne's first charge. The people of Dunipace lacked a vital ministry until Bonar reached them with the gospel. From this experience, M'Cheyne learned the crucial need for more churches to reach Scotland with the gospel. So, Andrew Bonar argues that it was at Larbert and Dunipace that M'Cheyne developed "such deep sympathy with the Church Extension Scheme."[127]

Robert Smith Candlish (1806–1873)

An overlooked influence on M'Cheyne is Robert Smith Candlish. M'Cheyne's senior by seven years, Candlish "was a wonderfully electric preacher of the Evangel; and in his public prayers, as he led the devotions of his people, he was described by Addison Alexander as praying like an inspired Hebrew prophet."[128] In 1834, Candlish became minister of St. George's in Edinburgh, the leading church in Scotland's capital. He became a prominent leader in the evangelical party, and, after 1843, he "was second only to Thomas Chalmers in his prestige in the new [Free Church], and he was its most prominent figure between Chalmers's death in 1847 and his own a quarter of a century later, being Moderator in 1861."[129] John Macleod refers to him as "one of the ablest Churchman

---

126. Quoted in Yeaworth, "Robert Murray M'Cheyne," 87. M'Cheyne's reaction was likely a youthful overreaction, for his sermons lengthened once installed at Dundee. Adam M'Cheyne remarks about his son's early sermons at St. Peter's: "He was not easily satisfied with what he had done. As a consequence, he was apt to prolong his pulpit services to too great a length. Hence many who had no great concern about spiritual things became disgusted with his long sermons." MACCH 2.7.50. Andrew Bonar concurs, saying it was not uncommon for M'Cheyne to be "too long in his addresses." *MAR*, 66.

127. *MAR*, 35.

128. Macleod, *Scottish Theology*, 271. For biographies of Candlish, see Watson, *Life of Robert*, and Wilson, *Memorials of Robert Smith Candlish*.

129. Wolffe, "Candlish, Robert Smith," 134.

in an age in which able Churchman were not few."[130] Charles Spurgeon described Candlish as "devout, candid, prudent and forcible."[131]

Candlish and M'Cheyne shared similar views on ministry, theology, and spirituality. Candlish mainly influenced M'Cheyne in the public matters of ecclesiastical life, as he played an outsized role in extending M'Cheyne's ministry throughout Scotland and England. Far from seeing M'Cheyne as a mere servant to his expansive ecclesiastical agenda, Candlish believed M'Cheyne was an ideal model of evangelical presbyterian ministry. He wrote to St. Peter's, three days after M'Cheyne's death, the following assessment of the young minister: "Assuredly he had more of the mind of his Master than almost any one I ever knew—and realized to me more of the likeness of the beloved disciple."[132]

In short, Candlish served as something like a denominational patron to M'Cheyne. He assisted him in his passage through the presbytery during ordination.[133] He lobbied for his appointment to St. Peter's. He paved the way for M'Cheyne's role on the mission of inquiry to Palestine. He "also showed a great interest in the 1839 awakening and McCheyne's part in it, and through him McCheyne was appointed to serve on various deputations and missions."[134] At Candlish's behest, M'Cheyne contributed articles to the *Scottish Christian Herald*, and published chapters in *Family Worship*[135] and *The Christian's Daily Companion*.[136] Candlish also sent M'Cheyne "to represent and explain the Church's position (on patronage) both in and out of Scotland."[137]

HISTORICAL INFLUENCES

M'Cheyne's sermons, letters, and diary reveal the extent to which he valued the insights and examples of those who had gone before him. Analysis of those sources found in his quotations and annotations reveals three key influences.

---

130. Macleod, *Scottish Theology*, 271.
131. Spurgeon, *Commenting and Commentaries*, 275.
132. Quoted in Yeaworth, "Robert Murray M'Cheyne," 141.
133. MACCH 2.6.42.
134. Yeaworth, "Robert Murray M'Cheyne," 90.
135. Church of Scotland, *Family Worship*.
136. Church of Scotland, *Christian's Daily Companion*, 105–42.
137. Yeaworth, "Robert Murray M'Cheyne," 341, 344.

The Reformers

Reformation giants such as Martin Luther, John Calvin, and John Knox seasoned M'Cheyne's ministry. Direct quotations from the Reformers are not extensive, but they nonetheless cast a long shadow over M'Cheyne's theological and spiritual program. M'Cheyne's hymn, "Jehovah Tsidkenu," has "the watchword of the Reformers" as its superscription. While at the Divinity Hall, M'Cheyne took extensive notes on Luther's teaching on justification as found in his commentary on Galatians.[138] The Reformer's recovery of the doctrine of righteousness by faith alone was central to M'Cheyne's preaching. According to Van Valen, "This was M'Cheyne's message: Christ our righteousness."[139] From Luther, M'Cheyne learned to how to preach Christ. M'Cheyne adopted Luther's vision of preaching as his own: "The gospel is the true alluring speech that draws the heart of man."[140] He also channeled Luther in speaking against "the splendid sins of humanity," urging hearers to cling to Christ alone for salvation.[141] Furthermore, Luther was a model of diligent and fervent prayer.[142]

After returning from the mission of inquiry, M'Cheyne's labor for the Jews and ongoing revival found him increasingly involved with Christians of all denominations. Bonar describes the trouble that came from his ecumenicity: "Indeed, he so much longed for a scriptural unity, that some time after, when the General Assembly has repealed the statute of 1799, he embraced the opportunity of showing his desire for unity, by inviting two dissenting brethren to his pulpit, and then writing in defense of his conduct when attacked."[143] One such writing was a letter to the editor of the *Dundee Warder*, dated July 6, 1842. In the letter, M'Cheyne called on John Calvin as a witness to prove that his ecumenical practice was thoroughly in step with Reformation principles.[144] Where John Calvin's teaching on the church gave a doctrinal spine to M'Cheyne's efforts

---

138. MACCH 1.1.
139. Van Valen, *Constrained by His Love*, 224.
140. *TPP*, 75.
141. *TPH*, 33.
142. *MAR*, 255, 366; *BOF*, 49.
143. *MAR*, 139.
144. *MAR*, 560, 562. M'Cheyne found it difficult to complete the account of the mission of inquiry. He wrote, "I find it hard to carry on the work of a diligent pastor and that of an author at the same time. How John Calvin would have smiled at my difficulties!" *MAR*, 142.

for ecumenicity, John Knox's spirit gave M'Cheyne a ministerial fire.[145] He found in Knox a model of spiritual courage that could conquer a country for Christ.

The Puritans

M'Cheyne also immersed himself in Puritan literature, freely referencing figures such as Thomas Boston,[146] John Flavel,[147] John Owen,[148] and John Bunyan.[149] Richard Baxter is especially prominent. After reading Baxter's *Call to the Unconverted*, M'Cheyne wrote,

> Though Baxter's lips have long in silence hung,
> And death long hush'd that sinner-wakening tongue;
> Yet still, though dead, he speaks aloud to us all;
> And from the grave still issues forth his, "Call."[150]

Baxter's zeal for souls captured M'Cheyne and caused him to declare in an ordination sermon, "O for a pastor who unites the deep knowledge of Edwards, the vast statements of Owen, and the vehement appeals of Richard Baxter!"[151]

Another Puritan who influenced M'Cheyne was Samuel Rutherford. He loved to feast on Rutherford's "flame of grace."[152] In one sermon, he remarked, "How humbling it is to read Rutherford."[153] James Hamilton recalled that Rutherford's *Letters* were M'Cheyne's "daily delight," and that

---

145. OTS, 168; MAR, 196.

146. MAR, 41; TPH, 88.

147. TPH, 93.

148. MAR, 363, 560.

149. HTD, 13. McLennan includes Jeremy Taylor (1613–1667) as one of two seventeenth-century divines who "had quite an influence on McCheyne." McLennan, *McCheyne's Dundee*, 48. Yet, the only mention of Taylor in the *Memoir* is Bonar's quotation of Taylor's dictum: "If thou meanest to enlarge thy religion, do it rather by enlarging thine ordinary devotions rather than thy extraordinary." MAR, 54. Bonar does not say Taylor was a direct influence on M'Cheyne as much as Taylor's maxim illustrated M'Cheyne's devotional pattern.

150. MAR, 25.

151. MAR, 363. For additional references to Baxter, see MAR, 55, 59, 74, 123–24, 560, 563.

152. MAR, 184. For additional references to Rutherford, see MAR, 117, 365, 562; TPH, 82, 169.

153. MACCH 1.10.

"like Rutherford his adoring contemplations naturally gathered round them the imagery and language of the Song of Solomon."[154] Rutherford's insistence on Christ's sweetness and loveliness shaped M'Cheyne's life and ministry. It was in Rutherford that M'Cheyne found a soulmate in Christ-centered spirituality.

Jonathan Edwards and David Brainerd

M'Cheyne interacts with Edwards and Brainerd far more than any other authors. Edwards edited and published the extremely influential *Life of David Brainerd*,[155] which represents his ideal of spirituality. Notable Edwards scholars Michael J. McClymond and Gerald R. McDermott write, "At the center of [Edwards's] evocations of the Christ-like minister was the figure of David Brainerd, immortalized in The Life of David Brainerd (1749). It was Brainerd, above all others, who exemplified Edwards's emerging themes of perseverance, obedience, separation from the world, solitariness (if need be), self-denial, asceticism, and self-sacrifice."[156]

Previous studies of M'Cheyne have failed to note that it was Chalmers who cultivated M'Cheyne's love of Edwards. Near the end of his life, Chalmers praised Edwards, noting how the New England theologian had shaped his thinking on predestination for nearly fifty years. Chalmers added, "His is by far the highest name which the New World has to boast of . . . Never was there a happier combination of great power with great piety . . . I would hold it as the brightest combination of great power with great piety . . . I would hold it as the brightest eulogy both on the character and the genius of any clergyman, that he copied the virtues and had imbibed the theology of Edwards."[157] Edwards's treatise, *Freedom of the Will*, persuaded Chalmers in his early life. He recalled,

---

154. Hamilton, *Church in the House*, 222. See also, *MAR*, 145.

155. For the edition likely read by M'Cheyne, see Edwards, *An Account of Life*.

156. McClymond and McDermott, *Theology of Jonathan Edwards*, 82–83. George Marsden suggests that "Edwards was much more interested in the sacrifice involved in Brainerd's mission than in its success." Marsden, *Jonathan Edwards*, 332. For further study on Edwards' use of Brainerd, see especially Weddle, "The Melancholy Saint," 297–318.

157. Quoted in Noll, "Thomas Chalmers," 763. For other treatments of Edwards' influence on Chalmers, see Piggin, "Expanding Knowledge of God," 269–70; Noll, "Jonathan Edwards," 193; McClymond and McDermott, *Theology of Jonathan Edwards*, 565.

> [There was] no book of human composition which I more strenuously recommend than his Treatise on the Will,—read by me forty-seven years ago, with a conviction that has never since faltered and which has helped me more than any other uninspired book, to find my way through all that might otherwise have proved baffling and transcendental and mysterious in the peculiarities of Calvinism.[158]

It is thus not surprising to find M'Cheyne reading Edwards after coming under Chalmers's tutelage. On March 20, 1832, he wrote in his diary: "Read part of the life of Jonathan Edwards. How feeble does my spark of Christianity appear beside such a sun! But even his was a borrowed light, and the same source is still open to enlighten me."[159] This first recorded encounter with the Northampton pastor was powerful enough to cause M'Cheyne to purchase Edwards's collected works three months later.[160] Bonar remarks, "It was [during his first pastoral charge] . . . that [M'Cheyne] began to study so closely the works of Jonathan Edwards— reckoning them a mine to be wrought, and if wrought, sure to repay the toil."[161] M'Cheyne's writings reveal his longing that his "heart and understanding may grow together" like Edwards.[162] He finds "help and freedom" from Edwards's instruction on prayer.[163] He encourages William Chalmers Burns to remember Edwards's "magnificent" resolutions.[164] And he proclaims Edwards's example as worthy of imitation.[165] Near the end of his ministry M'Cheyne called Edwards "one of the holiest and most eminent divines that ever lived."[166]

It was Edwards who gave M'Cheyne a theological vision for revival, and convinced him of how to preach God's sovereign grace in a way that infuses the affections with sweetness and love. Brainerd showed M'Cheyne what it means to center evangelism on Christ's loveliness. M'Cheyne told St. Peter's that "David Brainerd's people were most deeply

---

158. Quoted in Noll, "Jonathan Edwards," 320.
159. *MAR*, 14. See also, Loane, *They Were Pilgrims*, 146.
160. *MAR*, 15.
161. *MAR*, 33.
162. *MAR*, 16.
163. *MAR*, 56.
164. *MAR*, 242.
165. *MAR*, 363, 377. See also, *TPP*, 306.
166. *HTD*, 16.

affected because Christ was so lovely."[167] In another sermon, he declared, "I remember David Brainerd used to say that he loved to see souls saved, not so much for the sake of the souls that were saved, as for the joy and glory it gave to the Lord Jesus."[168]

CONCLUSION

The foregoing chapter has demonstrated that M'Cheyne ministered in a context that fostered his rise to prominence. In the ecclesiastical scene, evangelicalism reached new heights after "the dark age of the Church of Scotland."[169] Moderatism's dominance of theology and piety waned, and new vitality flooded the Scottish Church through evangelical ministers. The public was thus primed for a minister who preached the gospel, cared for the poor, exuded personal holiness, and participated in missionary endeavors.

In the philosophical sphere, common sense realism, descending from Thomas Reid, seeped into society. It was sensibility for the common man. A. T. B. McGowan argues that common sense philosophy "was a significant influence for good," even in the evangelical movement.[170] Classicism and empiricism receded as the mood of the moment searched for simple, universal principles available to all mankind. Thus, M'Cheyne's sensible sermons and rational appeals found ready audiences.

In the cultural context, romantic and burgeoning-Victorian ideals were dominant. A subjective and emotional component saturated the contemporary temperament. This disposition was one in which M'Cheyne flourished, for, as William G. Blaikie writes, he preached with an "almost feminine quality"—his ministry was full of tenderness, sympathy, and pathos.[171]

Not only did M'Cheyne's immediate context provide a suitable platform for him to succeed, but his ministerial influences helped to shape

---

167. *OTS*, 52.

168. *TPP*, 166. For additional references to Brainerd, see *MAR*, 16, 87, 198, 250, 427, 534–35; *NTS*, 139; *OTS*, 52; *TPP*, 26, 78, 147, 166; *TPH*, 125, 229; *HTD*, 42; *SC*, 72.

169. Quoted in Watson, *Life of Robert Smith Candlish*, 6.

170. McGowan, "Evangelicalism in Scotland," 79.

171. Blaikie, *Preachers of Scotland*, 294–95. Loane concurs, "The two most prominent qualities were his tremendous urgency and his exceeding tenderness... his heart was so wistful; his words were so tender." Loane, *They Were Pilgrims*, 173.

his convictions and cement his legacy. It was "Uncle Henry" Duncan who first gave M'Cheyne a glimpse of a faithful ministry, especially among children. Thomas Chalmers was the mold around which M'Cheyne's theology and piety formed. Chalmers's unquestioned influence in the Church of Scotland and appreciation for M'Cheyne meant that young M'Cheyne was primed to gain significance. John Bonar, minister at Larbert and Dunipace, offered a vibrant model of parish ministry fit for M'Cheyne. It was Bonar who stamped an assiduousness for Christ on to M'Cheyne. The final major influence on M'Cheyne was Robert Smith Candlish, the eminent church politician and preacher. M'Cheyne's ever-increasing role in the public courts can largely be traced to Candlish's able hand.

M'Cheyne represented the ideal evangelical presbyterian minister leading up to the Disruption. Ecclesiastical, philosophical, and cultural forces provided a stage on which M'Cheyne could shine. Influences such as Chalmers and Candlish ensured that he ascended to a position of prominence. The Reformers, the Puritans, Edwards, and Brainerd imparted and confirmed a passionate christological spirituality.

4

Knowing Christ
M'Cheyne's Theology

SPEAKING OF SCOTTISH EVANGELICALISM in the early Victorian era, John MacLeod declares, "Among the young men of that epoch who profited by the studies of such divines in sacred truth there was none that left his mark on the Evangelical Churches more than Robert Murray M'Cheyne."[1] Not everyone is as favorable in their opinion as MacLeod. Dr. John Duncan, the venerable missionary and professor of Hebrew, quipped, "M'Cheyne's mind plays about the lighter aspects of theology."[2] Is Duncan's critique accurate, or is M'Cheyne's theology more robust than generally assumed?

This chapter answers that question by highlighting the main contours of M'Cheyne's theology. It shows that he was sound in doctrine, and a more rigorous thinker than many assume. His theology was not primarily theoretical, but experiential. David Yeaworth rightly notes that M'Cheyne's doctrine "was not merely a matter of orthodoxy but an experience of utmost importance."[3] Similarly, Alexander Moody-Stuart writes, "With all his poetry [M'Cheyne] did not care for what was specu-

---

1. MacLeod, *Scottish Theology*, 277.

2. Moody-Stuart, *Recollections*, 47. David Yeaworth gives a fuller but similar conclusion: "While there is a strong undercurrent of doctrine in McCheyne's preaching, and although he kept abreast of contemporary thought as it was related to Evangelicalism, he did not consider it to be expedient to give a prominent place to theology as such, except as it touched upon his chief object of evangelism and Christian nurture." Yeaworth, "Robert Murray McCheyne," 228.

3. Yeaworth, "Robert Murray McCheyne," 231.

lative, but liked all that was practical; practical in theology, practical in spiritual exercise, practical in dealing with the conscience, practical in duty."[4]

This chapter considers M'Cheyne's commitment to the Westminster Standards, as evidenced in his understanding of four key motifs: (1) God's sovereignty; (2) man's depravity; (3) the Son's beauty; and (4) the Spirit's efficacy. M'Cheyne summarized his doctrinal system as an appropriation of Rowland Hill's three R's: "ruin by the fall, righteousness by Christ, and regeneration by the Spirit."[5] Such a focus inevitably centered his attention and affections on Christ, for he believed the system demanded that one "preach Christ for awakening, preach Christ for comforting, preach Christ for sanctifying."[6] The chapter concludes by demonstrating how these emphases led to M'Cheyne's chief goal—the free offer of salvation in Christ.

THE WESTMINSTER CONFESSION OF FAITH

In their history of the Victorian church in Scotland, Andrew Drummond and James Bulloch state, "If by some strange chance all the copies of the Westminster Confession had disappeared it would be totally impossible to reconstruct the barest outline of it from Victorian sermons. Even the writings of men like Robert Murray McCheyne and Andrew Bonar would have failed to tell clearly of its contents."[7] The historians are correct, in so far as a study of M'Cheyne's writings reveals that he scarcely mentioned the Westminster Standards, chapter and verse, in his ministry.[8] But it is wrong to conclude that M'Cheyne was anything less than a full supporter of the Standards. He subscribed to the Standards at his

---

4. Moody-Stuart, *Recollections*, 49.

5. *MAR*, 360. See also, *SOH*, 10. M'Cheyne declared, "The main thing in a Christian Church . . . is the righteousness of Christ that ought to be made known." *SOH*, 135. In writing his letter on ecumenicalism, M'Cheyne says, "My elders and people can bear witness that they have seldom heard any voice from its pulpit that did not proclaim ruin by the Fall, righteousness by Christ, and regeneration by the Spirit." *MAR*, 562.

6. *MAR*, 361.

7. Drummond and Bulloch, *Church in Victorian Scotland*, 301.

8. Exceptions include a quotation of Shorter Catechism, 37 in *NTS*, 186; a quotation of Shorter Catechism, 1 in *BOF*, 167; specific interaction with Westminster Confession of Faith 25.1 in *BOF*, 124. He also alluded to the Shorter Catechism by way of warning individuals not to rely on religious knowledge. *BOF*, 98; *TPP*, 32, 38, 39, 81; *TBJ*, 14, 44.

ordination, and never deviated from his vows.[9] "There was nothing [in M'Cheyne] that differed from the views of truth laid down in the standards of our Church," writes Bonar.[10] Yeaworth concurs, "McCheyne's theology was that which was laid down in the Westminster standards, which he thoroughly believed."[11] Although M'Cheyne did not quote the Confession directly in his sermons, it nonetheless provided the doctrinal foundation for M'Cheyne's theology and spirituality.

Covenant Theology

An example of M'Cheyne's commitment to the Westminster Standards, absent from previous M'Cheyne studies, is his exposition of God's covenant dealings with man. A covenantal substructure is one distinguishing feature of the Westminster Confession. In his study of the Confession, B. B. Warfield remarks, "The architectonic principle of the Westminster Confession is supplied by the schematization of the Federal theology, which had obtained by this time in Britain, as on the Continent, a dominant position as the most commodious mode of presenting the *corpus* of Reformed doctrine."[12] There is no record of M'Cheyne lecturing on the

---

9. For an overview of confessional subscription in the Scottish church tradition, see Duncan, "Owning the Confession," 77–92. See also, Raffe, "Presbyterians and Episcopalians," 570–98; Enright, "Preaching and Theology," 3–9; Cheyne, *Transforming of the Kirk*, 60–87.

10. *MAR*, 76. Crawford Gribben notes that Bonar's understanding of the antichrist necessarily led him to disagree with the Confession's assertion that the pope is the antichrist (*WCF*, 25.6). Gribben and Stunt, *Prisoners of Hope?*, 200. Bonar himself did not believe that allegiance to premillennialism struck at the vitals of the Confession. A contemporary magazine reports that "Dr. Andrew Bonar, on the occasion of his Jubilee, openly and boldly avowing his belief in it and attachment to it . . . he had no hesitation in telling the brethren that he had been true to the principles of the Free Church to this hour. But he would tell them more: he believed the whole of the Confession of Faith." *The Original Secession Magazine*, vol. 19 (1890), 60–61. Interestingly, Bonar did not oppose the Declaratory Act of 1892, in which the free church endeavored to adjust itself to historic Westminster theology in light of intellectual and religious developments of the time. Palmer, "Andrew A. Bonar," 411n1.

11. Yeaworth, "Robert Murray M'Cheyne," 227. L. J. Van Valen sounds the same note: "In his presentation of the doctrine, he heartily agreed with the Westminster Confession of Faith, which he had signed at his ordination. He was no theologian, and yet he emphasized certain aspects during his sermons which presupposed the influence of his predecessor, Thomas Chalmers." Valen, *Constrained by His Love*, 212.

12. Warfield, *Works of Benjamin*, 56 (emphasis original). See also, Fesko, *Theology of Westminster Standards*, 125–68; McWilliams, "Covenant Theology," 109–24; Letham,

covenants, nor are there any sermons in which he deals specifically with covenant theology at length. This helps to explain why prior studies have neglected to consider his covenant theology.[13] But a careful investigation of his writings reveals that a covenantal thread is woven richly into his theology and ministry.

M'Cheyne's sermon on Hebrews 8:6[14] reveals his covenant theology in miniature. He begins by "[inquiring] into the covenants that are spoken of in the Word of God."[15] He articulates a standard reformed perspective on the covenant of works, the covenants with Noah, Abraham, Moses, and the new covenant secured in Christ.[16] For M'Cheyne, covenant theology is not a speculative approach to redemptive history, but proof of "the *amazing love of God* . . . [for] the covenant which he made with Noah was a covenant of grace; and the covenant he made at Sinai, was also a covenant of grace; and the covenant that was made with Christ was a covenant of grace."[17] Noticeably absent from this sermon are the Davidic covenant and the covenant of redemption. While M'Cheyne gives scant attention to the former, he consistently extols the latter. In fact, the covenant of redemption—the intra-trinitarian covenant in eternity—saturates his preaching.[18] He delights in what it teaches about Christ's eternal love, declaring, "The Bible assures us that this feeling of compassion for sinners that care not for Him existed in the bosom of Christ before the world was. It was this feeling that moved Him to enter into covenant with His Father in the eternity that is past, that He would undertake the doing and suffering of all that was needful in the stead of guilty sinners."[19]

A further feature in M'Cheyne's covenantal thought is how it pivots on Christ. It does so in two ways. First, he situates the covenants

---

Westminster Assembly, 224–36; Venema, *Christ & Covenant*, 3–36. For J. B. Torrance's critique of Westminster's covenantal doctrine, see Torrance, "Covenant or Contract?," 51–76; Torrance, "Strengths and Weaknesses," 40–53. For a representative overview of covenant theology from Thomas Chalmers, see Chalmers, *Sermons*, 472–84.

13. Yeaworth, for example, never mentions M'Cheyne's view of the covenant.

14. "But now hath he obtained a more excellent ministry, by how much also he is the mediator of a better covenant, which was established upon better promises."

15. *SOH*, 109.

16. *SOH*, 109–12. For M'Cheyne's comments on the Shorter Catechism's teaching on the covenant of works and covenant of grace, see MACCH 1.7.

17. *SOH*, 112 (emphasis original).

18. *SOH*, 87; *TPH*, 400; *NTS*, 13; *MAR*, 375; *TPP*, 15; *SOH*, 118, 121–22.

19. *SOH*, 188. See also, *OTS*, 87; *TPH*, 400.

in relation to Christ. When speaking about the Mosaic covenant, he preaches, "I believe that we do not rightly understand the old covenant unless we understand it thus, unless we see it as making them long for the coming of Christ."[20] When defining the covenant of grace, he says, "God makes the covenant with a sinner when he brings the sinner to lay hold on Christ; then the covenant made with Christ is put into the sinner's hand, its conditions being all fulfilled already by Jesus."[21] He understands the new covenant as "the gospel covenant"[22] that joins us to Christ,[23] who is its surety and mediator.[24] Christ is a "covenant Saviour,"[25] "covenant head,"[26] and the "Angel of the Covenant."[27] Through Christ's saving work we are "brought into the bonds of the covenant,"[28] and thus become Christ's covenant people.[29] M'Cheyne's covenant Christology reaches its climax when he says that not only has God made "but one covenant—that is, with Christ and all in him,"[30] but Christ himself is the covenant.[31] In a sermon on Isaiah 42:5–8,[32] he affirmed,

---

20. *SOH*, 161. For further reflection on the Mosaic covenant, see *TPP*, 55; *SOH*, 122, 160–61, 184.

21. *TPP*, 15.

22. *TPP*, 50.

23. *TBJ*, 99.

24. *TPP*, 155.

25. *TPH*, 70.

26. *TPH*, 149.

27. *TPP*, 87; *MAR*, 307. In these contexts, M'Cheyne clearly had Malachi 3:1 in mind, which says, "Behold, I will send my messenger, and he shall prepare the way before me: and the Lord, whom ye seek, shall suddenly come to his temple, even the messenger of the covenant, whom ye delight in: behold, he shall come, saith the Lord of hosts."

28. *TPH*, 430.

29. *TPP*, 58.

30. *TPH*, 256.

31. *TPH*, 73; *TPP*, 124; *NTS*, 23. M'Cheyne appealed to Isaiah 42:6 for proof: "I the Lord have called thee in righteousness, and will hold thine hand, and will keep thee, and give thee for a covenant of the people, for a light of the Gentiles." M'Cheyne's position is congruent with Sinclair Ferguson's comments, "God's covenant with his people is not only *found in* Jesus Christ; it is Jesus Christ. The new covenant, the final covenant, the covenant in which is experienced the fullness of God's promise 'I will be your God and you will be my people' is made in him. In him all the (covenant) promises of God find their 'yes!' So when we rightly speak of 'Christ and the covenant,' this is ultimately the same as speaking of the 'Christ who *is* the covenant.'" Venema, *Christ & Covenant*, xi (emphasis original).

32. "Thus saith God the Lord, he that created the heavens, and stretched them

"I will give thee for a covenant of the people." ... God not only provided the Saviour, and upheld him, but he gave him—gave him away, to be a covenant Saviour of the people, and a light to the Gentiles ... He took his Son out of his bosom, and gave him away to be bound, to be a covenant Saviour of the people. There are not more wonderful words in the whole Bible than these: "I will give thee." ... Herein is love.[33]

M'Cheyne's covenant theology frames many of his characteristic exhortations to pursue Christ-centered piety. Perfect happiness and holiness "is all in the covenant."[34] Additionally, the covenant imparts confidence for the increase of grace, because through it we are united to Christ and thus "there is covenant certainty about our holiness. It shall abide forever, for the Spirit shall abide with us forever."[35] The covenant also led M'Cheyne to exhort his fellow believers to see suffering as an act of the covenant-keeping God to bring his children into deeper love.[36] He encouraged William Burns after a season of sickness: "I am truly thankful that you have been raised up again—renewed, I trust, both in the inner and outer man. 'I will cause you to pass under the rod, and I will bring you into the bond of the covenant.' Sweet rod that drives the soul into such a precious resting place."[37] The spiritual apex, for M'Cheyne, of covenant theology is sovereign christological love. In his exposition of the various types found in the tabernacle, M'Cheyne comes eventually to the precious ornaments placed on the priest's shoulders. He asserted, "These chains and sockets of gold are the love of Christ—his electing love—his drawing love—his covenant love."[38]

This brief interaction with M'Cheyne's covenant theology affords several important conclusions. First, M'Cheyne's covenant thinking

---

out; he that spread forth the earth, and that which cometh out of it; he that giveth breath unto the people upon it, and spirit to them that walk therein: I the Lord have called thee in righteousness, and will hold thine hand, and will keep thee, and give thee for a covenant of the people, for a light of the Gentiles; to open the blind eyes, to bring out the prisoners from the prison, and them that sit in darkness out of the prison house. I am the Lord: that is my name: and my glory will I not give to another, neither my praise to graven images."

33. *TPH*, 73.
34. *TPH*, 171.
35. *TPP*, 212.
36. *BOF*, 39. See also, *OTS*, 137–38; *MAR*, 241, 316.
37. *MAR*, 241. The Scripture reference is Ezekiel 20:37.
38. *MAR*, 485.

conforms clearly to the *Westminster Confession of Faith*, particularly its section entitled, "Of God's Covenant with Man."[39] While he never cites a specific chapter or article from the Confession, he believed and preached it. Second, M'Cheyne's covenantal teaching mirrors the approach found in George Hill's *Lectures in Divinity*, the systematic theology textbook M'Cheyne read while at the Divinity Hall. Hill scatters covenantal instruction throughout his work, but dedicates only nine pages to a detailed exposition of covenant theology.[40] Likewise, covenant theology grounds and animates M'Cheyne's entire scheme, but rarely receives prolonged treatment. Thirdly, as mentioned above, M'Cheyne's understanding of covenant theology provides a window into his theological and spiritual concerns. His doctrinal program is akin to a home with a cornerstone (Christ), a foundation (the covenant), and four main living areas (the doctrines of election, sin, salvation, and sanctification).

God's Sovereignty

David Yeaworth believes a "thoroughgoing Calvinism" was one of M'Cheyne's "most outstanding features."[41] That a Calvinistic soteriology would mark M'Cheyne is not surprising for two reasons. First, his ministry began at a time when "the Calvinism of the Westminster Standards was restored and adhered to by Moderates and Evangelicals alike, and was the popular religious thought of the day."[42] Second, God's sovereign

---

39. For a study of the reception and development of Westminster's convent theology, see Woolsey, *Unity and Continuity*, 80–102, 499–539. See also, Golding, *Covenant Theology*, 47–84.

40. Hill, *Lectures in Divinity*, 640–49. Hill interacts with the covenant in relation to diverse subjects: "External Evidences of Christianity" (70, 82, 83, 84); "Predictions Delivered by Jesus" (94); "Actions Ascribed to Jesus in His Pre-Existent State" (288, 289, 290, 294); "Disease for Which the Remedy is Provided" (406, 410); "Doctrine of the Atonement" (452, 454, 458, 476); "Eternal Life" (482, 491); "Opinions Concerning Predestination" (526); "Application of the Remedy" (535); "Justification" (614), "Prayer" (650–51); "Sacraments" (652, 654, 655); "Baptism" (660–65); and "The Lord's Supper" (670, 673, 675, 679). Jack Whytock reminds that Hill's theology was somewhat of a middle ground between moderatism and evangelicalism: George Hill, as a professor of divinity, did not neatly reflect the label evangelical. Thomas Chalmers summed it up well when he wrote concerning Hill's divinity lectures that "there will not often be substantial, but often at least a complexional difference between us.'" Whytock, "An Educated Clergy," 141.

41. Yeaworth, "Robert Murray McCheyne," 244.

42. Yeaworth, "Robert Murray McCheyne," 226–27. The clearest articulation of

decree was among the earliest subjects to which M'Cheyne devoted attention after his conversion.[43] He believed a focus on election ensured a correct understanding of how God relates to man: "God alone can bring you into the covenant . . . A Sovereign Almighty Jehovah must do it or it will be left undone."[44] He developed his convictions regarding God's decree while at the Divinity Hall, taking copious notes on "The Leading Doctrines of Christianity." No doctrine receives more attention in his notebook than the following truth: "Salvation is only by the Free Grace of God in Christ Jesus Our Lord."[45]

Since most of M'Cheyne's congregation adhered to Calvinism's major tenets, there was no need for the young pastor to give a careful defense of God's sovereign election.[46] Instead, he was able to assert, "Ah! my brethren, those who deny election, deny that God can have mercy. O it is a sweet truth that God can have mercy!"[47] In another sermon, he declared, "Brethren, all conversion comes from God. You might rather expect the icebergs of the Atlantic to melt without the sun than expect a sinner's heart to change without God."[48] Far from being a deterrent to evangelism or conversion, M'Cheyne believed God's sovereign work in salvation is a truth the Lord uses to draw the lowest of sinners to himself. He announced, "Salvation is by grace. When a man chooses an apple off a tree, he generally chooses the ripest, the one that promises best. It is not so with God in choosing the soul He saves. He does not choose those that have sinned least, those that are most willing to be saved; He often chooses the vilest of men, 'to the praise of his glorious grace.'"[49]

God's sovereignty in the Confession of Faith comes in the eight sections of chapter three: "Of God's Eternal Decree." The Confession states, "God, from all eternity, did, by the most wise and holy counsel of his own will, freely, and unchangeably ordain whatsoever comes to pass: yet so, as thereby neither is God the author of sin, nor is violence offered to the will of the creatures; nor is the liberty or contingency of second causes taken away, but rather established." *WCF*, 3.1.

43. *MAR*, 11.
44. *TPP*, 16. See also, *OTS*, 157.
45. *MACCH* 1.5.
46. The *Dundee Advertiser* said, "Far from being dissertations about the way of salvation, McCheyne's sermons were exhortations to accept it, so that he was judged to be 'persuasive rather than argumentative.'" Quoted in Yeaworth, "Robert Murray M'Cheyne," 229.
47. *BOF*, 47. See also, *MAR*, 468; *OTS*, 56.
48. *BOF*, 80. See also, *TPH*, 38.
49. *HTD*, 41. See also, *NTS*, 267. Another example is when M'Cheyne taught, "It

Although M'Cheyne locates the decree primarily in the Father's work, he does teach a trinitarian Calvinism. "Christ is entirely sovereign in saving souls," he stated.[50] Again, "How do any come? Christ makes them willing. Christ sends the rod of his strength out of Zion and then the people are willing in the day of his power."[51] M'Cheyne also concentrated on the Spirit's sovereignty, saying, "Conversion is not accomplished by might, nor by power, but by the Spirit of God."[52]

M'Cheyne emphasized God's election precisely because it undercuts man's tendency to believe he contributes something to his salvation. M'Cheyne explained why he accented God's sovereignty in salvation: "So long as a person has hope of saving himself, of reforming, praying, weeping out his sins, so long he keeps his religion up. But when he is brought to see that he can do nothing to save himself, that it signifies just nothing, his heart dies within him."[53] As his song, "I Am Debtor," shows, God's sovereignty produces gratitude:

> Chosen not for good in me;
> Wakened up from wrath to flee,
> Hidden in the Saviour's side,
> By the Spirit sanctified,
> Teach me, Lord, on earth, to show,
> By my love, how much I owe.[54]

Man's Depravity

James M. Gordon writes of M'Cheyne's preaching: "If a soul was to be awakened to 'its perilous condition,' then an honest statement of the spiritual facts was in order"—namely, the terrifying reality of sin.[55] For M'Cheyne, bold declarations about sin stemmed from his

---

was a mercy that made Him give His only begotten Son. It was mercy that made Him choose, awaken, and draw any sinner to Christ. He never saved any but out of free sovereign mercy. There is none so vile but God can save him without prejudice to His justice, truth, holiness, or majesty." *HTD*, 12. See also, *OTS*, 35.

50. *MAR*, 392.
51. *TPP*, 257. See also, *NTS*, 127; *SOH*, 37, 38.
52. *OTS*, 167. See also, *TPH*, 130; *TPP*, 168; *HTD*, 9.
53. *OTS*, 99.
54. *MAR*, 588.
55. Gordon, *Evangelical Spirituality*, 127.

self-examination.⁵⁶ On June 15, 1840, he wrote a letter to his good friend, Reverend Dan Edwards, urging, "Pray for more knowledge of your own heart—of the total depravity of it—of the awful depths of corruption that are there."⁵⁷ M'Cheyne regularly probed his heart and discovered a depth of iniquity that caused him to feel "broken under a sense of my exceeding wickedness."⁵⁸ M'Cheyne's diary entries and personal letters reveal two specific sins that plagued his life and ministry.

The first struggle M'Cheyne mentions repeatedly relates to pride. The struggle came from both external and internal realities. Nearly unbroken ministerial success caused the former, while innate stirrings to vanity motivated the latter. After unusually well-attended Lord's Day services, M'Cheyne asked, "Shall I call the liveliness of this day a gale of the Spirit, or was all natural? I know that all was not of grace; the self-admiration, the vanity, the desire of honour, the bitterness—these were all breaths of earth or hell."⁵⁹ Following another Sunday in which his preaching was praised, M'Cheyne remarked, "I fear some like the messenger, not the message; and I fear I am so vain as to love that love."⁶⁰ Sabbath services proved to be the regular soil in which the sin of pride grew. M'Cheyne wrote after a day of powerful preaching, "In both discourses I can look back on many hateful thoughts of pride, and self-admiration, and love of praise, stealing the heart out of the service."⁶¹ M'Cheyne believed that his pride caused his seasons of sickness, in which God was confronting him with his sin. During one prolonged period of illness, he told his sister Eliza that God had sent the disease to "teach me that He can save and feed the people without any help of mine."⁶²

Closely linked to M'Cheyne's struggle with pride was his struggle with lust. He believed "the lust of praise has ever been my besetting sin."⁶³ In his "Personal Reformation," he said, "I am tempted to think that I am

---

56. Yeaworth says, "It was out of a deep acquaintance with his own heart that he dwelt at great length upon the mark of guilt in others." Yeaworth, "Robert Murray McCheyne," 236.

57. *MAR*, 242.

58. *MAR*, 56. In a letter to Mrs. Collier, M'Cheyne wrote, "None but God knows what an abyss of corruption is in my heart." *MAR*, 213.

59. *MAR*, 44. See also, *MAR*, 23, 106.

60. *MAR*, 44.

61. *MAR*, 43. See also, *MAR*, 45.

62. M'Cheyne, *Familiar Letters*, 134–35.

63. *MAR*, 36.

now an established Christian—that I have overcome this or that lust so long . . . This is a lie of Satan."[64] He goes on to write, "I am helpless in respect of every lust that ever was, or ever will be, in the human heart."[65] An 1842 letter to R. Macdonald of Blairgowrie reveals the depth of M'Cheyne's struggle:

> I think I never was brought to feel the wickedness of my heart as I do now. Yet I do not feel it as many sweet Christians do, while they are high above it, and seem to look down into a depth of iniquity, deep, deep in their bosoms. Now, it appears to me as if my feet were actually in the miry clay, and I only wonder that I am kept from open sin. My only refuge is in the word, "I will put my Spirit within you." It is only by being made partakers of the *divine nature* that I can escape the corruption that is in the world through lust.[66]

M'Cheyne's sermons disclose that he understood "lust" in two ways. First, he spoke of lust in the broad sense of "sinful passion"—a temptation directed to many vices.[67] Second, he defined lust more narrowly as sinful sexual desire.[68] What specific lust, then, plagued M'Cheyne? While no particular answer can be given with confidence, it seems he waged a prolonged battle with those passions typical of an ambitious, young man.

M'Cheyne believed that discovering the depths of our sinful condition is essential to a true understanding of the gospel, for "the more you feel your weakness, the amazing depravity of your heart . . . the more need have you to lean on Jesus."[69] He was thus relentless in his declara-

---

64. MAR, 153.

65. MAR, 154. M'Cheyne also wrote, "Eve, Achan, David, all fell through lust of the eye. I should make a covenant with mine, and pray, 'Turn away mine eyes from viewing vanity . . . One of my most frequent occasions of being led into temptation is this—I say it is needful to my office that I listen to this, or look into this, or speak of this." MAR, 156–57.

66. MAR, 275 (emphasis original).

67. MAR, 351, 369, 387, 392, 400, 533; HTD, 63; BOF, 39, 92, 100, 104, 140, 171, 185; TPH, 39, 41, 42, 47, 101, 111, 115, 141, 146, 164, 168, 181, 210, 227, 230, 240–42, 260, 344, 367, 369, 375, 410, 421, 426, 450, 464, 474, 516; SOH, 13, 24, 42, 107, 170; NTS, 56, 58, 90, 121, 148, 229–30, 318; TPP, 64, 86, 87, 130, 164, 203, 223, 238, 243, 253, 282, 286, 331; OTS, 60.

68. MAR, 352, 437; HTD, 75; SOH, 23; TPP, 13, 45, 132, 224, 307; TBJ, 96; TPH, 74, 129, 250, 312, 421; BOF, 186; NTS, 80, 180, 277–79, 282, 307, 310.

69. MAR, 526–27. M'Cheyne exhorted St. Peter's to "get a deep acquaintance with your own heart. It is fearful to think how little young believers know of their own heart. Pray to get a deep sight of the desperate wickedness of your heart. I believe

tion of the doctrine of man's depravity. For example, he asserted, "The whole Bible bears witness that by nature we are dead in trespasses and sins—that we are as unable to walk holily in the world, as a dead man is unable to rise and walk."[70] It is not uncommon to find him impressing the terrible reality of sin upon his audience. For instance, he proclaimed, "Your *whole nature* is totally depraved. You are accustomed to think that you have some parts good; that though some part was depraved, yet some part remained sound. But learn that the whole head is sick, the whole heart is faint. Your *whole history* is covered with sin."[71]

M'Cheyne believed that self-righteousness,[72] pride,[73] and formality[74] were the most common sins in his parish, and thus he spoke consistently against them. He ministered in a context in which many outwardly moral people filled the pews at St. Peter's. He believed, however, that they remained unconverted. He directed some of his strongest statements toward this group, whom he called "almost Christians." He warned, "The deepest place in hell will be for almost Christians. In strict justice it will be so. The more sin the greater guilt and the deeper hell. And who has so much sin as the soul that comes nearest to Christ, yet is not ravished with His beauty, and attracted to Him by his loveliness. In the nature of things, the hell of the 'almost Christian' will be more severe than that of others."[75]

M'Cheyne's pronouncements regarding man's depravity had a christological and soteriological purpose. He knew it is only through a clear sense of sin that we are awakened to God's grace in Christ. He proclaimed, "Be determined to know the worst of yourself; for thus only will you see the desirableness of conversion—the excellency of Christ."[76]

---

that it is ignorance that is the cause of many of your falls. Ignorance is at the bottom of them." *BOF*, 67. Similarly, he proclaimed, "Sin is an infinite evil. It leaves a mark on the soul that nothing human can wipe away. Oh! pray for a discovery of the loathsomeness of sin." *TBJ*, 61. See also, *MAR*, 399–400. In one notebook, M'Cheyne spent extended time cataloging the sins included in the vice lists of 1 Cor 6:9, Gal 5:19, and Eph 5:3–6, concluding with various lessons Christians should learn from Paul's teaching. MACCH 1.3.

70. *MAR*, 341. See also, *SOH*, 20, 49; *TPP*, 165; *CIS*, 135.
71. *MAR*, 439 (emphasis original). See also, *HTD*, 19.
72. *BOF*, 34.
73. *OTS*, 116.
74. *TPH*, 152.
75. *NTS*, 102.
76. *TPH*, 43. In an ordination sermon for P. L. Miller, M'Cheyne said, "I believe we cannot lay down the guilt of man—his total depravity, and the glorious gospel of

M'Cheyne focused on sin's malady because it amplified the glorious love revealed in God's remedy: Christ. To remain in sin meant "refusing to come to so lovely, excellent and glorious a Saviour as Christ is."[77] He taught that the Holy Spirit makes men feel "the greatness of sin" and see it as "done against a God of love; done against Jesus Christ and His love."[78] What a wonder it is, M'Cheyne exclaimed, that "Christ should love *any*. The heart of an unconverted man is so frightful, so revolting, has got such depths of sin, it is amazing He should love *any*."[79] M'Cheyne's usual movement from sin's depravity to God's remedy in Christ is clearly seen in the following exhortation from his sermon on Psalm 69:1–3:

> I have shown you your sad condition. Now here behold the way of safety. You are every moment exposed to the wrath of God, and yet you are every moment exposed to the love of the Saviour. This love does not regard them as good and holy, but as ungodly, as sinners, as enemies. You always think that you must repent and mend your life to make yourself worthy of the Saviour's compassion. Learn that the Saviour came for the ungodly, for those who are not repenting, nor believing.

M'Cheyne's pivot from sin to salvation shows the centrality of love for Christ to his spirituality and ministry. In contrast to the typical view that a pastor should preach the terrors of the law to drive people to Christ, M'Cheyne was convinced that a preacher should lean on a more magnetic power—the love of Christ. He proclaimed, "You *may* be moved with fear, as Noah was, but you *must* be drawn by love. I believe that never a soul was converted without a sight of the God of glory."[80] He maintained that while the law's terror is a proper means to induce fear of judgment, it cannot cause a sinner to close with Christ. For that to happen, the sinner must look upon God's eternal love in Christ:

Christ, too clearly; that we cannot urge men to embrace and flee too warmly." *MAR*, 363.

77. *SOH*, 68.
78. *MAR*, 410.
79. *TBJ*, 59 (emphasis original).
80. *BOF*, 81 (emphasis original). See also, *OTS*, 65; *CIS*, 17, 30–31; *TPH*, 53–54. M'Cheyne similarly proclaimed, "It is quite true that none were ever brought to Christ by fear. We must be brought to Christ by a sight of his love. But then, it is quite as true that you will never be brought out of your own security but by fear; you must be drawn *out* by fear, and drawn *in* by love." *BOF*, 71 (emphasis original). See also, *TPH*, 380–81.

It is commonly thought that preaching the holy law is the most awakening truth in the Bible,—that by it the mouth is stopped, and all the world becomes guilty before God; and, indeed, I believe this is the most ordinary mean which God makes us of. And yet to me there is something far more awakening in the sight of a Divine Saviour freely offering Himself to every one of the human race.[81]

The Savior's Beauty

In 1844, the *Presbyterian Review* offered an assessment of M'Cheyne's pulpit ministry—the place where "he was at home." When it came to M'Cheyne's gospel heralding, the magazine declared, "His solicitude for the salvation of his hearers made him affectionate even beyond his natural tenderness."[82] Marcus Loane believes that M'Cheyne's affectionate gospel preaching was the secret of his success.[83] M'Cheyne's knowledge of sin and the Savior was a holy elixir for his faithful proclamation.[84] His sermons were nothing less than the overflow of his personal experience of Christ.[85] And nothing was more astonishing to M'Cheyne than Christ coming to save sinners. He thus centered every sermon on Christ who came to seek and to save the lost. He believed it must be so, for as he wrote to the Reverend Alex Gatherer, "Never forget that the end of a sermon is

---

81. *MAR*, 366.
82. Cited in Yeaworth, "Robert Murray M'Cheyne," 222.
83. Loane, *They Were Pilgrims*, 169–70.
84. In a letter to Mrs. Collier, M'Cheyne declared, "Who can preach so well as a sinner—who is forgiven much, and daily upheld by the Spirit with such a heart!" *MAR*, 215. Bonar comments, "His deep acquaintance with the human heart and passions often led him to dwell at greater length, not only on those topics whereby the sinner might be brought to discover his guilt, but also on marks that would evidence a change, than on 'the glad tidings.' And yet he ever felt that these blessed tidings, addressed to souls in the very gall of bitterness, were the true theme of the minister of Christ; and never did he preach other than a full salvation ready for the chief of sinners. From the very first, also, he carefully avoided the error of those who rather speculate or doctrinise about the gospel, than preach the gospel itself." *MAR*, 46.
85. Bonar agrees, "From the first he fed others by what he himself was feeding upon. His preaching was in a manner the development of his soul's experience. It was a giving out of the inward life. He loved to come up from the pastures wherein the Chief Shepherd had met him—to lead the flock entrusted to his care to the spots where he found nourishment." *MAR*, 34–35.

the salvation of the people."[86] He confessed to St. Peter's: "I have sought to preach to all, that the veil was rent and that every sinner might enter; that Christ was lifted up, and that every sinner might look to Him and live."[87] Apparently, his indefatigable gospel preaching troubled many who sat in the pews. He told of those who were "quite offended because we preach Christ to the vilest of sinners."[88] But M'Cheyne was undeterred, proclaiming, "This is the chief object of the Bible, to show you the work, the beauty, the glory, the excellency of this High Priest."[89] He promised he would not stop proclaiming "in accents of tenderness . . . the simple message of redeeming love—that the wrath of God is abiding on sinners, but that Christ is a Saviour freely offered to them, just as they are."[90]

M'Cheyne's sermons exude a Westminster Christology that revels in Christ's mediatorial ministry as our prophet, priest, and king.[91] He offers no new insight for orthodox Christology; he believed and preached it without apology.[92] One example of a typical gospel exhortation came in a sermon entitled, "Look to a Pierced Christ":

> Do any of you feel that you have been awakened to concern about your souls? You have been pierced through with an arrow of conviction. Look at that arrow; it came out of the bow of Christ. It was Christ that took it out of his quiver. Christ aimed it at your heart, he made it pierce your heart. The feather is marked

---

86. *MAR*, 329. A memorable illustration of M'Cheyne's passion for gospel preaching comes in the following conversation between Bonar and M'Cheyne: "Once, after preaching in St. Peter's, Dundee, upon the text, 'Thine eyes shall see the King in His beauty,' Mr. M'Cheyne said to him (Bonar) as they walked home together, 'Brother, I enjoyed your sermon; to me it was sweet. You and I and many, I trust, in our congregations shall see the King in His beauty. But, my brother, you forgot there might be many listening to you to-night, who, unless they are changed by the grace of God, shall never see Him in His beauty.'" Bonar, *Reminiscences*, 132.

87. *OTS*, 101.

88. *TPH*, 381. See also, *OTS*, 131; *SC*, 90–91.

89. *SOH*, 87. Similarly, M'Cheyne taught that "Christ is the main thing in the gospel . . . So I believe that Christ is the main thing in a believer's heart." *SOH*, 139.

90. *TPH*, 318. M'Cheyne's concentration on the gospel message goes all the way back to his days at the Divinity Hall. He recorded in a notebook: "Subjects for the Pulpit." One annotation reads, "In demonstrating the guilt and the remedy—the danger of rejecting the duty of embracing the gospel—you are dealing with the great elements of preaching." MACCH 1.7.

91. *WCF*, 8.

92. For M'Cheyne's theological notes on the christological sections of the Shorter Catechism (esp. 21–36), see MACCH 1.7.

with the blood of the pierced hand. That arrow came from the hand of love, from the hand that was nailed to the cross.[93]

M'Cheyne rarely preached on a gospel theme without reveling in the love of Christ.[94] A ruling elder at St. Peter's recalled, "How beautifully affectionate were M'Cheyne's addresses! He *draws* you to Christ."[95] M'Cheyne said it was Christ's love for sinners that compelled him to obey God's law in our stead,[96] become the sacrificial substitute for sinners,[97] undergo the horror of God's wrath for sin,[98] and unite us to his person.[99] Such "divine love" is the supreme argument to "persuades sinners now to believe on him."[100] This love even informed M'Cheyne's notions of saving faith.[101] True faith is when "the soul begins to feel a suitableness in the way of salvation by the Lord our righteousness and sweetly, humbly, calmly rejoices in Him ... He sees in the gospel plan, in the Person of Jesus, in His office and work, such a divine glory that there arises in his heart a sweet sense of the certainty of these things."[102] Faith, M'Cheyne explained, is little more than a believing look upon the "brightness and beauty of Christ."[103]

---

93. *TPH*, 225. Another characteristic appeal is as follows: "Sinner, have you received the Lord Jesus Christ? Has your heart melted at the sight of the heaven-provided Saviour? Have you known the gift of God? Have you seen and delighted in the *finished work* of Christ?" *HTD*, 45 (emphasis original).

94. Bonar writes, "He was sometimes a little unguarded in his statements, when his heart was deeply moved and his feelings stirred, and sometimes he was too long in his address; but this arose from the fulness of his soul." *MAR*, 65.

95. Lamb, *M'Cheyne from the Pew*, 31 (emphasis original).

96. *NTS*, 32. See also, *SOH*, 22; *TPH*, 58.

97. *SOH*, 59.

98. *TPH*, 72. See also, *TPH*, 72.

99. *TPP*, 261. See also, *OTS*, 64.

100. *CIS*, 140–41. See also, *TPP*, 211; *TPH*, 59, 385.

101. The Confession defines faith as "a saving grace, whereby we receive and rest upon him alone for salvation, as he is offered to us in the gospel" (*WCF*, 86). M'Cheyne did not disagree with this view. He merely added his peculiar tone and tenor.

102. *SOH*, 17. Likewise, M'Cheyne teaches that knowing Christ's righteousness means having "a sense of the preciousness and fitness of Christ, as he is revealed in the gospel." *TPH*, 324. He also writes, "A real discovery of the glory, suitableness, and freeness of the Lord Jesus Chris in the soul, is saving faith." *HTD*, 43.

103. *TPH*, 59. M'Cheyne's marveling at true faith is also expressed in his statement, "When once a fluttering sinner comes in sight of Christ, when once he has seen the atoning blood, the love and tenderness that are in the eye of Immanuel, he cannot withdraw." *OTS*, 65.

The love of Christ pervaded M'Cheyne's preaching, visiting, and writing, as he consistently called parishioners to behold Christ's beauty and glory. A Song-of-Songs-shaped Christology tinged his pleas with sinners. In one letter, he wrote,

> I do trust that you are seeking hard after Him whom your soul loveth. He is not far from any one of us. He is a powerful and precious Saviour, and happy are they who put their trust in Him. He is the Rose of Sharon, lovely to look upon, having all divine and human excellencies meeting in Himself; and yet he is the Lily of the Valleys,—meek and lowly in heart, willing to save the vilest. He answers the need of your soul. You are all guilt; He is a fountain to wash you. You are all naked; He has a wedding garment to cover you. You are dead; He is the life. You are all wounds and bruises; He is the Balm of Gilead. His righteousness is broader than your sin; and then He is so free.[104]

The central feature of M'Cheyne's theology is the knowledge of God's love in Christ. Centering his ministry on this love meant focusing on Christ who is "altogether lovely" and came to earth on an "errand . . . of purest love."[105] M'Cheyne believed that exalting Christ's fullness was the key to a faithful and fruitful ministry, as "the soul that has once seen the loveliness of Christ, leaves all for Him."[106] His primary endeavor, then, was the realization of John 3:14–15, "And as Moses lifted up the serpent in the wilderness, even so must the Son of man be lifted up: That whosoever believeth in him should not perish, but have eternal life."[107]

---

104. *MAR*, 322. In another letter to a seeker, M'Cheyne wrote, "The pure, full love of God streams through the blood and obedience of Jesus to every soul that is lying under them, however vile and wretched in themselves. Have you tried—have you tasted the holy love of a holy God? Thy love is better than wine. It is better than all creature love or creature enjoyments. Oh, do not live—oh, do not die, out of this sweet, sweet, sin-pardoning, soul-comforting love of God!" *MAR*, 262.

105. *TPH*, 180. M'Cheyne's teaching on Christ's loveliness and love for sinners is vast, saturating his entire sermon catalog. For representative sermons, see "The Love of Christ" on 2 Cor 5:14 in *TPH*, 44–54, and "Who Shall Separate Us from the Love of Christ?" on Rom 8:35–37 in *TPH*, 341–48.

106. *TBJ*, 84.

107. See *OTS*, 14, 101; *TPH*, 209, 295, 381, 403, 525; *TPP*, 94, 102; *NTS*, 26, 253; *MAR*, 239, 328. The "brazen serpent" was M'Cheyne's favorite Old Testament type of Christ. See *TPH*, 95, 258; *TPP*, 93–94, 102; *OTS*, 10; *NTS*, 15, 20, 26, 253; *SC*, 9; *TBJ*, 69; *SOH*, 82; *MAR*, 89, 160, 266, 328.

The Spirit's Efficacy

David Beaty's work on M'Cheyne rightly emphasizes the significance of the Holy Spirit in his life and ministry.[108] M'Cheyne was not a theologian of the Holy Spirit to the same degree as John Calvin,[109] but he cherished the person and work of the Holy Spirit. He thirsted for more of the "dew from heaven"—his preferred way of describing the Holy Spirit's influence upon believers.[110] His focus on the Holy Spirit is evident in his first sermon as pastor of St. Peter's. His chosen text was Isaiah 61:1–3, "The Spirit of the LORD God is upon me; because the LORD hath anointed me to preach good tidings."[111] He believed that "the more anointing of the Holy Spirit, the more success will the minister have."[112] Further, he extolled the Holy Spirit calling him "[the] greatest of all the privileges of a Christian,"[113] adding, "It is sweet to get the love of Christ; but I will tell you what is equally as sweet—that is to receive the Spirit of Christ."[114]

---

108. Beaty, *An All-Surpassing Fellowship*, 95–101. Yeaworth often mentions M'Cheyne's appropriation of the Holy Spirit, but does not see it as a unifying motif in M'Cheyne's theology.

109. Warfield, "John Calvin the Theologian," 484–87; Hesselink, *Calvin's First Catechism*, 177; Dantas, "Calvin," 128; Evans, "John Calvin," 94; Lopes, "Calvin," 38–49.

110. MACCH 1.16 contains M'Cheyne's systematic overview of the Holy Spirit's person and work. The reference to the Holy Spirit as "dew" comes from M'Cheyne's interpretation of 2 Sam 7:12, Exod 16:13, Isa 28:19, and Hos 14:5. He penned, "What is more lovely than dew? How sweet and refreshing is the dew to thirsty ground. Every green thing is revived by it. It comes when the earth is calm and still, it comes regularly, silently, unseen. Such is the Spirit of God. He comes on the soul when the soul is brought to rest in Christ. He comes silently on feet unseen and yet receives and refreshes the whole soul. Oh, how good a Spirit must he be who is like the dew unto Israel." TPP, 41. See also, TBJ, 111; TPH, 92, 151, 310, 451; OTS, 147–49; NTS, 109; MAR, 182, 215, 276, 361, 461, 501. M'Cheyne also employed the dew imagery when speaking about Christ's love for his people. His motivation for doing so comes from Song of Songs 5:2, "I sleep, but my heart waketh: it is the voice of my beloved that knocketh, saying, Open to me, my sister, my love, my dove, my undefiled: for my head is filled with dew, and my locks with the drops of the night." A typical application of this text is, "How often, how long has He stood at your hearts!—even until His head was filled with dew, and His locks with the drops of the night." SC, 74. See also, SC, 94; TBJ, 61; TPH, 338; BOF, 167; MAR, 434.

111. MACCH 3.3. M'Cheyne returned to this text each year on the anniversary of his installation. He changed little in the exposition from year to year, usually inserting new conclusions and applications after an additional twelve months of ministry.

112. MAR, 530.

113. OTS, 74.

114. BOF, 42. See also, TPP, 73.

M'Cheyne locates the Holy Spirit's work in two primary areas: regeneration and sanctification.[115]

The sovereign Spirit is God's agent unto conversion,[116] as he works through the preached Word to bring peace to sinners.[117] He is the Spirit of the new birth,[118] the "Spirit of Grace" who comes in and renovates the soul.[119] The Holy Spirit, M'Cheyne instructed, always makes us "look to a pierced Christ.[120] We come to an "abiding believing knowledge of the love of Christ" when the Father grants us "His free Spirit."[121] M'Cheyne taught that the Holy Spirit usually brings people to Christ in two stages: (1) by convincing them of their sin, and (2) by convincing them of Christ's righteousness. It is then that the Holy Spirit begins the work of sanctification.[122]

The Holy Spirit is full of "a tender desire" to make us holy, affirmed M'Cheyne.[123] Much of M'Cheyne's teaching on the Holy Spirit exalts his role in ensuring that we attain that holiness needed to see God. M'Cheyne was eager to emphasize that we did not come to Christ in our own power, and we do not advance in Christ-likeness by our own strength. He said, "In the sanctification of the people of God, though means are used, yet the word is not by might, nor by power, but by God's Spirit."[124] Further, M'Cheyne believed that the Spirit's working in sanctification brought confidence to a Christian. The Holy Spirit comes to purify the entire per-

---

115. M'Cheyne assumed the divine person and work of the Holy Spirit. He typically offered brief comments before proceeding to exhortation. On one occasion, he expounded eight truths concerning the Holy Spirit: (1) He is God (Isa 48:16; 61:1); (2) He is the Author of Regeneration (Gen. 1:2; Job 26:13; Ps 118:20; Eccl 11:5; Isa 52:13); (3) He is the Convincer of Sin; (4) He is the Leader to Christ (Num 11:9); (5) He is the Sanctifier and Sealer (Num 14:24; Pss 51; 139:7; 143:10); (6) He strives with men (Neh 9:20, 30; Ps 95; Heb 3:7); (7) Sins against the Spirit (Heb 3:7, 10; Ps 106:32); and (8) He is the Giver of Minister's Gifts (Num 11:17, 25-26; 27:18). MACCH 1.1.

116. *TPP*, 168. See also, *NTS*, 244; *TPH*, 314.

117. *OTS*, 168.

118. *NTS*, 126.

119. *TPH*, 226.

120. *TPH*, 228. See also, *TPH*, 100.

121. *HTD*, 53.

122. *NTS*, 105–6.

123. *TPH*, 97.

124. *OTS*, 168. The means that M'Cheyne has in mind are clear: "It is in learning, in reading, in remembering, in meditating on the Word of god that the Spirit works in us to will and do of God's good pleasure." *NTS*, 110. See also, *OTS*, 178.

son after Christ's image: "There is not a faculty, there is not an affection, a power, or passion of the soul, on which the Spirit does not descend... [as] the dew comes upon every leaf, the Spirit comes upon every thought and feeling of the inner man."[125] Additionally, it is the Holy Spirit who teaches us to behold God's glory in the face of Christ,[126] to pray,[127] and to put sin to death.[128] He also seals us for the day of glory.[129] Viewing communion with the Holy Spirit as vital, M'Cheyne warned against grieving him by (1) putting his work in the place of Christ's; (2) failing to lean all on him; (3) refusing to follow his leading; or (4) despising his ordinances.[130]

As with all his theological tenets, M'Cheyne's view of the Holy Spirit is supremely experiential.[131] His exhortations to pursue a Spirit-empowered life routinely focused on sweet communion with the third person of the Trinity. At the conclusion of a sermon on Ezekiel 36:27,[132] M'Cheyne preached,

> Learn to hold intimate communion with God. The Spirit of God will continually be lifting the heart to sweet adoring thoughts of God. Through Jesus we have access by one Spirit to the Father. The Spirit is one with the Father and the Son and wherever he dwells he will be lifting himself toward God. If you are the temple of the Holy Ghost, then what sweet fellowship you will have with the Father and the Son. Oh, what adoring looks at Jesus will not the Spirit make you cast.[133]

THE FREE OFFER OF THE GOSPEL

M'Cheyne's emphases on covenant theology, God's sovereignty, man's depravity, the Son's beauty, and the Spirit's efficacy ultimately come together

---

125. *OTS*, 148.
126. *TPH*, 100.
127. *BOF*, 102.
128. *TPH*, 101. See also, *MAR*, 462.
129. *BOF*, 103.
130. *BOF*, 103–4.
131. See *NTS*, 108, 110, 126, 244; *OTS*, 75, 165, 168; *TPH*, 97, 101; *HTD*, 53; *MAR*, 504; *BOF*, 67, 103–4; *SOH*, 153.
132. "A new heart also will I give you, and a new spirit will I put within you: and I will take away the stony heart out of your flesh, and I will give you an heart of flesh."
133. *TPP*, 72.

in his free offer of the gospel. The best way to describe M'Cheyne's homiletic identity is that he was *a preacher of the free offer of Christ's love for sinners*. The free offer of the gospel has a long—and controversial—history in Scotland.[134] David Dickson's classic work on pastoral theology raised the question: "How can this offer of grace to all hearers of the gospel . . . stand with the doctrine of election of some, and reprobation of others, or, with the doctrine of Christ's redeeming of the elect only, and not of all and every man?"[135] Significant Scottish figures who argued for the free offer include James Durham in the seventeenth century,[136] the Marrow Men in the eighteenth century,[137] and Thomas Chalmers in the nineteenth century.[138] Indeed, the free offer was a hallmark of Chalmers's preaching and theological instruction at the Divinity Hall.[139] One

---

134. Richard Mouw observes that the matter of the gospel offer "has been fiercely debated in just about every context where Calvinism has flourished. Indeed, it has probably stirred up more passions than any other theological topic within the Calvinist camp." Mouw, *Calvinism*, 45. Yet, John Roxborogh rightly explains, "That a high doctrine of election, such as that embodied in the Westminster Confession, can be compatible with evangelism, has often been more of a problem for those outside the Westminster tradition than those within." Davie, *New Dictionary*, 137. B. R. Oliphant takes a dimmer view, however, saying of Horatius Bonar's emphasis on the free offer, "When [Bonar] began his ministry in Kelso his congregation were unaccustomed to such emphasis being placed on the doctrine, and some regarded it as heretical teaching." Oliphant, "Horatius Bonar," 147. For an overview of Horatius Bonar's pamphlet conflict with John Kennedy over the free offer, see Hamilton, *A Scottish Christian Heritage*, 186–94.

135. Dickson, *Therapeutica Sacra*, 170–71.

136. See Maclean, "James Durham," 92–119.

137. See MacLeod, *Scottish Theology*, 154–66; Hall, "Marrow Controversy," 239–57; VanDoodewaard, "Marrow Theology," 399–416; Lachman, *Marrow Controversy*, 201–460; Henderson, *Religious Controversies*, 24–42; Blaikie, *Preachers of Scotland*, 185–95.

138. In 1814, Chalmers said, "I suspect both Edwards and Brainerd impair the freeness of the gospel offer and may embarrass and restrain a young convert in the outset of the work of seeking after God." Quoted in Roxborogh, *Thomas Chalmers*, 47.

139. William Hanna writes, "The discovery that pardon and full reconciliation with God are offered gratuitously to all men in Christ, had been the turning point in Mr. Chalmers's own spiritual history; and the most marked characteristic of his pulpit ministrations after his conversion was the frequency and fervour with which he held out to sinners Christ and His salvation as God's free gift." Hanna, *Memoirs of the Life*, 420. For summary comments from Chalmers on the free offer, see Hanna, *Select Works of Thomas Chalmers*, 3:49, 8:424–442; *Sermons*, 513; Chalmers, *Works of Thomas Chalmers*, 30; Chalmers, *Discourses*, 242–43; Chalmers, *Sermons Preached*, 324; Chalmers, *Works of Thomas Chalmers*, 7:340.

of Chalmers's final sermons was entitled, "The Fullness and Freeness of the Gospel Offer." According to John Roxborough, the title "summarizes . . . his basic understanding of the Christian message."[140] Chalmers explained the golden chain of salvation as follows:

> The natural depravity of man; his need both of regeneration and of an atonement; the accomplishment of the one by the efficacy of a divine sacrifice, and of the other by the operation of a sanctifying spirit; the doctrine that a sinner is justified by faith, followed up . . . by the doctrine that he is judged by works; the righteousness of Christ as the alone foundation of his meritorious claim to heaven, but this followed up by his own personal righteousness as the indispensable preparation for heaven's exercises and heaven's joys; the free offer of pardon even to the chief of sinners; but this followed up by the practical calls of repentance, without which no orthodoxy can save him; the amplitude of gospel invitations, and, in despite of all that has been unintelligently said about our gloomy and relentless Calvinism, the wide and unexplained amnesty that is held forth to every creature under heaven.[141]

Chalmers's zeal for the free offer was influential in his time,[142] and undoubtedly influenced young M'Cheyne as well. Annotations on the free offer of the gospel fill a seminary notebook from 1839.[143] An 1832 notebook finds M'Cheyne calling the free offer "the stamina of good preaching."[144] The free offer of Christ's love is found throughout his pulpit ministry because he believed ministerial faithfulness depended upon it: "A faithful watchman preaches a free Saviour to all the world. This was the great object of Christ's ministry."[145] M'Cheyne acknowledged the

---

140. Davie, *New Dictionary of Theology*.
141. Quoted in Roxborogh, "Chalmers' Theology," 180.
142. Roxborogh, "Chalmers' Theology," 180.
143. MACCH 1.5.
144. MACCH 1.6, 112. See also, *NTS*, 55.

145. *MAR*, 536. On October 10, 1840, Andrew Bonar wrote to M'Cheyne and confessed disappointment in his preaching. Bonar concluded that his "failure to dwell enough upon a free Gospel" was partly to blame. Quoted in Palmer, "Andrew A. Bonar," 381. Palmer's analysis of Bonar's ministry is that "Bonar felt that the doctrine of election did not adequately express the truth concerning the extent of Christ's offer of salvation." Bonar did not believe the Westminster Confession of Faith erred in teaching the free offer; rather, it did not say enough about Christ's universal love for sinners. Palmer, "Andrew A. Bonar," 380–81.

difficulty in reconciling God's election with the freeness of the gospel, yet he believed both because he found both in the Bible.[146] He taught that Christ nowhere invites "the elect" to come,[147] but everywhere invites all people to faith and repentance.[148] M'Cheyne's formulation of the free offer finds him regularly extolling Christ's desire to save all sinners. He preached a crucified Christ who willingly died for sinners and so now calls out to all with eager love: "The whole Bible shows that Christ is quite willing and anxious that all sinners should come to him. The city of refuge in the Old Testament was a type of Christ; and you remember that its gates were open by night and day. The arms of Christ were nailed wide open, when he hung upon the cross; and this was a figure of his wide willingness to save all."[149] M'Cheyne viewed preaching Christ's free love as the sum and substance of his work, for "His free love is all you need."[150] Additionally, he demonstrated how Christ's free love rebukes the self-righteous[151] and condemns those who remain in sin.[152] M'Cheyne understood the free offer of the gospel to be a most precious doctrine, and tender pleas fill his proclamation of Christ's love for all. He declared at St. Peter's, "The free offer of Christ is the very thing that pierces you to the heart. You hear that He is altogether lovely—that He invites sinners to come to Him—that He never casts out those who do come."[153]

For M'Cheyne, the free offer was not only a doctrine to preach, but a truth to sing. In one of his better-known hymns, he expressed the following:

> When free grace awoke me, by light from on high,
> Then legal fears shook me, I trembled to die;
> No refuge, no safety in self could I see,—
> Jehovah Tsidkenu my Saviour must be.

---

146. *NTS*, 199. Bruce McLennan concurs, "To McCheyne, there was no inconsistency in preaching the doctrine of God's sovereign electing grace and making a free offer of the gospel to whosoever will." McLennan, *McCheyne's Dundee*, 59.

147. *MAR*, 329.

148. *OTS*, 27, 54, 110, 116, 119; *SOH*, 85–86; *TPH*, 178, 295; *TPP*, 171; *MAR*, 327, 536, 546.

149. *TPH*, 295. See also, *TPH*, 178.

150. *MAR*, 461.

151. *TPH*, 318.

152. *MAR*, 330, 490.

153. *MAR*, 370. See also, *MAR*, 384; *NTS*, 27.

My terrors all vanished before the sweet name;
My guilty fears banished, with boldness I came
To drink at the fountain, life-giving and free,—
Jehovah Tsidkenu is all thing to me.[154]

A fair summation, then, of M'Cheyne's theology is the knowledge of God's free love in Christ. Looking upon the Savior's unmerited love for sinners undergirds M'Cheyne's theology. "Nothing is more wonderful than the love of Christ," hence everyone must "learn the freeness of the love of Christ."[155]

CONCLUSION

Like his mentor, Thomas Chalmers, M'Cheyne had no "new theology" to teach.[156] He ministered in harmony with the Westminster Standards. He happily subscribed to its teaching at his ordination, and he diligently propagated its doctrinal system. Thus, any account of M'Cheyne's theology must take into account his commitment to the Standards. First, his theology was *covenantal*. Previous works on M'Cheyne have not recognized the degree to which the covenant shapes his theology. It undergirds his preaching and provides the foundation for his understanding of key theological motifs. Second, his theology was *Calvinistic*. He preached God's sovereignty and man's depravity with equal enthusiasm. Such truths, in the hands of M'Cheyne, were never cold dogmas, but the basis of his winsome appeals. It is precisely because M'Cheyne was a profound feeler that his declarations of truth—even the hardest doctrines—exuded noticeable warmth. He was a minister captivated with Christ. Third, his theology was *christological*. Proclaiming Christ's person and work was his passion. It was impossible for him to speak for any length of time without referencing the Savior's majesty and beauty. A love for Christ filled his mind and animated his heart, and became the all-consuming fire in his theology. In a letter to Horatius Bonar, he asked, "Do you see increasing marks that Immanuel in His grace and beauty is with you, attracting souls by His loveliness and fitness, and transforming His own

---

154. *MAR*, 583.

155. *TPH*, 168.

156. Donald Fraser concludes, "Dr. Chalmers had no new theology to teach. His convictions were in harmony with that Westminster Confession of Faith." Fraser, *Thomas Chalmers*, 78.

people into His own lovely image?"[157] Convinced of the Holy Spirit's agency in ministry, M'Cheyne coupled his covenantal and christological convictions with a thoroughly evangelical ministry. Christ's free love to sinners was his chief message. He once declared, "*The love of Christ!* Such is our precious theme! Can we ever weary of it? Its greatness, can we ever know? It's plenitude, can we fully contain?"[158]

William Blaikie has captured the essence of M'Cheyne's theology best by saying that he "brought into the pulpit all the reverence for Scripture of the Reformation period; all the honour for the headship of Christ of the Covenanter struggle; all the freeness of the Gospel offer of the Marrow theology; all the bright imagery of Samuel Rutherford; all the delight of the Erskines in the fulness of Christ."[159]

---

157. Quoted in Bonar, *Life of the Rev.*, 36.
158. *NTS*, 137 (emphasis original).
159. Blaikie, *Preachers of Scotland*, 294.

5

Loving Christ
M'Cheyne's Devotion

JAMES HAMILTON EXPLAINS THAT the "striking characteristic of [M'Cheyne's] piety was absorbing love for the Lord Jesus."[1] M'Cheyne taught that the Sun of Righteousness in his beauty and glory is a ravishing sight,[2] which constrains believers to seek communion with him. Bruce Milne elaborates on this christological emphasis, saying, "[M'Cheyne's] unfailing awareness of the grace of God in Christ was the only possible basis of this new life: the new life is the life of the risen Christ expressed in the disciple's life through wholehearted devotion to and submission to the person of Jesus."[3] The present chapter highlights the christological communion of love in M'Cheyne's spirituality by (1) demonstrating how he employed the Song of Songs as a paradigm for genuine spirituality; (2) outlining the three pillars of his spirituality; and (3) demonstrating how his concept of holiness as renewal "in the whole man after the image of God"[4] was the fullest expression and experience of love.

---

1. Hamilton, *Church in the House*, 221.

2. M'Cheyne loved the Bible's depiction of Christ as "the Sun of Righteousness" (Mal 4:2). He said, "The Sun of Righteousness is the grand attractive centre, around which all his saints move." *TPH*, 54. See also, *MAR*, 33, 146, 173, 288, 373; *HTD*, 12; *SC*, 45; *TBJ*, 19, 49; *NTS*, 159, 165, 186; *TPH*, 45, 60, 342, 352, 361, 459. He preached, "The soul that has once seen the loveliness of Christ, leaves all for Him." *TBJ*, 84.

3. Lewis, *Dictionary*, 710.

4. *WSC*, 35.

THE EXPRESSION OF LOVE

David Yeaworth states, "M'Cheyne's favorite Old Testament book was the Song of Solomon, whose terms and pictures constantly found their way into his preaching of Christ."[5] The famed preacher Alexander Moody-Stuart waited two decades before preaching on the Song of Songs because he believed he had nothing to add to M'Cheyne's "singular sweetness" on the subject.[6] M'Cheyne's high esteem for the Song is most evident in his exposition of 2:8–17, his chosen text when he preached as a candidate at St. Peter's on August 14, 1836.[7] M'Cheyne declared at the sermon's outset: "There is no book of the Bible which affords a better test of the depth of a man's Christianity than the Song of Solomon."[8] He stated,

> [If a man] hath felt his need of [Christ], and been brought to cleave unto him, as the chiefest among ten thousand, and the altogether lovely, then this book will be inestimably precious to his soul; for it contains the tenderest breathings of the believer's heart toward the Saviour, and the tenderest breathings of the Saviour's heart again towards the believer.[9]

Any proper account of M'Cheyne's view of Christian living must reckon with his preaching on the Song, as it provided the grammar for his spirituality of love.[10] He viewed the Song as a spiritual parable representing

---

5. Yeaworth, "Robert Murray M'Cheyne," 200.

6. Moody Stuart, *Alexander Moody Stuart*, 119. For Moody-Stuart's exposition of the Song, see Moody-Stuart, *Song of Songs*.

7. *MAR*, 437–47.

8. *MAR*, 437. M'Cheyne also said, "There is no part of the Bible which opens up more beautifully some of the innermost experiences of the believer's heart." *MAR*, 440.

9. *MAR*, 438.

10. James M. Gordon rightly states, "In his search for an adequate vocabulary [M'Cheyne] resorted to the Song of Solomon." Gordon, *Evangelical Spirituality*, 129. Scholars have long recognized the immense influence of Bernard of Clairvaux's interpretation of the Song. Chaoluan Kao argues, "St. Bernard's *On Loving God* and *Sermons on the Songs of Songs*, were crucial works that changed the traditional understanding on Solomon's Song of Songs and medieval way of piety." Kao, *Reformation of Prayerbooks*, 94. Bernard McGinn states, "Expositions of union with God reached a high level of sophistication during the twelfth century, especially among the Cistercians"—with Bernard as the champion. McGinn, "*Unio Mystica*/Mystical Union," 204. McGinn describes St. Bernard's sermons on the Song of Songs as the Cistercian leader's "premier work . . . [and] one of the greatest works of mystical exegesis of the medieval period." McGinn, *Essential Writings*, 27. Kimberly Bracken Long says Bernard represents "the culmination of . . . interest (in mystical union)." Long, *Eucharistic*

the believer's communion with Christ.[11] His christological approach to the book has a rich heritage in the Puritan and Scottish tradition.[12] It was the typical view of those men who most influenced M'Cheyne: Samuel Rutherford, John Owen, Jonathan Edwards, and Thomas Chalmers.[13] For

---

Theology, 21. For an overview of Bernard's preaching on the Song, see Old, *Reading and Preaching*, 271–74. For a concise study of Bernard's spirituality of mystical union, as derived from the Song of Songs, see de Reuver, *Sweet Communion*, 27–63. Scholars continue to note John Calvin's adaptation of Bernard's spirituality of mystical union and its subsequent appropriation in the Reformed tradition. For relevant studies, see Reid, "Bernard of Clairvaux in the Thought of John Calvin," 127–45; Butin, *Revelation, Redemption, and Response*, 14; Fesko, *Beyond Calvin*, 106–10; Billings, *Calvin, Participation, and the Gift*, 19–22; Garcia, *Life in Christ*, 69–73; Tamburello, *Union with Christ*, 65–111;. Lane, *Calvin*, 115–50; Lane, *Calvin and Bernard*. Lane argues that Calvin's substantive use of Bernard came late in his development and that Calvin proved to be selective in his appropriation of Bernard. See Richard Muller's comments in Muller, *Unaccommodated Calvin*, 11–12. For a perspective on Bernard's influence on Lutheranism, see Rittgers, *Reformation of Suffering*, 219–25. Geddes Macgregor notes Bernard's attractiveness to Scottish piety, saying, "Bernard's interpretation of the Song of Solomon no doubt appealed to the Scots for two reasons: (*a*) for its implied emphasis on the doctrine of the Church, and (*b*) for the devotional values suggested in passages such as that in which Bernard remarks that there are many 'canals' in the Church, but too few 'reservoirs,' and in which he enjoins the reader to 'show yourself rather as a reservoir than as a canal.'" Macgregor, *Corpus Christi*, 99.

11. *MAR*, 437.

12. See Clarke, *Politics*, 105–33. See also Schwanda, *Soul Recreation*, 42–74. For the medieval background, see Matter, *Voice of My Beloved*, 49–85.

13. Rutherford's letters communicate the belief that the Song is ultimately about Christ's communion with the church. M'Cheyne wrote of the profit he received from Rutherford, who, "with ink and pen [points to] the gospel of the grace of God." *MAR*, 184–85. For divergent views on Rutherford's use of the Song, see Mullan, *Scottish Puritanism*, 161–63; and Innes, *Studies in Scottish History*, 17–18. For other treatments Rutherford's view on the Song of Songs, see Richard, *Supremacy of God*, 202–4, and Button, "Scottish Mysticism," 63–105. John Owen summarizes his understanding of the Song as follows: "Then may a man judge himself to have somewhat profited in the experience of a mystery of a blessed intercourse and communion with Christ, when the expressions of love in that holy Dialogue, the Song, do give light and life unto his mind, and efficaciously communicate unto him an experience of their power. But because these things are little understood by many, the book itself is much neglected, if not despised." Owen, *Christologia*, 95. Elsewhere, Owen says, "[The glory of Christ] was represented in the mystical account which is given us of his communion with his church in love and in grace. As this is intimated in many places of Scripture, so there is one entire book designed into this declaration. This is the divine Song of Solomon, who was a type of Christ and a penman of the Holy Ghost therein. A gracious record it is of the divine communications of Christ in love and grace unto his church, with their returns of love unto him, and delight in him . . . But because these things are little understood by many, the book itself is much neglected, if not despised." Owen,

example, Chalmers prayed when reading the Song: "My God, spiritualize my affections. Give me to know what it is to have the intense and passionate love of Christ. . . . Give me, O Lord, to love Christ both for what He is in Himself and for His love to me. May His love to me constrain me to love Him back again. I long for mutual and confiding intercourse."[14] A similar spiritualization of the Song was typical for those in the M'Cheyne group.[15] While M'Cheyne's teaching on the Song is not as exegetically rigorous as Rutherford's or Owen's, it contains his winsome and evangelistic zeal.

M'Cheyne typically began his sermons on the Song by explaining the text's original meaning. His comments were brief and pointed. The rest of his message then expounded the text's spiritual meaning about Christ's communion with the believer. Although M'Cheyne employs the Song to illustrate Christ's corporate relationship to the church, he chiefly used the book to portray the individual union between Christ and the believer. His sermon on Songs of Songs 2:3–4[16] is emblematic of his approach. It also illuminates the salient features of his teaching on the book. His main doctrine is personal, showing that "the believer is unspeakably precious in the eyes of Christ, and Christ is unspeakably precious in the eyes of

---

Meditations and Discourses, 115. See also, Kay, *Trinitarian Spirituality*, 165–69. For relevant treatments of Owen on the subject, see Ferguson, *John Owen*, 78–85; McGraw, *A Heavenly Directory*, 61–65; Gribben, *John Owen*, 131–32; Kay, *Trinitarian Spirituality*, 165–69. Jonathan Edwards wrote, "The whole book of Canticles used to be pleasant to me, and I used to be much in reading it . . . and found from time to time an inward sweetness that would carry me away in my contemplations." Edwards, *Works of President Edwards*, 16. See also, Sweeney, *Edwards the Exegete*, 113–36. Speaking against Dr. Pye Smith's view that the Song was uninspired, Chalmers says, "It would bespeak not only a more pious but a more philosophic docility, to leave that book in undisturbed possession of the place which it now enjoys, where it might minister, as in ages heretofore, to the saintly and seraphic contemplations of the advanced Christian, who discovers that in this poem a greater than Solomon is here, whose name to him is as ointment poured forth, and who, while he luxuriates with spiritual satisfaction over pages that the world has unhallowed, breathes of the ethereal purity of the third heavens, as well as their ethereal fervour." Chalmers, *On the Miraculous*, 421–22. See also, Burrowes, *A Commentary*, 25–27.

14. Chalmers, *Daily Scripture Readings*, 251.

15. See Bonar, *Andrew A. Bonar*, 48, 135, 215, 237; Burns, *Memoir of the Rev.*, 113; Bonar, *Land of Promise*, 182; Bonar, *Night of Weeping*, 22; Bonar, *Reflections on Canticles*, 7, 8, 37, 40, 44–45, 59, 66, 78, 80, 84–85, 86, 110, 176.

16. "As the apple tree among the trees of the wood, so is my beloved among the sons. I sat down under his shadow with great delight, and his fruit was sweet to my taste. He brought me to the banqueting house, and his banner over me was love."

the believer."[17] Having explained the text and expounded the doctrine, M'Cheyne commented on how the passage illustrates the communion between Christ and a Christian. He explained (1) what Christ thinks of the believer, and (2) what the believer thinks of Christ. Applications to the unconverted, the awakened, and the mature saturate his sermon. His penultimate exhortation was to remind his hearers that "everything you need is in Christ."[18]

From the Song, M'Cheyne generated a conception of spirituality best defined as the christological union and communion of love. He declared, "In seasons when Christ reveals himself afresh to the soul, shining out like the sun from behind a cloud, with the beams of sovereign, unmerited love—then no other words will satisfy the true believer but these, 'My beloved is mine, and I am his.'"[19] The Song's romantic language is the most suitable way to describe this communion because we are united to Christ by "chains of love."[20] Further, a believer grows in Christ as he "melts under [Christ's] love."[21] Such melting exemplifies a loving exchange meant to increase conformity to Christ: "When Christ chooses a sinner, and sets his love on the soul, and when he woos the soul and draws it into covenant with himself, it is [so] he may make the soul a sister—that he may impart his features—his same heart—his all to the soul."[22] For M'Cheyne, Christ brings sinners into covenant union, to make us a partaker of his holiness, "to change [our] nature—to make [us] sister to himself—of his own mind and spirit."[23] A spirituality of love thus means a growing likeness to the Savior.[24]

M'Cheyne also used the Song to develop a spirituality focused on obtaining "a larger acquaintance with Christ—with his person, work, and character,"[25] and expressing love for him in return. In his sermons on texts throughout Scripture's canon, he regularly applied the Song's

17. *MAR*, 311.
18. *MAR*, 316.
19. *MAR*, 445.
20. *MAR*, 344.
21. *MAR*, 339. See also, *TPH*, 233; *TPP*, 230.
22. *MAR*, 338.
23. *MAR*, 338.
24. M'Cheyne says, "Communion with Christ is always sanctifying. Oh! it is good for the soul to meet with Jesus." *TPH*, 216. See also, *TPH*, 81, 159, 291; *TPP*, 61, 64, 243.
25. *MAR*, 414.

titles to Christ (e.g., "Rose of Sharon" or "Lily of the valley"), revealing the degree to which the Song shaped his Christology.[26] His emphasis on Christ as a wooing bridegroom fueled his spirituality because

> Love is the best decider of casuistry. It is like the needle pointing to the north. Men without a compass may guess which is north and which is south, sometimes right, sometimes wrong, but he that hath the needle can say where is north. So love always points to God and doth his will. The believer loves Jesus and therefore the way of holiness is a plain one to him.[27]

The "way of holiness" meant a diligent use of the ordinary means of grace.[28] He declared, "Christ is not done with a soul when he has brought it to the forgiveness of sins. It is only then that he begins his regular visits to the soul."[29] And, for M'Cheyne, Christ's ordinarily visits his people through the means of grace.

Previous studies on M'Cheyne have concentrated on *how* he used the means of grace in his personal pursuit of holiness. What has eluded scholars, however, is the reason *why* M'Cheyne developed such an approach. The essential point to understand is that M'Cheyne diligently used the means of grace because he saw them as the primary vehicles through which Christ comes to believers in love, and believers respond to

---

26. For examples, see *BOF*, 10, 20, 88, 151; *TPH*, 55, 169-70, 189, 202, 342, 377, 490; *TBJ*, 19; *NTS*, 22; *MAR*, 282, 565.

27. *TPP*, 54.

28. Here M'Cheyne reveals his consistency with the Westminster tradition, which views spirituality as union and communion through the means of grace. "What doth God require of us that we may escape his wrath and curse due to us for sin? To escape the wrath and curse of God due to us for sin, God requireth of us faith in Jesus Christ, repentance unto life, with the diligent use of all the *outward means whereby Christ communicateth to us the benefits of redemption.*" *WSC*, 85 (emphasis added). The catechism goes on to explain, "The outward and ordinary means whereby Christ communicateth to us the benefits of redemption, are his ordinances, especially the word, sacraments, and prayer; all which are made effectual to the elect for salvation." *WSC*, 85. Sinclair Ferguson states, "Reformed teaching on sanctification has focused attention on . . . [where] the grace and duties of sanctification coincide. Together these constitute 'means of grace.'" Alexander, *Christian Spirituality*, 68. See also, Gundry, *Five Views*, 59-90.

29. *TPH*, 232-33. M'Cheyne explained, "The graces that Christ puts into the heart and brings out of the life are the very best, the richest, most pleasant, most excellent that a creature can produce. Love to Christ, love to the brethren, love to the Sabbath, forgiveness of enemies, all the best fruits that can grow in the human heart." *MAR*, 341.

him in love.[30] M'Cheyne's preference for speaking of the means of grace as "trysts"—meetings between lovers—further illuminates his idea of spirituality as a communion of love. He proclaimed,

> In the daily reading of the Word, Christ pays daily visits to the soul. In the daily prayer, Christ reveals himself to his own in that other way than he doth to the world. In the house of God Christ comes to his own, and says: 'Peace be unto you!' And in the sacrament he makes himself known to them in the breaking of bread, and they cry out: 'It is the Lord!' These are all trysting times, when the Savior comes to visit his own.[31]
>
> The Sabbath is Christ's trysting time with his church. If you love him, you will count every moment of it precious. You will rise early and sit up late, to have a long day with Christ.[32]
>
> The hour of daily devotion is a trysting hour with Christ, in which he seeks, knocks, and speaks and waits.[33]
>
> The Lord's Table is the most famous trysting place with Christ.[34]
>
> The sacraments especially, how sweet to the Christian—wells of salvation, Bethels, trysting-places with Christ! What sweet days of pleasure, love, and covenanting with Jesus![35]
>
> [Lord's Day worship] is a trysting place with Christ. It is the audience chamber where he comes to commune with us from the mercy-seat.[36]
>
> We love everything that is Christ's (word, prayer, sacrament, fellowship) . . . We love his House. It is our trysting-place with

---

30. M'Cheyne was careful to admonish his congregation not to pursue the means in and of themselves apart from Christ, "Now, it is quite right to make use of means, for God is the God of means, but do not make a Christ of them." *TPP*, 65.

31. *TPH*, 232–33. Similar language flowed forth in a sermon on Song 2:8–17, "My friend, you are no believer, if Jesus hath never manifested Himself to your soul in your secret devotions—in the house of prayer, or in the breaking of bread—in so sweet and overpowering a manner, that you have cried out, 'Lord, it is good for me to be here!'" *MAR*, 446.

32. *TPP*, 330. See also, *SOH*, 32–33.

33. *TPH*, 234.

34. *TPH*, 234.

35. *TPH*, 103.

36. *TPP*, 28.

Christ, where he meets with us and communes with us from off the mercy-seat.[37]

M'Cheyne's notion of the means of grace as "trysts" reveals a few keys to understanding his spirituality. First, it shows that he viewed spirituality as a thriving experience of Christ's love—what he called "the secret spring"[38] and "master-principle."[39] True spirituality must first grasp the objective love of Christ before moving on to our subjective response. Second, it displays M'Cheyne's conviction that personal holiness depends on the mutual exchange of love. Spirituality begins when we behold Christ's love. It continues as we express love for Christ in return, particularly by communing with him in the means of grace. M'Cheyne wanted to ensure that enjoying Christ was the point of the word, sacrament, and prayer. So, he said, "Now, it is quite right to make the most diligent use of means—ministers and Bible and Christian friends; but then you must fix your eye on Christ through them all."[40]

M'Cheyne's view of the Song not only shaped his understanding of the means of grace in particular, but it also influenced how he spoke about holiness in general. M'Cheyne prayed, "Lord, make me as holy as a pardoned sinner can be made,"[41] because he saw holiness as the mature expression and highest experience of love for Christ. To know Christ's love is to be made holy. To grow in Christ's love means increased holiness. Piety then, begins and ends, in a communion of christological love. He often used language from the Song of Songs speaking of spirituality. He recorded in his diary: "Rose early to seek God, and found him whom my soul loveth. Who would not rise early to meet such company?"[42] He counseled other Christians in his letters: "I do trust you are seeking hard after him whom your soul loveth."[43] He wrote to another, "If you cannot say, 'I found him whom my soul loveth,' is it not sweet that you can say, 'I am sick of love.'"[44]

---

37. *TPP*, 33.
38. *TPH*, 45.
39. *TPH*, 46. See also, *TPH*, 53.
40. *TPP*, 61.
41. *MAR*, 160.
42. *MAR*, 21. He had in mind Song 3:4, which states, "I found him whom my soul loveth." See also, *MAR*, 172.
43. *MAR*, 282. See also, *MAR*, 404–5, 421; *NTS*, 145–46, 303–4; *OTS*, 41; *TBJ*, 47; *TPH*, 116–17, 215, 235, 466.
44. *MAR*, 287. In 1842, M'Cheyne published a tract about the conversion of James

M'Cheyne's exhortations to love Christ were born out of his own experience. Just as the bride in the Song pants after her husband so M'Cheyne panted after Christ.[45] He told his sister Eliza: "May you and I be kept abiding in the Beloved to the end—nothing else is worth possessing."[46] More than anything, we need "childlike views of the glory and excellency of Christ,"[47] for "it is a discovery of the person, offices, beauty, finished work, and freeness of God our Saviour"[48] that satisfies the soul's longing for fellowship with Christ.

What then was M'Cheyne's system of spirituality, as derived from the Song of Songs? He said spirituality is best understood as loving communion with Christ, because knowing Christ's love for us begets our love for Christ.[49] Devotion to the means of grace was the logical outflow of this mutual love, for it is through these means that we meet the beloved. M'Cheyne's spirituality thus assumed the expressions of the romantic relationship between the bride and bridegroom.

THE DEMONSTRATION OF LOVE

On August 3, 1838, Andrew Bonar wrote in his diary: "Psalm i. 3 again occurred to me, keeping up our first love. This seems to me what Robert M'Cheyne is eminent for."[50] Out of this love flowed M'Cheyne's pursuit of

---

Laing, "a little boy in his flock, brought to Christ early, and carried soon to glory." *MAR*, 160. It is titled: *Another Lily Gathered*, which echoes Song 2:2. According to M'Cheyne, the beauty of Laing's godliness was found in his fondness for the Song, which opened many parts of Christ's person and work to the boy's soul. *MAR*, 508–9.

45. He told St. Peter's that all true Christians "pant after holiness." *TPH*, 406. Again, "Souls seeking after holiness pant after God." *MACCH* 1.1, 296. See also, *TBJ*, 122. He considered longing after holiness to be "the great mark of a work of the Holy Spirit." *NTS*, 91. While on his sickbed in the winter of 1835, he pleaded with Horatius Bonar to come for a visit, and "bring a book with you for me to read,—a quickening, wakening, stirring book, that tells about Jesus and His sufficiency." Quoted in Bonar, *Life of the Rev.*, 29n1.

46. M'Cheyne, *Familiar Letters*, 45.

47. *SOH*, 1.

48. *HTD*, 32. See also, *TPP*, 304; *NTS*, 146, 190.

49. *TPH*, 51.

50. Bonar, *Diary and Letters*, 66. Ps 1:3 says, "And he shall be like a tree planted by the rivers of water, that bringeth forth his fruit in his season; his leaf also shall not wither; and whatsoever he doeth shall prosper." Bonar also writes of M'Cheyne: "The love of God . . . was the true secret of his holy walk, and of his calm humility. . . . The sweeter love of God constrained him." *MAR*, 66. Bonar scatters wistful comments on

holiness. His pursuit rested on three pillars: (1) the necessity of holiness, (2) the power of holiness, and (3) the crucible of holiness.

The Necessity of Holiness

M'Cheyne believed growth in holiness is the essence of what it means to love Christ. His conviction rested on Christ's statement in John 14:5, "If ye love me, keep my commandments." M'Cheyne said, "If you have been saved by Christ and truly love him . . . you will not be perfect, far from it, but you will wish to be perfect even as your Father in heaven is perfect."[51] A zeal for holiness, therefore, is a mark of God's saving grace. M'Cheyne wrote to a parishioner: "I trust you feel real desire after complete holiness. This is the truest mark of being born again. It is a mark that he has made us meet for the inheritance of the saints."[52] He exhorted believers to "seek advance of personal holiness. It is for this that the grace of God has appeared to you."[53] Holiness is the reason Christ chose his people, died for them, and converted them.[54] M'Cheyne was especially persistent in his call for holiness in ministers. In an ordination sermon for one young pastor, he proclaimed, "Oh! study universal holiness of life. Your whole usefulness depends on this. Your sermon on Sabbath lasts but an hour or two—your life preaches all the week."[55]

M'Cheyne throughout his diary. On November 8, 1838, he records, "I was made to see that I was very far backward in point of real holiness, and was led much more to plead that I was the 'least of all saints,' though that is difficult with me because of the pride of my heart. O what I wonder at in Robert M'Cheyne more than all else is his simple feeling of desire to show God's grace, and to feed upon it himself." Bonar, *Diary and Letters*, 77. After M'Cheyne's death, Bonar records on Monday, March 27, 1843: "How very unlike Robert am I! 2 Kings ii. much in my mind. O that his mantle would fall upon me! Evil days are begun. He was so reverent toward God, so full also in desire toward Him, whether in family prayer or at common ordinary meetings. He never seemed unprepared. His lamp was always burning, and his loins always girt. I never knew it otherwise, even when we were journeying in Palestine." Bonar, *Diary and Letters*, 102. Bonar writes on Sunday, July 16, 1843, after visiting M'Cheyne's tomb: "The text came powerfully to mind, 'His banner of *him* was love,' for that was Robert's experience surely all his days! More nearness to God is what we need, more retirement, more prayer, more fellowship." Bonar, *Diary and Letters*, 109–10.

51. *TPP*, 137. See also, *TPP*, 302, 305.
52. *MAR*, 248. See also, *TPH*, 43.
53. *MAR*, 255. See also, *MAR*, 487.
54. *MAR*, 255. See also, *TPH*, 373; *NTS*, 232.
55. *MAR*, 365. See also, *MAR*, 276. M'Cheyne wrote to William Chalmers Burns

M'Cheyne embodied this priority. Bonar mentions that, while on the mission of inquiry, M'Cheyne's "unabated attention to personal holiness" challenged his own laxity. "[Personal holiness] was never absent from his mind," Bonar explains, "whether he was at home in his quiet chamber, or on the sea, or in the desert. Holiness in him was manifested, not by efforts to perform duty, but in a way so natural, that you recognised therein the easy outflowing of the indwelling Spirit."[56] Although many friends and congregants acknowledged M'Cheyne's striking conformity to Christ, M'Cheyne himself was never satisfied. He wrote, "I earnestly long for more grace and personal holiness, and more usefulness."[57] Nothing communicates M'Cheyne's longing more than his *Reformation*. Written in late 1842 or early 1843, it is his ten-page resolution for personal holiness. In the first section, he concentrated on "Personal Reformation," saying,

> I am persuaded that I shall obtain the highest amount of present happiness, I shall do most for God's glory and the good of man, and I shall have the fullest reward in eternity, by maintaining a conscience always washed in Christ's blood, by being filled with the Holy Spirit at all times, and by attaining the most entire likeness to Christ in mind, will, and heart, that it is possible for a redeemed sinner to attain to in this world.[58]

M'Cheyne proceeded to delineate a scheme for personal holiness that would enable him to live in increasing communion with Christ. The plan included strategies for confessing sin, reading Scripture, applying Christ

---

in September of 1840: "Oh, cry for personal holiness, constant nearness to God, by the blood of the Lamb. Bask in his beams—lie back in the arms of love—be filled with His spirit—or all success in ministry will only be to your own everlasting confusion . . . O to have Brainerd's heart for perfect holiness." *MAR*, 250. See also, *TBJ*, 92; *TPH*, 373.

56. *MAR*, 94–95.

57. *MAR*, 146. Bonar astutely says, "An experienced servant of God has said, that, while popularity is a snare that few are not caught by, a more subtle and dangerous snare is to be *famed for holiness*. The fame of being a godly man is a great a snare as the fame of being learned or eloquent. It is possible to attend with scrupulous anxiety even to secret habits of devotion, in order to get a name for holiness. If any were exposed to this snare in his day, Mr. M'Cheyne was the person. Yet nothing was more certain than that, to the very last, he was ever discovering, and successfully resisting, the deceitful tendencies of his own heart, and a tempting devil. Two things he seems never to have ceased from—the cultivation of personal holiness, and the most anxious efforts to save souls." *MAR*, 150. On the last sentence, M'Cheyne himself wrote, "I feel there are two things it is impossible to desire with sufficient ardour—personal holiness, and the honour of Christ in the salvation of souls." *MAR*, 242.

58. *MAR*, 151.

to the conscience, being filled with the Spirit, growing in humility, fleeing temptation, meditating on heaven, as well as studying specific christological subjects.

In the second section, M'Cheyne focused on "Reformation in Secret Prayer." He committed himself to the earnest use of all kinds of prayer—adoration, confession, thanksgiving, and intercession. His prayer plan included regular intercession for no less than twenty-five different groups or agencies. Prayer was essential to M'Cheyne's spirituality because he viewed it as the minister's "noblest and most fruitful employment, and is not to be thrust into any corner."[59] M'Cheyne was certain that ministers should be standard bearers when it comes to their personal piety. He said a pastor must continually cast himself "at the feet of Christ, [and] implore His Spirit to make [him] a holy man."[60]

The Power of Holiness

While M'Cheyne emphasized the word, sacraments, and prayer as the ordinary vehicles by which God communicates his grace, they are not the real power for holiness.[61] Only the exalted Christ, indwelling his people by the Spirit, can animate growth in grace.[62] As M'Cheyne concluded a sermon on John 14:6 with a word of exhortation: "Remember, then, my unbelieving friends, the only way for you to become holy is to become united to Christ. And remember you, my believing friends, that if ever you are relaxing in holiness, the reason is, you are relaxing your hold on Christ. Abide in me, and I in you; so shall ye bear much fruit. Severed from me, ye can do nothing."[63]

---

59. *MAR*, 159.

60. *MAR*, 366.

61. *Shorter Catechism* 91 points to this reality when it asks, "How do the sacraments become effectual means of salvation?" The answer is, "The sacraments become effectual means of salvation, not from any virtue in them, or in him that doth administer them; but only by the blessing of Christ, and the working of his Spirit in them that by faith receive them." *WSC*, 91. Apart from Christ and the Spirit, the means cannot impart grace.

62. M'Cheyne announced, "Living holiness is a gift of God and is all in Jesus. In him as a fountain inexhaustible, the Spirit dwells. Every member receives it freely and fully." *TPP*, 314.

63. *MAR*, 303. M'Cheyne also proclaimed, "There is but one way in which a believer can walk holily, that is, by abiding in Christ, so that Christ may abide in him, and he may bear much fruit." *NTS*, 189. In his letter on "Communion with Brethren of

Union with Christ is the fount of our holiness. Since our abiding in the vine is the way to vital godliness,[64] our endeavor after holiness must be rooted in Christ—for "the very use of being joined to Christ is to be made holy."[65] For M'Cheyne, a life rooted in Christ means increasingly beholding the love of Christ in his person and work: "[God] hath invented a way of *drawing us* to holiness. By showing us the love of the Son, he calleth forth our love."[66] In the same sermon, M'Cheyne proclaimed, "If Christ's love to us be the object which the Holy Ghost makes use of, at the very first, to draw us to the service of Christ, it is by means of the same object that he draws us onwards, to persevere unto the end."[67]

M'Cheyne believed that this view of Christ's love is transformative: "Oh, dear souls, if you got but a glimpse of the beauty of Jesus, you would leave all and follow him!"[68] He declared in a letter to a fellow Christian, "Lean much on the Lord Jesus. For every look at yourself, take ten looks at Christ. He is altogether lovely . . . Let your soul be filled with a heart-ravishing sense of the sweetness and excellency of Christ and all that is in Him. Let the Holy Spirit fill every chamber of your heart; and so there will be no room for folly, or the world, or Satan, or the flesh."[69]

M'Cheyne saw no tension between exalting Christ and emphasizing the Holy Spirit's role in godliness. "The love of Christ to man, continually presented to the mind by the Holy Ghost," he exhorted, "should enable

---

Other Denominations," M'Cheyne reminded, "Christ and him crucified [is] the only way of pardon, and the only source of holiness." *MAR*, 561. In another sermon, "As long as a man is out of Christ he never can walk in the way of holiness." *TPP*, 51. He preached, "It is only by abiding in Christ with a branchlike faith that you can become a partaker of Christ . . . Remember the devil will persuade you to seek holiness some other way." *TPP*, 264.

64. The image of abiding in Christ from John 15:1–10 was significant for M'Cheyne's conception of holiness. See *OTS*, 18, 65, 71, 137, 147; *MAR*, 45, 80, 133–34, 181–82, 185, 238, 268, 280, 288, 303, 312, 336, 415–16, 518; *TBJ*, 100–1; *TPH*, 119, 185, 249, 263, 288, 351, 366, 373; *TPP*, 63, 103, 122, 241, 264, 271; *SOH*, 147, 195; *NTS*, 94, 141, 161, 189, 317.

65. *TBJ*, 91.

66. *TPH*, 52 (emphasis original). See also, *TPH*, 380–81.

67. *TPH*, 53. Earlier in the same sermon M'Cheyne says, "The Spirit is given to them that believe; and that almighty Agent hath one argument that moves us continually—*the love of Christ*." *TPH*, 47 (emphasis original).

68. *MAR*, 267. See also, *MAR*, 260, 333–34; *OTS*, 28. M'Cheyne counseled, "Behold Him, behold Him. Keep your eye upon Him, keeps the arms of faith around Him, so 'that Christ may dwell in your heart by faith.'" *HTD*, 52.

69. *MAR*, 254.

any man to live a life of gospel holiness."[70] The Spirit was given so that we might behold the Son. M'Cheyne thus taught that an inseparable link exists between Christ and his Spirit. He said our daily pursuit of holiness means remaining "in the arms of Christ" by living "much upon the Holy Spirit."[71] He wrote to a ministerial friend: "Union to Jesus, and holiness from His Spirit flowing into us is our chief and only happiness."[72]

In early 1839, M'Cheyne spent extended time away from St. Peter's, recovering from an illness.[73] He began writing a series of pastoral letters to encourage his congregants.[74] In his fifth letter, M'Cheyne warned, "The most of God's people are contented to be saved from the hell that is *without*. They are not so anxious to be saved from the hell that is *within*. I fear there is little feeling of your need of the indwelling Spirit."[75] He reminded St. Peter's that it is only though the comforter's constant visits, in the Word and in the church, that a Christian can grow in holiness.[76]

M'Cheyne's *Reformation* further discloses the degree to which he lived in dependence upon the Holy Spirit for personal growth. He wrote, "I ought to study the Comforter more—his Godhead, his love, his almightiness. I have found by experience that nothing sanctifies me so much as meditating on the Comforter, as John xiv. 16. And yet how

---

70. *TPH*, 47–48. See also, *TPH*, 380–81; *BOF*, 186.

71. *TPP*, 298. See also, *TPH*, 100; *TPP*, 72–73; *BOF*, 186.

72. *MAR*, 231. M'Cheyne also underscored the importance of the Holy Spirit to every successful ministry. In his anniversary sermon of November 24, 1838, he penned, "The anointing of the Spirit is the first requisite for a minister." MACCH 1.1, 304.

73. The onslaught of communication in the extant letters from January 1839 reveals a profound anxiety in St. Peter's regarding M'Cheyne's health. MACCH 2.1. The various letters cite conflicting reports concerning M'Cheyne's condition (many heard M'Cheyne was on his deathbed, while many others were told he was on the mend). The congregation was concerned enough to "set apart a night in the week to pray for [his] recovery." MACCH 2.1, 58.

74. Andrew Nielson asked M'Cheyne for a short, weekly pastoral letter because "I need not tell you how anxious your people are to hear of you." MACCH 2.1.47.

75. *MAR*, 198 (emphasis original). M'Cheyne taught that one defining mark of the unbeliever is that he has "no gracious indwelling of the Spirit, enabling him to cleave to Jesus." *TPH*, 460.

76. M'Cheyne's dependence on the Song of Songs extended to his pneumatology. He wrote in a letter to the Rev. Macdonald: "I hope . . . that you have a continued interest in the blood which speaketh peace—a sense of forgiveness and acceptance in the beloved—that you feel 'his right hand under your head,' and the power of his indwelling Spirit dwelling in you and walking in you. These sweet experiences alone can make the minister's life calm and serene, like this autumnal evening." *MAR*, 274.

seldom I do this!"[77] If it were not for "the promise of the Comforter," we would be defenseless in the hour of temptation.[78] He urged every believer, therefore, to pray for the Holy Spirit in order to resist the devil, mortify the flesh, and overcome the world.[79] It is by the Spirit's power that grace advances in the heart and guards the mind in Christ.[80] "Remember," M'Cheyne declared, "without holiness you will never see the Lord; and without this indwelling Spirit you will never be holy."[81]

According to M'Cheyne, a Christ-centered and Spirit-empowered piety will inevitably focus on Scripture. This is because the Spirit presents Christ to a soul through the Word. M'Cheyne preached, "If ye be led by the Spirit, ye will love the Bible,"[82] for it is in the Word that "the Spirit will continually be lifting the heart to sweet adoring thoughts of God."[83] He was thus convinced that the Holy Spirit's primary work in sanctification is "to shine upon the Bible."[84] There is, however, another channel through which Christ visits the soul: suffering.

The Crucible of Holiness

A heretofore unrecognized facet of M'Cheyne's spirituality is his emphasis on suffering as a primary pathway for communing with Christ. He stated in a lecture on John 11:28–35, "Afflicting time is trysting time."[85] A survey of his sermons reveals why M'Cheyne was so confident that suf-

---

77. *MAR*, 155.

78. *MAR*, 274. See also, *MAR*, 361; *TPH*, 423. For a summary of M'Cheyne's teaching on "the Comforter," see *HTD*, 33–35.

79. *HTD*, 36.

80. *TPP*, 44.

81. *TPH*, 124. M'Cheyne also spoke of the inevitability of the believer's holiness, for "if you be risen by the indwelling of the Holy Ghost then you cannot but seek God and set your affections on God. God the Holy Ghost loves God the Father with an infinite love. Wherever he dwells he will be always lifting himself heavenward, just a flame always burns upward. Does God the Holy Ghost dwell in you? Then he will be constantly lifting your heart to burn upward as a holy flame toward the Father." *TPP*, 213.

82. *TBJ*, 95.

83. *TPP*, 72.

84. *TPP*, 72. M'Cheyne preached, "God's word is a hammer that breaks the rock in pieces. When the Word is in the hand of the Spirit, it must break hearts." *NTS*, 261. See also, *NTS*, 250.

85. *TPH*, 491.

fering increases loving participation in Christ. He taught that God sends affliction to "open the heart,"[86] thereby bringing us to Christ,[87] which leads us to choose him,[88] to see him more clearly,[89] to learn of his love,[90] to feel his comfort,[91] to know his presence,[92] to sense his sympathy,[93] to be assured of his grace,[94] and to pray to him.[95] "Afflictions," M'Cheyne said, "are sweet to the taste" of every true believer.[96] He concentrated on knowing Christ through suffering because of Scripture's teaching as well as his own experience.

M'Cheyne's third pastoral letter to St. Peter's is a meditation on God's providence, specifically on how God uses affliction to mature his people. After extended comments and applications from the book of Job, M'Cheyne concludes, "Affliction will *certainly* purify a believer."[97] He regarded God's purpose in his season of sickness was that he would "reflect on the sins and imperfections of [his] ministry."[98] He hinted at such a purpose in his first pastoral letter: "The only-wise Jehovah take[s] his ministers oftentimes away into darkness and loneliness and trouble, that he may sharpen and prepare them for harder work in his service."[99] As far back as 1834, M'Cheyne's writings reveal a conviction that suffering is both vital and valuable. A diary entry, dated November 21, 1834, records, "If nothing else will do to sever me from my sins, Lord send me such sore and trying calamities as shall awake me from earthly slumbers.

---

86. *TPP*, 45; *TPP*, 68.
87. *NTS*, 98; *BOF*, 134.
88. *TPH*, 519.
89. *TBJ*, 101.
90. *TPH*, 472.
91. *TPH*, 416.
92. *TPH*, 335.
93. *TPH*, 162, 79; *SOH*, 53, 61, 165.
94. *OTS*, 29.
95. *TPH*, 117.
96. *MAR*, 316.
97. *MAR*, 189 (emphasis original).
98. *MAR*, 180.
99. *MAR*, 180. M'Cheyne further encouraged St. Peter's: "Let it be your prayer that I may come out like gold, that the tin may be taken away, and that I may come back to you, if that be the will of God, a better man, and a more devoted minister. I have much to learn, and these words of David have been often in my heart and on my lips, 'I know that thy judgments are right, and that thou in faithfulness hast afflicted me.'" *MAR*, 180.

It must always be best to be alive to thee, whatever be the quickening instrument."[100] M'Cheyne encouraged his parishioners to see God's sanctifying hand in suffering. He proclaimed one Lord's Day, "Some believers are much surprised when they are called to suffer . . . [yet] go round everyone in glory—everyone has a different story, yet everyone has a tale of suffering."[101] Because God means for the rod of difficulty to purify the soul,[102] M'Cheyne exhorted, "Let affliction strike heavy blows at your corruptions, your idolatries, and self-pleasing and *worldly schemes*. Learn much of Christ at such an hour."[103] In September of 1837, he wrote to his parents, recounting Eliza's renewed struggle with rheumatism: "God sends these sicknesses and calamities to be hedges and thorns to bring us into Christ that we may be his."[104]

Moreover, M'Cheyne encouraged joyful submission to affliction, for through it God "brings out grace that cannot be seen in a time of health . . . [Affliction] draws forth submission, weanedness from the world, and complete rest in God. Use afflictions while you have them."[105] He was so sure of the necessity of suffering for spirituality that he spoke of it as "the daily bread of the believer,"[106] and warned those in danger of backsliding that "God *must* afflict [them]" lest they fall away.[107]

The necessity, power, and crucible of holiness are three central pillars to M'Cheyne's spirituality. They reveal that he viewed personal holiness as the necessary result of a redeemed heart. Through faith in Christ, we are "brought into union with Christ so that [we have] communion with Christ."[108] Therefore, we "learn to hold intimate communion with God."[109] They also reveal that he believed the Holy Spirit's work of exalt-

---

100. *MAR*, 25-26. M'Cheyne also said, "To me there is something sacred and sweet in all suffering; it is so much akin to the Man of Sorrows." *MAR*, 144-45.

101. *MAR*, 348. See also, *BOF*, 147; *SC*, 26, 28.

102. M'Cheyne spoke of afflictions as "covenant gifts." *MAR*, 316.

103. *MAR*, 272 (emphasis original).

104. MACCH 2.1.23.

105. *TPH*, 476. For an extended treatment of these points, see M'Cheyne's sermon on Job 43:31-32, "The Improvement of Affliction." *BOF*, 37-39.

106. *TPP*, 126.

107. *OTS*, 138 (emphasis original).

108. *TPP*, 263.

109. *TPP*, 72. How will such intimate communion happen? M'Cheyne explained, "The Spirit will continually be lifting the heart to sweet adoring thoughts of God." *TPP*, 72.

ing Christ provides the crucial strength to grow in genuine godliness.[110] Through the Word, the Holy Spirit brings "heart-filling views of the lovely person of Immanuel, [so that we] might draw from *him* rivers of comfort, life, and holiness."[111] Finally, they reveal that he embraced suffering as a significant means for cultivating holiness because it brings us into deeper fellowship with the Father and with his Son, Jesus Christ.

M'Cheyne expressed his desire for such a regular, experiential acquaintance with Christ to William Chalmers Burns: "Oh for closest communion with God, till soul and body—head, face, and heart—shine with divine brilliancy! but oh for a holy ignorance of our shining! Pray for this; for you need it as well as I."[112] Indeed, a complete reflection of Christ's likeness was M'Cheyne's lifelong pursuit—a desire that points to another aspect of M'Cheyne's devotion.

THE MANIFESTATION OF LOVE

In his biography of John Milne, Horatius Bonar engages in an extended comparison between Milne and M'Cheyne.[113] He reveals how M'Cheyne was short-sighted and generally wore spectacles. His countenance was commanding, his smile pleasant, his laughter ringing and surprisingly loud. He also notes that M'Cheyne was considerably above the average height. Most significantly for Bonar is how M'Cheyne radiated holiness, walking with "an agility that spoke of inward joy."[114]

M'Cheyne preached for the final time at St. Peter's on March 12, 1843. His texts for the day were Hebrews 9:15[115] and Romans 4:22-23.[116]

---

110. David Beaty is thus right so say, "In M'Cheyne's view, the great key to growth in holiness was reliance on the Holy Spirit." Beaty, *An All-Surpassing Fellowship*, 75.

111. *MAR*, 214 (emphasis original).

112. *MAR*, 131. See also, *MAR*, 27; *TPH*, 81.

113. Bonar, *Life of Milne*, 88-90. See also, Lamb, *M'Cheyne from the Pew*, 79-80.

114. Bonar, *Life of Milne*, 88-89. Bonar recalls, "I remember Robert M'Cheyne coming in one morning to a private prophetical reading which some of us had, before he went to Dundee, and saying, 'I felt so happy this morning that I could not refrain from skipping as I came along.' Like Philip Saphir of Pesth, he could say with gladness, 'I have got a religion for my whole man.'" Bonar, *Life of Milne*, 89.

115. "And for this cause he is the mediator of the new testament, that by means of death, for the redemption of the transgressions that were under the first testament, they which are called might receive the promise of eternal inheritance."

116. "And therefore it was imputed to him for righteousness. Now it was not written for his sake alone, that it was imputed to him."

The next week, when he lay with fever, a letter was delivered and placed on his desk. It went unopened until after M'Cheyne's death. The writer penned, "I hope you will pardon a stranger for addressing you a few lines. I heard you preach last Sabbath evening, and it pleased God to bless that sermon to my soul. It was not so much what you said, as your manner of speaking, that struck me. I saw in you a beauty in holiness that I never saw before."[117] Isabella Dickson, eventual wife of Andrew Bonar, expressed a similar sentiment after hearing M'Cheyne preach for the first time: "There was something singularly attractive about Mr. McCheyne's holiness . . . It was not his matter nor his manner either that struck me; it was just the living epistle of Christ—a picture so lovely, I felt I would have given all the world to be as he was, but knew all the time I was dead in sins."[118] People were regularly convicted of their sin through M'Cheyne's manner as much as his message. Andrew Bonar tells of how, at various evangelistic campaigns, preaching stations, and revival meetings, M'Cheyne's conduct left a profound mark. At Jedburgh, for example, "the impression left was chiefly that there had been among them a man of peculiar holiness. Some felt, not so much his words, as his presence and holy solemnity, as if one spoke to them who was standing in the presence of God; and to others his prayers appeared like the breathings of one already within the veil."[119] Contemporaries, such as Thomas Guthrie, tell of the extraordinary holiness attached to M'Cheyne's "person, appearance, and conversation."[120] William Lamb, an elder at St. Peter's, remarked that M'Cheyne's expression shined like that of Moses.[121] Alexander Smellie says M'Cheyne's appearance was as "pleasant to look upon as young David coming from the sheepfold to be anointed king."[122] John Roxburgh

---

117. Quoted in *MAR*, 162–63. See also, Smith, *A Modern Apostle*, 297, and Van Valen, *Constrained by His Love*, 414. Another said, "It was not what you said, nor even how you said it, but it was your look—it was so Christlike—the face of one shining from being in the presence of the Lord." Quoted in Van Valen, *Constrained by His Love*, 407.

118. Bonar, *Robert Murray M'Cheyne*, viii. M'Cheyne counseled a group of Christians to embody this very ideal: "Seek advance of personal holiness. It is for this the grace of God has appeared to you. See Titus ii. 11, 12. For this Jesus died—for this he chose you—for this he converted you, to make you holy men—living epistles of Christ—monuments of what God can do in a sinner's heart." *MAR*, 255.

119. *MAR*, 138. See also, *MAR*, 83, 160–61, 169.

120. Guthrie, *Autobiography of Thomas Guthrie*, 175.

121. Quoted in Van Valen, *Constrained by His Love*, 224.

122. Smellie, *Biography of R. M. McCheyne*, 60.

goes so far as to say, "Whether viewed as a son, a brother, a friend, or a pastor, often has the remark been made by those who knew him most intimately, that he was the most faultless and attractive exhibition of the true Christian which they had ever seen embodied in a living form."[123]

Allowance for potential hagiography does not negate that the Holy Spirit worked profoundly on M'Cheyne's whole being. This was in keeping with M'Cheyne's own ideal.[124] Holiness begins in the heart, and then manifests itself in life. He noted the order carefully. God looks not upon outward appearance, but on the heart of man.[125] He called formality "the most besetting sin of the human mind," and an enemy to authentic spirituality.[126] What God requires is spiritual sincerity. Such sincerity must always have an outward manifestation. M'Cheyne called believers to adorn their profession of Christ by pursuing complete renewal. "We must," M'Cheyne insisted, "be sanctified entirely through the Spirit."[127] So vital was this concern that he explained, "The great object of the gospel ministry is to get you entirely like Christ—to get you entire Christians—Christians in public and Christians in private."[128] Complete conformity to Christ meant living in Christ's love. In a sermon on Song of Songs 5:2, M'Cheyne spoke about true believers being "sick of love" for Christ.[129] He taught that when Christ thrives in a soul, a believer exudes an entire spiritual health. This is because "Christ is the health of the countenance. When I have him full in my faith as a complete surety, a calm tranquility is spread over the whole inner man, the pulse of the soul has a calm and easy flow, the heart rests in a present Saviour with a healthy, placid

---

123. *MAR*, 601.

124. It also keeps with the Westminster Standards' ideal for sanctification. The Shorter Catechism defines sanctification as: "The work of God's free grace, whereby we are renewed in *the whole man* after the image of God, and are enabled more and more to die unto sin, and live unto righteousness." *WSC*, 35 (emphasis added). The Confession states, "This sanctification is throughout, *in the whole man*; yet imperfect in this life, there abiding still some remnants of corruption in every part; whence ariseth a continual and irreconcilable war, the flesh lusting against the Spirit, and the Spirit against the flesh." *WCF*, 13.2 (emphasis added).

125. *MAR*, 487. See also, *NTS*, 157–58; *TPP*, 112; *TBJ*, 42; *TPH*, 145, 185, 212–13, 461.

126. *TPH*, 153. See also, *BOF*, 67; *TPP*, 257.

127. *BOF*, 186. See also, *BOF*, 182; *TBJ*, 70.

128. *BOF*, 77.

129. *TPH*, 231. See also *MAR*, 287, 316, 434; *NTS*, 145; *TPH*, 136–37.

affection."[130] M'Cheyne feared that the hearts of many believers were not full, did not "swim in the love of God," and thus did not reflect Christ on the outside.[131] He exhorted his hearers to live in the full countenance of Christ, permitting him to kiss them "with the kisses of His mouth."[132] He also taught that growing into the fullness of Christ is a blessing of the new birth. The almighty Spirit, M'Cheyne said, "Strengthens [believers] with all might in the inner man. He renews and changes every part of the soul."[133]

M'Cheyne thus pursued and modeled a spirituality marked by entire devotion to Christ. It was no mere performance. What ultimately convinced and convicted so many of his hearers was his sincerity—inward and outward.[134] The *Reformation* further proves this point, showing that M'Cheyne's pursuit of "entire likeness to Christ"[135] was an expression of his longing for the One who had captivated his soul.

CONCLUSION

After spending an evening with M'Cheyne, one minister was so struck by his godliness that he burst into tears, crying, "O, that is the most Jesus-like man I ever met with."[136] M'Cheyne's personal holiness befuddled even his closest friends. Robert Smith Candlish once remarked to Alexander Moody-Stuart: "I can't understand M'Cheyne; grace seems to be natural to him."[137] Previous studies agree that M'Cheyne's personal holiness was a magnetic force in his life and ministry. What these studies neglect to emphasize, however, is how M'Cheyne's communion of love with Christ animated his pursuit of holiness. It is such a central component of

---

130. *TPH*, 236.

131. *OTS*, 81. M'Cheyne used similar imagery in a sermon on Isaiah 42:18–21, calling the law-magnifying righteousness of Christ "an ocean of divine righteousness, and those who are plunged in it are, as it were, lost in divine righteousness. It is an atmosphere of light, ready to envelop the soul, so that the sinner may be covered entirely, and thus become divinely fair." *TPH*, 358.

132. *OTS*, 81. See also, *NTS*, 182; *MAR*, 439–40.

133. *TPP*, 307.

134. Robertson agrees, "A key to McCheyne's success is due to his sincerity and transparency." Robertson, *Awakening*, 23.

135. *MAR*, 151, 155–56.

136. Quoted in Hastings, *Great Texts of the Bible*, 89.

137. Quoted in Bonar, *Reminiscences*, 10.

M'Cheyne's spirituality because he viewed conformity to Christ as the supreme expression of love for Christ. M'Cheyne summed up this essential truth in a letter he wrote to his family in March of 1837: "Let us be glad in all that God gives so richly to enjoy—and use all for him. If we are all his children, washed in the blood of his Son, led by his holy spirit, [let us live] a life of prayer and reading of the word and growing in likeness and nearness to him."[138]

---

138. MACCH 2.1.10.

6

Communing With Christ
M'Cheyne's Sacramentalism

THE WESTMINSTER LARGER CATECHISM asks, "What are the outward means whereby Christ communicates to us the benefits of his mediation?" It answers, "The outward and ordinary means whereby Christ communicates to his church the benefits of his mediation, are all his ordinances; especially the word, sacraments, and prayer; all which are made effectual to the elect for their salvation."[1] M'Cheyne agreed wholeheartedly. He viewed the means of grace as the regular channels through which Christ meets his people.[2] He told St. Peter's, "It is quite right to make the most diligent use of means ... [but] you must fix your eye on Christ through them all."[3] Love for Christ permeates M'Cheyne's concept of the means of grace, for it is through them that Christ

> begins his regular visits to the soul. In the daily reading of the Word, Christ pays daily visits to sanctify the believing soul. In daily prayer, Christ reveals himself to his own in that other way than he doth to the world. In the house of God Christ comes to his own, and says: "Peace be unto you!" And in the sacrament

---

1. *WLC*, 154.
2. In his eighth pastoral letter, M'Cheyne reminded his church that "[The ordinances] are the channels through which God pours His Spirit. The Bible, prayer, the house of God—these are the golden pipes through which the golden oil is poured." *MAR*, 210. M'Cheyne also called the ordinances "the wells of salvation." *TPH*, 219.
3. *TPP*, 61.

> he makes himself known to them in the breaking of bread, and they cry out: "It is the Lord!" These are all trysting times, when the Saviour comes to visit his own.[4]

Word, sacrament, and prayer figure prominently in M'Cheyne's spirituality because he understood them to be sacred "trysting" times with Christ. They are, in other words, experiences and expressions of the communion of love between Christ and his people.

THE WORD OF GOD

Adam Philip believes M'Cheyne's "peculiar spiritual temperament" is primarily responsible for the young pastor's renown.[5] By temperament, he means M'Cheyne's devotional spirit. It is a spirit that has captured the attention of countless souls since his death, especially its earnest pursuit of holiness through devotional disciplines. Alexander Smellie describes M'Cheyne's devotional spirit as follows:

> His first concern was the nurture of his soul. Every morning he saw to it before he turned to anything else. He rose early that he might have time to spend with God . . . He would sing a Psalm, to tune his spirit into harmony with heavenly things. Then he sat down to read, mark, learn, and inwardly digest the living Word of his Lord, often studying three chapters in succession. Then he gave himself to prayer.[6]

M'Cheyne's Approach to the Word

M'Cheyne possessed an "insatiable" appetite for Scripture.[7] After the death of his older brother David in 1831, he "began to seek God to his soul, in the diligent reading of the Word."[8] While a student at the Divinity Hall, he aimed to read twenty-five verses in the original languages each

---

4. *TPH*, 232–33.
5. Philip, *Devotional Literature of Scotland*, 66.
6. Smellie, *Biography of R. M. McCheyne*, 73.
7. *MAR*, 91. Bonar also says, "His desire to grow in acquaintance with Scripture was very intense; and both Old and New Testament were his regular study. He loved to range over the wide revelation of God." *MAR*, 34. See also, *MAR*, 55.
8. *MAR*, 8.

day.[9] Throughout his ministry, he satisfied his hunger for Scripture by reading three chapters a day, with the goal of reviewing these on the Lord's Day. In 1837, he formulated a plan by which he would read through the entire Bible in one month—resulting in roughly fifty chapters each day.[10] James Dodds comments,

> [M'Cheyne was] unconsciously elevated, as it were, above most of his contemporaries by a zeal in the pursuit of sacred learning that seemed to know no bounds. His much-used, well-worn pocket Bible was never out of his hands at any spare moment . . . He searched and fed upon the Word of God with an eagerness which I have never seen equaled. All his studies seemed penetrated with prayer and the reading of the Scriptures . . . he appeared to breathe the very atmosphere of spiritual life.[11]

Comments regarding personal Bible reading appear regularly in M'Cheyne's correspondence. For example, he wrote to Alexander Somerville on January 31, 1839: "I have been reading the Book of Acts with great delight and encouragement . . . I have been reading also the 119th Psalm, with meditation. I love to muse over it, and seek that it may be engrained in my heart."[12]

In 1842, he put together a congregational reading plan called "Daily Bread: Being a Calendar for Reading through the Word of God in a Year." He wrote, "We must be driven more to our Bibles, and to the mercy seat, if we are to stand in the evil day."[13] It had long been his desire to devise such a plan so the congregation "might be feeding in the same portion

---

9. Van Valen, *Constrained by His Love*, 77.

10. MACCH 1.3. It is unclear how many times he used this ambitious plan.

11. Dodds, *Personal Reminiscences*, 73.

12. Smith, *A Modern Apostle*, 35. Late in 1842, M'Cheyne wrote to Horatius Bonar: "I love the Word of God, and find it sweetest nourishment to my soul. Can you help me to study it more successfully?" *MAR*, 274.

13. *MAR*, 571. M'Cheyne's plan remains popular today. Various church and parachurch ministries make it available at the beginning of each year as Christians resolve afresh to read God's word. D. A. Carson's whole-Bible commentary is framed by "Daily Bread." Carson, *For the Love of God*. Martyn Lloyd-Jones encouraged preachers to use M'Cheyne's plan because "the whole object of his scheme is to get people to go right through the Scriptures every year omitting nothing. That should be the very minimum of the preacher's Bible reading." Lloyd-Jones, *Preaching and Preachers*, 184. William Chalmers Burns said of "Daily Bread," "I have found of late the chapters in Mr. M'Cheyne's Calendar for the daily reading of the Scriptures exceedingly suitable to my wants." Burns, *Memoir of the Rev.*, 322.

of the green pasture at the same time."[14] He knew that certain dangers accompany a planned approach to reading Scripture; namely, formality, self-righteousness, careless reading, and a yoke too heavy to bear.[15] Yet, in M'Cheyne's mind, the advantages far exceeded the disadvantages. A plan like "Daily Bread" means (1) the whole Bible will be read through in an orderly manner each year; (2) Christians do not waste time in choosing the text to read; (3) parents have a regular subject upon which to examine their households; (4) the pastor knows where his flock is feeding; and (5) the "sweet bond of Christian love and unity" grow.[16] M'Cheyne's plan guided church members on average through four chapters per day. As a result, they read through the New Testament twice, the Psalms twice, and the rest of the Old Testament once per year.

M'Cheyne also counseled his parishioners in how to read the Bible. He wrote to a young seeker: "You read your Bible regularly, of course; but do try and understand it, and still more, to *feel* it. Read more parts than one at a time. For example, if you are reading Genesis, read a psalm also; or, if you are reading Matthew, read a small bit of an Epistle also."[17] In a sermon on Hebrews 3:16–19, he exhorted, "Learn to search the Scriptures; to lie down in these green pastures; to drink from those still waters. Take up your Bible with prayerful uplifted eyes. Turn its threatenings into confession; as dew draws out the odour from the flowers, so will the Holy Spirit draw out the fragrance of heaven from this garden of delights. All Scripture is given by inspiration of God."[18] Guidance on Scripture reading was an early concentration, as he recorded the following "Directions for Reading the Bible" in a college notebook:

> *Read it regularly*. Set apart an exact time for it.

---

14. *MAR*, 572.

15. *MAR*, 572–73.

16. *MAR*, 573. M'Cheyne forcefully encouraged reading of every page of Scripture: "He would be a sorry student of the Bible who would not know all that God has inspired; who would not examine into the most barren chapters to collect the good for which they were intended; who would not strive to understand all the bloody battles which are chronicled, that he might find 'bread out of the eater, and honey out of the lion.'" *MAR*, 34.

17. *MAR*, 48.

18. *TPP*, 273. He went on to say, "Take up your Bible with prayerful uplifted eyes. Turn its threatenings into confession; as dew draws out the odour from flowers, so will the Holy Spirit draw out the fragrance of heaven from this garden of delights." *TPP*, 273.

Read in more places than one. Thus, a *historical* piece and a *devotional* psalm, a *piece* of a gospel and a piece of an epistle.

Read with parallels. Either 2 or 3 verses. Or the most difficult parts, or the most interesting.

Read whole books. A whole epistle, or little prophet, and trace and overlook the divisions into chapter and verse.

Try to understand. Ask where you do not.

Pray before and after. In devotional parts turn every verse into prayer.[19]

Personal Bible reading was, for M'Cheyne, a necessary consequence of love for Christ. "If ye be led by the Spirit, ye will love the Bible . . . Be determined to learn something new out of the Bible every day . . . Oh, be wiser in your Bibles than in the newspaper."[20] Believing Scripture to be the place where Christ communicates with the his people fueled M'Cheyne's interest in daily Bible reading.

Communing with Christ in the Word

M'Cheyne asked St. Peter's, "Sometimes, when reading the Bible alone, has not the voice of Christ been louder than thunder?"[21] He urged them to see the devotional hour(s) as nothing less than a meeting with Christ.[22] Christians should not view the Bible primarily as a record of God's work in history, but as the revelation of Christ. He announced, "The whole Bible from beginning to end testifies of Christ."[23] Since "Christ is in the Bible, [which] is in [our] hand," we ought to meet him there.[24] He said,

> Spread out the record of God concerning His Son. The gospels are the narrative of the heart of Jesus, of the work of Jesus, of the grace of Jesus. Spread them out before the eye of your mind, till they fill your eye. Cry for the Spirit to breathe over the page, to make a manifested Christ stand out plainly before you; and the moment that you are willing to believe all that is there spoken

---

19. MACCH 1.7 (emphases original).
20. *TBJ*, 95.
21. *MAR*, 327.
22. See *TPH*, 232–33; *HTD*, 80.
23. *BOF*, 139. See also, *OTS*, 15, 60; *CIS*, 58; *TPH*, 419. M'Cheyne also declared, "The words of the Bible are just the breathings of God's heart." *TPH*, 170.
24. *OTS*, 11.

concerning Jesus, that moment you will wipe away your tears, and change your sighs for a new song of praise."[25]

When we root ourselves in Scripture, it is nothing less than laying hold of Christ—the incarnate Word—by faith. M'Cheyne revealed the symbiotic relationship between reading Scripture and communing with Christ in a letter to one student: "I thirst for the knowledge of the Word, but most of all of Jesus himself, the True Word."[26] God's Word, then, is the primary way God's Son abides in us. M'Cheyne urged his hearers to "come into the arms of [the Lord's] love." They were to come by reading the Bible, which brings them "into communion with him; daily walk with him."[27] His hymn, "Thy Word is a Lamp Unto My Feet, and A Light Unto My Path," sings,

> O grant in me thy Word to see
> A risen Saviour beckoning me.[28]

On a related note, M'Cheyne taught that because Scripture is the indispensable means for communing with Christ, it is the essential means of true holiness. "Go then," M'Cheyne proclaimed, "to Jesus for all you need; learn the means of sanctification—the Word. No holiness without the Bible!"[29]

THE SACRAMENTS

Past works on M'Cheyne's spirituality routinely emphasize his practice in the Word and prayer, while minimizing (or even ignoring) his use of the sacraments. The Westminster Confession of Faith teaches, "There be only two sacraments ordained by Christ our Lord in the Gospel; that is to say, baptism, and the Supper of the Lord."[30]

25. *MAR*, 334.
26. *MAR*, 134.
27. *TPH*, 80, 81.
28. *MAR*, 591.
29. *BOF*, 54. In the same sermon, M'Cheyne taught, "Learn, then, that there is no other means of sanctification, and without holiness no man shall see the Lord. Unless you love your Bibles, and feed upon them, you will never stand with the Lamb upon Mount Zion, with golden harps." *BOF*, 55.
30. *WCF*, 27.4. For a useful overview of baptism in the Scottish Reformed tradition, see Dunlop, "Baptism in Scotland," 82–99. See also, Henderson, *Church and Ministry*, 46–50.

M'Cheyne's Approach to the Sacraments

M'Cheyne's corpus reveals little about his view of baptism. David Wright argues that this reflects the prevailing attitude: "In Scotland, among Presbyterians, it is probably fair to say that a higher view of the Lord's Supper has prevailed than of baptism."[31] The extant literature occasionally refers to M'Cheyne's administration of baptism. Bonar tells of an event when M'Cheyne refused to baptize an infant because he believed the parent was presenting the child out of pure superstition.[32] Baptizing infants close to their birth was common, as he wrote to his parents in January of 1837: "On Sabbath I baptized a little one just entering the world."[33] In April of 1839, he said, "Saw the Baptismal service (at Hampstead)—far too long—too many kneelings, and the absurd signing with the cross on the forehead of the child. The sponsors, too, seemed ignorant clowns."[34]

M'Cheyne occasionally mentioned baptism from the pulpit. He warned those who come to the Lord's Table "to get baptism for your child."[35] He also advised communicants to come to the Table looking back on their "baptism with a soothing complacency," remembering that they are the Lord's and the Lord is theirs,[36] for God makes covenant promises to his children in baptism.[37] In keeping with the Westminster tradition, M'Cheyne reminded St. Peter's that physical baptism pointed to a spiritual reality: "Baptism [is] not merely external washing, but real and internal, signifying and sealing our union with Christ."[38]

M'Cheyne's most extensive treatment on baptism is found in his manuscript, "Form of Baptism."[39] His purpose was to guide the pastor in a baptismal service, particularly those of children. M'Cheyne explained that baptismal waters represent two main realities. First, "it represents the fountain opened up in the blood of Christ . . . believingly applied to

---

31. Cameron, *Dictionary of Scottish Church*, 739.
32. *MAR*, 72-73.
33. MACCH 2.1.4.
34. *FL*, 12.
35. *TPH*, 389. See also, *TPH*, 219; *TPP*, 203.
36. *TPH*, 154. Such counsel mirrors the Larger Catechism's instruction on improving one's baptism. *WLC*, 167.
37. *TPH*, 134.
38. *NTS*, 117. See also, *TPH*, 158. See also, *WCF*, 28.1.
39. MACCH 3.2.16. The Form is also transcribed in Robertson, *Awakening*, 109-10.

the conscience [that] washes out the guilt of all sin."[40] Secondly, baptism signifies "the gift of the Holy Ghost ... [who] purifies from all corruptions the heart of all them that believe."[41] He accentuated the need for faith in the recipient, saying, "Without faith on the part of the baptized the mere washing with water is of no avail."[42] M'Cheyne proceeded to uncover the covenantal background of baptism, calling it the sign of new covenant grace, which is "to you and your seed." He then presented parents with a series of five vows, after which he prayed for the child, and concluded with the administration of the sacrament.[43]

M'Cheyne gave far greater attention to the Lord's Supper, for which he had a deep affection. In his tract, "This Do in Remembrance of Me," he explained, "The Lord's Supper is the sweetest of all ordinances."[44] He added, "Christ is the Alpha and Omega of the Lord's Supper; it is all Christ and Him crucified. These things have a peculiar sweetness to the broken bread and poured-out wine."[45] So sweet was the supper in M'Cheyne's mind that he wanted St. Peter's to observe it with greater frequency. It was the church's practice to observe the supper twice per year. He moved to administer the supper at least four times per year—a practice "regarded as an innovation."[46]

40. MACCH 3.2.16.
41. MACCH 3.2.16.
42. MACCH 3.2.16.
43. Andrew Bonar's tract on baptism may afford more elaboration on M'Cheyne's view. Because the friends were so similar in the essentials of presbyterian practice, it is no stretch to believe that Bonar's comments on baptism would reflect M'Cheyne's. In 1844, Bonar published a twenty-four page tract on baptism: *Baptism Briefly Opened Up*. Bonar's work represents an elaboration of the salient features found in M'Cheyne's *Form*, and thus it is right to believe Bonar's statements are ones with which M'Cheyne would agree heartily. Necessary for this study is Bonar's comment, "The written Word in every part leads us to Christ, and all of the ordinances of the Lord's appointment are intended for the same end." Bonar further states, "Like the telescope that fixes the eye on the one object which it is meant to magnify, sacraments fix us intently on Christ and his benefits—the Sun of Righteousness and his healing rays." Bonar, *Baptism*, 3. Bonar saw little fruit from his early ministry at Collace, outside his writing projects. He wrote, "The *Memoir of M'Cheyne* and my tract on *Baptism* seem to me the chief way in which the Lord has been using me to any extent." Quoted in Bonar, *Reminiscences*, xviii. See also, Palmer, "Andrew A. Bonar," 393–94.
44. *MAR*, 522.
45. *MAR*, 522.
46. Lamb, *M'Cheyne from the Pew*, 70. Robertson notes that M'Cheyne preferred weekly communion. Robertson, *Awakening*, 107. See also M'Cheyne's comments on the desirableness of frequent communion in *MAR*, 468. For a useful analyses of the

By the time of M'Cheyne's ministry the Lord's Supper was observed during what was called "communion seasons."[47] Likeminded ministers assisted with the administration of the sacrament, as the communion seasons lasted several days and involved much preaching.[48] The quarterly celebration at St. Peter's typically began on the Lord's Day before the sacrament was scheduled to be administered. The following Thursday saw assisting ministers join M'Cheyne for two "Fast Day" services for prayer and "humiliation."[49] Both Friday and Saturday had a service in

---

Lord's Supper in Scottish church history, see Burnet, *Holy Communion*, 265–91; Sefton, "Continuity and Discontinuity," 53–58; Forrester and Murray, *Studies in History*, 73–106; Cheyne, *Transforming of the Kirk*, 105–6; Maxwell, *A History of Worship*, 171–75; Adamson, *Christian Doctrine*, 79–131.

47. Yeaworth, "Robert Murray McCheyne," 150.

48. See MACCH 2.2–2.3, for letters M'Cheyne exchanged with other ministers, usually containing an invitation to assist in an upcoming communion season. For an accessible example, see *MAR*, 130. William Lamb says the ministers who most commonly assisted M'Cheyne were Andrew Bonar, Horatius Bonar, Robert Macdonald, and James Grierson. Lamb, *M'Cheyne from the Pew*, 69.

49. It is clear that M'Cheyne engaged regularly in fasting. There are, however, too few remarks on the subject to construct his full views on the subject. A side comment in one sermon shows he thought of fasting as an ordinance. *OTS*, 176. Most mentions of fasting, however, are simple recordings of a day's practice. On July 7, 1832, he recorded, "After finishing my usual studies, tried to fast a little, with much prayer and earnest seeking of God's face, remembering what occurred this night last year. (Alluding to his brother's death.)" *MAR*, 17. On August 14, 1834, he wrote, "Partial fast, and seeking God's face by prayer. This day thirty years, my late brother was born." *MAR*, 24. Two years later, on June 11, he said, "After the example of Boston, whose life I have been reading, examined my heart with prayer and fasting." *MAR*, 41. On September 27, 1837: "Devoted chief part of Friday to fasting. Humbled and refreshed." *MAR*, 56. On November 11, 1838, he mentioned, "Fast-day." While his normal practice centered on personal fasting, M'Cheyne also participated in fasts called for by presbytery or the larger church. On April 1, 1840, he talked about "Presbytery day . . . A fast-day fixed for the present state of the Church." *MAR*, 127. During the Sabbath-Railway Controversy, "believers were urged to rise two hours earlier to fast and confess personal, family, and national sin." Yeaworth, "Robert Murray M'Cheyne," 327. Bonar comments on M'Cheyne's practice: "He did occasionally set apart seasons for special prayer and fasting, occupying the time so set apart exclusively in devotion." *MAR*, 54. It appears that M'Cheyne typically used fasting as a means of confession and humiliation. He wrote sometime in December of 1839 regarding the ministerial prayer meeting: "Meeting in St. David's vestry. The subject of fasting was spoken upon. Felt exceedingly in my own spirit how little we feel real grief on account of sin before God, or we would often lose our appetite for food." *MAR*, 130–31. He sounds a similar note in the *Reformation*: "I ought to have a stated day of confession, with fasting—say, once a month." *MAR*, 152 He stated further, "Whatever I say to be sin, I ought from this hour to set my whole soul against it, using all scriptural methods to mortify it—as, the Scriptures, special

preparation for communion Sunday. Yeaworth writes, "The day of the Communion was long, and the dispensing of the elements often lasted from six to seven hours."[50] If St. Peter's was full, and it usually was for a communion Sunday, seven hundred communicants were present.[51]

The supper began with the "Action Sermon," which exalted Christ's loving invitation to sinners.[52] In a representative sermon on Romans 8:35–37, M'Cheyne asked those who are soon to commune with Christ at the table: "How shall [you] know that [you are] in the love of Christ?" He answered,

> By your being drawn to Christ: "I have loved thee with an everlasting love, therefore with loving-kindness have I drawn thee." Have you seen something attractive in Jesus? The world [is] attracted by beauty, or dress, or glittering jewels—have you been attracted to Christ by his good ointments? This is the mark of all who are graven on Christ's heart—they come to him; they see Jesus to be precious.[53]

After the "Action Sermon," M'Cheyne gave a brief address on "Fencing the Table." It simultaneously warned against partaking of Christ in an unworthy manner and welcomed the lowest of sinners. Although many ministers's fencing of the table was stern and fear-inducing,[54] M'Cheyne's wooing of sinners shone through: "If there is anyone who feels that they are all sin, and if you are willing to be righteous in the righteousness of another, then you are welcome."[55] Yeaworth correctly concludes, "[M'Cheyne's] supreme aim was to prevent the Sacrament from being taken lightly without meaning."[56] To aid young communicants in prepa-

---

prayer for the Spirit, fasting, watching." *MAR*, 156.

50. Yeaworth, "Robert Murray M'Cheyne," 151. The dispensing of the sacrament typically lasted from 1 p.m. to 7 p.m. Lamb, *M'Cheyne from the Pew*, 73–74.

51. *MAR*, 274.

52. For examples of an "Action Sermon," see *MAR*, 374–80, 425–31; *TPH*, 171–78, 178–85, 185–91, 224–31, 341–48, 359–65, 396–403, 423–28; *BOF*, 52–56; *OTS*, 83–88.

53. *TPH*, 344.

54. Henderson, *Church and Ministry*, 46.

55. *BOF*, 63. M'Cheyne offered warnings in a tone of love. He says, "Many of you know that a work of grace has never been begun in your heart; you never were made to tremble for your soul; you never were made to pray, 'God be merciful to me a sinner,' you never were brought to 'rejoice, believing in God.' Oh, beloved, let me say it with all tenderness, this table is not for you." *MAR*, 524.

56. Yeaworth, "Robert Murray McCheyne," 152.

ration, M'Cheyne established a communicants class. When the class concluded, he left the young members to examine their hearts with the following questions:

> Is it to please your father or mother, or any one on earth, that you think of coming to the Lord's Table?
>
> Is it because it is the custom, and your friends and companions are coming?
>
> It is because you have come to a certain time of life?
>
> What are your real motives for wishing to come to the Lord's Table? Is it to thank God for saving your soul? Psalm cxvi. 12, 13; to remember Jesus? Luke xxii. 19; to get near to Christ? John xiii. 23; or it is for worldly character? to gain a name? to gain money? Matt. xxvi. 15.
>
> Who do you think should come to the Lord's Table? Who should stay away?
>
> Do you think any should come but those who are truly converted? And what is it to be converted?
>
> Would you come if you knew yourself to be unconverted?
>
> Should those come who have had deep concern about their soul, but are not come to Christ?
>
> Do you think you have been awakened by the Holy Spirit? Brought to Christ? Born again? What makes you think so?
>
> What is the meaning of the broken bread and poured out wine?
>
> What is the meaning of taking the bread and wine into your hand? Have you truly received the Lord Jesus Christ?
>
> What is the meaning of feeding upon them? Are you as truly living upon Christ?
>
> What is the meaning of giving the bread and wine to those at the same table with you? Do you as truly love the brethren?[57]

After "fencing the table" on the communion Sunday, small groups of communicants came forward and assembled at an individual table, where a minister distributed the elements. The minister offered short comments before the taking of the elements. After everyone was served, M'Cheyne concluded the day's services with another brief homily, giving a series of Scriptures for further meditation.[58] Monday was considered "The Day of Thanksgiving," and a corresponding service was held. In total, the Lord's

---

57. *MAR*, 529.

58. For examples of these addresses from a communion Sunday, see *BOF*, 52–68 and *MAR*, 425–436.

Supper occupied no less than twelve Sundays per year in St. Peter's sacramental calendar.[59]

Communing with Christ in the Supper

Love for Christ motivated M'Cheyne's passion for the supper. He agreed with the Westminster Confession, believing that the Lord's Supper is a "perpetual remembrance of the sacrifice of himself in his death; the sealing all benefits thereof unto true believers, their spiritual nourishment and growth in him, their further engagement in and to all duties which they owe unto him; and, to be a bond and pledge of their communion with him, and with each other, as members of his mystical body."[60]

In addition to the action sermons, M'Cheyne's exhortations before and after the supper emphasized especially the sacrament as a meal of remembrance and participation in Christ.[61] M'Cheyne understood the Lord's Supper to be "an appropriating act"[62] in which we "do feed on

---

59. Yeaworth, "Robert Murray McCheyne," 151.

60. *WCF*, 29.1. J. V. Fesko notes, "[The Lord's Supper] was one of the most hotly contested doctrines during the Reformation." Fesko, *Theology of Westminster Standards*. Scholars have long described four different views on Christ's presence in the supper: transubstantiation (Roman Catholic), consubstantiation (Lutheran), memorialist (Zwinglian), and real spiritual presence (Calvin/reformed). For a summary of each view, see Gerrish, "Lord's Supper," 224–43. The Westminster Confession of Faith rejects transubstantiation in *WCF*, 29.2, 29.6, and it also denies supper as a mere remembrance in *WCF*, 29.1. For a representative Puritans work of polemics on the subject, see Hall, *No Peace with Rome*; Morton, *Lord's Supper*; Primrose, *Table of the Lord*. The Assembly refuted the Lutheran view of consubstantiation, saying, "Worthy receivers, outwardly partaking of the visible elements, in this sacrament, do then also, inwardly by faith, really and indeed, yet not carnally and corporally but spiritually, receive, and feed upon, Christ crucified, and all benefits of his death: the body and blood of Christ being then, not corporally or carnally, in, with, or under the bread and wine; yet, as really, but spiritually, present to the faith of believers in that ordinance, as the elements themselves are to their outward senses." *WCF*, 29.7. Such is the sacramental tradition in which M'Cheyne stood. J. Stephen Yuille has demonstrated how the Puritans' doctrine of the real spiritual presence of Christ built on the work of John Calvin. Yuille argues, "By and large the Puritans follow Calvin's lead" in their view of Christ's presence in the supper. Yuille, *Puritan Spirituality*, 171. See also, Tylenda, "Calvin and Christ's Presence," 65–75; Roberts, "'Cup of Blessing,'" 55–71; Jones, "Reformation Concepts," 134–67.

61. *MAR*, 523–24. See also, *TPP*, 28.

62. *MAR*, 523. See also, *MAR*, 525–26.

Christ."⁶³ Communion at the table is the Lord's invitation to "come and dine" upon him.⁶⁴ Additionally, through the elements of bread and wine, Christ "giveth himself to us," that we might grow in his likeness.⁶⁵ Attendance at the Lord's Table was a most solemn, yet joyful act, as Christ nourishes his bride. M'Cheyne heralded the bread and wine as "a living picture of the dying Saviour."⁶⁶ He further explained, "The broken bread and poured-out wine represent the broken body and shed blood of Christ. Oh, it is enough to melt the heart of the stoutest to look at them!"⁶⁷

It is in the action sermons that M'Cheyne scaled the high summits of Christ's love for sinners. In one such sermon, he declared,

> You could hardly imagine it possible that anyone could hate the Lord Jesus. "He is altogether lovely." There is no perfection in God but it dwelt in him; there is no loveliness in man but it shone in him. And then his errand was one of purest love. He came to seek and save that which was lost. He healed all that came—he spoke lovingly to all. Even his threatenings were mingled with tears of compassion? How could they hate him?⁶⁸

In another action sermon on "Christ's Silence Under Suffering," M'Cheyne extolled Christ's love: "The cords with which the soldiers bound him were tight and strong; but, oh! his love bound him more firmly on than all. The nails that pierced his hands and feet held him firmly on the bloody cross; but, oh! his love was the strongest nail—it was stronger than death."⁶⁹ M'Cheyne believed that Christ knocks on our heart with special love in the Lord's Supper. Christ presents himself to the physical senses in the elements of bread and wine, desiring to communicate his person to his people. Thus, M'Cheyne taught, "The Lord's Table is the most famous trysting-place with Christ. It is then that believers hear him knocking,

---

63. *BOF*, 62.
64. *MAR*, 433.
65. *MAR*, 434.
66. *MAR*, 309.
67. *MAR*, 432. See also, *TPH*, 191.
68. *TPH*, 180. He later announced, "Ah! brethren, herein was infinite love. Infidels scoff at it, fools despise it; but it is the wonder of all heaven. The Lamb that was slain will be the wonder of eternity. Today Christ is evidently set forth crucified among you. Angels, I doubt not, will look down in amazing wonder at that table. Will you look on with cold, unmoved hearts? It is a sight of the Lamb slain that moves the hosts of heaven to praise him (Revelation 5:8) . . . Will you not praise Him?" *TPH*, 182.
69. *TPH*, 401.

saying: 'Open to me.'"[70] Further demonstrating his view of the supper as an expression of christological love is his statement, "The sacraments especially . . . [are] trysting-places with Christ! What sweet days of pleasure, love, and covenanting with Jesus!"[71]

For M'Cheyne, the Lord's Supper was a means of grace for several reasons. First, it was a striking portrayal of and sensible participation in Christ, with all his blessings and benefits. Christ "is the beginning, middle, and end" of the supper.[72] It is the place where we are made to lean peacefully on Christ, just as the beloved apostle.[73] The meal is preeminently a feast—a "feeding upon Christ."[74] With tenderness, he urged all communicants to nourish their souls on Christ: "The more you feel your weakness, the amazing depravity of your heart, the power of Satan, and the hatred of the world, the more need you have to lean on Jesus, to feed on this bread and wine—you are all the more welcome."[75]

Second, the supper was a catalyst to pursuing holiness. M'Cheyne's "After Communicating" homilies aimed to guide communicants in holy living, for communion with Christ is a sanctifying ordinance. On one communion Sunday, he told the congregation that Christ alone, signified and sealed in the elements of bread and wine, can satisfy the soul. Such satisfaction necessarily stirs sanctification. M'Cheyne asked, "Do you want to be holy?" Then, "Let us now (in view of this holy meal) live to him. Let us give ourselves away to Christ—solemnly to him; give your wills and affections to him for time and for eternity."[76] He also announced,

---

70. *TPH*, 324.

71. *TPH*, 103. M'Cheyne said, "We love his table. It is his banqueting house, where he feasts the souls of his own. It is the place where he makes our hearts burn." *TPP*, 28. M'Cheyne knew his valuation of the sacrament could unintentionally create a congregational environment in which members' piety relied too much on the special sacramental seasons. Thus, he advised, "Remember it is not a sight of Christ on a sacrament Sabbath that will give you constant peace. Feed on the manna day by day if you would live." *TPP*, 262. See also, *TPH*, 84.

72. *MAR*, 522. He further commented, "Christ is the Alpha and Omega of the Lord's Supper; it is all Christ and Him crucified. These things give a peculiar sweetness to the broken bread and poured out wine." *MAR*, 522.

73. *MAR*, 525.

74. *MAR*, 525.

75. *MAR*, 526–27.

76. *BOF*, 65.

"If you are not made holy, then it is in vain for you that the Sacrament is spread."[77]

PRAYER

Prayer was crucial to M'Cheyne's spirituality. He wrote, "You will get more holiness from immediate conversing with God, than from all other means of grace together."[78] As with the other means of grace, he viewed prayer as a means of communing with Christ. Therefore, he encouraged the congregation, "Penetrate through every veil to the living Saviour, the living God. Do not rest in a form of prayer if you find not Christ."[79]

M'Cheyne's Approach to Prayer

M'Cheyne believed prayer was indispensable in the Christian life. He explained, "No person can be a child of God without living in secret prayer; and no community of Christians can be in a lively condition without unity in prayer."[80] M'Cheyne labored for consistency and fervency both in secret and corporate prayer. His goal was to start each day with prayer. He purposed to rise at 6:30 a.m., spending two hours in prayer and meditation on Scripture. From 8:30 to 10 a.m., he sat for breakfast and led family devotions.[81] His Sabbath routine was even more strenuous, as he

77. *TBJ*, 91. M'Cheyne further declared, "It is for this very end that Sacraments are given, that you may thereby be strengthened to cleave to Christ, to overcome the world, and to live above it while in it." *TBJ*, 91.
78. *TPH*, 81.
79. *HTD*, 80.
80. *MAR*, 236.
81. These devotions included the servants in the house. M'Cheyne ardently supported regular family worship. *MAR*, 573–74; *TPH*, 131–34. He said, "If you do not worship God in your family, you are living in positive sin; you may be quite sure you do not care for the souls of your family. If you neglect to spread a meal for your children to eat, would it not be said that you did not care for their bodies? And if you do not lead your children and servants to the green pastures of God's Word, and to seek the living water, how plain is it that you do not care for their souls! Do it regularly, morning and evening. It is more needful than your daily food, more needful than your work. How vain and silly all your excuses will appear, when you look back from Hell! Do it fully. Some clip off the psalm, and some the reading of the Word; and so the worship of God is reduced to a mockery. Do it in a spiritual, lively manner, go to it as to a well of salvation." *TPH*, 132–33. M'Cheyne even warned St. Peter's: "You may not know that an elder who does not keep worship in his family may be suspended from

set aside a total of six hours for prayer and Bible reading.[82] Bonar states, "None were more regular at the hour of prayer than he, and none more frequently led up our praises to the throne."[83]

M'Cheyne's devotion to prayer grew through the crucible of suffering. He exhorted a newly ordained minister: "Give yourself to prayer and to the ministry of the Word. If you do not pray, God will probably lay you aside from your ministry, as he did me, to teach you to pray."[84] The specific occasion M'Cheyne had in mind was the illness that laid him aside in the winter of 1838–1839. He wrote to a friend: "I am persuaded that I have been brought into retirement to teach me the value and need of prayer. Alas! I have not estimated aright the value of near access to God."[85] Later that same month, January of 1839, he sent his first pastoral letter to St. Peter's. He asked the congregation to pray that he might receive the refining benefits of suffering. He felt the special lesson he needed to learn was that "a calm hour with God is worth a whole lifetime with man. Let it be your prayer that I may come out like gold . . . a more devoted minister."[86]

Until the end of his life, M'Cheyne yearned for increasing communion with Christ through prayer. The second half of his *Reformation* concentrates on "Reformation in Secret Prayer," and it gives clear insight into his struggles with and ideals for secret prayer. He wrote,

> I ought to pray before seeing anyone. Often when I sleep long, or meet others early, and then have prayer, and breakfast, and forenoon callers, often it is eleven or twelve o'clock before I begin secret prayer. This is a wretched system. It is unscriptural. Christ rose before day, and went into a solitary place. David says, "Early I will seek thee; thou shalt early hear my voice." Mary Magdalene came to the sepulchre while it was yet dark. Family prayer loses much of its power and sweetness; and I can do no good to those who come to seek me. The conscience feels guilty, the soul unfed, the lamp not trimmed. Then, when secret prayer comes, the soul is often out of tune. I feel it is far better to begin with

---

that office." *BOF*, 120.

82. Yeaworth, "Robert Murray M'Cheyne," 103. See also, Robertson, *Awakening*, 129.

83. *MAR*, 26–27.

84. *MAR*, 366.

85. *MAR*, 172.

86. *MAR*, 180.

God—to see his face first—to get my soul near him before it is near another.[87]

M'Cheyne battled against the indwelling sin that kept him from bowing the knee. His diary conveys his struggle: "Mind quite unfitted for devotion. Prayerless prayer." Again, "Some wrestling in social prayer. But my prayers are scarcely to be called prayer."[88] In 1839, he wrote, "It is not easy to get my soul into tune for prayer; and often, when that is accomplished, I have no more strength to pray. Still, I love to pray; and often my heart is near God."[89]

M'Cheyne's love of secret prayer permeates the *Reformation* as he endeavors to grow in all parts of the work—confession, adoration, thanksgiving, petition, and intercession. His intention in intercession was pronounced. The *Reformation* lists no less than twenty-eight categories of individuals and groups for whom he planned to intercede.[90] An extract from one prayer diary reveals the following subjects for intercession:

> Prayer List 1: People
> *Relations*: home/William/Hunters/Dicksons/cottage.
> *Friends:* Macgregors/Grahams—Lizzy/Sommer/Bonars/Campbells/Thain
> *People:* careless/anxious (followed by a list of names)/Brought to peace (eighteen names listed)/Christians (included a list of ruling elders and their districts).
> *People:* Female club/young men's club/young communicants/Sabbath Schools (at least three mentioned)/the sick (twenty names recorded)
> *Dying:* three names.
> That God would raise up elders and Sabbath School teachers and prayer meetings.
> Preached word on Sabbath/visitation/preached word on week evening/prayer meeting/small prayer meetings.
> *Ministers:* Friends, young ministers, all ministers in Dundee/Edinburgh/the land. All missionaries—India (three

---

87. *MAR*, 158. M'Cheyne also says, "In general, it is best to have at least one hour *alone with God*, before engaging in anything else. At the same time, I must be careful not to reckon communion with God by minutes or hours, or by solitude." *MAR*, 158 (emphasis original).

88. *MAR*, 18, 31. See also, *MAR*, 56.

89. Quoted in Smith, *A Modern Apostle*, 34.

90. *MAR*, 158.

names)/China/Africa. Against Popery/Jews ("Here I am send me. Thy kingdom come.")

Those suffering persecution.

Prayer List 2: Subject Headings

For an abundant gift of the Holy Spirit.

For the purity and unity of the Church of Christ.

For her majesty and the Queen and all in authority under her and for a special blessing upon our country.

That God may raise up in great numbers fit persons to serve in the ministry of his church.

That a blessing may accompany the ministrations of the Word of God, in order that it may have free course and be glorified.

For the propagation of the gospel among the heathen.

For the fulfilment of God's promises to his ancient people.

For a special blessing on all the members of the Assembly and Church.[91]

Because M'Cheyne believed prayer to be the Christian's "noblest and most fruitful employment,"[92] he actively promoted larger prayer gatherings. At the Divinity Hall, he helped lead a Saturday prayer meeting in Thomas Chalmers's vestry.[93] He began a corporate prayer time on Thursday evenings soon after his ordination at St. Peter's, and it grew to over seven hundred regular attendees.[94] He also initiated a Dundee ninety-minute ministerial prayer meeting on Monday mornings.[95] Additionally,

---

91. Quoted in Robertson, *Awakening*, 130–31.

92. *MAR*, 159.

93. *MAR*, 22.

94. M'Cheyne started the meeting by giving a Scripture suitable for meditation—"generally a promise of the Spirit or the wonderful effects of his outpouring." Prayer happened before and after the meditation. He then read some story of revival from church history, making comments throughout the reading. More prayer followed. M'Cheyne especially cherished the Thursday meetings, believing, "They will doubtless be remembered in eternity with songs of praise." On another occasion he said of the meeting, "There is a stillness to the last word—not as on Sabbaths, a rushing down at the end of the prayer, as if glad to get out of God's presence." *MAR*, 63.

95. M'Cheyne told Andrew Bonar, "Of course, we do not invite the colder ministers; that would only damp our meetings. Tell me if you think this is right." *MAR*, 119–20. See also, Bonar, *Life of the Rev.*, 94. Horatius Bonar also mentions a monthly concert of prayer started by M'Cheyne. "For several years a few brethren in different parts of the country had been in the habit of observing some day in each month (generally, though not always, the first Monday), as a day of special private prayer, that they might seek help and wisdom in 'taking heed to themselves and to their ministry.' The practice was suggested and begun by Robert M'Cheyne; and each of us in turn

M'Cheyne and his brother pastors covenanted to pray for one another on Saturday evening because they knew faithful preaching required the Spirit's power—power that comes only through prayer. He was once asked if the busyness of parish business crowded out prayerful preparation on Saturday. He responded, "What would my people do if I were not to pray?"[96] "If a minister is to thrive in his own soul, and be successful in his work," M'Cheyne said, "he must be the half of the time on his knees."[97] He also gathered frequently with like-minded ministers "to spend the whole day in confession of ministerial and personal sins, with prayer for grace."[98] His earnest promotion of prayer bore great fruit, as during the Dundee revival he reported that thirty-nine different prayer meetings connected to the church took place each week—five were conducted and attended exclusively by little children.[99]

Further, M'Cheyne participated in promoting special days of prayer in the church. St. Peter's was one of the first congregations in Scotland to begin a series of monthly prayer meetings for the church's future, stemming from a recommendation of the 1840 Assembly.[100] He published a widely read editorial in *The Witness* calling for a day of national prayer during the Sabbath Railway Controversy.[101] In 1841, St. Peter's joined in a ten-day "Prayer Union Service" happening in congregations throughout the country. Eight to nine hundred people gathered every weekday morning at 8:00 a.m., and over one thousand came on the Lord's Day to pray.[102] The ten days of special prayer continued in succeeding years with

---

wrote the monthly letter, reminding the brethren of the day, and noting thoughts and subjects that might seem particularly suitable. It was a happy bond." Bonar, *Life of the Rev.*, 94.

96. *MAR*, 51. See also, *MAR*, 547.

97. *BOF*, 119. A similar quote often attributed to M'Cheyne is as follows: "What a man is on his knees before God, that he is—and nothing more." No source exists in those secondary resources that reference it, nor has one yet been found. It sounds very similar to a statement attributed to John Owen that "a minister may fill his pews and communion roll but what he is on his knees in secret before God Almighty, that he is and no more." Thomas, *A Puritan Golden Treasury*, 192.

98. *MAR*, 71.

99. *MAR*, 498. See also, Van Valen, *Constrained by His Love*, 319–26. For insight into the specific meetings, see McLennan, *McCheyne's Dundee*, 95–97.

100. Yeaworth, "Robert Murray M'Cheyne," 346. See also, Macgregor, *Proceedings*, 262.

101. Yeaworth, "Robert Murray M'Cheyne," 327.

102. For a series of letters from M'Cheyne to Horatius Bonar on the prayer union

success. Additionally, after the Convocation of 1842, M'Cheyne presented a proposal for united prayer that circulated throughout the country.[103]

Communing with Christ in Prayer

M'Cheyne said, "We must study prayer more, [and so] be instant in prayer."[104] His studies led to several points of emphasis. First, he understood that prayer is founded on the Triune God's work: "When a believer prays, he is not alone—there are three with him: the Father seeing in secret, His ear open; the Son blotting out sin, and offering up the prayer; the Holy Ghost quickening and giving desires. There can be no true prayer without these three."[105] Ultimately, M'Cheyne taught that our prayers are to the Father, through union with Christ, and by the Spirit of adoption.[106] He gave special attention to Christ's work as intercessor, saying,

> See how surely Christ's prayer will be answered for you, beloved. He does not plead that you are good and holy; He does not plead that you are worthy; He only pleads His own loveliness in the eye of the Father. Look not on them, He says, but look on Me. Thou lovedst Me before the foundation of the word. Learn to use the same argument with God, dear believers. This is asking in Christ's name, for the Lord's sake; this is the prayer that is never refused.[107]

Christ's intercession should give us immense confidence before the throne of grace, for "Christ is with [us] in prayer."[108] M'Cheyne wrote in the *Reformation*: "If I could hear Christ praying for me in the next room, I would not fear a million of enemies. Yet the distance makes no difference; He is praying for me."[109] He believed that secret prayer is the most powerful work in which we engage, for "prayer moves him that moves

---

services, see Bonar, *Life of Milne*, 37–39.

103. Yeaworth, "Robert Murray M'Cheyne," 342.

104. *MAR*, 172. See also, *MAR*, 131, 242. M'Cheyne also exhorted, "Pray to be taught to pray." *MAR*, 256.

105. *MAR*, 466.

106. *MAR*, 191. "When God brings a soul into Christ," M'Cheyne instructed, "He covenants to hear his prayer." *OTS*, 72.

107. *MAR*, 427.

108. *TPH*, 336.

109. *MAR*, 155.

the universe."[110] Faith is the necessary ingredient for successful prayer, as "he that believes most the love and power of Jesus will obtain most in prayer."[111]

Secondly, M'Cheyne said prayer is the delightful duty of genuine Christians. He explained, "Christ loved secret prayer. Ah, you are no Christian, if you do not love secret prayer. O brethren! a prayerless man is an unconverted man."[112] M'Cheyne expected private prayer and family prayer to flourish in any true Christian. He stated, "If ye be heads of families, and yet refuse to kneel with them before the God of families, you are not Christians."[113] While he extolled earnestly the duty of prayer, he was even more intent to preach about prayer's delight in such a way that a believer cannot help but grow in communing with Christ at the mercy seat. He asked where is the "spring-time of love, Immanuel coming over the mountains of Bether?"[114] His answer focused on secret prayer. Through prayer, M'Cheyne said, "The soul enjoys great nearness to God, enters within the veil, [and] lies down at the feet of Jesus."[115] Prayer also gives the believer "glimpses of the reconciled countenance of God," and thus is "a sweet duty to a believer."[116] Personal prayer is sanctifying communion with Christ, the place where Christ loves to meet his people.[117] Ultimately, then, it is not the mere practice of prayer that vindicates the reality of conversion. Instead, M'Cheyne said, "There is no better test of the soul than delight in prayer, unobserved and unknown by man."[118]

M'Cheyne also exhorted his fellow pastors to understand the necessity of prayer for gospel ministry. He declared, "A minister that is fervent on his knees is always mighty when he labours among a people."[119] He knew preachers are apt to spend the bulk of their time proclaiming the word, yet "prayer is more powerful than preaching. It is prayer that gives preaching all its power."[120] Discovering prayer's power for preaching

---

110. *TPH*, 279.
111. *CIS*, 19. See also, *MAR*, 190.
112. *BOF*, 49.
113. *TBJ*, 95. See also, *TPH*, 286–87.
114. *HTD*, 5. "The mountains of Bether" refers to Song 2:17.
115. *TPH*, 419.
116. *TPP*, 319.
117. *TPH*, 216–17.
118. *TPH*, 223.
119. *TBJ*, 44.
120. *TPH*, 83. M'Cheyne also exhorted ministers to consider the example of Paul:

ought to lead ministers to "engage more in secret prayer," for through prayer Christ pours out His Spirit in power.[121] M'Cheyne summarized his convictions by stating, "Prayer must be added to preaching, else preaching is in vain."[122]

M'Cheyne's letters offer counsel on how to grow in the practice of prayer. Of particular note, for M'Cheyne, is that God's people pray in a scriptural manner. He told a young Christian, "Turn the Bible into prayer. Thus, if you were reading the 1st Psalm, spread the Bible on the chair before you, and kneel and pray, 'O Lord, give me the blessedness of the man,' & 'Let me not stand in the counsel of the ungodly.' This is the best way of knowing the meaning of the Bible, and of learning to pray."[123] Additionally, he taught St. Peter's about the value of planning to pray:

> If you are a child of God, you will find some secret place to pray. It will not do to say, you will pray when walking, or at your work, or in the midst of company. It will not do to make that your praying time throughout the day. No; Satan is at your right hand. Get alone with God. Spend as much time as you can alone with God every day; and then, in sudden temptations and afflictions, you will be able to lift your heart easily even among the crowd to your Father's ear.[124]

A perusal of the *Reformation* shows the degree to which M'Cheyne pursued biblical variety in prayer. He believed "the heart is selfish" and so tends to rush to petition, thereby omitting adoration, confession, thanksgiving, and intercession. He wisely concludes, "Perhaps every prayer need not have all these; but surely a day should not pass without some space being devoted to each."[125] Additionally, he examined his ordinary day to discover those parts most conducive to prayer, and then resolved to dedicate them solemnly to God in prayer.[126]

"O that all ministers could pray like Paul. Probably no man ever lived who was the means of saving so many souls as Paul. Probably no minister was ever made the instrument of bringing his people to such a height of holiness as Paul. How was this? Look at his prayers for an answer." *HTD*, 50.

121. *NTS*, 250; *OTS*, 81.
122. *TPH*, 277.
123. *MAR*, 48–49.
124. *TPH*, 502.
125. *MAR*, 157.
126. *MAR*, 159.

As his influence grew, M'Cheyne received many inquiries on how to cultivate prayer in local churches and how best to lead prayer gatherings. In a letter to a fellow Christian, M'Cheyne gave the following helps for conducting prayer meetings:

1. One great rule in holding [prayer meetings] is, that they really be meetings of disciples.
2. The prayer-meeting I like best is where there is only praise and prayer, and the reading of God's word.
3. Meet weekly, at a convenient hour.
4. Be regular in attendance. Let nothing keep you away from your meeting.
5. Pray in secret before going.
6. Let your prayers in the meeting be formed as much as possible upon what you have read in the Bible. You will thus learn variety of petition, and a Scripture style.
7. Pray that you may pray to God, and not for the ears of man.
8. Pray for the outpouring of the Spirit on the Church of Christ and for the world; for the purity and unity of God's children; for the raising up of godly ministers, and the blessing of those that are so already.
9. Pray for the conversion of your friends, of your neighbours, of the whole town.
10. Pride is Satan's wedge for splitting prayer-meetings to pieces: watch and pray against it.
11. Watch against seeking to be greater than one another; watch against lip-religion.
12. Above all, abide in Christ, and He will abide in you.[127]

M'Cheyne's final appeal concentrates on the central pulse of his piety—loving communion with Christ. All the means of grace, including prayer, are vehicles in which the Christian and Christ meet in love and delight.

---

127. *MAR*, 237–38.

CONCLUSION

M'Cheyne continues to captivate those who find in him a model of how to pursue personal holiness.[128] Many hear his story, read his diary, and conclude with L. J. Van Valen that "the enabling strength behind M'Cheyne's ministry originated from his communion with God."[129] While this conclusion is true at one level, it ultimately does not go far enough. Love for Christ saturated M'Cheyne's spirituality. He saw the means of grace as preeminently the communication of love:

> Increase thy diligence in the means of grace. If you have truly found the Lord Jesus, be often at the spot where you have met with him. If you have found Him in the Word, be faithful and diligent in meeting Him there. If you begin to let your Bible slip, you are beginning to let Jesus slip. If you found Him in secret prayer, give more earnest heed to meet Him often there. It is a sweet-trysting place with Jesus, "within the vail." If you let slip the throne of grace, you let Him slip who sits thereon. Have you found Jesus in the sanctuary, then "love the habitation of his house, and the place where his honour dwelleth" (Psalm 26:8). Has he revealed Himself to you in the breaking of bread, then "continue steadfastly in the apostles' doctrine, and in fellowship, and in breaking of bread, and in prayer" (Acts 2:42).[130]

M'Cheyne thus understood the means of grace chiefly through the lens of a "tryst." In the Word, Christ speaks lovingly to his people. In the

---

128. Yeaworth agrees, "McCheyne's personal spiritual equilibrium and depth had been a constant cause for marveling among his acquaintances, and have inspired millions to this day. Next to his dependence upon the Spirit of God, much of his success was due to the consistency and conspicuousness of his Christian character as a pastor among his people who knew that his week-days were merely the sequel to his Sabbaths." Yeaworth, "Robert Murray McCheyne," 352. Yeaworth seems to be echoing the sentiments of *The Presbyterian Review and Religious Journal*, which states, "The occasion for his uncommon success was *the consistency and conspicuousness of his Christian character* . . . He was everywhere 'the man of God.'" *The Presbyterian Review and Religious Journal*, 221–22. Edinburgh: William Whyte & Co., 1845..

129. Van Valen, *Constrained by His Love*, 156. David Estrada similarly says, "Communion with Christ was for [M'Cheyne] the true secret of holiness." Estrada, "Robert Murray M'Cheyne," 31. Van Valen does properly identifies the source of the power of M'Cheyne's ministry when he says, "'The love of Christ constraineth us.' This was the motive for his powerful ministry." Van Valen, *Constrained by His Love*, 218. The shortcoming in Van Valen's work, however, is that he neglects what must be emphasized in any study of M'Cheyne: his all-consuming love for Christ.

130. *HTD*, 80.

sacraments, especially in the supper, there is an exchange of love as Christ gives himself to believers and they feed on him. In prayer, the believer speaks lovingly to his beloved. Each is, therefore, a spiritual meeting between lovers. This view explains M'Cheyne's diligence in his pursuit and practice of the means of grace, for the person who loves Christ delights above all else to commune with him in the Word, the sacraments, and prayer.

7

Proclaiming Christ
M'Cheyne's Preaching

M'Cheyne preached the gospel when "the old evangelical sermon" thrived in Scotland.[1] The day's demand was for an educated and popular preacher who, above all else, proclaimed Christ as the Savior of sinners. Evangelical congregations expected their ministers to "preach Christ and him crucified" every Lord's Day. M'Cheyne happily ministered in such a context, being convinced that as "weak and foolish as it may appear, [preaching] is the grand instrument which God has put into our hands, by which sinners are to be saved, and saints fitted for glory."[2] Preaching is the minister's "grand business,"[3] the ordinary means by which God awakens cold and callous hearts. This chapter demonstrates the centrality of preaching to M'Cheyne's spirituality by considering his method, manner, and message.

M'CHEYNE'S METHOD

William Enright has demonstrated how M'Cheyne's preaching stood squarely within the homiletic style "that dominated the [Scottish] pulpit

---

1. Enright, "Preaching and Theology," 207–12.
2. *MAR*, 360.
3. *MAR*, 359.

throughout the first half of the nineteenth century."[4] The style employed hermeneutics "as the springboard" for "doctrinal discourses."[5] M'Cheyne's hermeneutical approach to Scripture is best described as "a doctrinal-typological method."

Chalmers instructed M'Cheyne in a three-pronged hermeneutical method: "the philological, the contextual, the doctrinal."[6] Enright shows that although Chalmers argued occasionally for a balanced relationship between the three approaches, the doctrinal approach proved ultimate: "It was the final classification, the net result of the philological and the contextual. He dismissed the philological as 'unimportant' and argued that 'what is true of the doctrinal is true . . . in a less degree of the contextual.'"[7] Under Chalmers tutelage, M'Cheyne imbibed an essentially doctrinal approach to Scripture. Chalmers warned his students away from asking, "What does this text mean?" He urged them to "specifically ask whether or not this particular doctrine is the meaning of the text."[8] He advised preachers not to tarry on linguistic arguments or exegetical precision, but to arrive speedily at the text's main doctrine. He declared,

> The very utterance of your text will generally be enough for gaining their assent to the doctrine which it enunciated, or, at the most, the concurrence of a few decisive testimonies from other parts of Scripture, will abundantly suffice in the way of argument . . . I would curtail the formal proof of a doctrine, that

---

4. Enright, "Preaching and Theology," vi. He includes M'Cheyne in "the older evangelical sermon tending toward pietism [that] accentuated the conversion experience and . . . [demanded] a radical religion of the heart." Enright, "Preaching and Theology," v. James E. Mathieson maintains that M'Cheyne belonged "to that pietistic order who . . . attracted to the Free Church all that was best in Scotland." Quoted in Moody Stuart, *Alexander Moody Stuart*, 70.

5. Enright, "Preaching and Theology," 234.

6. Quoted in Enright, "Preaching and Theology," 235.

7. Enright, "Preaching and Theology," 235.

8. Enright, "Preaching and Theology," 236. Enright goes on to say, "Since systematic theology was concerned with 'the whole subject-matter' of the Bible and the philological and the contextual hermeneutic with usually only a word, sentence, or passage, it was the task of systematic theology as the sum of doctrine 'to sit in judgment' over the whole interpretation of the Bible. In effect this meant for Thomas Chalmers, and most of the older evangelicals, doctrine formed the essence and determined the meaning of any given text." Enright, "Preaching and Theology," 237.

room might be left for an object ulterior to that, and in which the mere verifying of the proof is conviction.⁹

M'Cheyne's sermons show how he adapted Chalmers's instruction. After a few exegetical comments, M'Cheyne states his main doctrine, and then weaves his subsequent exposition through extended exhortations and applications.¹⁰ The main doctrinal force of each sermon is christological, as he revels in the Redeemer's love for sinners.

The second facet of M'Cheyne's hermeneutical method is its esteem for typology. Patrick Fairbairn, a contemporary of M'Cheyne, defines typology as follows:

> It is admitted by general consent, first, that in the character, action, or institution, which is denominated the *type*, there must be a resemblance in form or spirit to what answers to it under the Gospel; and secondly, that it must not be *any* character, action, or institution, occurring in Old Testament Scripture, but such only as had their ordination of God, and were designed by Him to foreshadow and prepare for the better things of the gospel.¹¹

The closest M'Cheyne comes to defining typology is in "Some Notes on the Types Found in the Tabernacle." He writes, "When you would teach a little child in the simplest and most interesting way, you do it by means of pictures."¹² M'Cheyne ransacked the Scriptures for typological portrayals of Christ. He noticed Abraham's offering of Isaac,¹³ the Passover Lamb,¹⁴ Moses and Joshua,¹⁵ the tabernacle's furniture and features,¹⁶ the cities

---

9. Quoted in Enright, "Preaching and Theology," 238.

10. M'Cheyne was capable of, and often engaged in, detailed exegesis. For examples of his exegetical work in the original languages see MACCH 1.7, 3.1.34–40.

11. Fairbairn, *Typology of Scripture*, 59. For Fairbairn's five principles of biblical typology, see 138–66. For modern interaction with Fairbairn's work, see Nicole, "Patrick Fairbairn," 765–76; Stek, "Biblical Typology," 133–62.

12. *MAR*, 483.

13. *BOF*, 26.

14. *TPH*, 280.

15. *TPP*, 247, 258. According to M'Cheyne, Moses' "chief honour was that he was a type." *TPP*, 258.

16. *MAR*, 438–95. See also, *NTS*, 26, 268; *SOH*, 98.

of refuge,[17] the temple,[18] and the two olive trees of Zechariah 4.[19] His notebooks contain his typological comments on twenty additional types of Christ.[20] Although M'Cheyne ordinarily spoke on christological types, he also elaborated on other doctrinal types representing the covenant of grace,[21] the devil,[22] the church,[23] the Holy Spirit,[24] eternal rest,[25] and Pentecost.[26] So pervasive was his typological outlook that a sermon on Christ's healing of the deaf and mute man became an extended commentary on how the event is a "type of the way in which Jesus saves a poor sinner."[27]

M'Cheyne's "doctrinal-typological" interpretive approach yielded sermons that typically, in the words of David Yeaworth, were in "haste to preach Christ."[28] To this hermeneutic he married a homiletical model geared towards preaching Christ.

M'CHEYNE'S MANNER

William Enright says a formal structure marked the "older evangelical sermon," marked by a "distinct proposition and outline, and . . . [a] straight-forward yet personal style."[29] Such features were undoubtedly true of M'Cheyne's pulpit ministry. His standard practice was to expose promptly the sermon's central doctrine and then proceed to illuminate its truth along a series of headings.[30] One of his most-preached sermons was,

---

17. *OTS*, 9–18. M'Cheyne also viewed the manna, the water from the rock, the pillar of fire, and the brazen serpent, as types.
18. *NTS*, 77.
19. *OTS*, 163.
20. *TPP*, 90–120.
21. *SOH*, 110.
22. *NTS*, 54.
23. *OTS*, 39, 160.
24. *SOH*, 113; *TPH*, 310.
25. *SOH*, 33; *TPP*, 28–29, 34.
26. *TPH*, 119.
27. *NTS*, 42–51.
28. Yeaworth, "Robert Murray M'Cheyne," 32.
29. Enright, "Preaching and Theology," 245.
30. A friend observed, "The heads of his sermons were not the mile stones that tell you how near you are to your journey's end, but they were nails which fixed and fastened all he said. Divisions are often dry; but not so *his* divisions—they were so

"Jesus Christ the Same Yesterday, Today, and Forever."[31] His doctrine was "Christ is an unchangeable Savior." He proceeded to divide the sermon under four headings: (1) Christ is Unchangeable in His Compassion; (2) Christ is Unchangeable in His Tenderness to Weary Sinners; (3) Christ is Unchangeable in His Completeness as a Savior; and (4) Christ is Unchangeable in His Compassion to the Afflicted. Further, his preaching was discriminatory in its application, with customary exhortations directed at the unbeliever, the awakened, the backslider, the afflicted, and the true believer.[32] Bonar notes how M'Cheyne's applications flowed naturally from his doctrine:

> [His sermon manuscripts] may convey a correct idea of his style and mode of preaching doctrine. But there are no notes that give any idea of his affectionate appeals to the heart and searching applications. These he seldom wrote; they were poured forth at the moment when his heart filled with his subject; for his rule was to set before his hearers a body of truth first—and there was always a vast amount of Bible truth in his discourses—and then urge home the application. His exhortations flowed from his doctrine, and thus had both variety and power.[33]

Indeed, the extant manuscripts reveal how M'Cheyne routinely truncated his written comments near the end of the sermon, giving the impression that his homiletic peroration was usually extemporaneous.[34] Such extemporaneity signals M'Cheyne's evolving convictions related to preaching. While at the Divinity Hall, M'Cheyne learned to write out his sermons in full. From a lecture on "Composition of Sermons," he carefully notes,

---

textual and so feeling, and they brought out the spirit of a passage so surprisingly." *MAR*, 64 (emphasis original).

31. *SOH*, 187–97. M'Cheyne preached this sermon in three different locations (St. Peter's, Abernyte, and Dunipace) in 1837. Other notable—and apparently preferable—sermons that he preached at least three times in three different locations are: "Having Therefore Boldness, Let Us Draw Near" on Heb 10:19–22; "Desiring to Depart and Be with Christ" on Phil 1:23; "A New Creature in Understanding" on 2 Cor 5:17; "A New Creature in Affections" on 2 Cor 5:17; "The Work of the Spirit in the Heart" on Rom 5:5; "Lydia and the Jailer" on Acts 16:12–36; "The Lord Hearkening to His People" on Mal 3:16.

32. This category of "awakened" hearers appears in most sermons. By "awakened" M'Cheyne meant "souls that have been a long time under the awakening hand of God. God has led them into trouble, but not into peace... These are thirsty souls." *TPH*, 84.

33. *MAR*, 65.

34. See also, Enright, "Preaching and Theology," 194.

"The extemporaneous is a good temptation to indolence and is apt to lead you always into the same strain of preaching. The bulk of your parish preparations should be in writing, but in a rapid style of writing."[35] M'Cheyne took the instruction to heart and began his pulpit ministry by writing out his sermons and lectures at length, but he never fell into the practice of reading them.[36] He worked to memorize the essential substance of his manuscript and then preach with relative liberty. A crucial moment for change came one Lord's Day

> as he rode rapidly along to Dunipace, his written sermons were dropped on the wayside. This accident prevented him from having the opportunity of preparing in his usual manner; but he was enabled to preach with more than usual freedom. For the first time in his life, he discovered that he possessed the gift of extemporaneous composition, and learned, to his own surprise, that he had more composedness of mind and command of language than he believed.[37]

As he matured, and as preaching opportunities increased significantly, M'Cheyne's manuscripts inevitably became more concise. The shorter notes still reveal a concern for order and clarity of argument. He told James Hamilton, "I used to despise Dr. Welsh's rules at the time I heard him; but now I feel I *must use* them, for nothing is more needful for making a sermon memorable and impressive than a logical arrangement."[38] M'Cheyne valued clarity and purpose in preaching. He critiqued Andrew Bonar's habit of being unclear, telling his friend, "Study to express yourself very clearly. I sometimes observe obscurity of expression. Form your sentences very regularly . . . It sometimes strikes me you begin a sentence before you know where you are to end it, or what is to come in at the end."[39] Such attention to articulation did not produce in M'Cheyne's preaching the veneer of polished rhetoric, but natural eloquence joined to evident sincerity.[40] James Dodds recalled,

---

35. MACCH 1.6, 107.

36. McLennan mentions that, at the moment of M'Cheyne's nomination to St. Peter's, "several people wanted to know whether McCheyne read his sermons or not (a habit developed in the days of the Moderates). [John] Roxburgh answered he did not." McLennan, *McCheyne's Dundee*, 42.

37. *MAR*, 38.

38. *MAR*, 29 (emphasis original).

39. Quoted in Bonar, *Reminiscences*, 7.

40. Yeaworth notes how George Gilfillan, the Dundee minister-literary critic,

> On several occasions I heard Mr. M'Cheyne preach in Edinburgh; and I can testify to the singular earnestness and unction of his ministrations. He never aimed at high argument or eloquence, or anything very profound or original... His extraordinary spirituality and earnestness, the elegance of his action, and the simple beauty of his language, soon overcame all prejudices, and deeply impressed every hearer that had any discernment or love of spiritual things. His views of the Gospel truth were full and clear; his deep knowledge of Scripture was manifest in almost every sentence he uttered; and his acquaintance with the human heart was wonderfully complete in one so young.[41]

In addition to order and sincerity, M'Cheyne flooded his sermons with tenderness. Marcus Loane's conclusion is representative of most memorials: "The great secret of his success in the pulpit was his combination of faithfulness to the Word of God with tenderness for the souls of men."[42] "The new element," Blaikie concludes, "he brought to the pulpit, or rather which he revived and used so much that it appeared new, was *winsomeness*."[43]

While many remark on M'Cheyne's natural tenderness, they miss that he believed Scripture mandated tenderness in gospel preaching. In a diary entry on May 15, 1836, he recorded, "Large meeting in the evening. Felt very happy after it, though mourning for *bitter speaking of the gospel*. Surely it is a gentle message, and should be spoken with angelic tenderness, especially by such a needy sinner."[44] Bonar says M'Cheyne's zeal for tenderness in gospel proclamation was all-consuming, leading him to despair unnecessarily on certain occasions.[45] He believed a minister must

---

listed M'Cheyne with Thomas Carlyle and Edward Miall as the three most sincere men he had ever known. Yeaworth, "Robert Murray McCheyne," 223.

41. Dodds, *Personal Reminiscences*, 77. Dodds knew M'Cheyne from his time at Ruthwell and remembered that his earliest attempts behind the pulpit were "full of fine fancy and Hebrew learning." In time and with maturity, M'Cheyne's language "became plainer." Dodds, *Personal Reminiscences*, 75. For similar comments on M'Cheyne's elegant simplicity, see Yeaworth, "Robert Murray McCheyne," 208–9.

42. Loane, *They Were Pilgrims*, 172–73. For nearly congruent comments on M'Cheyne's tenderness in preaching, see Dodds, *Personal Reminiscences*, 76; Van Valen, *Constrained by His Love*, 220; Stewart, *Robert Murray McCheyne*, 35; Yeaworth, "Robert Murray McCheyne," 220; Cameron, *Memorials of John Roxburgh*, 13; Smellie, *Biography of R. M. McCheyne*, 62; MAR, 57.

43. Blaikie, *Preachers of Scotland*, 294–95 (emphasis original).

44. MAR, 42 (emphasis original).

45. MAR, 42. One example of such introspection comes in the following diary

reflect the Holy Spirit who empowers the preacher: "Ah! brethren, if the Spirit, whose very breath is all gentleness and love—whom Jesus hath sent into the world to bring men to eternal life—if he begins his work in every soul that is to be saved by convincing of sin, why should you blame the minister of Christ if he begins in the very same way?"[46] As he proclaimed in another sermon, preachers are to offer the gospel in peaceful tones because it is the good news of peace.[47] Imitation of Christ is also necessary for the minister on this point because Christ "was a tender-hearted Saviour upon the Cross, and so now He is a tender-hearted Saviour upon the throne."[48] M'Cheyne's preaching, then, reflected those spiritual fruits distinctive of his ordinary life—eloquence, tenderness, and affection. He strove to present the gospel of Christ with spiritual sincerity and biblical simplicity, for "it is the truth of God in its naked simplicity that the Spirit will most honour and bless."[49]

M'CHEYNE'S MESSAGE

M'Cheyne's purpose in preaching was to direct every hearer to gaze upon the beauty and glory of Christ. "Faithful ministers," he declared, "preach Jesus Christ as Lord."[50] He was so eager to present Christ that he made

---

entry: "Preached with some tenderness of heart. Oh, why should I not weep, as Jesus did over Jerusalem?" *MAR*, 39. Bonar also recalls "on one occasion, when we met, he asked what my last Sabbath's subject had been. It had been, 'The wicked shall be turned into hell.' On hearing this awful text, he asked, 'Were you able to preach it *with tenderness?*'" *MAR*, 42 (emphasis original). This manner of sermon critique was apparently common between the two. On another occasion, Bonar records, "After preaching in St. Peter's, Dundee, upon the text, 'Thine eyes shall see the King in His beauty,' Mr. M'Cheyne said to him as they walked home together, 'Brother, I enjoyed your sermon; to me it was sweet. You and I and many, I trust, in our congregations shall see the King in His beauty. But, my brother, you forgot there might be many listening to you to-night, who, unless they are changed by the grace of God, shall never see Him in His beauty.'" Bonar, *Reminiscences*, 132.

46. *TPH*, 310. See also, *TPH*, 318; *NTS*, 277.
47. *TPP*, 112.
48. *TPH*, 192.
49. *MAR*, 361. M'Cheyne also wrote, "Let us learn that a simple word may be blessed to the saving of precious souls. Often we are tempted to think there must be some deep and logical argument to bring men to Christ. Often we put confidence in high-sounding words. Whereas it is the simple exhibition of Christ carried home by the Spirit, which awakens, enlightens, and saves." *HTD*, 21.
50. *BOF*, 6.

few comments on his text's original meaning and application. He raced to Calvary as fast as possible to behold the love of a Savior crucified for sinners, being convinced "this is the sum of all preaching."[51] David Yeaworth concludes correctly, "It was the love of Christ for wicked man that Robert M'Cheyne sought most to proclaim to his congregation. His own life exuded confidence in this love, and there was scarcely a sermon which failed to include some allusion to it."[52]

Enright asserts that the sermons of older nineteenth-century Scottish evangelicals emphasized soteriology at the expense of Christology.[53] His critique is surely fair for a select few, but requires far too much nuance to be of great use. M'Cheyne's pattern proves the point. His pulpit ministry shows how christological preaching is inescapably soteriological. In M'Cheyne's mind, Christ indeed is Savior, but he is also Lord, King, prophet, and judge, and should be heralded as such. "Preach Christ for awakening, Christ for comforting, Christ for sanctifying," he announced.[54] Thus, M'Cheyne's sermons were not merely presentations of Christology, but proclamations of Christ. As Bonar notes, "It was not *doctrine* alone that he preached; it was *Christ*, from whom all doctrine shoots forth as rays from a centre. He sought to hang every vessel and flagon upon him."[55]

M'Cheyne hinted at this nuance when he recorded, "It is strange how sweet and precious it is to preach directly about Christ, compared with all other subjects of preaching."[56] In a notebook, he listed series of vital doctrines for Christianity and Christian preaching. They include subjects such as sin, repentance, faith, holiness, prayer, and perseverance.[57] He rightly understood that it was possible to proclaim such essential truths in a way that relegates Christ in the hearer's mind, and not elevate Christ as the magnetic center of all truth. M'Cheyne exhorted his congregation to cling steadfastly to Christ as the center. He did not call St. Peter's merely to hold fast to Christ's blessings or benefits but to cling

---

51. *SOH*, 87.
52. Yeaworth, "Robert Murray McCheyne," 233.
53. Enright, "Preaching and Theology," 217.
54. *MAR*, 361.
55. *MAR*, 65 (emphasis original).
56. *MAR*, 65.
57. MACCH 1.5.

to Christ himself. He critiqued most Scottish evangelical preaching as weak on pleading:

> I would observe what appears to me *a fault in the preaching of our beloved Scotland*. Most ministers are accustomed to set Christ before the people. They lay down the gospel clearly and beautifully, but they do not urge men to enter in. Now God says, Exhort,—beseech men,—persuade men; not only point to the open door, but compel them to come in. Oh to be more merciful to souls, that we would lay hands on men and draw them in to the Lord![58]

M'Cheyne was careful not to let his preaching of Christ become an exercise in reduction, focusing only on a few facets of his person and work. He aimed to present Christ in all his fullness.

Christ our Surety

In one sermon, M'Cheyne said, "I have often explained that Christ came to be a surety, not only in suffering for sinners, but in obeying also, obeying inwardly and outwardly the law of His Father."[59] On another occasion, he reminded his congregation, "We often set forth Immanuel, the Surety of perishing sinners."[60] His conception of Christ our surety aligned with the Westminster Larger Catechism, which asks, "How is justification an act of God's free grace?" The catechism answers:

> Although Christ, by his obedience and death, did make a proper, real, and full satisfaction to God's justice in the behalf of them that are justified; yet inasmuch as God accepteth the satisfaction from a *surety*, which he might have demanded of them, and did provide this *surety*, his own only Son, imputing his righteousness to them, and requiring nothing of them for

---

58. *MAR*, 362 (emphasis original). M'Cheyne said in another sermon: "Some set forth Christ plainly and faithfully, but where is Paul's *beseeching* men to be reconciled? We do not invite sinners tenderly; we do not gently woo them to Christ; we do not authoritatively bid them to the marriage; we do not *compel* them to come in; we do not travail in birth till Christ be formed in them the hope of glory." *MAR*, 544.

59. *NTS*, 31.

60. *OTS*, 55. M'Cheyne regularly employed "Surety" as a title for Christ. For example, see, *NTS*, 116, 244, 254; *OTS*, 93; *TPP*, 24.

their justification but faith, which also is his gift, their justification is to them of free grace.[61]

According to the catechism, Christ's surety-work is a forensic act, which brings legal benefits such as justification. M'Cheyne's heralding of Christ as surety matches this focus, for he consistently highlighted the judicial nature of Christ's work.

First, Christ is an obeying surety. When he cried out at calvary, "It is finished!" He announced the completion of his obedience. "It is finished! It is finished! His whole work as a Surety in the place of sinners is finished," M'Cheyne declared. "The whole undertaking is completed. The whole obedience to the law is done."[62] Everything that Christ did in this world, he did in the stead of sinners. Before dying as surety, Christ lived as surety: "Through his whole life Christ was fulfilling all righteousness . . . It was not on his own account that he went through that life of willing obedience, delighting to do the will of God." All Christ's obedience, M'Cheyne said, was "as a surety in the stead of sinners, that any sinner may clothe himself with obedience and have a right to eternal glory."[63] Thus, to take Christ as our surety is to lay hold of his perfect obedience.[64]

Preaching Christ in this way led M'Cheyne to revel in the wonders of imputation. He proclaimed, "Behold thy Surety! How fully He obeyed in your stead. Ah! cling you to Him and all the merit of His holy obedience is yours. You are complete in Him."[65] "When a sinner accepts Christ as Surety," M'Cheyne deduced, "He accepts His obedience, His infinitely pure and lovely obedience. This is all put upon the believing sinner. This is the 'clothing wrought of gold.'"[66]

Second, Christ is a suffering surety. M'Cheyne marveled at Christ's suffering. In a sermon on the enemies of the cross, he said,

> Through his whole life Christ was a suffering surety, but he was especially so in his dying. Had he stood for himself he would

---

61. *WLC*, 71 (emphasis added).

62. *TPP*, 198. In "The Free Obedience of Christ," M'Cheyne asserts, "The death of Christ is, my friends, the most wonderful event past, present, or future in the whole universe." *BOF*, 24.

63. *TPP*, 209–10.

64. *TPH*, 186

65. *NTS*, 32.

66. *NTS*, 134.

have had no sufferings, for he knew no sin, neither was guile found in his mouth. But though he knew no sin, yet God made him to be sin for us. God made him as if he were all sin from head to foot . . . God charged him with the ten thousand thousand sins of all that ever had believed.[67]

M'Cheyne stressed Christ's suffering because it satisfied God's wrath against sinners. He extolled Christ's sufferings, because through faith they are counted as our own.[68] A sinner's hope is thus "all in Christ . . . in his work of suffering as surety."[69] M'Cheyne further rejoiced, "His sufferings are ours, his obedience is ours. Oh, this is true happiness—of a sinner to be a partaker of Christ."[70] Undergirding M'Cheyne's preaching of Christ as man's surety is his clear understanding of the nature and penalty of sin. He believed man was sinful from birth, utterly corrupt, and under the just punishment for his transgression. Therefore, the redemption and reconciliation of sinners demand a price. That payment, M'Cheyne taught, was Christ's blood.

Third, Christ is an atoning surety. M'Cheyne's focus on Christ's blood as the payment for sin came from a soul steeped in the typological significance of the Old Testament ceremonies. He knew that blood flowed like a torrential river in the old covenant. The sacrificial system announced that blood must be shed for a person to enter God's presence. Man's blood could never atone for sin—it has the vile stain and stench of iniquity. Such an offering could not grant entrance into God's holy presence. Also, the blood of sacrificial animals could not permanently stay God's wrath. Yet, "He that offers to be your Surety," M'Cheyne declared, "offers to cover all your sins with His own blood."[71] It is the blood of Christ that heals all wounds.[72] Christ our surety erases sin "with His bloody hand."[73] The blood of Christ saves, provides entrance into God's presence, and takes away the guilt of sin forever.[74] Without the blood of

---

67. *TPP*, 198.
68. *NTS*, 134.
69. *TPP*, 314.
70. *TPP*, 261.
71. *NTS*, 272.
72. *TPP*, 198.
73. *OTS*, 55.
74. *SOH*, 155.

the surety, no one can enter heaven.[75] M'Cheyne called every sinner to cry, "Here, Lord, am I; wash my in thy blood, or else I die."[76]

For M'Cheyne, Christ's role as an obeying, suffering, atoning surety proved God's love for sinners: "Oh, be persuaded to accept of Christ as your surety. Believe the love in the bosom of God which provided such a surety."[77] Experiencing this love leads to love for Christ. M'Cheyne exhorted, "God has brought you to a Surety, where you have received of the Lord's hand double for your sins. Prize this Surety!"[78] In another sermon, he declared, "The heart of Christ is revealed—his love to the lost, his undertaking for them, his suretyship obedience, his suretyship sufferings. Glorious Christ! Precious Christ!"[79] In addition to verifying Christ's love, M'Cheyne believed an understanding of Christ as surety empowered praise,[80] peace,[81] delight,[82] confidence,[83] and rest.[84] Ultimately though, the highest spiritual reward from this surety is communion with Christ: "Your sins may be infinite, but so is His atonement. If the Mighty God is my Surety, I cannot doubt for a moment that He is enough for me and His work sufficient to save me. I am complete in Him!"[85]

Christ our Savior

M'Cheyne was relentless in pursuing the conversion of sinners because he considered it to be the minister's noblest work. "Conversion," he announced, "is the most glorious work of God."[86] He reminded, "The great use of the ministry—engrave it on your hearts, tell it to your children—that the use of ministry is to convert your soul."[87] Again, "The

---

75. *SOH*, 185.
76. *TPH*, 206.
77. *TPP*, 211. See also, *TPH*, 230.
78. *BOF*, 160.
79. *TPH*, 58.
80. *NTS*, 193.
81. *TPH*, 221.
82. *TPP*, 26.
83. *SOH*, 31. See also, *TPP*, 195; *TPH*, 222.
84. *TPH*, 406.
85. *OTS*, 54. See also, *TPP*, 197; *TPH*, 35.
86. *TPH*, 224.
87. *BOF*, 77. M'Cheyne also said, "Every heart and eye must be intent on that

conversion of a soul is by far the most remarkable event in the history of the world."[88] By any measurable standard, M'Cheyne cared deeply about the work of conversion and gave himself to it. He saw himself mirroring the work of his Savior who "was always seeking the conversion of souls."[89] He pursued conversion with such zeal that he said some in his church were "angry that I speak so much of conversion."[90] He focused on conversion because he believed it exalted Christ. It contains, he said, "the superior power of Christ's almighty, victorious, and saving grace."[91] In Christ, there is "completeness and all-sufficiency" to bear the load of conversion.[92] Therefore, when a converted soul springs forth from sin's grip, Christ receives all honor: "The conversion of a sinner and honour of the Savior of sinners are inseparably united."[93]

For M'Cheyne, conversion was not strictly a christological work. While he preached that Christ comes in power to melt hearts unto conversion,[94] and saw Paul's encounter with Christ on the road to Damascus as a quintessential conversion experience,[95] he nonetheless extolled conversion as a trinitarian wonder. He referred regularly to the Father as the author of conversion[96] and the Holy Spirit as the sovereign agent. Ev-

---

grand achievement, the conversion of the world." *TPP*, 140.

88. *BOF*, 97.
89. *TPH*, 530.
90. *TPH*, 349. See also, *NTS*, 201.
91. *NTS*, 62.
92. *TPP*, 176.
93. *TPP*, 158.
94. *NTS*, 261; *TPP*, 257.
95. *BOF*, 176. For M'Cheyne, the typological function of Paul's Damascus encounter lay not in the revelatory experience of the risen Christ. Instead, he believed it essential for sinners to encounter the blinding power of Christ in true gospel preaching. While M'Cheyne saw preaching as the ordinary means of conversion, it is not the *sole* means. Bonar remarks, "During all his ministry he was careful to use not only the direct means appointed for the conversion of souls, but also those that appear more indirect, such as the key of discipline." *MAR*, 72. M'Cheyne confirmed this when, in a sermon on ruling elders, he admitted that early in his ministry he thought his "great and almost only work was to pray and preach." So devoted was he to praying and preaching that "when cases of discipline were brought before me and the elders, I regarded them with something like abhorrence." In time, he came to see that God uses discipline for his converting purposes. "It pleased God," M'Cheyne said, "to bless some of the cases of discipline to the manifest and undeniable conversion of souls of those under my care." *BOF*, 119.
96. *OTS*, 175. See also, *BOF*, 35, 81.

ery hearer needed to "learn that conversion is not in your own power. It is the Spirit alone who convinces of sin, and he is a free agent."[97] Without the Holy Spirit, all his preaching for conversion would be powerless.[98] M'Cheyne underscored the Spirit's sovereignty in conversion because it always led to Christ: "When the Spirit of God is really working in the heart (for conversion), he makes the man look to a pierced Christ."[99]

If Christ is peculiarly interested in and glorified by conversion, what does this mean for spirituality? The most obvious implication was the need for men, women, and children to close with Christ: "The call of Christ is to immediate conversion," M'Cheyne proclaimed.[100] When we close with Christ, the fruits of conversion inevitably follow. In a sermon titled, "On the Difficulty and Desirableness of Conversion," M'Cheyne said conversion's ordinary fruits include (1) peace with God, (2) a holy life, and (3) a joyful and thankful heart.[101] Other than his appeal to close with Christ, his most common appeal was to brokenhearted, evangelistic prayer:

> If you were to mingle with poor unconverted souls in the God-forgetting companies, where they dance, drink, are gay and merry, singing their own songs, and enjoying themselves in their accustomed manner, what could you expect to do for their conversion? You should weep over them, and seek their salvation, rather than let down your Christianity and join them in worldliness, forgetfulness of God, carnal mirth, and giddy folly. If you would do them good, you must seek God's Holy Spirit to give you a heart to weep for them.[102]

In other places, M'Cheyne lamented that too many fathers do not pray for their children's conversion.[103] He also criticized ministers who lacked passionate prayer for the conversion of their flock.[104] What these pastors needed was christological awakening.

97. *TPH*, 314, 91.
98. *TPH*, 530.
99. *TPH*, 228.
100. *TPH*, 22.
101. *TPH*, 42.
102. *NTS*, 87–88. M'Cheyne remarked, "I fear there are few among us who weep in secret place over the pride of unconverted souls. Cultivate this spirit, I beseech you!" *OTS*, 121.
103. *TPH*, 132.
104. *TPH*, 88.

Ministers are apt to sleep, and forget the power of God's word. We are apt to despair. Oh, that we could only believe and wait on God! There may be a breaking-up in this quarry yet! As the water gushed, so, when Christ is received, the soul flows toward Him. Oh, that He would reveal Himself to you! Oh, that you knew His loveliness, His excellence, His glorious freeness! Your hearts would surely melt and run to Him. The fire of His love would melt the hard wax of your hearts.[105]

Christ our Judge

M'Cheyne announced, "The deepest place in hell will be for . . . [anyone who] is not ravished with His beauty, and attracted to Him by his loveliness."[106] M'Cheyne believed that the Bible is a "blessed book full of the clearest declarations of God's wrath against sin."[107] He preached accordingly. His sermons reveal his faithful and fervent warnings to the lost: "God's Rectitude in Future Punishment" (Pss 11:6–7); "The Day of Great Slaughter" (Isa 30:25–26); "The Sword Over the Ungodly" (Ezek 21:9–10); "Future Punishment Eternal" (Mark 9:44); "Enemies of the Cross" (Phil 3:17–21); "Do Not Provoke God" (Heb 3:16–19); and "The Eternal Torment of the Dead, Matter of Eternal Song to the Redeemed" (Rev 19:3). M'Cheyne's preaching of God's punishment of sinners was persistent enough that some in his congregation urged him to lessen his emphasis on judgment. "Sometimes you wonder at our anxiety for you," he told St. Peter's. "Sometimes you say, 'Why are you so harsh?' O poor soul! It is because the house is on fire . . . Every day that passes is bringing you nearer to the judgment-seat."[108] What then were the contours of his preaching of coming judgment?

M'Cheyne's view of the final judgment walked hand in hand with the Westminster Confession of Faith: "And the souls of the wicked are cast into hell, where they remain in torments and utter darkness,

---

105. *NTS*, 261.
106. *NTS*, 102.
107. *OTS*, 60.

108. *BOF*, 80. It seems M'Cheyne thought his warnings were not strong enough or consistent enough. In the same sermon, he says, "Oh! I fear that many may reproach me on a death-bed, or in hell, that I did not tell you oftener that there was a hell. Would to God I had none to reproach me at last!" *BOF*, 80.

reserved to the judgment of the great day."[109] The Westminster divines also declared, "The wicked, who know not God, and obey not the gospel of Jesus Christ, shall be cast into eternal torments, and be punished with everlasting destruction from the presence of the Lord, and from the glory of his power."[110] With such confessional rooting, it is not surprising to see that M'Cheyne included references to hell,[111] destruction,[112] misery,[113] dread,[114] damnation,[115] terror,[116] groaning and shrieking,[117] torment, darkness, and weeping and gnashing of teeth.[118] Heralding such truth usually led to a simple exhortation: "Ah! dear souls, flee now the wrath to come!"[119] For M'Cheyne, the Bible is clear: eternal punishment awaits those who remain apart from Christ. While the self-evident nature of future judgment should be enough to lead sinners to flee to Christ,[120] it is nonetheless powerless to move any. What is needed is God's effectual call for salvation: "If you are not effectually called, dear fellow sinner, you will remember you had the outward call when in hell."[121] He further extolled God's sovereignty by proclaiming,

> Remember, God can only give you this conviction. Lie at the feet of God as a sovereign God—a God who owes you nothing but punishment. Lie at his feet as the God who alone can reveal Christ unto you. Cry night and day that he would reveal Christ unto you—that he would shine into your darkness, and give you

---

109. *WCF*, 33.1.

110. *WCF*, 33.2.

111. *BOF*, 154. M'Cheyne makes it clear that the coming punishment is not annihilation: "Some weak and foolish men think and please their fancy with the thought that hell will burn out, and they will come to some place where they may bathe their weary soul. Ah! you try to make an agreement with hell; but if ever there come a time when the flame that torments your soul and body shall burn out, the Jesus will be a liar, [for he says] it shall never be quenched." *BOF*, 153.

112. *NTS*, 219.

113. *OTS*, 133.

114. *SC*, 54. See also, *TPH*, 534.

115. *SOH*, 20.

116. *TBJ*, 31.

117. *TPH*, 276.

118. *TPP*, 148.

119. *NTS*, 152. See also, *OTS*, 14, 23, 58, 116–17, 127–28; *SOH*, 83, 85, 194; *TPP*, 60, 79, 86, 266; *TPH*, 177, 221, 243, 249, 250–51, 255, 278, 351.

120. *NTS*, 228.

121. *SOH*, 183.

the light of the knowledge of the glory of God in the face of Christ. One glimpse of that face will give you peace. It may be you shall be hid in the day of the Lord's anger.[122]

If awakening sinners of their terrible plight is God's work, why then did M'Cheyne permeate his preaching with warnings of judgment? A few answers can be given. First, he believed it was his responsibility: "By nature your hearts are as hard as adamant, and even demonstration will not make you flee from hell; yet, 'knowing the terrors of the Lord, we persuade men.'"[123] Secondly, he believed he would give an account: "We must acquit our conscience and if you go to the judgment-seat unpardoned, unsaved, your blood will be upon your own heads ... Therefore, brethren, I must warn you, I must tell you about hell."[124] He also clearly believed that such preaching was a specifically ordained means to awaken sinners to their condition and danger.

M'Cheyne directed his warnings toward the unconverted and the "almost Christian." He warned the unconverted that they lie sleeping over hell. "He that believeth not the Son, the wrath of God abideth on him," M'Cheyne warned. "Not only is God angry every day, but every moment of the day. There is not a moment of an unconverted man's life, but God's wrath abideth on him ... Unconverted souls walk and sleep over hell."[125] Reminiscent of Jonathan Edwards in "Sinners in the Hands of an Angry God," M'Cheyne told the lost, "Your days are numbered. You are hanging by a thread over the mouth of hell."[126] He reserved his severest warnings for those who draw near to Christ without ever resting in him:

> The deepest place in hell will be for almost Christians. In strict justice it will be so. The more sin the greater guilt and the deeper hell. And who has so much sin as the soul that comes nearest to Christ, yet is not ravished with His beauty, and attracted to Him by his loveliness. In the nature of things, the hell of the "almost Christian" will be more severe than that of others. To be almost saved, and yet to be lost; to be not far from the kingdom of God,

---

122. *TPH*, 327 (emphasis original).
123. *TPH*, 276. "Adamant" refers to a stone, such as a diamond, believed to be of impenetrable strength.
124. *BOF*, 151.
125. *TPH*, 220.
126. *TPH*, 220.

and yet to fall into the kingdom of wrath—Oh, that will be an awful thought to all eternity!"[127]

A sense of urgency filled M'Cheyne's preaching. Sinners stood on the precipice of eternity, soon to find Christ's judgment falling on them. How could a faithful preacher not warn them? M'Cheyne's love led him to strive for the salvation of lost sinners in danger of judgment. Love motivated all his warnings. He proclaimed, "Learn that it is in love we beseech you. Am I become you enemy, because I tell you the truth? When we speak of sins, your lost condition, the wrath that is over you, the hell beneath you, it is in love."[128] Additionally, in M'Cheyne's estimation, the truth of God's judgment served to magnify, not minimize, Christ's love to sinners: "[Christ] hates sin. He is angry with the wicked every day. He has created an eternal hell to show his utter abhorrence of sin, and yet he came and died for the ungodly."[129] M'Cheyne never stopped reveling in the glorious gospel. For him, the warning of judgment only increased the beauty of Christ. He preached,

> *The dying of the Lord Jesus is the most awakening sight in the world* . . . Why did he lie down in the cold rocky sepulchre? Was it not that there was wrath infinite and unutterable lying upon men? Would Christ have wept over Jerusalem if there had been no hell beneath it? Would he have died under his Father's wrath if there were no wrath to come? Oh! secure sinners, triflers with the gospel, polite hearers, who say often: 'Sir, we would see Jesus,' but who never find him, go to Gethsemane, see his unspeakable agonies; go to Golgotha, see the vial of wrath poured upon his breaking heart.[130]

"Admire the love of Jesus," M'Cheyne said, "Oh, what a sea of wrath did he lie under for you!"[131] A failure to see the indescribable love of Christ, which caused him to endure the horror of God's justice, was heartbreaking to M'Cheyne. "This is an awful sight," he said, "To see a [sinner] not subdued by the love of Jesus."[132]

---

127. *NTS*, 102.
128. *NTS*, 277.
129. *OTS*, 25.
130. *TPH*, 208–9 (emphasis original).
131. *TPH*, 191.
132. *TPP*, 69.

M'Cheyne believed loving tenderness was the appropriate tone for preaching of hell's horror. In a sermon on Malachi 1:6, he concluded that "earthly virtues may accompany a man to hell," adding, "I desire to speak with all reverence and with all tenderness upon so dreadful a subject. The man who speaks of hell should do it with tears in his eyes."[133] The reality of Christ's judgment should not only promote tenderness in the preacher, but compassion in all Christians. "O beloved!" M'Cheyne cried, "Think of hell. Have you no unconverted friends, who are treasuring up wrath against the day of wrath? . . . Oh, have you no compassion on them—no mercy's voice to warn them?"[134]

M'Cheyne's preaching of Christ was, in summary, an expression of his love for Christ. Trusting in Christ was to taste his love. The love of Christ was the central motif of his preaching because he was convinced that we can point sinners "to no other remedy than the love of Christ."[135]

CONCLUSION

David Robertson concludes that M'Cheyne's preaching is ordinary: "When one reads McCheyne's sermons there is not a great deal that is outstanding." He adds, "McCheyne's sermons were not literary classics and they generally do not translate well to the printed page."[136] This chapter takes a much more positive view of M'Cheyne's preaching ability, agreeing with David Yeaworth's assessment:

> To [his] natural talents and skills, McCheyne added his singular manner of delivery, which was but an extension of his own personality. He was confident, and yet preached with humility; his sermons were forceful, and yet gentle; critical although sympathetic; sober, and yet with feeling. More than any other human element, it was this personal factor which enabled him

---

133. *TPH*, 35.

134. *BOF*, 154. M'Cheyne informed ministers that "they that most love in their hearts speak most of hell." M'Cheyne, *Sermons*, 166.

135. M'Cheyne, *Sermons*, 8.

136. Robertson, *Awakening*, 127, 191. Contemporary publications did not always favor M'Cheyne's style. The *Dundee Advertiser* claimed, "His command of Scripture, imagery and illustration is intensive: but some of his figures he pursued rather too far. His voice has considerable power; but it is rather deficient in flexibility." Quoted in Robertson, *Awakening*, 105.

continually to draw 1100 hearers throughout the seven years of his ministry.[137]

When the Holy Spirit works through a minister, no one remains untouched. The Word is like a hammer that breaks the hard-hearted, a fire that warms the weary, an ointment that soothes the hurting, and a light that guides the lost. The power of M'Cheyne's preaching resulted from two realities.

First, M'Cheyne's preaching exalted Christ—crucified, buried, resurrected, and glorified. In every sermon, he set forth Christ and called upon people to look and live.[138] Christ's love is the most arresting reality because "the more ministers have Christ in their sermons, the more they faithfully preach."[139] M'Cheyne did not try to answer every specific objection, question, or need that lay before him. To be sure, he dealt with several in each sermon. But his chief aim was to direct his listeners's attention to Christ, who alone is the remedy for every ailment: "O yes, my friends, we have utterly failed in our preaching of Jesus if we have not set Him forth to you as 'a feast of fat things, of wines on the lees refined.'"[140] A recent assessment of M'Cheyne's preaching comes from L. J. Van Valen, who says, "Sometimes it was as if [M'Cheyne's] soul was overwhelmed by the love of Christ. Both in and out of the pulpit, this theme was the expression of his heart: 'The love of Christ constraineth us!' He never tired of proclaiming the precious name of his Redeemer: 'The Love of Christ. Such is our precious theme!'"[141]

The second reason for M'Cheyne's success in preaching was his spirituality. Experiential communion with Christ fortified M'Cheyne's soul, and infused his preaching with power. Bonar described M'Cheyne's preaching as "a giving out of the inward life. He loved to come up from the pastures wherein the Chief Shepherd had met him."[142] M'Cheyne said proper preaching cannot be done any other way. He said, "Faithful

---

137. Yeaworth, "Robert Murray McCheyne," 218. M'Cheyne's sermons should be read aloud to feel the force and appreciate the pathos of his preaching.

138. *OTS*, 14.

139. *BOF*, 28.

140. *NTS*, 4.

141. Van Valen, *Constrained by His Love*, 201. Van Valen adds, "Just as John was known as the apostle of love, so M'Cheyne rightly can be called the preacher of love!" Van Valen, *Constrained by His Love*, 201.

142. *MAR*, 34–35.

ministers preach from personal experience."[143] Christ-exalting preaching rises when a minister makes "a discovery to the soul of the wisdom, love, grace and power of God, manifested in the face of a dying Redeemer . . . Oh! it is then that a minister speaks with power, holy admiration, and urgency."[144] The secret of M'Cheyne's success lies herein: he preached with peculiar power precisely because he relished Christ's love. His preaching was so captivating because his love for Christ was on full display.[145]

Not only did M'Cheyne's sermons overflow with his love for Christ, but they were designed to inflame the same love in his hearers. He cried, "We preach Jesus Christ the Lord, that you may be holy."[146] M'Cheyne was convinced that true spirituality cannot be severed from the person and work of Christ. The ordinary way we come to know and adore Christ is through the preached Word. Therefore, M'Cheyne labored to preach the Bible because "Jesus pervades the Bible—it is the standing witness to Jesus."[147]

---

143. *NTS*, 155.
144. *NTS*, 155–56.
145. See also, Smellie, *Biography of R. M. McCheyne*, 47.
146. *BOF*, 6.
147. Quoted in Prime, *Robert Murray McCheyne*, 67.

8

Offering Christ
M'Cheyne's Evangelism

CHRIST CAPTIVATED M'CHEYNE'S SOUL and stirred in him a zeal to capture others for Christ. He was a "fisher of men," casting his net wherever Christ sent him. The portrait of M'Cheyne that hangs in the hallowed halls of church history concentrates on his inward life—his "seraphic devotion."[1] What receives less attention is how his inward life of loving Christ influenced his ministry. He understood his calling to be preeminently that of an evangelist. David Yeaworth rightly observes that "McCheyne's ministry from the beginning was essentially evangelistic."[2]

---

1. Steel, *Achievements of Youth*, 328. One nineteenth century periodical remarks how M'Cheyne "left behind the memory of an ethereal saintship and a burning evangelistic power." Cheyne, *Christian Monthly*, 22. M'Cheyne understood how congregations tend to amplify the preacher—his personality or ability—and unintentionally minimize Christ. He thus warned St. Peter's: "Ministers only shine as long as they are in the hand of Christ. People now look too much to ministers; they expect to get wisdom from them; but we are not put up to be between you and Christ. As I have told you before, the only use of the pole was to hold up the brazen serpent. No one thought of looking at the pole: so are we here to hold up Christ in the sight of you all; we are to give testimony to the truth; we are witnesses for Christ; we are to hold up Jesus before you, and before ourselves too: so that we shall disappear, and nothing shall be seen but Christ." *SC*, 9. In a letter to St. Peter's, he said, "I fear I will be a swift witness against many of my people in the day of the Lord, that they looked to me, and not to Christ, when I preached to them." *MAR*, 89. M'Cheyne would have preferred his legacy to be little more than that of a witness to Christ.

2. Yeaworth, "Robert Murray M'Cheyne," 284.

M'Cheyne's personal writings communicate his zeal to win souls for Christ. He declared, "I feel there are two things it is impossible to desire with sufficient ardour—personal holiness, and the honour of Christ in the salvation of souls."[3] In a sermon on the gospel ministry, he confessed, "I think I can say, I have never risen a morning without thinking how I could bring more souls to Christ."[4] Between house visitations, children's classes, revival labors, and preaching tours, M'Cheyne spent the bulk of his ministry in evangelism. His ordinary Lord's Day sermons aimed to evangelize each congregant. Van Oosterzee states that M'Cheyne's preaching was "the oratory of a heart penetrated with the vital truths of the gospel," and thus thoroughly bent towards soul-winning.[5]

M'Cheyne's passion for soul-winning caused him to consider a call to labor as an evangelist late in his ministry. Andrew Bonar recalled how M'Cheyne "had sometimes seriously weighed the duty of giving up his charge, if only the Church would ordain him as an evangelist."[6] Marcus Loane is more certain: "It is clear that M'Cheyne felt the power of that call (to be an evangelist); he was rapidly moving to a decision to leave the church and parish so that he might devote himself without reserve to the proclamation of the gospel."[7] Indeed, M'Cheyne wrote to Eliza on March 7, 1842, just weeks before his death: "I think the church should give me a roving commission at once. I can almost say, as Wesley did to the Bishop

---

3. *MAR*, 242.

4. *BOF*, 77.

5. Quoted in Garvie, *Christian Preacher*, 227.

6. *MAR*, 139. An insight into M'Cheyne's evangelistic zeal appears in his sermon, "The Office of The Ruling Elder." He declared, "I thought that my great and almost only work was to pray and preach. I saw your souls to be so precious, and the time so short, that I devoted all my time and care, and strength to labour in word and doctrine. When cases of discipline were brought before me and the elders, I regarded them with something like abhorrence. It was a duty I shrank from: and I may truly say it nearly drove me from the work of my ministry among you altogether." *BOF*, 119. M'Cheyne admits that he eventually came to see that "if preaching be an ordinance of Christ, so is church discipline." *BOF*, 119. It is clear from M'Cheyne's later endeavors that church governance was never something in which he delighted. He routinely left St. Peter's to preach the gospel in diverse places, causing his friends to believe he "erred in the abundant frequency of his evangelistic labours at a time when he was still bound to a particular flock." *MAR*, 60. In the pattern of Ephesians 4:11, M'Cheyne was more comfortable in the office of evangelist than that of pastor-teacher.

7. Loane, *They Were Pilgrims*, 162. See also, McLennan, *McCheyne's Dundee*, 114–15.

of London . . . 'The world is my parish.'"[8] William Chalmers Burns had already encouraged him in the same direction, saying,

> I know not how it is, but it seems more clear to me that you must without delay give up your charge, and enter on that tempting field in which I am honoured to be. The fields are white. . . . Do not wait for a *Church* call. Christ's call is better. Souls are perishing! Let us to the rescue, and leave others to abide by the *stuff*. You understand me; I do not undervalue *pastoral work*. But there must be a *spiritual* flock gathered first."[9]

Whether M'Cheyne would have left St. Peter's to minister as an evangelist is not germane to this work. What is worth noting is the depth to which his soul thrived on mission for the honor of Christ.[10] This chapter

---

8. Quoted Smellie, *Biography of R. M. McCheyne*, 146–47.

9. Quoted in Smellie, *Biography of R. M. McCheyne*, 146 (emphasis original). Smellie thus concludes, "It is among the might-have-beens, of which there are scores in the regions of history and biography, that, had McCheyne's life been spared through a few weeks longer, he would have resigned his pastorate in St. Peter's, and gone out over broad Scotland to publish and comment the love of God in Christ Jesus our Lord." Smellie, *Biography of R. M. McCheyne*, 147. See also, Steel, *Burning and Shining Lights*, 163.

10. It is worth noting that although M'Cheyne's longing was to evangelize and promote revival throughout Britain, mission had a strong pull on his heart. Born in 1813, M'Cheyne entered the world at a time when the Church of Scotland was dreaming about missionary endeavors. Britain's colonial expansion, coupled with the aftershocks of the evangelical revival, helped organize evangelical causes for missions. Henderson, *Church of Scotland*, 210. William Carey's departure for India in 1793 further stimulated a conversation regarding foreign missions in the Scottish Church. It was at the 1796 General Assembly that the Church first heard overtures calling for missionary activity in other lands. David Yeaworth, adapting from Henderson says, "Following an historic and vehement debate the overtures untimely, and a more gradual course was followed for the next three decades." Yeaworth, *Robert Murray M'Cheyne*, 259. (Yeaworth remarks that the Dissenters took this patient process as their official position.) The Church's deliberate action reached a climax when, in 1829, Alexander Duff of Moulin left his homeland for India as the Church of Scotland's widely celebrated first missionary. The first rumblings of M'Cheyne's missionary spirit are found as far back as 1831 when he was a first-year student at the Divinity Hall. In April of that year, his older brother William took a medical post in India with the Bengal Medical Service. Henceforth India was often in M'Cheyne's mind. A November 12, 1831 diary entry finds M'Cheyne, "Reading H. Martyn's *Memoirs*. Would I could imitate him, giving up father, mother, country, house, health, life all—for Christ." *MAR*, 11. Diary entries from the summer of 1832 show a young man wrestling with missionary desires. He writes on May 19, "Thought with more comfort than usual of being a witness for Jesus in a foreign land." *MAR*, 15. In early June, he talks about conversing with Alexander Somerville had "on missions" and the missionary's necessary heart condition for

describes M'Cheyne's ordinary evangelistic labors in four main areas: (1) house visitation, (2) ministry to children, (3) revival, and (4) church extension. It concludes by demonstrating the place of Christ in M'Cheyne's evangelism.

EVANGELISM AND VISITATION

M'Cheyne's earliest models of gospel ministry were Henry Duncan, Thomas Chalmers, and John Bonar—men who extolled and embodied zeal for visitation.[11] They urged regular home visitation throughout the parish for pastoral care and evangelism. David Yeaworth agrees that they influenced M'Cheyne's practice of visitation: "In his general visitation, McCheyne adopted the system he first learned from Chalmers and used in Larbert."[12] The system aimed to minister to the entire parish, not merely to the communicant members of the local congregation. M'Cheyne visited some twelve to fifteen families per day while at Larbert, and the number increased to roughly twenty homes when he moved to Dundee.

---

fruitful service. *MAR*, 15. By June 27, he finds inspiration in another historical figure by reading, "*Life of David Brainerd* . . . Tonight, more set upon missionary enterprise than ever." *MAR*, 16. Missionary zeal continued its presence during his second year of theological study. The following summer's diary provides a longer, introspective entry on the subject: "Why is a missionary life so often an object of my thoughts? Is it simply for the love I bear to souls? Then, why do I not show it more where I am? Souls are as precious here as in Burmah. Does the romance of the business not weigh anything with me?—the interest and esteem I would carry with me?—the nice journals and letters I should write and receive? Why would I so much rather go to the East than to the West Indies? Am I wholly deceiving my own heart? And have I not a spark of true missionary zeal?" *MAR*, 20–21. It was also during these early years of theological study that M'Cheyne functioned as secretary of "The Missionary Society" for students at the Divinity Hall. Bonar says M'Cheyne, in this role, "interested himself deeply in details of missionary labors. Indeed, to the last day of his life, his thought often turned to foreign lands." *MAR*, 27. Bonar believed this restlessness never left his dear friend. "Though engaged night and day with his flock in St. Peter's, Mr. M'Cheyne ever cherished a missionary spirit. 'This place hardens me for a foreign land,' was his remark on one occasion." *MAR*, 84. M'Cheyne's zeal left a mark on Alexander Duff, as Duff said of M'Cheyne and Somerville, "If any number of the divinity students were like those, the India Mission would never lack men worthy of it." Smith, *Life of Alexander Duff*, 125.

11. Chalmers said, "A house-going minister makes a church-going people." Quoted in Murray, *Scottish Christian Heritage*, 328. For an overview of Chalmers's methods, see Hanna, *Memoirs of Thomas Chalmers*, 431–32. See also, Brown, *Thomas Chalmers*, 100–1. For a representative argument for the value of home visitation in the free church tradition, see Blaikie, *For Work of Ministry*, 259–66.

12. Yeaworth, "Robert Murray McCheyne," 157.

On average, he spent six hours a day visiting parishioners.[13] His method was to notify the family the day before he was to visit them, and to gird himself "for the combat."[14] He aimed to make each visit brief and to the point. He began by discovering the home's religious affiliation. Then he read and commented on relevant Scripture passages, urging everyone present to trust in Christ. If children were in the house, M'Cheyne asked them a few questions from the catechism. He was especially careful to speak of Christ whenever guests were present. One notebook recorded "Rules Worth Remembering," and begins with the command, "When visiting a family whether ministerially or otherwise, speak particularly to the strangers about eternal things—perhaps God has brought you together just to save the soul."[15] Before leaving the home, M'Cheyne invited the household to an evening meeting in the neighborhood, which often attracted some two hundred people "in a large home or on some back green."[16] It was not unusual for M'Cheyne's evening lecture to last for ninety minutes.

M'Cheyne's notebooks reveal the painstaking attention he gave to visitation. He sketched maps of various districts to ensure he could

---

13. *MAR*, 84.

14. MACCH 2.1.11. While in Larbert, M'Cheyne wrote home of his amusement at an elder's common practice of warning a household "the day before (visiting), so that their houses and bairns are all as clean and shining as pennies new from the mint." MACCH 2.9.21.

15. MACCH 1.10, 29. See also, Yeaworth, "Robert Murray McCheyne," 157-58. Rule 2 stated, "Read Part IV of Bridges on the Christian ministry. Would it not be right always to read something about ministry to stir up the gift that is in me?" Rule 3 asked, "Ought a minister not have a list of those of his people he thinks Christians that he pray for them by name—also of awakened persons—also of those who have particularly asked his prayers?" MACCH 1.10, 29.

16. Yeaworth, "Robert Murray McCheyne," 158. Blaikie calls these meetings "cottage lectures." He adds, "The cottage lecture derives its special charm from its domestic character, being a meeting of a few neighbouring families to hear the Word and join in praise and prayer. It is family worship on a larger scale. It has a kind of hallowing effect on the house and on the neighbourhood; the simplicity, ease, and affectionateness of the service have a great charm, especially for the rural mind, and it tends, perhaps, to gender more of a kindly, neighbourly, Christian spirit than even the Lord's Day service, where many of the people are unacquainted, and a distant feeling towards one another much to some degree prevail." Blaikie, *For Work of Ministry*, 210. M'Cheyne's diary records: "Visited eighteen families and met them in the evening in James Donald's green and preach to upwards of 200 on Ezekiel 20:35—I will bring you into the wilderness—with more freedom than usual—some of the anxious souls bowed down their heads and wept. May it be a time of power." Quoted in Robertson, *Awakening*, 116-17.

return to homes situated in the byways. In each entry, he wrote down those whom he visited, and the date of the last visit. He made brief comments on their spiritual state, and recorded in red ink the Scripture passages he commented on. He devoted a separate section to the sick.[17] A representative entry includes the following information:

> Anne Moodie (House West of Millers): Nice looking, intelligent woman—sat, in chapel shade. *Visit 31, Jan. 1837*: His faithfulness in affliction—all taught of God. [She's] seemingly a woman of God—very humble and meek in appearance & affectionate. *Visit 7, Feb.*: She not better. Hosea v. Spoke plainly—tho' searching in the dark not knowing whether she be a child of God or not. *Visit 21, Feb.*: Better. Xt (Christ) the intercessor for us. Xt having prayed for us in his agony are assured that he now intercedes.[18]

M'Cheyne devoted extra attention to those near death, especially if they were children.[19] He wrote of a young girl named Jean:

> Fine girl of eleven or twelve dying of water in head—spoke to her 1st day on the good shepherd gathering the lambs—she cautiously speaks but seems to love the word. 2nd day 23rd Psalm—much the same—asked her if she would like to lie on the shoulders of the Good Shepherd—she said yes. 3rd day—Prodigal son—she seems to listen with peace and joy. 4th day—Noah and the ark—she heard plainly. Died 23rd March 1838—I hope in peace. When the schoolmaster had been speaking to her she said, "I wish he could have spoken to me all night."[20]

---

17. The leading page of Notebook XIV includes these words: "Jesus: 'I was sick, and ye visited Me.' Believers: 'When saw we Thee sick or in prison?' Jesus: 'Verily, I say unto you, Inasmuch as ye have done it unto one of the least of these my brethren, ye have done it unto Me.'" MACCH 1.14. Interestingly, M'Cheyne seems to have used certain cases of illness to exercise his personal interest in medicine. He occasionally recorded "the pulses of the sick, and even noted the symptoms and his diagnoses, mentioning such examinations as: 'Listened at her back and heart and heard work of death going on fearfully.'" Yeaworth, "Robert Murray McCheyne," 159. Van Valen tells about M'Cheyne often warning individuals away from whiskey when prescribed by the doctor. He could at times frustrate doctors, and on one occasion he noted, "Dr. Tennant has forbidden all disturbance from ministers. So the body doctor has thrust out the soul doctor." Quoted in Van Valen, *Constrained by His Love*, 176.

18. MACCH 1.14.

19. See also, Smellie, *Biography of R. M. McCheyne*, 48.

20. MACCH 1.14.

Because the parish duties were immense, and M'Cheyne routinely visited certain families multiple times over the course of a month, the ruling elders of St. Peter's assisted him in visitation, especially during times of an epidemic.[21] M'Cheyne also appointed deaconesses to visit widows and comfort them in their loneliness.

David Robertson suggests that the vast majority of M'Cheyne's evangelism was done "through the regular visitation."[22] The statement is misleading as M'Cheyne's entire ministry was evangelistic. He spoke of Christ every day, wherever he found himself. He was part of a ministerial school directed at winning entire parishes, and thus the culture as a whole, to Christ. Thomas Chalmers taught his students to see diligent visitation as an integral part of achieving the goal of a godly country.[23] M'Cheyne possessed a realistic view of his efforts, however, considering them average at best. He urged Alexander Somerville (his friend and replacement as John Bonar's assistant): "Take more heed to the saints than I ever did . . . Speak boldly. What matter in eternity the slight awkwardness of time!"[24] Undoubtedly, his affectionate personality added an uncommon vitality to his visitation. He knocked on doors full of Christ's sympathy and tenderness. This is why he had such an impact on those soon to pass into eternity; his sincere compassion gave power to his pleadings to close with Christ. M'Cheyne's notebooks reveal occasional difficulties—even debates[25]—during visits; but, in the main, God blessed his labors. "All through his ministry," Smellie explains, "it was patent that McCheyne attached no less importance to the visitation of his people from house to house than to their instruction from the pulpit."[26]

---

21. Yeaworth, "Robert Murray McCheyne," 159.

22. Robertson, *Awakening*, 118.

23. See also, Brown, *Thomas Chalmers and the Godly Scottish Commonwealth*, 1–42, and Chalmers, *Discourses on the Application of Christianity*, 52.

24. *MAR*, 49.

25. A notation from December 12, 1836 mentions a visit with one Thomas Fyrie who was zealous to engage M'Cheyne in a debate about hell and annihilation. MACCH 1.14.

26. Smellie, *Biography of R. M. McCheyne*, 48.

EVANGELISM AND CHILDREN

M'Cheyne always aimed the gospel at the hearts of young children.[27] He published a well-received tract entitled, *Reasons Why Children Should Fly to Christ*.[28] It summarized and codified many standard refrains from his sermons. He proclaimed, "Youth is the best time to be converted."[29] Again, "Youth is a day of grace. If you intend to come to Jesus and be saved, there is not time so seasonable as the time of one's youth."[30] It is in the days of youth that the heart is tender, soft, and impressionable. He explained,

> Most people who are ever converted are converted in youth. Conviction of sin and conviction of righteousness are most easily wrought into the youthful mind ... Now, although conversion be a supernatural work, yet it is true of conversion also, that it is far oftener wrought in youth than afterwards. My young friends, this is your day of grace; remember, it quickly passes, the twilight is at hand; the night cometh when no man can believe.[31]

M'Cheyne consistently applied his sermons to children, and devised strategic measures to bring them Christ.[32] One measure was advocacy for a Sabbath Sunday School. He instituted the school in early 1837, and it was something of a novelty in the Scottish Church.[33] St. Peter's scheduled a special worship service for children at 8 a.m. on Sundays, and a Sabbath

---

27. McLennan says two convictions motivated M'Cheyne's love for young people: (1) his recognition of the brevity of life; and (2) his belief that young people can believe and be saved. McLennan, *McCheyne's Dundee*, 118.

28. *MAR*, 537–42.

29. *OTS*, 104.

30. *NTS*, 85.

31. *NTS*, 85.

32. For examples of exhortations to children, see *MAR*, 315, 322–24, 348, 351, 397, 399, 456, 540, 570; *BOF*, 67, 87, 94, 98; *NTS*, 85, 198, 233, 311; *OTS*, 44, 47, 49, 59, 104–5; *TPH*, 25, 26, 130, 205, 229–30, 297, 349, 350, 428, 458; *TPP*, 49, 85, 109, 146, 223. See also his hymns, "Children Called to Christ" and "The Child Coming to Jesus." *MAR*, 589, 596–97.

33. Yeaworth says St. Peter's was "often cited as [a good example] for the rest of the country." Other churches made similar efforts as M'Cheyne, but the "novelty of youth work may be seen in that it was not until 1872 that the Free Church took its first steps in creating a department for this age group." Yeaworth, "Robert Murray McCheyne," 165. In the decade after M'Cheyne's death, the free church sought to move toward a unified strategy for Sabbath School, but there was strong opposition as late as 1850. Yeaworth, "Robert Murray McCheyne," 167.

School from 6–8 p.m. By 1839, at least one hundred and fifty children were present for the evening class.[34] M'Cheyne's instruction utilized all manner of resources—the Bible, the catechism, hymns, tracts, and poems. He aimed "to entertain them to the utmost and at the same time to win their souls."[35] "I gather all sorts of interesting scraps to illustrate the catechism," M'Cheyne told his parents, "and try to entice them to know and to love the Lord Jesus."[36] He urged the Sabbath School teachers to see special joy in their work, for "to bring one child to the bosom of Christ would be reward for all our pains to eternity."[37] He also encouraged them to visit the children during the week, which allowed them to press home vital gospel truths and prove their genuine spiritual interest to the children's parents.[38]

A second strategy for reaching youth was the Tuesday night meeting for those too old to attend the Sabbath School. As many as two hundred and fifty teenagers frequented these classes in which M'Cheyne focused on simple Bible instruction and the catechism. The classes concentrated on the nature of sin because, he declared, "The greatest want in the religion of children is generally *sense of sin*."[39] An illuminating example of his method is his teaching on Shorter Catechism 19.[40] His exposition flowed through three heads: (1) What we have lost; (2) What we have come under; and (3) What are we liable to.[41] His notes represent a clear commentary on the features found in the catechism's answer. He reminded the students that "as children you are *all* under" God's wrath and curse. He also penned the following poem to help cement the lesson's truth:

> Stop poor sinner, stop and think
> Before you further go

---

34. Van Valen, *Constrained by His Love*, 151; Prime, *Robert Murray McCheyne*, 70.

35. Quoted in Van Valen, *Constrained by His Love*, 128.

36. Quoted in Van Valen, *Constrained by His Love*, 128. M'Cheyne's diligence in the Sabbath School belied his longing for the time when "there was no need for Sabbath Schools, for every family was a Sabbath school." Quoted in Yeaworth, "Robert Murray McCheyne," 167.

37. *MAR*, 255.

38. *MAR*, 254.

39. *MAR*, 513.

40. "Q. What is the misery of that estate whereinto man fell? A. All mankind by their fall lost communion with God, are under his wrath and curse, and so made liable to all miseries in this life, to death itself, and to the pains of hell forever."

41. MACCH 1.7.

Will you sport upon the brink
Of never ending woe.
Once again I charge you stop
For unless you warning take
Ere you are aware you drop
Into the burning lake.[42]

M'Cheyne's instruction on Tuesday evenings bore great fruit as young people crowded the communicant's class seeking full communion at St. Peter's. He enjoyed the Sabbath School and Tuesday evening catechism classes, but the communicant's class was his chief delight in evangelizing youth. Smellie says these classes were "more intimate and sacred."[43] Interacting with the prospective communicants afforded M'Cheyne a steady stream of those conversations he enjoyed most—discussing one's eternal state before God.

A third scheme for reaching children with the gospel was the weekday school of St. Peter's. M'Cheyne designed it for the church's children so that "the blessings of religion and the benefits of knowledge may be imparted together."[44] The school met in the evenings as most of the Dundee children worked in factories during the day. Over three hundred children enrolled. M'Cheyne ensured that the church's spiritual mission was of first importance. He reminded, "The chief use of the school is to convert the souls of the children."[45] His spiritual interest in the children is further demonstrated in that he sought to employ teachers who, above all, "can love the souls of little children."[46]

---

42. MACCH 1.7.

43. Smellie, *Biography of R. M. McCheyne*, 63. For M'Cheyne's notes on the communicants class, see MACCH 1.7.

44. Quoted in Yeaworth, "Robert Murray McCheyne," 165. Yeaworth recounts how M'Cheyne actively promoted education throughout the Presbytery: "He was a leader in seeking the 'best most of promoting the interests of education,' and served on several Presbytery committees to this end." Yeaworth, "Robert Murray McCheyne," 166. *The Home and Foreign Missionary Record* commended the Presbytery's efforts, saying in 1841, "We have oftener than once had occasion to advert to the zeal of the Presbytery of Dundee in the cause of education." Quoted in Yeaworth, "Robert Murray McCheyne," 166.

45. MACCH 3.3.38.

46. *MAR*, 62. He said any teacher who wanted for this would prove to be "a curse rather than a blessing." For a moving account of M'Cheyne's affection for children, see his tract, "Another Lily Gathered," in *MAR*, 504–21.

While Parish visitation and weekly ministry to children were consistent components in M'Cheyne's evangelistic efforts, he recognized that something more was needed. He told St. Peter's, "We may preach publicly, and from house to house; we may teach the young, and warn the old, but all will be in vain; *until* the Spirit be poured upon us from on high."[47] The Spirit's outpouring fell in 1839 and lasted for many months, stamping a mark on Scottish evangelicalism.[48]

EVANGELISM AND REVIVAL

The "remarkable times" of revival in Scotland long fascinated M'Cheyne.[49] Iain Murray argues that "the subject of revival was in the forefront" of his thinking when he arrived at St. Peter's.[50] Indeed, M'Cheyne had prayed for awakening at Larbert and Dunipace, urging Andrew Bonar to join him in petitioning God.[51] Seeing that most of Scotland lay in spiritual slumber, M'Cheyne examined possible reasons for the Holy Spirit's silence. He concluded, "Perhaps, one reason we are not favoured with revival is, that we are not ready for it; the minister would not be able to direct people in their alarms."[52] He thus arrived at St. Peter's thirsty for showers from the Holy Spirit. Upon his ordination, he immediately steered St. Peter's to gather for corporate prayer on Thursday nights. The consistent plea in the meetings was for the Holy Spirit to fall again on God's people.

In 1837, M'Cheyne preached a well-publicized sermon from Jeremiah 14:8–9, entitled, "Why is God a Stranger in the Land?"[53] It represents his detailed thinking on revival—what it is and how it comes.

47. *TBJ*, 117 (emphasis original).

48. Barbour, *Life of Alexander Whyte*, 24.

49. MACCH 3.2.46. For analyses of revival in Scotland, see Yeaworth, "Robert Murray McCheyne," 281–84; Smart et al., *Pentecostal Outpourings*, 100–32; Couper, *Scottish Revivals*; MacRae, *Revivals in Highlands*; Fawcett, *Cambuslang Revival*; Jeffrey, *When the Lord Walked*; Gillies, *Historical Collections*.

50. Murray, *Scottish Christian Heritage*, 104. See also, Yeaworth, "Robert Murray McCheyne," 284. In June of 1837, M'Cheyne told his father that one reason for his turning down a call to Perth was because, "There is an awakening look about my people and I really fear I dare not leave them." MACCH 2.1.17.

51. Bonar, *Andrew A. Bonar*, 39, 41.

52. Bonar, *Diary and Letters*, 27.

53. *MAR*, 542–47. The sermon was eventually published as a tract. M'Cheyne's sermon on "God Let None of His Words Fall to the Ground," from 1 Sam 3:19, takes up similar themes.

M'Cheyne described in detail what happens "when God is present with power in any land." First, "There are always many awakened to a sense of sin and flocking to Christ."[54] Second, "Not only are unconverted persons awakened and made to flee to Christ, but those who were in Christ before receive new measures of the Spirit."[55] Third, "Open sinners, though they may remain unconverted, are often much restrained. There is an awe of God upon their spirits."[56] While recognizing that God was making himself known in such ways in parts of Scotland, M'Cheyne lamented the spiritual deadness pervading most of the nation. In his estimation, the apathy called for ministers who were eager and equipped for revival.

M'Cheyne's program for revival began with proper preaching. He called ministers to "*yearn over* men in the bowels of Jesus Christ," and to preach tenderly and persuasively.[57] Too many preachers, he believed, did not make "it the end of their ministry to testify of Jesus as the hiding-place for sinners."[58] He also said ministers must preach Christ if revival was to come. He complained about typical preaching in the Church: "We do not invite sinners tenderly, we do not gently woo them to Christ; we do not *compel* them to come in; we do not travail in birth till Christ be formed in them the hope of glory. Oh, who can wonder that God is such a stranger in the land?"[59] M'Cheyne then turned his attention to the failings of ordinary Christians. He accused the average church member of having little regard for hearing the Word and prayer.[60] As he looked out on St. Peter's, he saw reasons for both confidence and concern. In his second pastoral letter, he penned,

> I bless God for all the tokens He has given us that the Spirit of God is not departed from the Church of Scotland, that the Glory is still in the midst. Still the Spirit has never shed on us "abundantly." The many absentees in the forenoon of the Sabbaths, the thin meetings on Thursday evenings, the absence of men from all meetings from the worship of God, the few private prayer meetings, the little love and union among Christians—all show

---

54. *MAR*, 542 (emphasis original).
55. *MAR*, 543.
56. *MAR*, 543.
57. *MAR*, 544.
58. *MAR*, 544.
59. *MAR*, 544.
60. *MAR*, 544–45.

[why] the plentiful rain has not yet fallen to refresh our corner of the heritage.[61]

One month later, M'Cheyne wrote his eighth pastoral letter, which mirrored his sermon, "Why is God a Stranger in This Land?" He began with self-examination, and concluded that many reasons for the Holy Spirit's silence are "to be sought in *your minister*."[62] M'Cheyne singled out his preaching, considering it full of "innumerable deficiencies," and his shepherding, which engaged too often in "fruitless intercourse."[63] He did not shoulder the entire blame, however. He was sure that the congregation had also "hindered in great measure God's work in the parish."[64] First, there was a lack of holiness. True revival always begins in the hearts of church members. They must be made living epistles of Christ, "having the Holy Spirit filling [them] with a sweet, tender, chaste, compassionate, forgiving love to all the world."[65] Second, M'Cheyne announced that St. Peter's had hampered God's work by their lack of prayer. The salvation

---

61. *MAR*, 185.

62. *MAR*, 207 (emphasis original). Early in his ministry, M'Cheyne read 1 Thess 2 in his morning Bible reading. He noted twenty-six characteristics of what constitutes a healthy minister: (1) bold in our God—having the courage of one who is near and dear to God, and who has God dwelling in him; (2) to speak the Gospel—he should be a voice to speak the gospel, an angel of glad tidings; (3) with much agony—he should wrestle with God, and wrestle with men; (4) not of uncleanness—he should be chaste in heart, in eye, in speech; (5) not of deceit or guile—he should be open, having only one end in view, the glory of Christ; (6) allowed of God to be put in trust—he should feel a steward, entrusted of God; (7) not as pleasing men, but God; he should speak what God will approve, who tries the heart; (8) neither flattering words—he should never flatter men, even to win them; (9) nor a cloak of covetousness—not seeking money or presents, devoted to his work with a single eye; (10) nor of men sought we glory—not seeking praise; (11) gentle as a nurse; (12) affectionately desirous of you—having an inward affection and desire for the salvation and growth of his people; (13) willing to impart our own souls—willing to suffer loss, even of life, in their cause; (14) laboriousness night and day; (15) to preach without being chargeable, to any of his people; (16) holily; (17) justly; (18) unblameably; (19) the daily walk; (20) exhorted every one—individuality of ministry; (21) as a father—authority and love; (22) thank we God—he should be full of thanksgiving without ceasing; (23) should be with his people in heart, when not in presence; (24) endeavoured to see you—his people, his hope, that which animates him; (25) joy—immediate delight; (26) and crown of rejoicing—when he looks beyond the grave. MACCH 1.1. See also, Smellie, *Biography of R. M. McCheyne*, 73-74.

63. *MAR*, 208.

64. *MAR*, 208.

65. *MAR*, 209.

of souls depends on God's children asking for it. "I often think it strange that ever we should be in heaven," M'Cheyne wrote, "and so many in hell through our soul-destroying carelessness."[66] Prayer, in the private closet and public meeting, is the means by which the Holy Spirit comes in power. If the church does not gather regularly for prayer, she has no reason to expect Christ's blessing.[67]

By the time he left for the mission of inquiry to Palestine, M'Cheyne was hopeful that revival would come during his absence—maybe even *because* of his absence. He wrote to Andrew Bonar:

> I sometimes think that a great blessing may come to my people in my absence. Often God does not bless us when we are in the midst of our labours, lest we shall say, "My hand and my eloquence have done it." He removes us into silence, and then pours "down a blessing so that there is no room to receive it"; so that all that see it cry out, "It is the Lord!" . . . May it really be so with my dear people.[68]

Therefore, when the Holy Spirit blew through St. Peter's in William Chalmers Burns's preaching, M'Cheyne was neither surprised nor jealous.[69] He had written to Burns in March 1839: "You are given in answer to prayer, and these gifts are, I believe, always without exception blessed. I hope you may be a thousand times more blessed among them than I ever was."[70] The week after returning home, M'Cheyne told his parents that Burns is "certainly a remarkable preacher. I find him in private much more humble and singlehearted than I would have believed from the

---

66. *MAR*, 210.

67. *TPH*, 82.

68. *MAR*, 86. M'Cheyne's optimism for revival is seen as far back as 1837, when he announced that in his lifetime "we shall have a time of reviving yet." MACCH 3.1.6.

69. M'Cheyne reckoned Burns to a be an unusually powerful preacher. He wrote to Bonar: "There is a great deal of substance in what [Burns] preaches, and his manner is very powerful,—so much so, that he sometimes made me tremble." *MAR*, 118. For evidence of the rich friendship that developed between M'Cheyne and Burns, see MACCH 2.4.1–29.

70. *MAR*, 89. Burns' ministry was indeed especially blessed. By September of 1839, the *Dundee, Perth and Cupar Advertiser* reported that the "revival in St. Peter's parish . . . [brings] public worship almost every night of the week, and continued to a very late hour, and attended by overflowing audiences." Quoted in Robertson, *Awakening*, 163.

reports circulated . . . I have no desire but the salvation of my people by whatever instrument."[71]

While many in Scotland celebrated the Dundee awakening, it also generated strong opposition.[72] Leading ecclesiastical figures supported the work, while others sought additional information before celebrating. One such body was the Presbytery of Aberdeen. In December of 1840, it appointed a committee to inquire into the various revivals that had taken place. The committee sent M'Cheyne fifteen different questions related to the awakening at Dundee.[73] He answered each in turn, and his responses were published as *Evidences on Revival*. His comments provide the clearest overview of the Dundee revival.

M'Cheyne's response began with a history of the revival to demonstrate its veracity: "A very remarkable and glorious work of God, in the conversion of sinners and edifying of saints, has taken place in this parish and neighborhood."[74] He believed the work began with his coming in 1836, "but it was much more remarkable in the autumn of 1839, when I was abroad on a Mission of Inquiry to the Jews, and when my place was occupied by the Rev. W. C. Burns."[75] He said the revival began when "the word of God came with such power to the people here" that "for nearly four months it was found desirable to have public worship almost every night."[76] What distinguished the awakening from previous periods of fruitful preaching was the "remarkable solemnity" that struck St. Peter's. M'Cheyne recounted how the fear of God's justice fell on the masses, and led them to find "pardon and purity in the blood of the Lamb, and by the

71. Quoted in Yeaworth, "Robert Murray McCheyne," 297.

72. McLennan, *McCheyne's Dundee*, 138–41. Robert Candlish had hinted at the potential problems when he wrote to M'Cheyne on November 8, 1839, "We hear much that is cheering and encouraging of what is going on in Dundee. At the same time there are circumstances which lead me to suggest that it will be necessary for you, coming in at this particular stage of the work, to proceed with due caution and deliberation, and even in some particulars with a certain reserve and suspense of judgment, for a time. I say this to you frankly and confidentially . . . I cannot conceal from you that there are . . . some points of considerable delicacy, and I feel persuaded that both in regard to the wholesome progress of the work at Dundee, and the general cause of the revival of religion, and the judgment to be formed respecting it, much may depend upon you." MACCH 2.1.80. For a concise account of the opposition, see Yeaworth, "Robert Murray McCheyne," 315–16.

73. *MAR*, 496–97.

74. *MAR*, 497.

75. *MAR*, 497.

76. *MAR*, 497.

Spirit of our God."⁷⁷ Sinners traded open wickedness for sanctity, and so testified to the Holy Spirit's power that M'Cheyne reported, "The change they have undergone might be enough to convince an atheist that there is a God, or an infidel that there is a Saviour."⁷⁸

M'Cheyne proceeded to remark how individual conversions had a significant influence on the general population. Citizens took notice of the work and even partook of St. Peter's services. The Lord's Day was observed with greater reverence, private meetings for prayer were frequent and sweet, solemnity pervaded gathered worship, extraordinary tenderness sounded forth in the singing of psalms and hymns, and the Sabbath schools overflowed with children.

M'Cheyne's theology of revival allowed for physical responses to the Holy Spirit's work. He spoke of the people's feelings being unrestrained while the awakening was in its fullness:

> I have observed at such times awful and breathless stillness pervading the assembly; each hearer bent forward in the posture of rapt attention; serious men covered their faces to pray that the arrows of the King of Zion might be sent home with power to the hearts of sinners. Again, at such a time, I have heard a half-suppressed sigh rising from many a heart, and have seen many bathed in tears . . . I have also, in some instances, heard individuals cry aloud, as if they had been pierced through with a dart.⁷⁹

Several issues contributed to the success of the 1839 awakening. The first cause was theological: the sovereign work of God's Spirit. M'Cheyne believed no pastor could manufacture a revival, for the Holy Spirit moves when and how he likes:

> [The Holy Spirit] comes like the pouring rain; sometimes like the gentle dew. Still I would humbly state my conviction, that it is the duty of all who seek the salvation of souls, and especially the duty of ministers, to long and pray for such solemn times, when the arrows shall be sharp in the heart of the King's enemies and our slumbering congregations shall be made to cry out, "Men and brethren, what shall we do?"⁸⁰

---

77. *MAR*, 498.
78. *MAR*, 498.
79. *MAR*, 501.
80. *MAR*, 501.

The second and third causes were ministerial—revival comes through preaching Christ and praying for the Holy Spirit. "Nothing but preaching the pure gospel of the grace of God" brings about awakening.[81] Burns's preaching ignited the revival and M'Cheyne's preaching stoked the flames. David Yeaworth concurs that their preaching was the earthly fuel for the revival, for they "declared an old message with a new vibrancy, such as had not been heard for years."[82] M'Cheyne described this new vibrancy as seeking "the *immediate* conversion of the people" and believing that "under a living gospel ministry, success is more or less the rule, and want of success is the exception."[83]

M'Cheyne emphasized prayer even more than preaching in his pursuit of revival. Not only was prayer of pivotal importance to the start of the awakening, but it was clear evidence of revival. Prayer calls upon the Holy Spirit to descend in power and to continue to do so. M'Cheyne believed that anointed revival preachers are "peculiarly given to secret prayer; and they have also been accustomed to have much united prayer when together, and especially before and after engaging in public worship."[84] Congregations played a key role as well: "If we go on in faith and prayer . . . God will hear the cry of His people and . . . we shall yet see days such as never before shone upon the Church of Scotland."[85]

EVANGELISM AND CHURCH EXTENSION

The fourth emphasis in M'Cheyne's evangelism came in the area of church extension. "The Church Extension scheme," Bonar writes, "had in view as its genuine, sincere endeavour, to bring to overgrown parishes the advantage of a faithful minister, placed over such a number of souls as

---

81. *MAR*, 503.

82. Yeaworth, "Robert Murray McCheyne," 320.

83. *MAR*, 503.

84. *MAR*, 503. Andrew Bonar noted of Burns' passion for prayer: "The lesson God is teaching me is this, that William Burns is used as the instrument where others have been labouring in vain, because he is much in prayer, beyond all of us. It is not the peculiar words he uses that God blesses." Bonar, *Diary and Letters*, 85. McLennan notes how Burns attributed the St. Peter's revival "in large part to the prayers of [M'Cheyne], who had been praying for them even on his sickbed in Smyrna when revival came." McLennan, *McCheyne's Dundee*, 86.

85. *TPH*, 166.

he could really visit."[86] M'Cheyne's concern for church extension stretched back as far as May 1833, as is evident from a diary entry in which he expressed concern over a motion regarding chapels of ease.[87] Bonar argues that M'Cheyne's experience at Larbert and Dunipace catalyzed his involvement in church extension as he understood, for the first time, how the plan was "a truly noble and Christian effort for bringing the glad tidings to the doors of a population who must otherwise remain neglected."[88]

M'Cheyne participated in official posts for establishing new churches. In 1837, he became the secretary of the Committee for Church Extension in Forfarshire, a committee chaired by John Roxburgh.[89] His passion for the work is seen in a letter to Roxburgh:

> Every day I live, I feel more and more persuaded that [church extension] is the cause of God and of his kingdom in Scotland in our day. Many a time, when I thought myself a dying man, the souls of the perishing thousands in my own parish, who never enter any house of God, have lain heavy on my heart. Many a time have I prayed that the eyes of our enemies might be opened, and that God would open the hearts of our rulers, to feel that their highest duty and greatest glory is to support the ministers of Christ, and to send these to every perishing soul in Scotland.[90]

---

86. *MAR*, 69. M'Cheyne spoke of the problem in his own parish in a sermon on February 25, 1838: "The flocks are too large to be cared for by the shepherd. My own flock is just four times the size a flock used to be in the days of our fathers, so that I am called upon to do the work of four ministers, and am left like Issachar, couching down between two burdens." *TPH*, 89. In May 7, 1840, he preached, "In our town, I suppose there are the least 15,000 still living in practical heathenism without having a pastor to look after them. I bless God that there are two new churches nearly ready to be opened and trust all God's children will pray that we may get pastors after God's own heart. Still, what are these among so many? I do wonder that Christians who have money can live at ease and see these multitudes going down. It is a crying sin." *TPP*, 48.

87. *MAR*, 20.

88. *MAR*, 35.

89. Cameron, *Memorials of John Roxburgh*, 12–14.

90. Quoted in *MAR*, 69–70. The letter alludes to the controversy between moderates and evangelicals in the 1830s. Moderates saw the evangelicals' zeal for church planting to be a scheme to saturate the presbyteries with like-minded ministers. For commentary on M'Cheyne's involvement in these debates over church planting, see Yeaworth, "Robert Murray McCheyne," 332–34.

M'Cheyne also served as secretary of the Dundee Association for Church Extension.[91] His service led to the erection of nearly two hundred churches and the collection of more than 300,000 pounds over seven years.[92] His labors were so successful that Thomas Brown placed him alongside Thomas Chalmers as the champion for church extension.[93] David Robertson rightly says, "[M'Cheyne's] view of church planting was that God would send the showers and the churches were the cisterns to collect the rain."[94] M'Cheyne wrote a short poem that summarizes his prayer for the extension scheme:

> Give me a man of God the truth to preach,
> A house of prayer within convenient reach,
> Seat-rents the poorest of the poor can pay,
> A spot so small one pastor can survey,
> Give these—and give the Spirit's genial shower,
> Scotland shall be a garden all in flower![95]

---

91. M'Cheyne's told St. Peter's: "We are building in this town new churches, and we want ministers, and we are apt to fear that we may not succeed; but let us trust Christ, let us go forward in power, let us go forward in simple faith, looking unto Jesus." SC, 42–43.

92. Yeaworth, "Robert Murray McCheyne," 335. Such a sum would be roughly equivalent to £28 million or $39 million in 2017.

93. Brown, *Annals of Disruption*, 1:45. For Chalmers's view on Church Extension, see Chalmers, *On Church Extension*. M'Cheyne's work in "a District extending from Seaton's Close" is mentioned on p. 149.

94. Robertson, *Awakening*, 185. Robertson is adapting Bonar's words from the *Memoir*, where Bonar writes, "These new churches were to be like cisterns—ready to catch the shower when it should fall, just as his own did in the day of the Lord's power." MAR, 70. M'Cheyne's passion is also seen in the following words: "One-hundred-and-eight new churches have been established—ministers have been appointed, congregations have been formed. Of those in Glasgow some of them are overflowing—yet the old churches are better filled than ever. In my case every seat was taken before there was a minister—I preach to 600 or 700 who had no seat in any house of worship . . . In most of these a small parish is annexed—elders appointed—every family is visited as are the sick and dying—the ministers can go from house to house and are recognised by each man, woman and child—men of God who are now really labouring. In most of these there is a school—with a godly teacher going hand in hand with the minister, in my own case 300 children." Quoted in Robertson, *Awakening*, 185.

95. MAR, 70. Yeaworth says M'Cheyne understood the prohibition that came with seat renting, or "seat letting," and so "advocated their complete removal, or at least their reduction" in price. Yeaworth, "Robert Murray McCheyne," 147. See also, McLennan, *McCheyne's Dundee*, 29–30.

M'Cheyne's participation in the mission of inquiry further reveals his passion for church extension. The mission's stated purpose was "to discover what means had previously been employed for [the Jewish people's] spiritual good, and the success of such enterprises; and to seek possible locations for mission stations."[96] The Church intended for the mission stations to function as ecclesiastical outposts in the evangelization of the Jews.

CONCLUSION

David Beaty writes, "For M'Cheyne and the church he served, evangelism was a priority. This focus did not come about because evangelism was a strategy for church growth; instead, it was a result of M'Cheyne's communion with God. Time spent with God resulted in his having more of the Lord's compassion for those without Jesus."[97] While M'Cheyne's communion with God through the ordinary means of grace indeed fueled his evangelism, a more foundational impulse was at work—love for Christ. The connection between M'Cheyne's evangelism and spirituality is clear: souls that love Christ speak of Christ.

M'Cheyne began his eighth pastoral letter by recounting a testimony he had heard from an English minister, who told of missionaries serving amidst great poverty and disease in Africa. M'Cheyne asked, "Who will forsake father and mother, houses and land, to carry the message of a Saviour to these poor lepers?"[98] He told of the Moravian missionaries "impelled by a divine love for souls" who chose such a field for harvest. He saw in these missionaries a paradigm for biblical evangelism: "Ah! my dear friends, may we . . . [be like] these men in vehement, heart-consuming love to Jesus and the souls of men."[99] Zealous evangelism was, for M'Cheyne, a quintessential proof of one's love for Christ and neighbor. He thus believed saving souls was the "chief business" of ordinary

---

96. Yeaworth, "Robert Murray McCheyne," 263. For M'Cheyne's presentation to the 1840 General Assembly, see Scott, *The Evangelist*, 8:84–87. For a detailed overview of the trip and subsequent report, see Huie, *History of the Jews*, 337–62.

97. Beaty, *An All-Surpassing Fellowship*, 142–43.

98. *MAR*, 200.

99. *MAR*, 200.

Christians.[100] When the heart burns with love for Christ, we inevitably share the good news of Christ.

---

100. *TPP*, 295. M'Cheyne declared, "Your *chief business* in this world ought to be to save the souls of others" (emphasis original).

9

Delighting in Christ
M'Cheyne's Sabbatarianism

GOD LOVES HIS PEOPLE; they are the "apple of His eye" (Deut 32:10; Ps 17:8). He thus rises to protect them when they are threatened (Zech 2:8). As those made in his image, God's children likewise fight for their Father's honor when he is wronged. Throughout church history passion pours from pens and pulpits to defend God's glory. A simple maxim holds true: to know what people treasure, identify what they guard most earnestly. Such is the case with M'Cheyne.

M'Cheyne's personal piety tends to overshadow his activity for the broader church. David Yeaworth reminds us that "although Robert McCheyne is primarily known for his personal religious devotion and his work in evangelism and revival, he was also keenly aware of and interested in the controversial and ecclesiastical affairs of the church."[1] David Robertson agrees, "McCheyne is sometimes portrayed as a pietist who had little interest in church questions, whereas the reality is that he was a real enthusiast for the evangelical party and continued to be active in church courts throughout his ministry."[2] Both biographers offer their statements with a particular event in view—the Sabbath Railway Controversy.

In the 1840s, the major rail companies in Scotland planned for and then began to open their tracks on Sundays. Was this permissible on the

1. Yeaworth, "Robert Murray McCheyne," 322.
2. Robertson, *Awakening*, 178.

Sabbath? Would riding the rails break the fourth commandment? The ensuing debate occupied Scottish evangelicals for over two decades. It was in the contest's early days that M'Cheyne's love for Christ caused him to engage in public polemics. His cultural and ecclesiastical labor for "the entire sanctification of the Lord's day"[3] earned him monikers such as the "wild man from Dundee,"[4] "fanatic" and "zealot,"[5] and the man full of "invective."[6] While these depictions might seem to disprove the more common portrayals of M'Cheyne as "sweet" and "saintly," they serve to demonstrate the depth of his devotion.

This chapter shows how M'Cheyne's passion for the Sabbath expressed his love for Christ. He believed Sunday belonged to Christ; it was *the Lord's Day*. He proclaimed, "The Sabbath is Christ's trysting time with his church. If you love him, you will count every moment of it precious. You will rise early and sit up late, to have a long day with Christ."[7] He further understood Sabbath-keeping to play an integral part in pastoral piety: "Can you name one godly minister, of any denomination in all Scotland, who does not hold the duty of the entire sanctification of the Lord's day?"[8] For M'Cheyne, sanctifying the Lord's Day was the delightful response of the soul in love with Christ.[9]

This chapter considers M'Cheyne's view of the Sabbath and Sabbath-keeping by (1) reviewing his role in the Sabbath Railway Controversy; (2) surveying his defense of Sabbatarianism; (3) analyzing his practice

---

3. *TPP*, 32.

4. Bonar, *Reminiscences*, 9. The minister said, "[Andrew Bonar] is bad enough, but [M'Cheyne] is ten times waur!" Bonar, *Reminiscences*, 9.

5. Yeaworth, "Robert Murray M'Cheyne," 327.

6. Yeaworth, "Robert Murray M'Cheyne," 325.

7. *TPP*, 330.

8. *MAR*, 553.

9. *MAR* includes one hundred sixty-five entries from M'Cheyne's diary. Two diary entries do not include the day of record. Of the one hundred sixty-three remaining, eighteen were written on a Monday, nineteen on a Tuesday, seventeen on a Wednesday, twenty-one on a Thursday, eleven on a Friday, sixteen on a Saturday, and sixty on a Sunday. M'Cheyne's spirituality depends, to a great extent, on how he spent his Sabbaths—in public and in private. For example, one oft-quoted statement from M'Cheyne's diary is: "Rose early to seek God, and found Him whom my soul loveth. Who would not rise early to meet such company?" *MAR*, 21. Many have used the quote to illustrate M'Cheyne's zeal to redeeming every moment for Christ. Such sentiment is true in the most basic form, but in reality it misses how M'Cheyne ordered his Sabbath devotions in a special manner. He rose earlier than usual on the Lord's Day and spent extra hours in his devotional practices.

of Sabbath-keeping; and (4) examining how he exhorted the St. Peter's congregation to increased Sabbath observance.

THE SABBATH RAILWAY CONTROVERSY

In 1839, Sir Andrew Agnew of Locknaw became the first chairman of the recently-formed "Scottish Society for Promoting the Due Observance of the Lord's Day." The society was founded to fight against planned expansion of rail traffic to Sunday. Agnew used his first speech as chairman to thunder against "the threatened invasion of Sabbath-breaking customs from England by the railways."[10] Sunday trains had been running for some time in England, but the strategy had not made its way north. C. J. A. Robertson says, "Unlike England, Scotland was accustomed to almost total cessation of public transport on Sundays, and the proposal of the [Edinburgh & Glasgow] company to institute two Sunday trains in each direction from the opening of the line in 1842 was indeed 'a great and startling *innovation*.'"[11] Throughout 1841, the company postponed any official decision on opening the rails on Sunday as an onslaught of literature from kirk sessions and Sabbatarian partisans occupied their attention. Then, on November 16, 1841, the company announced they would lay the matter before shareholders at the next meeting in February 1842.

It was in this milieu that M'Cheyne entered the debate.[12] He convened the "Sabbath Observance Committee" in his presbytery.[13] In February 1841, the presbytery commissioned him to write a letter to the Dundee and Arbroath rail company concerning mail delivery by rail on Sundays. He so strongly worded the letter that Yeaworth says, "It required modification by other ministers before being posted."[14] Just one month

---

10. T. McCrie, quoted in Robertson, "Early Scottish Railways," 145. Robertson's article provides the most concise history of the controversy. Other related sources include, Wigley, *Rise and Fall*; Murray, "The Sabbath Question," 319–30; Brooke, "The Opposition," 95–109; Harrison, "Sunday Trading Riots," 219–45.

11. Robertson, "Early Scottish Railways," 153 (emphasis original). James Gilfillan says, "From the Reformation to the present time (1862), the Scottish Church has had but one doctrine on the subject; and that for a long period general acclaim accorded to the nation a distinction above all others for a sacred regard to the Lord's Day." Gilfillan, *Sabbath*, 157.

12. Bonar notes, "It was during this year (1841) that the Sabbath question began to interest him so much." *MAR*, 140.

13. Yeaworth, "Robert Murray McCheyne," 324.

14. Yeaworth, "Robert Murray McCheyne," 324.

later, M'Cheyne penned an overture, later approved by the presbytery and submitted to the General Assembly, calling for the excommunication of Sabbath breakers.[15]

M'Cheyne's first public offensive against what he saw as "Sabbath desecration" came on December 1, 1841. He posted a letter to Alexander M'Neill, director of the Edinburgh & Glasgow company. The conservative periodical, *The Witness*, published M'Cheyne's notice on December 11. M'Cheyne opened by saying, "I take leave to express in this manner the deep feelings of righteous indignation."[16] The substance of his argument is a plea for forthrightness: "Ah! sir, speak out your mind. Tell what it is that lies at the bottom of your enmity to the entire preservation of the Lord's day."[17] M'Cheyne did not want to judge the director's motive(s); M'Neill's ambiguity merely vexed him. M'Neill's initial statement acknowledged the need to submit to God's law,[18] but M'Cheyne could not understand how the director reconciled this sentiment with his actions. He wrote, "I do not know whether the motion has come entirely from your own mind, or whether several have agreed with you in it; but I here freely state my convictions, formed upon the calm and deliberate study of the motion, and without the slightest desire to use a harsh or improper term, that THE MOTION IS BLASPHEMOUS."[19] M'Cheyne then proceeded to offer a relatively standard defense of Sabbath-observance. By the end of the letter, he set aside any "concerns" about judging M'Neill's motives, declaring, "You prove, even to the blind world, that you are not journeying toward the Sabbath above, where the Sabbath-breaker cannot

---

15. *Dundee Advertiser*, April 8, 1842.

16. *MAR*, 555.

17. *MAR*, 555.

18. The proposed motion stated, "Whereas it is the duty of the directors of the company to give implicit obedience to the law of God . . . this meeting resolves that it is not inconsistent with the duty of the directors as aforesaid, and they are hereby enjoined to provide trains to be run from the cities of Edinburgh and Glasgow respectively, in the morning and in the evening of Sunday."

19. *MAR*, 556 (capitalization original). M'Cheyne introduced his sermon as follows: "The Sabbath is the Lord's Day . . . As a servant of God in this dark and cloudy day, I feel constrained to lift up my voice on behalf of the entire sanctification of the Lord's Day. The daring attack that is now made by some of the Directors of the Edinburgh and Glasgow Railway on the Law of God and the peace of our Scottish Sabbath, the blasphemous motion which they mean to propose to the Shareholders in February next, and the wicked pamphlets which are now being circulated in thousands, full of all manner of lies and impieties, call loudly for the calm, deliberate testimony of faithful Ministers and private Christians on behalf of God's holy day." *TPP*, 32.

come."[20] M'Cheyne concluded with a postscript appealing to the law of 1690 that secured strict observance of the Sabbath.[21]

M'Cheyne's public opposition to the rail companies only increased as December 1841 advanced. He preached several sermons calling for Sabbath-keeping. On December 18, 1841, *The Witness* published his tract, *I Love the Lord's Day*.[22] The tract contains much of his natural winsomeness, but, as in the case of his letter to M'Neill, it is ultimately militant. His verdict on Sabbath-breakers is resolute: they are infidels, scoffers, men of unholy lives, enemies of all righteousness, moral suicides, sinners against light, traitors to their country, robbers, and murderers.[23] His sermon, "The Stone the Builders Refused," on which *I Love the Lord's Day* was based, concluded with a broadside: "Dear brethren, pray that their hearts may be turned or else if that may not be, that the Railway may be swept off the face of the earth."[24]

Two days before the shareholders voted in February 1842, M'Cheyne published a letter in *The Witness* calling for a national day of prayer. He longed for a united prayer "THAT THE DESIGNS OF THE RAILWAY

---

20. *MAR*, 557.

21. For background on the 1690 Act, see Lyall, *Church and State*, 205. M'Cheyne stood in the long line of presbyterian ministers who viewed Scotland as a covenanted country. As Yeaworth states, "McCheyne viewed this impending calamity in a way not unlike the Covenanters. It was largely due to the sin of the nation and the Church that this was brought upon them." Yeaworth, "Robert Murray McCheyne," 327. If Israel was God's chosen nation, Scotland was closest to them: "Scotland is the likest of all lands to ancient Israel," *MAR*, 196. Again, "In many respects, Scotland may be called God's second Israel. No other land has its Sabbath as Scotland has." *MAR*, 449. Therefore, disregarding the fourth commandment invited God's judgment on the nation. In early December 1841, M'Cheyne announced to his congregation: "If the day shall ever come in Scotland when our railways shall be opened on the Sabbath, it will be one of the finishing mark that the people of this land are not the people of God." *SOH*, 33.

22. Yeaworth explains, "'I Love the Lord's Day' ... was circulated widely throughout Britain, and together with the letter to [M'Neill] was translated into Dutch." Yeaworth, "Robert Murray M'Cheyne," 326. The tract was adapted from a sermon M'Cheyne preached at least twice, under two different titles: "The Stone the Builders Refused," in *TPP*, 27–32 (date unknown); "The Sabbath is the Lord's Day" (December 18, 1841) in *TPP*, 32–39. *The Witness* commended the tract as "so excellent, and on so vital a subject, [that it] is deserving of universal circulation." *The Witness*, March 30, 1842.

23. *MAR*, 553. Robertson sees M'Cheyne's reaction as "predictable" and apparently not worth much attention. See also, Robertson, "Early Scottish Railways," 153. *The Witness* said M'Cheyne's writings for Sabbath sanctification displayed "that *engagingness*, which so remarkably characterizes both Mr. McCheyne's writing and his speaking." Quoted in Yeaworth, "Robert Murray McCheyne," 183.

24. *TPP*, 31. This appeal was not included in "I Love the Lord's Day."

SABBATH-BREAKERS MAY BE ENTIRELY DEFEATED."²⁵ Yeaworth comments, "Believers were urged to rise two hours earlier to fast and confess personal, family, and national sin; family worship was to center around this theme; ministers were asked to intercede for the conversion of the Sabbath-breakers."²⁶ M'Cheyne's efforts (and prayers) proved unsuccessful as the railways soon opened for Sunday service. In response, the Church leaders redoubled their efforts. For three months, William Chalmers Burns preached every Lord's Day at the Haymarket Station, heralding the Lord of the Sabbath to all passengers.²⁷ By 1845, Sunday travel was stopped, and it did not renew until 1865.²⁸

M'Cheyne's public interactions during the Sabbath Railway Controversy were vigorous. Did his convictions veer into that treacherous abyss called "legalism"? L. J. Van Valen answers in the negative: "Pharisaical piety was strange to him; his scrupulous conduct of life emerged from a fervent love for God and His commands."²⁹

DEFENSE OF SABBATH-KEEPING

M'Cheyne was no doctrinal innovator; he subscribed to the theology of the Westminster Standards with head, heart, and hand. Yeaworth notes, "McCheyne's attitude toward the Sabbath may be regarded as typical of the Evangelical position. He considered the validity of the fourth commandment to be beyond question; it was to be obeyed by Christians and non-Christians alike."³⁰

---

25. M'Cheyne, "To the Children of God of Every Name in Scotland," in *The Witness*, February 19, 1842 (capitalization original).

26. Yeaworth, "Robert Murray McCheyne," 327.

27. Michael McMullen explains, "Whilst Burns was still at St. Luke's, the first Sabbath train to run between Haymarket Station in Edinburgh and Glasgow was planned to take place, and this stirred Burns to begin a major protest against what he saw as a major and unnecessary desecration of the Lord's Day. For the next three months, Burns' usual Sabbath duties consisted of four services: two he held at the railway station and two at St. Luke's. He considered the railway development to be so grave that he resolved to hold prayer meetings for this issue, every Monday, Wednesday, and Friday at noon." McMullen, *God's Polished Arrow*, 74.

28. For a history of this twenty-year period, see Robertson, "Early Scottish Railways," 154–67.

29. Valen, *Constrained by His Love*, 379.

30. Yeaworth, "Robert Murray M'Cheyne," 322. M'Cheyne's Sabbatarian convictions were common among evangelical presbyterians at the time, and stood squarely

DELIGHTING IN CHRIST   195

The following survey of M'Cheyne's teaching on the Sabbath concentrates on his tract, *I Love the Lord's Day*, along with six sermons preached on the topic.[31] Four of these sermons were preached in the months of November and December of 1841 when the Sabbath controversy was near its zenith.[32] Collectively, the expositions present M'Cheyne's biblical and theological views as forged in the furnace of debate. His teaching consistently emphasized six aspects of the Lord's Day.

First, the Lord's Day follows the creator's pattern. M'Cheyne said God's resting on the seventh day (Gen 2:2-3) "was not for His own sake."[33] He is the almighty creator who "fainteth not, neither is weary" (Isa 40:28). He rested for our sakes "that He might set an example to man."[34] We also learn of the importance of this day from Christ: "Just as God rested on the seventh day from all His works, wherefore God blessed the Sabbath day, and hallowed it; so the Lord Jesus rested on this day

---

in the Westminster tradition. For the Westminster Standards teaching on the Sabbath, see *Westminster Confession of Faith* 21.7-8; *Westminster Larger Catechism* 115-121; *Westminster Shorter Catechism* 57-62 in *The Westminster Standards*. For a representative Puritan work defending Sabbatarianism, see Owen, *A Sacred Day of Rest*, 2:263-460. For modern interactions with Puritan Sabbatarianism, see Dennison, *Market Day of Soul*; Parker, *English Sabbath*; Primus, *Holy Time*; Solberg, *Redeem the Time*; McGraw, "Principles of Sabbath-Keeping," 316-27; Hinson, "Redemption of Time," 11-15; Vasholz, "Amusements on Sabbath," 24-28; Primus, "Calvin and Puritan Sabbath," 40-75. For contemporary treatments of the Lord's Day congruent with M'Cheyne's approach and convictions, see Campbell, *On the First Day*; Chantry, *Call the Sabbath*; McGraw, *Day of Worship*; Pipa, *Lord's Day*; Clark, *Recovering Reformed Confession*, 295-305.

31. The six sermons are (1) "The Rest that Remains," in *SOH*, 28-34; (2) "The Stone the Builders Refused," in *TPP*, 27-32; (3) "The Sabbath is the Lord's Day," in *TPP*, 32-39; (4) "Christians Should Be Like Christ," in *TPP*, 326-32; (5) "Delighting in the Sabbath," in *OTS*, 89-97; (6) "The Sabbath Made for Man," in *NTS*, 35-41. For an overview of the Sabbath literature published in Scotland, see Gilfillan, *The Sabbath*, 157-72. Gilfillan says Thomas Chalmers preached a sermon in 1823 entitled, "On the Christian Sabbath," of which the late Bishop of Calcutta said, "It is in the most powerful and awakening manner of its author, and of itself settles the question." Gilfillan, *The Sabbath*, 166. Gilfillan highlights other noteworthy works such as: Drummond, *Jewish Sabbath*; Fairbairn, *Typology of Scripture*; Haldane, *Sanctification*; Innes, *Christian Sabbath Vindicated*. Robert Cox, *Literature of the Sabbath*.

32. "The Rest that Remains" was preached in late November 1841. "The Sabbath is the Lord's Day" was preached on December 18, 1841. "Christians Should be Like Christ" and "The Sabbath was Made for Man" were both preached on December 26, 1841 (one in the morning service and the other in the afternoon service).

33. *NTS*, 37.

34. *NTS*, 37.

from all His agony, and pain, and humiliation."[35] It is our responsibility, therefore, to reflect the divine example by keeping it holy.

Second, the Lord's Day is commanded. M'Cheyne's exposition of Mark 2:27[36] eventually brought him to the fourth commandment. "When God took Israel to be a peculiar people to Himself," M'Cheyne explained, "He revived, in a very clear and terrible manner, the holy law which was written on man's heart in the day of his creation."[37] By twice writing the Ten Commandments with his own finger on the stone tablets, God demonstrated that they are "perpetual."[38] M'Cheyne asserted, "All the other nine commandments are binding upon all men, so that there cannot be the shadow of a doubt that the fourth commandment is also binding upon all."[39]

Third, the Lord's Day is typological. M'Cheyne argues that the Christian Sabbath is "a relic of Paradise and type of Heaven."[40] Simply put, "a well-spent Sabbath . . . [is] a day of heaven upon earth."[41] He connected the present Sabbath with the Sabbath rest to come:

> When a believer lays aside his pen or loom, brushes aside his worldly cares, leaving them behind him with his week-day clothes, and comes up to the house of God, it is like the morning of the resurrection, the day when we shall come out of great tribulation into the presence of God and the Lamb. When he sits under the preached word, and hears the voice of the shepherd leading and feeding his soul, it reminds him of the day when the Lamb that is in the midst of the throne shall feed him and lead him to living fountains of waters. When he joins in the psalm of praise, it reminds him of the day when his hands shall strike the harp of God. When He retires, and meets with God in secret in his closet, or, like Isaac, in some favourite spot near his dwelling, it reminds him of the day when "he shall be a pillar in the house of our God, and go no more out" (Rev 3:12).

---

35. *MAR*, 556.

36. "And he said unto them, 'The sabbath was made for man, and not man for the Sabbath.'"

37. *NTS*, 38.

38. *NTS*, 38.

39. *NTS*, 38.

40. *NTS*, 596.

41. *MAR*, 550. See also, *SOH*, 31.

Fourth, the Lord's Day is evangelistic. M'Cheyne taught that God is especially pleased to exercise his power on the Lord's Day for the conversion of sinners. He claimed, "All God's faithful ministers in every land can bear witness that sinners are converted most frequently on the Lord's day—that Jesus comes in and shows Himself through the lattice of ordinances oftenest on His own day."[42] For M'Cheyne, the point is a logical one. Because the church gathers on Sundays for preaching, prayer, fellowship, and the sacraments, she should believe an extraordinary power will be present. It is through these means that God breathes life into dead bones. M'Cheyne maintained, "There is nothing superstitious in believing that we may expect more visits of Christ and of the Spirit on the Lord's Day than on other days."[43] Furthermore, Christ's visitation on the Sabbath tends to bring salvation because "it is the day in which God is peculiarly seeking your salvation."[44] In his tract, *Reasons Why Children Should Fly to Christ*, he declared, "The Sabbath is the great day for gathering in souls—it is Christ's market-day. It is the great harvest-day of souls."[45]

Because God intends to use the Sabbath for conversion, it is the day of greatest spiritual warfare. M'Cheyne explained, "Surely it is the devil that makes you hate the very season when Christ is seeking you."[46] A day of rest does not imply a respite from striving against Satan. True Sabbath-keeping is a great assault the church makes on the gates of hell, as she submits to Christ and thrives under his blessing.

Fifth, the Lord's Day is blessed. When God set apart the Sabbath in paradise, He made it a day of blessing (Gen 2:3). M'Cheyne believed that Christ followed the same pattern: "When the Lord Jesus rose from the

---

42. *MAR*, 551.

43. *TPP*, 331. M'Cheyne made a similar point in "Delighting in the Sabbath," teaching that the Sabbath "is the great meeting-day of the soul with God. Oh! meet with God in secret prayer, in the family, in the house of prayer." *OTS*, 95.

44. *TPP*, 332. In another sermon, M'Cheyne proclaimed, "The Sabbath is the great day for seeking souls and finding them. I believe most people have been found by God upon the Sabbath day. If, then, you neglect this holy time and spend it with worldly people, this shows you are neglecting the great salvation." *SOH*, 8.

45. *MAR*, 540.

46. *TPP*, 332. Speaking to "awakened persons" (those under conviction, but who have not fully closed with Christ), M'Cheyne said something similar: "It is common for Satan to beguile awakened persons back to their sins and he generally tries to do it on the Sabbath." *TPP*, 332. He further explained that the spiritual struggle over the Sabbath hearkens back to the Garden of Eden: "Learn, then, first, not to wonder at the opposition made to the Sabbath day. It is an old quarrel between the seed of the serpent and the seed of the woman." *NTS*, 41.

dead on the first day of the week before dawn, He revealed Himself the same day to two disciples going to Emmaus, and made their hearts burn within them" (Luke 24:13).[47] M'Cheyne pointed to Christ's appearances on the Lord's Day as proof (John 20:19; 20:26). On these occasions, Christ blessed the disciples with peace. Additionally, it was the Lord's Day when he poured out the Holy Spirit at Pentecost (Acts 2:1; Lev 23:15–16). "That beginning of all spiritual blessings," declared M'Cheyne, "that first revival of the Christian Church, was on the Lord's Day."[48] He also appealed to John's example. He was blessed with the Holy Spirit when he was taken up to heaven on the Lord's Day (Rev 1:10). M'Cheyne concluded, "So that in all ages, from the beginning of the world, and in every place where there is a believer, the Sabbath has been a day of double blessing. It is so still."[49]

Sixth, the Lord's Day is Christian. The Shorter Catechism asks, "Which day of the seven hath God appointed to be the weekly Sabbath?" The catechism answers, "From the beginning of the world to the resurrection of Christ, God appointed the seventh day of the week to be the weekly Sabbath; and the first day of the week ever since, to continue to the end of the world, which is the Christian Sabbath."[50] M'Cheyne affirmed that Sunday is the Christian Sabbath. His position was so widely accepted that he gave little attention to proving that the Sabbath had been changed from Saturday to Sunday. He assumed the change, as is evident in his exposition of Acts 20:6–7.[51] He proclaimed, "Here Paul waited over the Jewish Sabbath and preached and broke bread on the Lord's Day. Upon the same day did Paul command religious contributions to be made (1 Cor 15:1–2)."[52] To bolster his point, M'Cheyne did something unusual for him—he appealed to a secondary source: "From a Christian writer who lived fifty years after John, we learn that 'all the Christians that live either in the town or country meet together at the same place upon the

---

47. *MAR*, 550.

48. *MAR*, 550. M'Cheyne made the same points, in truncated fashion, in his sermon, "Christians Should Be Like Christ." *TPP*, 329.

49. *MAR*, 551.

50. *WSC*, 59.

51. "And we sailed away from Philippi after the days of unleavened bread, and came unto them to Troas in five days; where we abode seven days. And upon the first day of the week, when the disciples came together to break bread, Paul preached unto them, ready to depart on the morrow; and continued his speech until midnight."

52. *TPP*, 329.

day called Sunday, where the writings of the prophets and apostles are read."[53]

Objections Considered

M'Cheyne was aware of those that opposed his Sabbatarianism. Wanting to convince them of the importance of this day, he addressed several common objections.

Objection 1: Sabbath observance belongs to the Old Covenant order of Judaism. Paul writes, "Let no man therefore judge you in meat, or in drink, or in respect of an holy day, or of the new moon or of the Sabbath days, which are a shadow of the things to come, but the body is of Christ" (Col 2:16–17). M'Cheyne responded by pointing to the Sabbath rest in Eden: "The enemies of the Sabbath generally say that the Sabbath was a Jewish ceremony. But they altogether forget that the first Sabbath dawned on a sinless world. Even in paradise man needed a Sabbath."[54] Therefore, a believer needed to see the Sabbath as a creation ordinance that preceded the Mosaic economy.

Objection 2: "What about Matthew 5:17? Does not Jesus 'fulfill' the law?" M'Cheyne replied, "Christ says expressly, 'I am not come to destroy, but to fulfill' (Matt v. 17). And therefore He did not come to destroy the fourth commandment. In the new covenant, God says, 'I will put my law in their inward parts, and write in their hearts (Jer. xxxi. 33). In the old covenant, He wrote the law upon stones. The change is in the tablet, not in the law."[55] The law once externalized on stone tablets is now internalized as the Holy Spirit writes it on every redeemed heart. Thus, M'Cheyne reasoned that the fourth commandment is still binding in the new covenant age.

Objection 3: Every day should be a Sabbath day. The objectors asked, "Why single out Sunday as a special day of rest?" M'Cheyne cared little for this complaint: "This is a vain and unscriptural statement. It is not every day that Christ comes over the mountains, leaping on the mountains and skipping on the hills. True, Christ is always on His throne, and we

---

53. *TPP*, 329. The quote is from Justin Martyr's *Apology for the Christians*. See also, Macfarlan, *A Treatise*, 69. For additional commentary, see "The Lord's Day," in Kitto et al., *Journal of Sacred Literature*, 274.

54. *NTS*, 37.

55. *NTS*, 38.

may seek Him and find Him every day and hour, but there are peculiar days when He graciously manifests himself. There are market days and trysting days."[56]

Objection 4: What evidence have you that the day was changed from the seventh to the first day of the week? M'Cheyne admitted that "we have no express command to this purpose."[57] However, standing in the Westminster tradition, he reasoned that the change from Saturday to Sunday was a "good and necessary consequence" of Scripture's teaching.[58] Surprisingly, he did not marshal an army of Scripture texts, but proclaimed, "Christ revealed the truth to the disciples only as they were able to bear it . . . And so out of tenderness for the Jews who clung very much as they do still to their old Sabbath with all its ceremonies, Christ did not reveal to them till John wrote the Revelation, that it was to be changed for the Lord's Day. Still He gave many proofs all along that it was to be changed."[59]

M'Cheyne sought to be biblical in defending his position. He took God's Word simply and completely. Little in his defense-of-Sabbath-observance was novel. He reflected the standard puritan and presbyterian position.

PERSONAL DEVOTION TO SABBATH-KEEPING

M'Cheyne believed that joy in the Sabbath was a mark of a renewed heart. He defined his unconverted state as that of a Sabbath-breaker: "I know that I was very happy when I was unforgiven. I know that I had a great pleasure in many sins—in Sabbath-breaking for instance." M'Cheyne had no taste for "the unreal beauties of the Sabbath day."[60] However, when he came to Christ in faith, the glories of Christ's day became real.[61] Andrew

---

56. *SOH*, 31.

57. *TPP*, 327.

58. *WCF*, 1.6 states, "The whole counsel of God concerning all things necessary for his own glory, man's salvation, faith and life, is either expressly set down in Scripture, or *by good and necessary consequence* may be deduced from Scripture" (emphasis added).

59. *TPP*, 327.

60. Quoted in Yeaworth, "Robert Murray McCheyne," 325.

61. A regular lament from M'Cheyne while on the "Mission of Inquiry" to Palestine was how often he observed "Sabbath desecration." While traveling through Paris, he wrote, "Alas! poor Paris knows no Sabbath, all the shops are open, and all

Bonar summarizes his friend's experience as follows: "Mr. M'Cheyne's own conduct was in full accordance with his principles in regard to strict yet cheerful Sabbath observance. Considering it the summit of human privilege to be admitted to fellowship with God, his principle was, that the Lord's Day was to be spent wholly in the enjoyment of that sweetest privilege."[62]

M'Cheyne purposed to lie down early Saturday evening so that he could rise especially early on the Lord's Day. Saturday diary entries reveal how he prepared for the Sabbath. For example, on June 11, 1836, he recorded, "To-day sought to prepare my heart for the coming Sabbath. After the example of Boston, whose life I have been reading, examined my heart with prayer and fasting."[63] He understood Saturday to be "an awkward day for ministers," and so he aimed diligently to set his thoughts in order for the Sabbath.[64] One means of preparation was visiting those church members who were on their deathbed. He did this "with the view of being thus stirred up to a more direct application of the truth to his flock on the morrow, as dying men on the edge of eternity."[65]

After waking on Sunday, M'Cheyne spent extended time—a few hours ideally—in private prayer,[66] and then he read God's Word. He also examined his notes from the previous week's devotional readings, giving attention to those verses marked for meditation.[67] He refused to edit his sermons for the day. Bonar remarks, "[M'Cheyne] never laboured at his

---

the inhabitants are on the wing in search of pleasures—pleasures that perish in the using. I thought of Babylon and of Sodom as I passed through the crowd. I cannot tell how I longed for the peace of a Scottish Sabbath." *MAR*, 212. Or, in another place, Bonar remarks, "I well remember the indignation that fired his countenance, when our Arab attendants insisted on traveling forward on the Sabbath-day, rather than continue sitting under a few palm-trees, breathing a sultry, furnace-like atmosphere, with nothing more than just such supply of food sufficed. He could not bear the thought of being deprived of the Sabbath-rest." *MAR*, 92.

62. *MAR*, 141.
63. *MAR*, 41.
64. *MAR*, 55.
65. *MAR*, 76.
66. Andrew Bonar's house-servant said, "Oh, to hear Mr. M'Cheyne at prayers in the morning! 'Ye would hae thocht (sic) the very walls would speak again. He used to rise at six on the Sabbath morning, and go to bed at twelve at night, for he said he likit (sic) to have the whole day alone with God." Quoted in Bonar, *Reminiscences*, 9.
67. *MAR*, 158.

sermons on a Sabbath. That day he kept for its original end, the *refreshment of his soul*."[68]

A growing Christian once asked M'Cheyne if it was permissible to spend time recording meteorological observations on the Sabbath. He responded by expressing his reluctance to bind another man's conscience, but that he himself could not spend Sabbath hours in such practices.[69] "The more entirely I can give my Sabbath to God," he said, "And half forget that I am not before the throne of the lamb, with my harp of gold, the happier I am." He continued, "This is the noblest science, to know how to live in hourly communion with God in Christ."[70]

M'Cheyne's ordinary course of Lord's Day ministry involved many hours in visitation, evangelism, and spiritual conversation. He also gave a special place to confession of sin: "I ought, on Sabbath evenings . . . to be especially careful to confess the sins of holy things."[71] Not only did M'Cheyne see confession on Sunday as a God-honoring practice, but he viewed Sunday itself as a unique season of temptation. For instance, one Sabbath he wrote, "I know that all [of my Sabbath labor] was not of grace; the self-admiration, the vanity, the desire of honour, the bitterness—these were all breaths of earth or hell."[72] At the end of another Lord's Day, he said, "Two things that defile this day in looking back, are love of praise running through all, and consenting to listen to worldly talk at all."[73] Yeaworth explains, "It was common for him to chide himself for being 'too little devotional' on that day."[74] The tendency was extra problematic because M'Cheyne believed, "All sin is double sin on the Sabbath. It is a day of double blessing and double cursing."[75]

---

68. *MAR*, 56 (emphasis original).

69. M'Cheyne's sermons speak of many different actions he considered impermissible on Sunday. From his personal writings, it is clear another practice he would not engage in on Sunday was writing and sending letters, which he loved to do on other days. See *MAR*, 172.

70. *MAR*, 141.

71. *MAR*, 152.

72. *MAR*, 44.

73. *MAR*, 45.

74. Yeaworth, "Robert Murray M'Cheyne," 322.

75. From his class notes on the catechism quoted in Yeaworth, "Robert Murray M'Cheyne," 322–23.

CONGREGATIONAL EXHORTATION TO SABBATH-KEEPING

M'Cheyne's sermons reveal a pastor enraptured with Christ. He could not contain his affection for the Redeemer. His mind soared in wonder and admiration at the Savior. Nor could he be stopped from defending the One whom he loved. Convinced that the Sabbath was a means of grace[76] and a special "trysting" day with Christ,[77] he spoke ardently about the Lord's Day to his congregation at St. Peter's. Tenderness and earnestness fill his exhortations. He declared, "How sweet is the Sabbath morning!"[78] He also reminded church members, "The Sabbath day of which you once said, 'What a weariness is it!' and 'When will it be over, that we may set forth corn?' is now a 'delight' and 'honourable'—the sweetest day of all the seven."[79]

When thinking about Sabbath-keeping, Christians usually race to ask, "What am I allowed to do on the Lord's Day?" Although M'Cheyne offered specific answers, the burden of his exhortation did not focus on what was permissible on the Sabbath. Instead, he preferred to use Sabbath-observance as a mirror for our true spiritual condition. He asked, "I do not ask you if you have been . . . more quiet and more orderly in keeping the Sabbath, more regular in the house of God. But I ask, have you get a new heart?"[80] His Sabbath exhortations fell into four main categories.

First, M'Cheyne called for sincerity. In his sermon, "The Sabbath Made for Man," M'Cheyne declared, "I do not ask if you love the *externals* of the Sabbath day, the exciting sermon, the meeting with friends, the singing of praises. But do you love the *internals* of a holy Sabbath? The communion with God; the delighting in Him; loving, adoring, admiring Him."[81] Formal observance of the Sabbath is no more pleasing to God than no observance. Like the prophet Isaiah, he exhorted his church not to give mere lip service to the King (Isa 29:13). "It is an easy thing to keep the Sabbath outwardly, even with an old, wicked heart. There are many formalists who keep their foot from profaning the Sabbath, but they do

---

76. *TPH*, 254.
77. *TPP*, 330; *SOH*, 32.
78. *TPH*, 103.
79. *TPH*, 158.
80. *TPP*, 68.
81. *NTS*, 41 (emphasis original).

not keep their heart from profaning it."[82] He made the spiritual dichotomy evident, declaring, "To God's children, it is a day of great delight . . . to a new heart the Sabbath is the sweetest day of all seven."[83] Conversion to Christ means a sincere love for the Lord's Day—a love expressed by outward obedience and inward delight.[84]

Second, M'Cheyne called for examination. "There cannot be a better test of whether you are saved or lost than whether you delight in the Sabbath," M'Cheyne announced.[85] Never one to eschew an opportunity to call hearers to examine themselves to determine if they are in the faith, M'Cheyne found Sabbath-observance to be a simple test for true faith. He provided various trials and tests in his teaching on the Lord's Day:

1. "The Sabbath is Christ's trysting time with his church. If you love him, you will count every moment of it precious."[86]
2. "Did you ever meet with a child of God, one who bore the image of Christ, who did not love to spend a holy Sabbath day?"[87]
3. "Everyone that has a new heart regards the Sabbath as holy ground."[88]
4. "If anyone has come to Christ, he will not make it either a day of merchandise or a day of pleasure excursions."[89]
5. "Only believers spend the Sabbath in exalting Christ in their own hearts, getting their hearts more and more rooted and built up in him."[90]
6. "Have you a peculiar taste for the Sabbath day? Do you love a well-spent Sabbath? If so, you have one mark that you are passed from death to life."[91]

While he directed most examinations to the subject of salvation, he also pointed toward sanctification. He told St. Peter's, "Many of you complain

---

82. *OTS*, 92.
83. *OTS*, 93.
84. *OTS*, 91–92.
85. *SOH*, 33.
86. *TPP*, 332.
87. *NTS*, 39.
88. *OTS*, 91.
89. *OTS*, 91.
90. *OTS*, 95.
91. *NTS*, 40.

that you have little of the Spirit, that you have a hard heart, little love to Christ, frequent falls into sin, much coldness. See if these be not one main cause that you do not seek to be in the Spirit on the Lord's Day . . . See whether you prize every moment of holy time, looking up for a constant supply of the Spirit."[92] For those who fail the test, M'Cheyne proceeded to plead earnestly through evangelistic warnings.

Third, M'Cheyne called for repentance. He proclaimed, "You that love not a Sabbath here, learn that you will never enjoy a Sabbath in eternity."[93] Those who have no taste for the present heaven (Sunday) will never partake of the new heaven when Christ returns. Instead, their "portion" will be in hell where "there are no Sabbaths."[94] His view of the Lord's Day as a converting day provided another impetus for his warnings: "Oh! what a tormenting thought it will be in hell that God gave you a peculiar day for seeking conversion and these were the days when you sealed your damnation."[95]

M'Cheyne's warnings were direct, but they were not intended to destroy.[96] His loving concern motivated him to ask, "Are there not many hearing me today who feel themselves condemned by this word of God? Are there none of you, my dear friends, who make the Sabbath day a day of merchandise?"[97]

Fourth, M'Cheyne called for obedience. Christ is the model of true piety, and thus the epitome of faithful Sabbath-keeping. M'Cheyne reminded his church, "[Jesus] loved the holy Sabbath."[98] He told St. Peter's that Sabbath-days "are like milestones" guiding us along the way to holiness.[99] The Lord's Day is for weary souls in need of rest and for hungry souls in need of food. For those who wanted to know how to observe the Sabbath, M'Cheyne encouraged them to consider the saints's work in heaven. The chief joy of heaven is meeting with God; thus we ought to spend our Sabbaths in God's presence.[100] We must "especially do what

92. *TPP*, 331.
93. *NTS*, 41.
94. *NTS*, 41.
95. *TPP*, 332.
96. In one section of "Delighting in the Sabbath," he cried, "Ah, my dear friends, if I could speak with divine tenderness, I would do it." *OTS*, 89.
97. *OTS*, 91.
98. *TPH*, 357.
99. *MAR*, 343.
100. *OTS*, 96.

Moses did, lift up the brazen serpent." He exhorted, "So lift up Christ. It is the business of the eternal Sabbath. Let it be the great mark of your Sabbath: Glorify Christ!"[101] Lastly, M'Cheyne maintained that true Christians fill the Sabbath day with unceasing praise: "Praise is very much the work of the eternal Sabbath in heaven . . . The happiest and most experienced Christians spend much of the Sabbath in praise."[102]

The essence of M'Cheyne's heart for Sabbath-keeping is found in his oft-repeated call to see the Sabbath as a "delight."[103] Many view keeping the Lord's Day as a drudgery. M'Cheyne's remedy for this was not to lead his church into Sabbath-observance as mere duty. Formal observance of the Lord's day neither glorifies God nor exalts Christ. What M'Cheyne preached—and practiced—was a Sabbath-shaped life of delight as an expression of love for Christ.

CONCLUSION

I Love the Lord's Day is a brief tract, but it offers considerable insight into M'Cheyne's spirituality. It shows that he was a man of his time.[104] He was not a pastor confined to the prayer closet or reading room. His private life of devotion always had a *telos*: public exaltation of Christ. Few places reveal this as vividly as his labor to see St. Peter's—and Scotland—love the Lord's Day. He decried Sabbath-desecration because it was an offense against the Lord of the Sabbath. The Railway Sabbath Controversy gave him a unique opportunity to defend "him whom [his] soul loveth."[105] His defense of Christ's day was so fervent precisely because his love for Christ was so passionate.

The title of his tract, *I Love the Lord's Day*, is itself extremely significant,[106] as it heralds the impulse behind M'Cheyne's convictions

---

101. *OTS*, 95.

102. *OTS*, 96.

103. *TPP*, 330; *OTS*, 92; *MAR*, 549; *NTS*, 179; *SOH*, 31.

104. In fact, this is the larger thesis of Yeaworth's whole project. He believes that M'Cheyne "typified the Evangelical spirit of the early nineteenth century." Yeaworth, "Robert Murray McCheyne," xi. He goes on to say, "The purpose of this thesis is to portray McCheyne as a typical Evangelical minister—not merely a 'saint' but a man—whose spark was an intense spirituality, and yet whose human involvements were sane and well balanced." Yeaworth, "Robert Murray McCheyne," xii.

105. *MAR*, 21.

106. Van Valen, *Constrained by His Love*, 379.

concerning the Sabbath—love for Christ. He believed that Christ had marked off this day for himself. "This is the reason why we love it, and would keep it entire," M'Cheyne asserted. "We love everything that is Christ's . . . We love the *Lord's day*, because it is His."[107] A child-like simplicity saturates M'Cheyne's spirituality, as his Sabbatarianism shows. He believed Christ pours grace into a redeemed soul, thereby producing the best fruit: "Love to Christ, love to the brethren, [and] love to the Sabbath."[108]

---

107. *MAR*, 548 (emphasis original).
108. *MAR*, 341.

10

Looking For Christ
M'Cheyne's Millenialism

IN HIS ASSESSMENT OF M'Cheyne's ministry, Islay Burns writes,

> Robert Murray M'Cheyne . . . was already widely known throughout Scotland as one of the most gifted, holy, and successful ministers of recent times . . . An overflowing congregation, of every class and degree in life, drawn together, many of them, from considerable distances in the town and country round, accustomed to *the charm of a peculiar ministry*.[1]

What contributed to M'Cheyne's "peculiar ministry"? Many points are worth mentioning—his love for God, pursuit of holiness, and devotion to Scripture. One underemphasized point is M'Cheyne's longing for Christ's return. In eschatological terms, he was a millenarian.[2] He believed that

---

1. Burns, *Memoir of the Rev.*, 59.

2. Gribben and Stunt say, "The familiar terms—'premillennial,' 'postmillennial,' and 'amillennial'—are not ideally suited to describe the eschatological flexibility of earlier exegetes. The terms themselves were popularized only in the nineteenth century and seem insufficiently fluid to represent an immense variety of millennial beliefs in a range of historical periods . . . Even in the period in which the terms were being established, 'the categories . . . hardly seem applicable to most of the early-nineteenth-century British works on biblical prophecy.'" Swartz and Zindars-Swartz, quoted in "Introduction," in Gribben and Stunt, *Prisoners of Hope?*, 3–4. See also, Gribben, "Eschatology of Puritan Confessions," 51–78. More common in M'Cheyne's day was the distinction between a "millenialist" and "millenarian." "Conventionally, scholars working in millennial studies have followed Tuveson in distinguishing 'millennialists'

God would bring about a glorious ingathering of ethnic Jews at the end of the age, and that this Jewish revival would immediately precede Christ's millennial reign on earth. As John MacLeod observes, "Among the Scottish Evangelicals of their age [M'Cheyne was] regarded as being in this respect peculiar."[3] According to Iain Murray, M'Cheyne's millenarianism was so irregular in his day that it earned adherents the label "the Evangelical Light Infantry."[4]

This chapter explains M'Cheyne's millenarianism and its influence on his spirituality. It examines (1) his eschatological influences; (2) his millenarian theology with reference to his view of Israel; (3) the implications of his eschatology for spirituality; and (4) his emphasis on living in light of eternity.

INFLUENCES

M'Cheyne did not arrive at his millenarian views in a vacuum. Two eschatologically-interested pastors who contributed most to M'Cheyne's unique view were Edward Irving and Andrew Bonar.

Edward Irving (1792–1834) served as Chalmers's assistant for a time in Glasgow. In 1821, he accepted a call to pastor Caledonian Church in London where he soon attracted massive crowds, including the most influential people from high society. His popularity faded in 1833, when the Church deposed him for christological heresy.[5] He died the following year, leaving his fledgling Catholic Apostolic Church to lay a foundation for the coming wave of Pentecostalism. In the opinion of Washington Wilks, Irving's ministry was linked to "unknown tongues, unfulfilled predictions, and unintelligible polemics."[6] While debate continues over

---

(believers who adopt *post-millennial*, optimistic, and gradualist theologies) from 'millenarians' (believers who adopt *premillennial*, pessimistic, and radical theologies)." See Gribben and Holmes, *Protestant Millennialism*, xi.

3. MacLeod, *Scottish Theology*, 227.

4. Murray, *Scottish Christian Heritage*, 217. See also, Yeaworth, "Robert Murray McCheyne," 254. Light Infantry soldiers were used as a skirmishing screen. They were smaller in number and deployed to slow down the advancing enemy, ahead of the main infantry's advance.

5. For study on Irving's Christology see Dorries, "Edward Irving," 183–85; MacLeod, "Doctrine of Incarnation," 40–50; McFarlane, "Edward Irving," 217–29; McFarlane, *Christ and Spirit*.

6. Wilks, *Edward Irving*, 265. Also informative is David Bebbington's incisive overview in Bebbington, *Evangelicalism in Modern Britain*, 75–104.

Irving's lasting legacy, Mark Patterson argues, "[Irving] was a theologian of the millennium, and it is from this perspective, alone, that the real Irving, the whole Irving, may be understood."[7]

In the mid-1820s, Irving made waves with his millenarian propaganda. First, he predicted that Christ would return in 1864.[8] Then, he discovered the millenarian work of Manuel Lacunza, a South American Jesuit, and published it under the title, *The Coming of the Messiah in Glory and Majesty*.[9] Lacunza espoused a literalist view of interpretation "which had resulted in its being banned by Roman Catholic authorities, but which more than any other work drove the increasing respectability of premillennial thinking in southern parts of England."[10] Irving later republished John Lacy's defense of the Camisards's prophetic claims, entitled, *General Delusion of Christians Touching the Ways of God's Revealing Himself*.[11] Through his participation at the Albury Conference (1826–1830) and his publication of the *Morning Watch* (or *Quarterly Journal of Prophecy*), Irving spread his millenarian views throughout the world. Henry Drummond summarizes the major tenets of Irving's view:

1. That the present Christian dispensation is not to pass insensibly into the millennial state by gradual increase of the preaching of the gospel; but that it is to be terminated by judgments, ending in the destruction of this visible church and polity, in the same manner as the Jewish dispensation has been terminated.

2. That during the time that these judgments are falling upon Christendom, the Jews will be restored to their own land.

3. That the judgments will fall principally, if not exclusively, upon Christendom, and will begin with that part of the church of God which has been most highly favored, and is therefore most deeply responsible.

---

7. Patterson, "Designing the Last Days," 150.

8. For an analysis of Irving's predictions, see Grass, "Edward Irving," in Gribben and Stunt, *Prisoners of Hope?*, 98.

9. Lacunza, *Coming of Messiah*.

10. Gribben, *Evangelical Millennialism*, 79. Lacunza advocates a literal hermeneutic leading to futurism, premillennialism, and a one-stage coming of Christ. J. N. Darby read Irving's translation of Lacunza not long after it was published and believed it "profitable and timely." Stunt, "Influences in the Early Development of J. N. Darby," in Gribben and Stunt, *Prisoners of Hope?*, 57.

11. Lacy, *Introduction*.

4. That the termination of these judgments is to be succeeded by that period of universal blessedness to all mankind, and even to the beasts, which is commonly called the millennium.

5. That the second advent of Messiah precedes or takes place at the commencement of the millennium.

6. That a great period of 1,260 years commenced in the reign of Justinian, and terminated at the French Revolution; and that the vials of the Apocalypse began then to be poured out; that our blessed Lord will shortly appear, and therefore it is the duty of all, who so believe, to press these conclusions on the attention of all men.[12]

What influence did Irving have on M'Cheyne? Irving enchanted Edinburgh audiences in meetings throughout 1828–1830. James Gordon argues that M'Cheyne was present at an 1829 meeting.[13] However, Yeaworth asserts, "There is no evidence ... that McCheyne had heard Irving at that time. McCheyne was not as yet so concerned about Christianity as he was after 1831, and it was not until then that he became intimate with the Bonars. Thus, the exuberant power of Irving was lacking when the doctrine was relayed to him."[14] M'Cheyne surely conversed with the Bonars on their experience of Irving's teaching. He also read Irving, and logged a list of "Rules for Interpreting Symbolical Prophecy."[15] On November 9, 1834, he recorded the following entry in his diary: "Heard of Edward Irving's death. I look back upon him with awe, as on the saints and martyrs of old. A holy man in spite of all his delusions and errors. He is now with

---

12. Drummond, *Dialogues on Prophecy*, ii–iii. For an additional analysis of Irving's millenarianism, see Ice, "Did Edward Irving?" 57–73. Brown offers helpful context: "Irving's belief in the literal and imminent personal return of Christ was the most distinctive aspect of his appeal and a significant innovation in Evangelical doctrine. While the prophetic texts of the Bible had been extensively studied during the eighteenth century, this scholarship was not essentially millenarian. It formed part of the rationalist approach to Scripture that typified the Churches' response to Deism. Old Testament prophecies that seemed to have been fulfilled in the New Testament Gospels were felt to be amongst the strongest evidence that could be used against the Deists ... Little attention was devoted to the unfulfilled prophecies of the Bible or to the second coming of the Messiah." Brown, "Victorian Anglican Evangelicalism," 679.

13. Gordon, *Evangelical Spirituality*, 138. Gordon apparently bases this conclusion on one of M'Cheyne's notebooks (MACCH 1.3, 9–11), which records a series of notes on "Edward Irving on Daniel's Four Beasts—1829." Yet, the notebook records M'Cheyne's writing from 1835–1837.

14. Yeaworth, "Robert Murray McCheyne," 254.

15. MACCH 1.3, 9–15.

his God and Saviour, whom he wronged so much, yet, I am persuaded, loved so sincerely."[16] Irving scaled the summit of eschatological influence before M'Cheyne's conversion, yet his writings were still in circulation by the time M'Cheyne entered the Divinity Hall in 1831.[17]

Once there, M'Cheyne befriended Andrew Bonar (1810–1892). Only Chalmers surpassed Bonar in influence upon M'Cheyne. Bonar arrived at the Divinity Hall as an earnest millenarian. In 1828—before his conversion—he sat spellbound under Irving's lectures on premillennialism. On May 25, 1829, Bonar wrote, "Have been hearing Mr. Irving's lectures all the week, and am persuaded now that his views of the Coming of Christ are truth. The views of the glory of Christ opened up in his lectures have been very impressive to me."[18] Soon after his conversion, Bonar recorded, "More and more convinced that the time of Christ's Coming is before the thousand years; often grieved by hearing opposition to this."[19] At the Divinity Hall, Bonar found a perfect outlet for his millenarian views in Chalmers's Exegetical Society. Unsurprisingly, the subject of the millennium arose during the society's morning meetings. George Smith provides insight into these discussions:

> Millenarian theories were discussed, *chiefly under Andrew Bonar's influence*. McCheyne looked with interest on these, but did not commit himself to adopting them fully. Somerville denounced such speculation as 'dangerous,' but always with shrewd humour... The point was referred to [Chalmers], who took McCheyne's position. He had not so fully studied these views as his young friends, but saw no danger in holding them.[20]

16. *MAR*, 25.

17. Yeaworth, "Robert Murray McCheyne," 253–54.

18. Bonar, *Andrew Bonar*, 5.

19. Bonar, *Andrew Bonar*, 17. For an overview of Bonar's eschatological development, see Palmer, "Andrew A. Bonar," 47–50.

20. Smith, *A Modern Apostle*, 18 (emphasis added). Disagreement exists as to Chalmers's position on the millennium. Crawford Gribben notes, "[Chalmers's] published statements... seem to suggest a distinctively apocalyptic philosophy of history combined with a firm postmillennialism." Gribben and Stunt, *Prisoners of Hope?*, 185. There is, however, important evidence to the contrary. Bonar says Chalmers himself adopted premillennial views and said to John Welsh: "I tell you, Dr. Welsh, the millennium will come in with a hammer smash." Bonar, *Reminiscences*, xiii. In April of 1836, Chalmers wrote, "I am now far more confident than I wont to be, that there is to be a coming of Christ which precedes the millennium—a millennium to be ushered into the world by a series of dreadful visitations, for which, I fear, we are fast ripening." Hanna, *Letters of Thomas Chalmers*, 326. Bonar also declared that Chalmers, before

Smith's observation is important when it comes to determining M'Cheyne's eschatological influences. In the meetings of the Exegetical Society two close friends (M'Cheyne and Bonar) engaged in a regular study of theological subjects. Bonar was a convinced millenarian, who affirmed and defended his position at every opportunity. On the other hand, M'Cheyne, while in general agreement with Bonar, was not nearly as dogmatic. The marked difference in the degree of their conviction became evident in other ways.

First, Bonar's millenarianism cost him several church appointments. On September 9, 1837, he recounted in his diary that he was feeling "cast down" because he had been "kept out of several appointments" because of his "millenarianism chiefly."[21] This rejection continued. After M'Cheyne's death, St. Peter's Church refused to extend a call to Bonar because, by his own account, "many of the electors could not bear my views of Christ's advent."[22] Gribben posits, "Perhaps [St. Peter's] received news of Bonar's eschatological beliefs with some degree of surprise. Despite their close friendship and literary co-operation, overt premillennialism had not been a feature of Bonar's public interactions with McCheyne."[23] Moreover, Bonar's millenarian views were well known in the church whereas M'Cheyne's were not.[24]

The differing degrees in their conviction regarding millenarianism was also evident in that Bonar never wavered in his views, whereas M'Cheyne's commitment was far more tenuous. Yeaworth correctly notes,

> In spite of his intimacy with [millenarianism] McCheyne... never adopted it and its ramification fully. So indecisive was he that

---

his death, confessed "to be on the side of the Pre-millenarians." Quoted in Palmer, "Andrew Bonar," 50.

21. Bonar, *Diary and Letters*, 57. Bonar's millenarian zeal threatened to derail his appointment to the mission of inquiry. Yeaworth quotes a letter from Somerville to M'Cheyne as follows: "The sentiment seemed to prevail in the meeting that it was highly important that a Mission (to Israel) should take place, as proposed. The difficulty lies with the choice. They seem to feel the youth of the individuals a good deal—but all agreed that *you* should go. As to Andrew, I feel his millenarianism will knock the prospect of *his* going upon the head." Yeaworth, "Robert Murray McCheyne," 267.

22. Bonar, *Diary and Letters*, 105.

23. Gribben and Stunt, *Prisoners of Hope?*, 186.

24. One need only consider his journey of discovery to Israel and the subsequent publication of the mission. Additionally, Andrew's theological affinity with his brother Horatius was common knowledge. Horatius had edited the *Quarterly Journal of Prophetic Prophecy* for several years by this point.

as late as 1843 he began a list entitled: "Passages that seem to be anti-millenarian." . . . McCheyne repeatedly admitted to uncertainty as to the details which surrounded the second coming, emphasizing only the basic factors.[25]

Bonar himself acknowledged the difference in their commitment to premillennialism, writing,

> At a time when he was apparently in his usual health, we were talking together on the subject of the Premillennial Advent. We had begun to speak of the practical influence which the belief of that doctrine might have. At length he said, "that he saw no force in the arguments generally urged against it, though he had difficulties of his own in regard to it. And perhaps (he added), it is well for you . . . to be so firmly persuaded that Christ is thus to come."[26]

The point is that M'Cheyne was a hesitant forerunner of the premillennial scheme that soon engulfed evangelicalism within the English-speaking world. Chalmers's view on the subject was non-committal.[27] His mentorship put M'Cheyne on a collision course with Bonar, the beloved friend, who so admired Irving's eschatology. While Bonar's millenarianism was pronounced and even divisive, M'Cheyne's was full of that quality so evident in his ministry—winsomeness.

EXPECTATIONS

On November 17, 1839, days after returning from his mission to Israel, M'Cheyne ascended St. Peter's sacred desk and preached a sermon titled: "Our Duty to Israel." His chosen text was Romans 1:16.[28] If ever the stage were set for M'Cheyne to espouse his millenarian manifesto, this

---

25. Yeaworth, "Robert Murray McCheyne," 254.

26. *MAR*, 84. Surprisingly, Yeaworth states, "A. Bonar, who was never hesitant to point out those who agreed with him in this teaching, never so much as hinted in the *Memoir* that McCheyne was one of them." Yeaworth, "Robert Murray McCheyne," 254.

27. Palmer writes, "When Bonar first heard Edward Irving's eschatological views, he and three or four other students sought Chalmers's opinion and advice. Chalmers replied, 'Go on, gentlemen; proceed in your study of the Word; this thing will do you no manner of harm.'" Palmer, "Andrew Bonar," 49–50.

28. *MAR*, 447–54. Smellie notes that M'Cheyne delivered the same sermon almost two years prior. Smellie, *Biography of R. M. McCheyne*, 79.

was it. It is telling, therefore, that M'Cheyne made no mention of the millennium or anything remotely related to millenarianism. Instead, he focused on the need to evangelize the Jews. M'Cheyne developed the following doctrine from the text: "That the gospel should be preached first to the Jews." From this starting point, he gave four reasons for a specific mission to the Jews: (1) judgment will begin with them; (2) God cares first for them; (3) there is a peculiar access to the Jews; and (4) the Jews will give life to the dead world.

This sermon typifies M'Cheyne's "millenarianism." He took for granted that Christ will return before his thousand-year reign on earth.[29] He never used the word "millennium" in any of his published sermons, nor did he ever reference a thousand-year period following Christ's return. M'Cheyne's writings demonstrate that, when it came to the millennium, he was less concerned with what will happen after Christ returns than with what happens before Christ returns. He believed the Jews would be restored to their ancient land immediately preceding Christ's return, and that their widespread conversion would announce the soon-splitting skies. His view of eschatological Israel may be summarized under four points.

First, Israel is a chosen people. In one sermon, M'Cheyne announced, "God took Israel to be a peculiar people to Himself."[30] On another occasion, he declared that Israel is "the name of His peculiar people."[31] He wanted his church at Dundee to understand that "Israel is a people near to [God]."[32] To that end, he regularly extolled God's special election of the Jews as God's "ancient people."[33]

Second, Israel is a distinct people. When preaching from Hosea 2:14 on God's love for and leadership of Israel, M'Cheyne proclaimed, "I know well that many people are afraid to understand all these things literally and dare not believe in the real restoration of Israel. And still I cannot but think that if you will prayerfully consider the matter, you will come to see that all these things are truly promised."[34] M'Cheyne's

---

29. Yeaworth says, "He did not give this doctrine any more significance than that it was a fact, and since it was so, it should result in watchful diligence and urgency." Yeaworth, "Robert Murray McCheyne," 255.

30. *NTS*, 38.

31. *OTS*, 149.

32. *OTS*, 164.

33. *BOF*, 89.

34. *TPP*, 77.

pastoral hesitance regarding eschatological views is on display here. He did not use the Spirit's sword to draw eschatological lines in the doctrinal sand. Instead, he exhorted with patience and consideration. The same emphasis came in a letter to Mr. George Shaw, who enquired about M'Cheyne's eschatology: "I feel deeply persuaded, from prophecy, that it will always be difficult to stir up and maintain a warm and holy interest in outcast Israel." M'Cheyne responded, "The lovers and pleaders of Zion's cause will, I believe, be always few . . . [nevertheless I believe the Old Testament prophecies are for] *literal* Israel."[35] When preaching the Old Testament, M'Cheyne routinely began his sermons by situating the passage or prophecy in its immediate context:

> These words apply, first of all, to God's ancient people, the Jews.[36]
>
> In these words God describes the mercy yet in store for His ancient people, the outcast of Israel.[37]
>
> These words do, first of all apply to ancient Israel.[38]
>
> It seems to be the universal testimony of Scripture that the Jews who are at this day scattered among all nations shall yet be brought back to their own land. Though they have been sifted among all nations as corn is sifted in a sieve, yet the least grain shall not fall to the earth.[39]

Third, Israel is a remembered people. At this point, M'Cheyne clearly diverged from the Westminster divines.[40] He believed in a "final conversion" of Israel,[41] a world-changing event "yet to come."[42] He said God will "awaken the Jews in the latter day"[43] and that Israel will be "restored" to their ancient land."[44] "They are, at present, of all nations the most

---

35. MAR, 252. In a sermon, M'Cheyne proclaimed, "The moment a man begins to take the statements of the Word of God as literally true, that moment he begins to care for Israel." Quoted in Yeaworth, "Robert Murray McCheyne," 265.

36. *TPH*, 113.
37. *OTS*, 67.
38. *TPP*, 66.
39. *TPP*, 49.
40. See Gribben and Stunt, *Prisoners of Hope?*, 180–81.
41. *TPH*, 429.
42. *TPH*, 224.
43. *TPH*, 439.
44. *OTS*, 156.

hard-hearted and far from righteousness. But the time is fast approaching when God will turn them and they shall be turned . . . He will yet restore them to their own land and wholly changed their nature."[45] By the late 1830s, there was growing affinity with his conviction. According to Yeaworth, "At the Assembly of [1838], no less than sixteen overtures were presented concerning the Jews. Moderates and Evangelicals were united in looking for the conversion of the whole race and its return to Palestine. Churchmen took great pride was taken in the fact that this was the first such act by any Christian denomination."[46] The 1838 assembly appointed M'Cheyne to a committee to advance a mission to the Jews. His eschatological sympathies may not have been as earnest as Bonar's, but they were nonetheless considered important in the church.

Fourth, Israel is a paradigmatic people. If M'Cheyne's first reading of Old Testament prophecies regarding Israel was literal, his second—and more extensively employed reading—was typological. He began a sermon on Psalm 137:1-6 by preaching, "Israel was a typical people. They were typical of God's Church in all ages of the world. And they were typical of the soul of every individual believer."[47] M'Cheyne usually reminded St. Peter's that the Old Testament text in view was meant originally for Israel. Yet, he soon turned his attention to its contemporary explanation and application, spending the vast majority of his sermon on Israel's typological identity for the new covenant church.

IMPLICATIONS

M'Cheyne engaged carefully in private study while avoiding open discussion of his views. The Christ of eschatology interested him much more than the order of eschatology.[48] And it is this emphasis that deeply affected his spirituality in several different ways.

---

45. *TPP*, 66.

46. Yeaworth, "Robert Murray McCheyne," 263.

47. *TPH*, 429. His sermon on Deuteronomy 33:29 offers a full extension of this theme: "No man can read the Old Testament intelligently without seeing that the people of Israel were a typical people." *TPH*, 258.

48. Dodds, *Personal Reminiscences*, 78. Dodds says, "He firmly believed in their ultimate restoration to the land of their fathers; but about other and kindred prophetical subjects he expressed himself with much caution, like one unable to form a decided opinion. He spoke to me in the liveliest terms of his travels in the East, of the downcast present state and future spiritual glory of Israel: and his views on many subjects

For M'Cheyne theology was a labor of love. In all facets of his ministry, he desired his people to know Christ's love and to love Christ in return. This pastoral concern extended to his eschatology. In a sermon on Mark 13:34-37, he declared,

> I am far from discouraging those who seek to enquire from prophecy when the coming of the Saviour shall be—it is a most interesting enquiry—and it shows us little caring about the Saviour if we care little about the time. Neither am I an enemy to those who argue from what they see in the church and the world that the time is at hand . . . But what we are taught is . . . (1) Christ shall come; (2) He shall come suddenly.[49]

M'Cheyne's interest in eschatology was fueled by his interest in the Christ of eschatology. For him, it was a means to increase his service and affection for Christ.

When he sat on the Church of Scotland's committee of Jewish inquiry, M'Cheyne did not expect to join in the actual mission. Soon after his appointment to the committee, he lay with heart palpitations upon his bed. His doctor suggested that M'Cheyne travel on the Church's planned "Mission of Inquiry," because it would benefit his health. And so it was that M'Cheyne, from April to November 1839, journeyed to Israel.[50] Bonar recalled, "Mr. M'Cheyne found himself all at once called to carry salvation to the Jew, as he had hitherto done to the Gentile, and his soul was filled with joy and wonder."[51] This joyful wonder overflowed not only from M'Cheyne's deep love of evangelism but from his eschatological revivalism. He wrote to his parents:

> To seek the lost sheep of the house of Israel is an object very near to my heart, as my people know it has ever been. Such an enterprise may probably draw down unspeakable blessings on the Church of Scotland, according to the promise, "they shall prosper who love thee" . . . I feel convinced that if we pray that the world may be converted in God's way, we will seek the Good

---

seemed coloured by the experiences of his mission." Dodds, *Personal Reminiscences*, 78. See also, Murray, *Puritan Hope*, 307.

49. *NTS*, 42–43.

50. A full history of the mission is found in Bonar and M'Cheyne, *Narrative of a Mission*. The book became an instant bestseller. Newspapers published letters from the team while the mission was active. For an analysis of the theology found in the *Narrative*, see Gribben and Stunt, *Prisoners of Hope?*, 187–88.

51. *MAR*, 86.

of the Jews, and the more we do so, the happier we will be in our own souls. You should always keep up a knowledge of the prophecies regarding Israel.[52]

If revival were to come to Dundee, M'Cheyne believed it would come through determined efforts to preach the gospel to the Jews. It is tempting to read M'Cheyne's missionary action as primarily Israel-centered, when in fact his view is ultimately Christ-centered. The Jews are God's special people and—like every gentile—need the salvation that Christ alone can give. Thus, any gentile endeavoring to bring Christ to the Jews should humbly expect God to reward that work with a fresh outpouring of Christ. According to Bonar, M'Cheyne agreed with the prevailing sentiment of his day: "We might anticipate an *outpouring of the Spirit when our Church should stretch out its hands to the Jew as well as to the Gentile*."[53] That revival came to Dundee while he was on his mission to Israel only solidified M'Cheyne's view.

It is thus not surprising to find him, in the months after his return, rousing up more interest in missions to the Jews. His diary records many occasions when he visited individuals and churches "relating the things seen and heard among the Jews of Palestine and other lands."[54] If people could not carry the gospel to the Jews, M'Cheyne urged them to pray for and give to such work.[55] The logic behind his view was clear: the conversion of the Jews "will give life to this dead world" and hasten the return of Christ.[56]

According to Bonar, M'Cheyne remarked regularly, in relation to missions to the Jews, that "we should be like God in his peculiar affections; and the whole Bible shows that God has ever had, and still has, a peculiar love to the Jews."[57] In his sermon, "Our Duty To Israel," M'Cheyne exhorted his flock not to rest in the joy of forgiveness alone, for "our truest joy is to *be like Him* . . . Long for the day when Christ shall appear, and we shall be fully *like Him*, for we shall see Him as He is."[58] The chief point

52. *MAR*, 88.
53. *MAR*, 88 (emphasis original).
54. *MAR*, 125. See also, *MAR*, 127, 134, 139, 175.
55. *MAR*, 223, 464.
56. *TPH*, 224.
57. *MAR*, 88.
58. *MAR*, 449 (emphasis original). M'Cheyne's emphasis on the beatific vision is harmonious with his puritan forebears. Francis J. Bremer states, "The climax of heavenly blessedness would be the *beatific vision*, a term Puritans used in common with

in M'Cheyne's eschatology is the beatific vision. As we wait for Christ's blessed appearing, we are being conformed into his image from one degree of glory to the next. For M'Cheyne, such conformity means renewal in God's "*peculiar affections*."[59] He believed the essential eschatological affection was found in God's "strange, sovereign, most peculiar love [for the Jews]! . . . Should we not be like God in this peculiar affection?"[60]

M'Cheyne's millenarianism is thus another area of truth for God's people to walk in *imitatio Christi*. It was not a topic meant for division or affliction, but for holy affection, which is one reason why M'Cheyne's public handling of eschatology lacked Bonar's doctrinal bite. A true understanding of "the last things" enables God's people to know and walk in God's love.

THE CHRIST OF ETERNITY

M'Cheyne's millenarianism was a distinguished element in his broader eschatological ethic—an ethic of "living in light of eternity."[61] He declared, "[A believer] sees *eternity* as Christ does. Christ looked at everything in light of eternity."[62] Therefore, "believers should look on everything in light of eternity."[63] An eternal perspective fueled the crucial features of

---

medieval theologians." Bemer, *Puritans and Puritanism*, 405. Heaven's glory, according to Christopher Love, is found firstly in that "there shall be a beatific vision of God." Love, *Works of Christopher*, 473. See also, Boston, *Complete Works of Thomas Boston*, 334. John Owen writes, "The enjoyment of God by sight, is commonly called the beatific vision, and, it is the sole fountain of all the actings of our souls in the state of blessedness." Owen, *Glorious Mystery of Person*, 383. See also, Howe, *Select Practical Works*, 38. For analyses of the puritan focus on the beatific vision, see McDonald, "Beholding Glory of God," 141–58; Beeke and Jones, *A Puritan Theology*, 824–25. Randall J. Peterson argues that the puritans wrote "of the eternal beatific vision, especially to encourage private devotion and meditation as a 'foretaste' and reward for Christian duty and felicity." Peterson, *Unity in Diversity*, 188. See also, Cocksworth, *Evangelical Eucharistic Thought*, 46; Watson, *Saint's Spiritual Delight*, 50; Ambrose, *Looking Unto Jesus*, 673.

59. *MAR*, 449 (emphasis original).

60. *MAR*, 451.

61. Beaty, *An All-Surpassing Fellowship*, 85–94.

62. *MAR*, 416 (emphasis original).

63. *TPH*, 199. In another sermon, M'Cheyne declared, "You only are truly wise who live for eternity, who live as you shall wish you had done when you come to die." *TPH*, 450. The opposite is true of the unbeliever, for "the mind of a natural man shrinks back from contemplating the realities of God and of the eternal world." *HTD*, 67. See also,

M'Cheyne's spirituality. The week after graduating college, he said, "Life itself is vanishing fast. Make haste for eternity."[64] The hope of eternity with Christ gave a purpose for pursuing holiness, an urgency to his preaching, and a heavenly homesickness to his living. He thought he regularly fell short of the ideal, however. When a church member encouraged him to rest from his constant labor, he responded, "Time is short, my time especially, and souls are precious; and I fear many are slumbering because I watch not with sufficient diligence, nor blow the trumpet with sufficient clearness."[65]

M'Cheyne exhorted St. Peter's to see how a mind focused on eternity gave joy and zeal in God's service. He said, "I believe they are happiest who are living only for eternity, who have no object in this world to divert their hearts from Christ."[66] Wise Christians, then, "let nothing dim the eye that is looking on eternal realties."[67] His letters further display the degree to which eternity shaped his counsel. He wrote to an evangelistic society, "Live for eternity. A few days more, and our journey is done."[68] He exhorted Andrew Bonar, "Speak to your people as on the brink of eternity."[69] To Mrs. Thain, he encouraged, "Live near to God, and so all things will appear to you little in comparison with eternal realities."[70] The motto with which he sealed most his letters was, "The Night Cometh."

M'Cheyne's longing for eternity gave special fervency to his gospel ministry.[71] He did not expect to live a long life, and so he aimed to "speak very plainly" of Christ.[72] He cried, "Oh, believers, it is the duty of ministers

---

NTS, 203, 260.

64. MAR, 27.

65. MAR, 244. Bonar says a "motive to incessant activity was the decided impression on his mind that his career would be short. From the very first days of his ministry he had a strong feeling of this nature." MAR, 84.

66. MAR, 463.

67. HTD, 3.

68. MAR, 256. See also, BOF, 89.

69. MAR, 87. Van Valen captures this element in M'Cheyne's preaching: "The scope of his preaching was focused on eternity. Perhaps this subject was uppermost in his thoughts because he himself felt he was nearing his own end. He spoke as a dying man to those who were dying." Van Valen, *Constrained by His Love*, 355, 395.

70. MAR, 244. See also, NTS, 114.

71. Robertson agrees, "McCheyne was motivated by his consciousness of the shortness of time, the love of Christ and the lostness of human beings without God." Robertson, *Awakening*, 73.

72. In January of 1843, M'Cheyne wrote, "I do not expect to live long. I expect a

to preach with this solemn day in their eye (Judgment Day)! . . . Would not this take away fear of man? Would not this make us urgent in our preaching? You must either get these souls into Christ, or you will yet see them lying down in everlasting burnings."[73] Also, the Sabbath was a taste of eternity, and thus eternal business should fill each Lord's Day activity. He told a ministerial friend,

> May your mind be solemnized, my dear friend, by the thought that we are ministers but for at time; that the Master may summon us to retire into silence, or may call us to the temple above; or the midnight cry of the great Bridegroom may break suddenly on our ears. Blessed is the servant that is found waiting! Make all your services tell for eternity; speak what you can look back upon with comfort when you must be silent.[74]

M'Cheyne's preaching of eternal realities compelled growth in godliness. One Lord's Day, after preaching on Christ's second coming, he wrote, "Felt its (Christ's imminent return) power myself more than ever before, how the sudden coming of the Saviour constrains to a holy walk separate from sin."[75] How can a Christian tarry in sin when Christ could appear at any moment?[76] Looking at life through the lens of eternity kept Christ ever before the eye, and so enabled the believer to keep a close communion with Christ.[77] M'Cheyne also emphasized the nature of God's heavenly rewards for a life of holiness. He said, "Christians will differ as one star from another in glory. Some will have an entrance, some an

---

sudden call some day—perhaps soon, and therefore I speak very plainly." *MAR*, 160. McLennan believes M'Cheyne's preaching in the spring of 1843 "took on a more judgmental tone," as a result. Bruce McLennan, *McCheyne's Dundee*, 109. M'Cheyne may have been more urgent, but his 1843 sermons do not reveal a harsher spirit. McLennan does not see how sermons on hell and eternal punishment were common throughout M'Cheyne's ministry.

73. *MAR*, 359. See also, *BOF*, 90–91, 130, 140, 154–55, 161, 163, 169; *HTD*, 77; *NTS*, 43, 133–34, 158; *OTS*, 22–23; *TPH*, 263, 270, 350; *TPP*, 140; *SOH*, 15. Smellie records a poem from M'Cheyne on this point: "Up then, and be stirring! Let's work whilst 'tis day, / For soon shall come darkness and sorrow. / Up, up! Let us handle the plough whilst we may, / Unswerving, undaunted, pursuing our way: / We never may see a To-morrow." Smellie, *Biography of R. M. McCheyne*, 34.

74. *MAR*, 172.

75. *MAR*, 82.

76. *TPH*, 249.

77. *MAR*, 446. See also, *SOH*, 18, 83; *TBJ*, 101.

abundant entrance. Every lust indulged is lessening your eternal glory? Oh! will you give away something of heaven for that base lust?"[78]

Thus, as with all parts of his piety, M'Cheyne's eschatological ethic centered on Christ. He wrote in a popular magazine article: "May we be among the number of those who 'love his appearing,' who are 'looking for that blessed hope,' and who are 'waiting for his Son from heaven, even Jesus, which delivered us from the wrath to come.' Surely they have but cold love to Jesus that do not burn with desire to see the fair brow that was crowned with thorns."[79] A heart that loves Christ, longs to be with Christ.[80] M'Cheyne's piety embodied the apostle Paul's cry: "For to me to live is Christ, and to die is gain."[81] It is in heaven that we shall see Christ

---

78. *NTS*, 279. Few debate the reality of good works bringing heavenly rewards; rather, the debate centers on the nature of those rewards. M'Cheyne's view reflects the Westminster and reformed traditions. The confession states, "The persons of believers being accepted through Christ, their good works also are accepted in him; not as though they were in this life wholly unblamable and unreprovable in God's sight; but that he, looking upon them in his Son, is pleased to accept and reward that which is sincere, although accompanied with many weaknesses and imperfections." *WCF*, 16.6. John Calvin proclaims, "Anyone who closely studies the Scriptures, they promise believers not only eternal life but a special reward for each." Calvin, *Institutes*, 1,006. Such reward results in differing degrees of glory in heaven. Calvin, *Institutes*, 1,005. See also, Raith, *After Merit*, 169–72; Lane, *Calvin and Bernard*, 52–53; Quistrop, *Calvin's Doctrine*, 174. Francis Turretin agrees with Calvin, writing of the Parable of the Talents, "[The various talents ascribed] could not be said unless there was granted a diversity of reward corresponding in a certain proportion to the disparity of labor." Turretin, *Institutes of Elenctic Theology*, 621–30. For Puritan views on good works, rewards, and degrees of glory, see Bunyan, *Works of John Bunyan*, 735; Brooks, *Works of Thomas Brooks*, 366–68; Boston, *Complete Works*, 224; Burroughs, *Moses His Choice*, 711; Sibbes, *Works of Richard Sibbes*, 280; Love, *Works of Christopher Love*, 477–81; Owen, *Glorious Mystery of Person*, 457. See also Chalmers, *Works of Thomas Chalmers*, 14. For modern treatments on the topic that are similar to M'Cheyne's view, see Jones, *A Christian's Pocket Guide*; Grudem, *Systematic Theology*, 1143–45; Gaffin, *By Faith*, 114–18.

79. *HTD*, 1. See also, *HTD*, 11. M'Cheyne stated, "I know that if any of you have tasted the sweetness of being in Christ, you could be content to hide in him for an eternity." *TPH*, 287.

80. M'Cheyne said, "The Lamb that was slain will be the wonder of eternity." *TPH*, 182.

81. Phil 1:21. M'Cheyne preached, "Oh, let this make you willing to depart, and make death look pleasant, and heaven a home . . . It is the world of holy love, where we shall give free, full, unfettered, unwearied expression to our love forever." *MAR*, 459–60.

and "eternally gaze on His uncreated loveliness. Oh, what praises shall this draw from our burning hearts to all eternity!"[82]

CONCLUSION

The Jewish Mission stood before the General Assembly to deliver their report on May 22, 1840. Presbyters later remembered that, in M'Cheyne's address, "his youthful face beamed with love, and his soft, yearning voice thrilled."[83] He called on his fellow ministers to remember God's priority to the Jews. Should they neglect this responsibility, they had little reason to expect faithfulness in other areas of the ministry.

> Shall we be ashamed to be like God—to remember the tears shed on Mount Olivet over Jerusalem . . . Shall we be ashamed to join Emmanuel in the cry of tenderness . . . Shall we be ashamed to drink deep of the same spirit of which the mighty Paul drank, and to have the same heart—shall we not wish that every Christian in Scotland might love as Paul love and pray as Paul prayed?[84]

M'Cheyne may not have shared Bonar's ardency in defending premillennialism, even if he did share Bonar's basic interpretation. He may not have found affinity with Irving's excesses in eschatology. He may not have been in complete agreement with the millenarian wave soon to encompass the church.[85] But he did possess a peculiarly inviting view of "the last things." The truth of eschatology was revelation to be experienced. If M'Cheyne's eschatology had a sprinkle of strangeness to its doctrinal formulations, its spiritual applications were anything but odd for his spiritual program. God's love for the Jews and the reality of Christ's second coming afforded yet another reason for God's people to labor in the conversion of sinners. Eschatology and eternity were truths to increase obedience to Christ and express love for Christ. A life lived in love for Christ was M'Cheyne's primary concern. He wielded every part of Scripture to that end—even his view of the last things.

---

82. *NTS*, 194. See also, *TPH*, 146, 382, 394–95; *NTS*, 298; *OTS*, 181.

83. Rainy and Mackenzie, *Life of William Cunningham*, 152.

84. Quoted in Yeaworth, "Robert Murray M'Cheyne," 277.

85. For a skillful survey of how millenarianism took over the Free Church of Scotland, see Gribben and Stunt, *Prisoners of Hope?*, 193–202.

11

Conclusion

ACCORDING TO JAMES GORDON, "M'Cheyne seemed to have a heightened awareness of the reality and near presence of Christ, and sensed in him a fragrance and loveliness that was breathtaking in power and attraction. The suffering of the crucified Christ kindled an ardor and devotion he could sometimes barely contain."[1] A perusal of M'Cheyne's ministry confirms that he could not "contain" his "ardor" for Christ. His sermons magnify Christ in all his comeliness, loveliness, preciousness, sweetness, fullness, freeness, and fitness. "The chief object of the Bible," M'Cheyne acknowledged, is "to show you ... the beauty ... of [Christ]."[2] In a sermon on Mark 7:31–37, he addressed the unconverted: "He pities you. He wishes to be a Savior to you ... Oh! weary soul, look to a sighing Savior, with His inmost heart He desires to be your Savior and Lord."[3] Christ's willingness is, for M'Cheyne, the supreme expression of his love: "Brethren, look at the love of Christ, that he should be willing to be made sin for us."[4] With great enthusiasm, M'Cheyne presented the freeness and fullness of a Savior who longs to convert sinners. At the same time, however, he exalted Christ's sovereignty in salvation:

---

1. Gordon, *Evangelical Spirituality*, 128–29.
2. *SOH*, 87.
3. *NTS*, 49. M'Cheyne declared, "The whole Bible shows that Christ is quite willing and anxious that all sinners should come to him ... There is no unwillingness in the heart of Jesus Christ." *TPH*, 295.
4. *BOF*, 10.

> Everyone that becomes a [believer] becomes so willingly. We cannot force men to be concerned, to pray, to seek Christ, to believe and be saved. No, they must come willingly. But who makes them willing? Unconverted men are like stones: speak to them, they hear not; warn them, they feel not; beseech them, they move not. Sooner shall the rocks start from the caves of the ocean or from under the load of the mountains than unconverted men come of themselves to Christ. Ah, there is a load of guilt over them heavier than the ocean. There are bands of sin above them more binding than the ribs of mountains. *How do any come? Christ makes them willing.*[5]

M'Cheyne thus saw his role as heralding a sovereign Savior who allures sinners through his willingness to save. "A sight of his beauty draws us to follow him," he announced. "There is an indescribable loveliness in Christ that draws the soul to follow him." M'Cheyne affirmed that unbelievers's chief problem is that they do not see Christ's "loveliness" and, for this reason, they have "never tasted the sweetness of God's love."[6] This is the height of "folly."[7] "Sinner," M'Cheyne queried, "do you not think there must be something wrong about the state of your mind, that sees no beauty in the death of Christ?"[8] M'Cheyne's remedy for this dreadful "state of mind" was to proclaim a captivating Christ while ultimately resting in Christ's power to captivate.

M'Cheyne was convinced a glimpse of Christ's loveliness is transformative. He declared, "The soul that has once seen the loveliness of Christ, leaves all for him."[9] We must, therefore, look continually to Christ that we might follow him wholeheartedly. In a sermon entitled, "Follow the Lord Fully," M'Cheyne proclaimed, "Keeping the eye upon the Lord this was what enabled Caleb to follow the Lord fully."[10] To follow Christ fully is to see his beauty, for it is the captivating love of Christ that empowers whole-hearted love to Christ.

It is this conviction that animated M'Cheyne's Christocentric spirituality. He encountered in the Song of Solomon a vocabulary which gave voice to his union and communion with Christ. He discovered in

5. *TPP*, 257 (emphasis added).
6. *TPH*, 313.
7. *SOH*, 177.
8. *BOF*, 25.
9. *TBJ*, 84.
10. *TPH*, 380.

the pursuit of holiness the ultimate declaration of his love for Christ—namely, his growth in conformity to Christ. He approached the means of grace (the Word, sacraments, and prayer) as "trysts" in which he enjoyed blessed communion with the object of his love. He entered the pulpit with Christ before him, and extolled his beauty while inviting all to taste of his sweetness and behold his loveliness. He stressed devotion to and delight in the Sabbath because he was convinced that his love for Christ required love for his day. He was eager to evangelize the Jews out of a burning zeal for Christ's honor among all peoples. He lived each day with eternity in view because he longed for his Beloved's return.

While each of these expressions of M'Cheyne's spirituality could be a dissertation in its own right, the purpose of the present work has been to demonstrate that the common driving force behind them is M'Cheyne's communion of love with Christ. This observation is important as it provides a better understanding of M'Cheyne's spirituality while serving to reorient the field of M'Cheyne studies away from the *how* of his spirituality to the more fundamental issue of *why*.

At the same time, this dissertation has taken into account various factors that facilitated and encouraged this particular emphasis in M'Cheyne's spirituality. He was committed to a theological tradition encapsulated in the Westminster standards, and he was part of an exegetical tradition surrounding the Song of Solomon. Moreover, he stood at a unique ecclesiastical, philosophical, and cultural moment in Scottish history. He was also influenced by the towering theologians of his day and of previous generations. While a deeper analysis of these influences merits further study, this dissertation has at the very least demonstrated their importance to the formulation, expression, and appeal of M'Cheyne's spirituality.

James Gordon notes that M'Cheyne's ministry set off "vibrations" that are still felt "generations later."[11] This statement is true of his ardent pursuit of holiness and tireless proclamation of the gospel. It is also true of his commitment to foreign missions and involvement in spiritual revivals. The statement is true of M'Cheyne's passionate devotion to the means of grace and uncompromising observation of the Lord's Day. It is true of his relatively short life, expended in the cause of Christ. But behind all of these stands M'Cheyne's greatest legacy—his vision of the Christian pilgrimage as a communion of love with Christ.

11. Gordon, *Evangelical Spirituality*, 145.

Appendix
Robert Murray M'Cheyne's Manuscripts at New College Library, Edinburgh University

THE FOLLOWING MANUSCRIPTS, HOUSED at New College Library, Edinburgh University, were used in this work:

NOTEBOOKS

MACCH 1.1: Sermon outlines and reading notes (1837–1838)
MACCH 1.2: Poems and Sketches (1827–1831)
MACCH 1.3: Sermons, outlines, reading notes, texts to be preached, contents in back (1835–1837)
MACCH 1.4: Sixteen letters to family while on trip to Palestine (1839)
MACCH 1.5: "Leading doctrines of Christianity."
MACCH 1.6: Class notes: Chalmers. (1832)
MACCH 1.7: Class notes: Chalmers. Hebrew notes. Sermon outlines. Catechism notes. Notes for communicants class and list of class members. (1832–1841).
MACCH 1.8: Diary of sketches of Palestine trip. "Personal Reformation." Article on James Laing. (1839–1842)
MACCH 1.9: Diary of trip to Palestine. Sketches, poetry, etc. (1839)
MACCH 1.10: Visitation notebook. Sermon outlines and notes. Notes on Jews and religious state of towns affected by revival of 1839. (1835–1840)
MACCH 1.11: Diary and sketches of trip to Palestine. (1839)
MACCH 1.12: Sermons. (1842)
MACCH 1.13: Trips to Ireland, Newcastle and Aberdeen. Sermon notes. (1841–1843)

MACCH 1.14: Dundee visitation notes of records of interview. (1836–1838)

MACCH 1.15: Outlines of talks for "free Presbyterian church," Jewish missions, etc. Poems. (1839–1842)

MACCH 1.16: Convocation notes. Itineration. Sermon notes. (1842–1843)

MACCH 1.17: Poetry scrapbook compiled by David M'Cheyne and Robert Murray M'Cheyne. (1820–1832)

MACCH 1.18: Poetry scrapbook given by Mary Macgregor to Robert Murray M'Cheyne. Many poems and sketches by both. (1831–1832)

MACCH 1.19: Poetry scrapbook of Isabella Dickson. (1811–1813)

MACCH 1.20: Poetry scrapbook of David M'Cheyne. (1821)

MACCH 1.21: Notebook in Eliza M'Cheyne's hand. (1848)

LETTERS

MACCH 2.1 (ninety-one letters from 11/30/1837–12/31/1839)

MACCH 2.2 (twenty-seven letters from 4/29/1837–3/28/1843)

MACCH 2.3 (ninety letters from 6/8/1841–4/27/1843)

MACCH 2.4 (twenty-nine letters from 3/1/1839–12/16/1842)

MACCH 2.5 (eight letters concerning prayer meetings of different groups during revival)

MACCH 2.6 (forty-two letters from 8/31/1827–1/27/1828)

MACCH 2.7 (fifty-four letters from 4/24/1841–3/27/1843)

Bibliography

Adamson, Robert M. *The Christian Doctrine of the Lord's Supper.* Edinburgh: T. & T. Clark, 1905.
Adamson, Steven C. "The Apologetic Distinctives of Thomas Chalmers." *Scottish Bulletin of Evangelical Theology* 32 (2014) 63–74.
Alexander, Donald L., ed. *Christian Spirituality: Five Views of Sanctification.* Downers Grove, IL: InterVarsity Press, 1988.
Ambrose, Isaac. *Looking Unto Jesus: A View of the Everlasting Gospel; or, the Soul's Eye of Jesus.* Pittsburgh: Luke Loomas & Co., 1832.
Anton, Peter. *Kilsyth: A Parish History.* Glasgow: John Smith & Son, 1893.
Arnot, William. *Life of James Hamilton, D.D., F.L.S.* New York: Robert Carter and Brothers, 1870.
Barbour, G. F. *The Life of Alexander Whyte, D.D.* London: Hodder & Stoughton, 1923.
Bates, Cleveland Buchanan. "A Sociological and Demographic Analysis of Patterns of Church Membership in the Church of Scotland in the Urban City (Dundee)." PhD diss., University of St. Andrews, 1985.
Beaty, David. *An All-Surpassing Fellowship: Learning from Robert Murray M'Cheyne's Communion with God.* Grand Rapids: Reformation Heritage, 2014.
Bebbington, David. *The Dominance of Evangelicalism: The Age of Spurgeon and Moody.* Downers Grove, IL: InterVarsity, 2005.
———. "Evangelical Christianity and the Enlightenment." *Crux* 25 (December 1989) 29–36.
———. *Evangelicalism in Modern Britain: A History from the 1730s to the 1980s.* London: Routledge, 1988.
Beeke, Joel R. *Living for God's Glory: An Introduction to Calvinism.* Lake Mary, FL: Reformation Trust, 2008.
———. *Puritan Reformed Spirituality.* Darlington, England: Evangelical Press, 2006.
Beeke, Joel R., and Mark Jones. *A Puritan Theology.* Grand Rapids: Reformation Heritage, 2012.
Begg, Alistair, and Derek Prime. *On Being a Pastor: Understanding Our Calling and Work.* Chicago: Moody Publishers, 2004.
Begg, Alistair, and Sinclair B. Ferguson. *Name Above All Names.* Wheaton, IL: Crossway, 2013.
Bell, Charles Dent. *Reminiscences of a Boyhood in the Early Part of the Century.* London: Sampson Low, Marston, Searle & Rivington, 1889.

Bemer, Francis J., and Tom Webster, eds. *Puritans and Puritanism in Europe and America: A Comprehensive Encyclopedia*, vol. 1. New York: ABC-Clio, 2006.
Bennett, David Malcolm. *Edward Irving Reconsidered: The Man, His Controversies, and the Pentecostal Movement*. Eugene, OR: Wipf & Stock, 2014.
Beveridge, William. *Makers of the Scottish Church*. Edinburgh: T. & T. Clark, 1908.
Billings, J. Todd. *Calvin, Participation, and the Gift: The Activity of Believers in Union with Christ*. Oxford: Oxford University Press, 2007.
Blaikie, William G. *For the Work of Ministry: A Manual of Homiletical and Pastoral Theology*. London: Daldy, Isbister & Co., 1878.
———. *The Preachers of Scotland: From the Sixth to the Nineteenth Century*. 1888. Reprint, Edinburgh: Banner of Truth, 2001.
Blanning, Tim. *The Romantic Revolution: A History*. New York: Modern Library, 2012.
Bloom, Jon. *Things Not Seen: A Fresh Look at Old Stories of Trusting God's Promises*. Wheaton, IL: Crossway, 2015.
Boice, James Montgomery. *Renewing Your Mind in a Mindless World: Learning to Think and Act Biblically*. Grand Rapids: Kregel, 1993.
Bonar, Andrew A. *Andrew A. Bonar, D.D. Diary and Letters*. Edited by Marjory Bonar. London: Hodder & Stoughton, 1894.
———. *Baptism Briefly Opened Up and Applied*. London: James Nisbet, 1844.
———. *The Life of Robert Murray M'Cheyne*. 1844. Reprint, Edinburgh: Banner of Truth, 1962.
———. ed. *Memoir and Remains of the Rev. Robert Murray M'Cheyne*. Dundee: Middleton, 1845.
Bonar, Andrew A., and Robert Murray M'Cheyne. *Narrative of a Mission of Inquiry to the Jews from the Church of Scotland in 1839*. Edinburgh: William Whyte & Co., 1842.
Bonar, Horatius. *The Land of Promise: Notes of a Spring-Journey from Beersheba to Sidon*. New York: Carter and Brothers, 1858.
———. *The Life of the Rev. John Milne of Perth*. London: James Nisbet and Co., 1868.
———. *The Night of Weeping: Or, Words for the Suffering Family of God*. New York: Robert Carter, 1847.
———. *Reflections on Canticles: Or, The Song of Solomon with Illustrations from Modern Travelers and Naturalists*. London: S.W. Partridge & Co., 1870.
Bonar, Marjorie, ed. *Reminiscences of Andrew A. Bonar*. London: Hodder & Stoughton, 1895.
Boston, Thomas. *Complete Works of Thomas Boston*, vol. 6. London: William Tegg & Co., 1853.
———. *Complete Works of Thomas Boston*, vol. 8. London: William Tegg & Co., 1853.
Bradley, Ian. *The Call to Seriousness: The Evangelical Impact on the Victorians*. London: Macmillan, 1976.
Broadie, Alexander, ed. *The Cambridge Companion to the Scottish Enlightenment*. Cambridge: Cambridge University Press, 2003.
Brooke, David. "The Opposition to Sunday Rail Services in North Eastern England, 1834–1914." *Journal of Transport History* 6 (1963) 95–109.
Brooks, Thomas. *Works of Thomas Brooks*, vol. 4. Edinburgh: Banner of Truth, 1980.
Brown, David Blayney. *Romanticism*. London: Phaidon, 2001.
Brown, Ralph. "Victorian Anglican Evangelicalism: The Radical Legacy of Edward Irving." *The Journal of Ecclesiastical History* 58 (October 2007) 675–704.

Brown, Stewart J. "Dean Stanley and The Controversy Over His History of the Scottish Church, 1872." *Records of the Scottish Church History Society* 31 (2001) 145–72.

———. *Thomas Chalmers and the Godly Commonwealth in Scotland*. Oxford: Oxford University Press, 1982.

Brown, Stewart J., and Michael Fry, eds. *Scotland in the Age of Disruption*. Edinburgh: Edinburgh, University Press, 1993.

Brown, Thomas. *Annals of the Disruption: Consisting Chiefly of Extracts from the Autograph Narratives of Ministers Who Left the Scottish Establishment in 1843*. Edinburgh: MacNiven & Wallace, 1883.

———. *Church and State in Scotland: A Narrative of the Struggle for Independence from 1560–1843*. Edinburgh: Macniven and Wallace, 1891.

———. *Selected Writings*. Edited by Thomas Dixon. Exeter: Imprint Academic, 2010.

Bryce, James. *Ten Years of the Church of Scotland: From 1833–1843*. 2 vols. Edinburgh: William Blackwood and Sons, 1850.

Buchanan, Robert. *The Ten Years' Conflict: Being the History of the Disruption of the Church of Scotland*. Edinburgh: Blackie and Son, 1849.

Bunyan, John. *Works of John Bunyan*. 2 vols. Edinburgh: Banner of Truth, 1991.

Burnet, George B. *The Holy Communion in the Reformed Church of Scotland, 1560–1960*. Edinburgh: Oliver and Boyd, 1960.

Burns, Evan. *A Supreme Desire to Please Him: The Spirituality of Adoniram Judson*. Eugene, OR: Pickwick, 2016.

Burns, Islay. *Memoir of the Rev. Will. C. Burns, Missionary to China for the English Presbyterian Church*. London: James Nisbet & Co., 1870.

Burroughs, Jeremiah. *Moses His Choice: With His Eye Fixed Upon Heaven: Discovering the Happy Condition of a Self-denying Heart. Delivered in a Treatise Upon Heb. 11. 25, 26*. London: John Field, 1641.

Burrowes, George. *A Commentary on the Song of Solomon*. Philadelphia: William S. Martien, 1853.

Butin, Philip Walker. *Revelation, Redemption, and Response: Calvin's Trinitarian Understanding of the Divine-Human Relationship*. Oxford: Oxford University Press, 1995.

Button, C. N. "Scottish Mysticism in the Seventeenth Century, with Special Reference to Samuel Rutherford." PhD diss., University of Edinburgh, 1927.

Calvin, John. *Institutes of the Christian Religion*, vol. 2. Translated by Ford Lewis Battles. Philadelphia: Westminster, 1960.

Cameron, George G., ed. *Memorials of John Roxburgh*. Glasgow: David Bryce and Son, 1881.

Cameron, Nigel M. de S., et al., eds. *Dictionary of Scottish Church History and Theology*. Edinburgh: T. & T. Clark, 1993.

Campbell, Iain D. *On the First Day of the Week: God, the Christian and the Sabbath*. Leominster: Day One, 2005.

Campbell, Murdoch. *Diary of Jessie Thain*. Edinburgh: Murdoch Campbell, 1955.

Campbell, R. H., and Andrew S. Skinner, eds. *The Origins and Nature of the Scottish Enlightenment*. Edinburgh: John Donald Publishers, 2003.

Carson, D. A. *For the Love of God: A Daily Companion for Discovering the Riches of God's Word*. Wheaton, IL: Crossway, 2006.

———. *Praying with Paul: A Call to Spiritual Reformation*. Grand Rapids: Baker, 2014.

———. ed. *Telling the Truth: Evangelizing Postmoderns*. Grand Rapids: Zondervan, 2000.
Chalmers, Thomas. *Butler's Analogy, Paley's Evidences of Christianity, and Hill's Lectures in Divinity*. Edinburgh: Thomas Constable and Co., 1852.
———. *Daily Scripture Readings*, vol. 3. Edinburgh: Thomas Constable and Co., 1852.
———. *Discourses on the Application of Christianity to the Commercial and Ordinary Affairs of Life*. Edinburgh: Thomas Constable and Co., 1848.
———. *Discourses on the Christian Revelation View in Connection with the Modern Astronomy Together with Six Sermons Embracing the Last Occasioned by the Death of the Princess Charlotte of Wales*. Andover, MA: Mark Newman, 1818.
———. *Memoirs of the Life and Writings of Thomas Chalmers*. 4 vols. Edinburgh: Thomas Constable and Co., 1849-1852.
———. *On Church Extension*. Glasgow: William Collins, 1838.
———. *On the Miraculous and Internal Evidences of the Christian Revelation; and the Authority of Its Records*. New York: Robert Carter and Brothers, 1850.
———. *Posthumous Works of the Rev. Thomas Chalmers*. New York: Harper, 1855.
———. *Sermons by the Late Thomas Chalmers: Illustrative of Different Stages in His Ministry*. Edinburgh: Thomas Constable and Co., 1849.
———. *Sermons of the Late Thomas Chalmers: Illustrative of Different Stages in His Ministry: 1798-1847*. Edited by William Hanna. New York: Harper, 1860.
———. *Sermons Preached in St. John's Church, Glasgow*. Glasgow: Chalmers and Collins, 1823.
———. *The Works of Thomas Chalmers*. New York: Robert Carter, 1841.
———. *The Works of Thomas Chalmers: Minister of the Tron Church, Glasgow*. Hartford, CT: George Goodwin and Sons, 1820.
———. *Works of Thomas Chalmers*, vol. 3. Glasgow: William Collins, 1836.
Chantry, Walter J. *Call the Sabbath a Delight*. Edinburgh: Banner of Trust, 1991.
Cheney, Virginia Robinson. "Approaches to the Spiritual Problem of Young People as Found in a Study of the Life and Works of Robert Murray McCheyne." MRE diss., Biblical Seminary, 1954.
Cheyne, A. C., ed. *The Practical and the Pious: Essays on Thomas Chalmers (1780-1847)*. Edinburgh: St. Andrew Press, 1985.
———. *Studies in Scottish Church History*. Edinburgh: T. & T. Clark, 1999.
———. *The Ten Years' Conflict and The Disruption: An Overview*. Edinburgh: Dunedin Academic Press, 2005.
———. *The Transforming of the Kirk: Victorian Scotland's Religious Revolution*. Edinburgh: St. Andrew Press, 1983.
The Christian Monthly and Family Treasury for 1881. London: T. Nelson and Sons, 1881.
Church of Scotland. *The Christian's Daily Companion: Presenting an Entire View of Divine Truth, in a Series of Meditations for Every Morning and Evening Throughout the Year*. Edinburgh: Blackie & Son, 1841.
———. *Family Worship: A Series of Prayers, with Remarks on Passages of Sacred Scripture, By Clergymen of the Church of Scotland*. Edinburgh: Blackie & Son, 1841.
Clark, G. Kitson. *The Making of Victorian England*. New York: Routledge, 1962.
———. "The Romantic Element: 1830-1850." In *Studies in Social History: A Tribute to G. M. Trevelyan*, edited by J. H. Plumb, 226-42. London: Libraries Press, 1955.
Clark, R. Scott. *Recovering the Reformed Confession: Our Theology, Piety, and Practice*. Phillipsburg, NJ: P&R, 2008.

Clarke, Elizabeth. *Politics, Religion and the Song of Songs in Seventeenth-Century England*. New York: Macmillan, 2011.

Cockburn, Henry. *Journal of Henry Cockburn: Being a Continuation of the Memorials of His Time*. Edinburgh: Edmonston and Douglas, 1874.

Cocksworth, Christopher J. *Evangelical Eucharistic Thought in the Church of England*. Cambridge: Cambridge University Press, 1993.

Coleman, James J. *Remembering the Past in Nineteenth Century Scotland: Commemoration, Nationality and Memory*. Edinburgh: Edinburgh University Press, 2014.

Coleman, Robert. *The Heart of the Gospel: The Theology Behind the Master Plan of Evangelism*. Grand Rapids: Baker, 2011.

Couper, W. J. *Scottish Revivals*. Dundee: James P. Mathew and Co., 1918.

Cox, Robert. *The Literature of the Sabbath Question*. 2 vols. Edinburgh: MacLachlan and Stewart, 1865.

Cuneo, Terence, and René van Woudenberg, eds. *The Cambridge Companion to Thomas Reid*. Cambridge: Cambridge University Press, 2004.

Cunningham, John. *The Church History of Scotland: From the Commencement of the Christian Era to the Present Time*. Edinburgh: James Thin, 1882.

Currie, David Alan. "The Growth of Evangelicalism in the Church of Scotland, 1793–1843." PhD diss., University of St. Andrews, 1990.

Dabundo, Laura, ed. *Encyclopedia of Romanticism: Culture in Britain, 1780s–1830s*. London: Routledge, 1992.

Dallimore, Arnold. *The Life of Edward Irving: Fore-Runner of the Charismatic Movement*. Edinburgh: Banner of Truth, 1983.

Dantas, Elias. "Calvin, the Theologian of the Holy Spirit." In *John Calvin and Evangelical Theology: Legacy and Prospect*, edited by Jung Wook Chung, 128–41. Milton Keynes, UK: Paternoster, 2009.

Dargan, Edwin C. *A History of Preaching: From the Close of the Reformation Period to the End of the Nineteenth Century*, vol. 2. New York: Hodder & Stoughton, 1912.

Davie, George. *A Passion for Ideas: Essays on the Scottish Enlightenment*. Edinburgh: Polygon, 1994.

Davie, Martin, et al., eds. *New Dictionary of Theology: Historical and Systematic*. Downers Grove, IL: IVP Academic, 2016.

Dennison, James. *The Market Day of the Soul: The Puritan Doctrine of the Sabbath in England, 1532–1700*. Morgan, PA: Soli Deo Gloria, 2001.

Devine, T. M. *The Scottish Nation: A History, 1700–2000*. New York: Viking, 1999.

Dickson, David. *Therapeutica Sacra*. Edinburgh: Evan Tyler, 1664.

Dinwiddie, John L. *The Ruthwell Cross and the Ruthwell Savings Bank: A Handbook for Tourists and Students*. Dumfries, Scotland: Robert Dinwiddie, 1933.

Dodds, James. *Personal Reminiscences and Biographical Sketches*. Edinburgh: Macniven & Wallace, 1887.

Dorries, David W. "Edward Irving: The Forgotten Giant." *The Evangelical Quarterly* 59 (1987) 183–85.

Drummond, Andrew L., and James Bulloch. *The Church in Victorian Scotland, 1843–1874*. Edinburgh: St. Andrews Press, 1975.

———. *The Scottish Church, 1688–1843: The Age of the Moderates*. Edinburgh: St. Andrew Press, 1973.

Drummond, D. T. K. *The Jewish Sabbath: What it Was Not, and What it Was*. Edinburgh: Scottish Society Promoting Due Observance of the Lord's Day, 1862.

Duncan, George John C. *Memoir of the Rev. Henry Duncan D.D.* Edinburgh: William Oliphint and Sons, 1848.

Duncan, J. Ligon. "Owning the Confession: Subscription in the Scottish Presbyterian Tradition." In *The Practice of Confessional Subscription*, edited by David Hall, 77–92. Lanham, MD: University Press of America, 1995.

Dunlop, A. *Sermons by the Late Reverend David Welsh D.D. with a Memoir*. Edinburgh: W.P. Kennedy, 1846.

Dunlop, A. I. "Baptism in Scotland after the Reformation." In *Reformation and Revolution: Essays Presented to the Very Reverend Hugh Watt, D.D.*, edited by Duncan Shaw, 82–97. Edinburgh, St. Andrew Press, 1967.

Edwards, Jonathan. *An Account of the Life of the Late Reverend Mr. David Brainerd, Missionary to the Indians, Chiefly Taken from His Own Diary, and Other Private Writings*. Edinburgh: J. Ogle, 1798.

———. *The Works of President Edwards in Four Volumes*. New York: Robert Carter and Brothers, 1879.

Edwards, O. C. *A History of Preaching*. Nashville: Abingdon Press, 2004.

Enright, William Gerald. "Preaching and Theology in Scotland in the Nineteenth Century: A Study of the Context and the Content of the Evangelical Sermon." PhD diss., University of Edinburgh, 1968.

Estrada, David. "Robert Murray M'Cheyne: The Shining Light of Scotland." *Christianity and Society: The Biannual Journal of the Kuyper Foundation* 14 (October 2004) 28–37.

Evans, Eifon. "John Calvin: Theologian of the Holy Spirit." *Reformation and Revival* 10 (2001) 83–104.

Fairbairn, Patrick. *The Typology of Scripture; or The Doctrine of Types Investigated in Its Principles, and Applied to the Explanation of the Earlier Revelations of God, Considered as Preparatory Exhibitions of the Leading Truths of the Gospel*. Philadelphia: Daniels & Smith, 1852.

———. *The Typology of Scripture: Viewed in Connection with the Entire Scheme of the Divine Dispensations*. Philadelphia: Smith & English, 1854.

Fawcett, Arthur. *The Cambuslang Revival: The Scottish Evangelical Revival of the Eighteenth Century*. Edinburgh: Banner of Truth, 1971.

Ferguson, Sinclair B. *In Christ Alone: Living the Christ Centered Life*. Lake Mary, FL: Reformation Trust, 2007.

———. *John Owen on the Christian Life*. Edinburgh: Banner of Truth, 1987.

Fergusson, David, ed. *Scottish Philosophical Theology*. Exeter: Imprint Academic, 2007.

Fernando, Ajith. *Acts. The NIV Application Commentary*. Grand Rapids: Zondervan, 1998.

———. *The Call to Joy & Pain: Embracing Suffering in Your Ministry*. Wheaton, IL: Crossway, 2007.

Fesko, J. V. *Beyond Calvin: Union with Christ and Justification in Early Modern Reformed Theology (1517–1700)*. Göttingen: Vandenhoeck & Ruprecht, 2012.

———. *The Theology of the Westminster Standards: Historical Context & Theological Insights*. Wheaton, IL: Crossway, 2014.

Finlayson, Sandy. *Thomas Chalmers*. Darlington, England: Evangelical Press, 2015.

Forrester, Duncan, and Douglas Murray, eds. *Studies in the History of Worship in Scotland*. Edinburgh: T. & T. Clark, 1996.
Frame, John M. *History of Western Philosophy and Theology*. Phillipsburg, NJ: P&R, 2015.
Fraser, Donald. *Thomas Chalmers, D.D., LL. D.* New York: A.C. Armstrong and Son, 1882.
Fry, Michael. *Patronage and Principle: A Political History of Modern Scotland*. Aberdeen: Aberdeen University Press, 1991.
Gaffin, Richard B. *By Faith, Not By Sight: Paul and the Order of Salvation*. Phillipsburg, NJ: P&R, 2013.
Garcia, Mark A. *Life in Christ: Union with Christ and Twofold Grace in Calvin's Theology*. Eugene, OR: Wipf & Stock, 2008.
Garretson, James M. *Thoughts on Preaching and Pastoral Ministry: Lessons from the Life and Writings of James W. Alexander*. Grand Rapids: Reformation Heritage, 2015.
Garvie, Alfred Earnest. *The Christian Preacher*. New York: Charles Scribner's Sons, 1921.
Gavreau, Michael. *The Evangelical Century: College and Creed in English Canada from the Great Revival to the Great Depression*. London: McGill-Queen's University Press, 1991.
George, David, ed. *A Passion for Ideas: Essays on the Scottish Enlightenment*. Edinburgh: Polygon, 1994.
Gerrish, Brian. "The Lord's Supper in the Reformed Confessions." *Theology Today* 23 (1966) 224–43.
Gilfillan, James. *The Sabbath: Viewed in the Light of Reason, Revelation, and History with Sketches of Its Literature*. New York: American Tract Society, 1862.
Gillies, John. *Historical Collections of Accounts of Revival*. Edinburgh: Banner of Truth, 1981.
Golding, Peter. *Covenant Theology: The Key of Theology in Reformed Tradition and Thought*. Fearn, Scotland: Mentor, 2004.
Goodwin, Thomas. *A Habitual Sight of Him: The Christ-Centered Piety of Thomas Goodwin*. Edited by Joel R. Beeke and Mark Jones. Grand Rapids: Reformation Heritage, 2009.
Gordon, James M. *Evangelical Spirituality*. 1991. Reprint, Eugene, OR: Wipf & Stock, 2006.
Graham, Gordon, ed. *Scottish Philosophy in the Nineteenth and Twentieth Centuries*. Oxford: Oxford University Press, 2015.
———. "Scottish Philosophy in the 19th Century." In *The Stanford Encyclopedia of Philosophy*, Winter 2015. Edited by Edward N. Zalta. Accessed September 1, 2017. https://plato.stanford.edu/archives/win2015/entries/scottish-19th/.
Grass, Tim. *Edward Irving: The Lord's Watchman*. Milton Keynes, UK: Paternoster, 2011.
———. *The Lord's Watchman: A Life of Edward Irving (1792–1834)*. Eugene, OR: Pickwick Publications, 2012.
Gribben, Crawford. "The Eschatology of the Puritan Confessions." *Scottish Bulletin of Evangelical Theology* 20 (2000) 51–78.
———. *Evangelical Millennialism in the Trans-Atlantic World, 1500–2000*. New York: Palgrave Macmillan, 2011.

———. *John Owen and English Puritanism: Experiences of Defeat*. Oxford: Oxford University Press, 2016.

Gribben, Crawford, and Andrew R. Holmes, *Protestant Millennialism, Evangelicalism, and Irish Society, 1790-2005*. Basingstoke, UK: Macmillan, 2006.

Gribben, Crawford, and Timothy C. F. Stunt, eds. *Prisoners of Hope? Aspects of Evangelical Millennialism in Britain and Ireland, 1800-1880*. Milton Keynes, UK: Paternoster, 2004.

Grudem, Wayne. *Systematic Theology: An Introduction to Biblical Doctrine*. Grand Rapids: Zondervan, 1994.

Gundry, Stanley N., ed. *Five Views of Sanctification*. Grand Rapids: Zondervan, 2011.

Guthrie, Thomas. *Autobiography of Thomas Guthrie. D.D.: And Memoir by His Sons*. Detroit: Craig and Taylor, 1878.

Haldane, Robert. *Sanctification of the Sabbath: The Permanent Obligation to Observe the Sabbath Or Lord's Day*. Edinburgh: W. Whyte, 1842.

Hall, Joseph H. "The Marrow Controversy: A Defense of Grace and the Free Offer of the Gospel." *Mid-America Journal of Theology* 10 (1999) 239–57.

Hall, Joseph. *No Peace with Rome: Wherein Is Proved, That, as Terms Now Stand, There Can be No Reconciliation of the Reformed Religion with the Romish*. London: William Pickering, 1852.

Hall, Sophy. *Dr. Duncan of Ruthwell, Founder of Savings Banks*. Edinburgh: Oliphant, Anderson & Ferrier, 1910.

Hamilton, James. *The Church in the House: And Other Tracts*. London: James Nisbet, 1847.

———. *The Departure of the Free Church of Scotland Out of the Erastian Establishment*. London: James Nisbet, 1843.

Hanna, William. *Memoirs of Thomas Chalmers*. Edinburgh: Edmonston and Douglas, 1867.

———. ed. *A Selection from the Correspondence of the Late Thomas Chalmers*. Edinburgh: Thomas Constable and Co., 1848.

———. ed. *Letters of Thomas Chalmers*. Edinburgh: Banner of Truth, 2007.

———. ed. *Memoirs of the Life and Writings of Thomas Chalmers, D.D. LL.D*. Edinburgh: Thomas Constable and Co., 1852.

———. ed. *Select Works of Thomas Chalmers*. 8 vols. Edinburgh: Thomas Constable and Co., 1856.

Harper, J. Wilson. *The Social Ideal and Dr. Chalmers's Contribution to Christian Economics*. Edinburgh: Macniven and Wallace, 1910.

Harrison, B. H. "The Sunday Trading Riots of 185." *Historical Journal* 8 (1965) 219–45.

Hart, Hendrik, Johan Van Der Hoeven, and Nicholas P. Wolterstorff, eds. *Rationality in the Calvinian Tradition*. Eugene, OR: Wipf & Stock, 2011.

Hastings, James, ed. *The Great Texts of the Bible: II Corinthians and Galatians*. Edinburgh: T. & T. Clark, 1913.

Haykin, Michael A. G. *The God Who Draws Near: An Introduction to Biblical Spirituality*. Darlington, England: Evangelical Press, 2007.

Haykin, Michael A. G., and Kenneth J. Stewart, eds. *The Advent of Evangelicalism: Exploring Historical Continuities*. Nashville: B&H Academic, 2008.

Helopoulos, Jason. *The New Pastor's Handbook: Help and Encouragement for the First Years of Ministry*. Grand Rapids: Baker, 2015.

Henderson, G. D. *Church and Ministry: A Study in Scottish Experience*. London: Hodder & Stoughton, 1951.
———. *The Church of Scotland*. Edinburgh: Church of Scotland Youth Committee, 1939.
———. *Heritage: A Study of the Disruption*. Edinburgh: Oliver and Boyd, 1943.
———. "Thomas Chalmers as Preacher." *Theology Today* 4 (October 1947) 346–56.
Henderson, H. F. *The Religious Controversies of Scotland*. Edinburgh: T. & T. Clark, 1905.
Herman, Arthur. *How the Scots Invented the Modern World: The True Story of How Western Europe's Poorest Nation Created Our World & Everything in It*. New York: Crown, 2001.
Hesselink, I. John. *Calvin's First Catechism: A Commentary*. Louisville: Westminster John Knox, 1997.
Hildebrand, Lloyd. *Praying the Psalms Changes Things*. Alachua, FL: Bridge Logos, 2014.
Hill, George. *Lectures in Divinity*. Philadelphia: Herman Hooker, 1842.
Hinson, Edward Glenn. "The Redemption of Time: The Puritan Concern for the Sabbath." *Liturgy* 8 (1989) 11–15.
Holland, H. W. *The Kilsyth Revival*. London: Hamilton, Adams, & Co., 1867.
Hopkins, Mark *Nonconformity's Romantic Generation: Evangelical and Liberal Theologies in Victorian England*. Eugene, OR: Wipf & Stock, 2004.
Howe, John. *Select Practical Works of Rev. John Howe and Dr. William Bates*. New York: G. & C. & H. Carvill, 1830.
Hudson, J. Harrison, Thomas W. Jarvie, and Jock Stein. *Let the Fire Burn: A Study of R. M. McCheyne, Robert Annan, and Mary Slessor*. Dundee: Handsel Publications, 1978.
Hughes, Barbara. *Disciplines of a Godly Woman*. Wheaton, IL: Crossway, 2013.
Huie, James A. *The History of the Jews, from the Taking of Jerusalem by Titus, to the Present Time, Containing an Account of Their Wanderings, Persecutions, Commercial Enterprises and Literary Exertions: With an Account of Various Efforts Made for Their Conversion*. Andover, MA: M. A. Berk, 1843.
Hywel Roberts, "'The Cup of Blessing': Puritan and Separatist Sacramental Discourses." In *Union and Communion*, 55–71. London: Westminster Conference, 1979.
Ice, Thomas. "Did Edward Irving Invent the Pre-Trib Rapture View?" *The Master's Seminary Journal* 27 (2016) 57–73.
Innes, Alexander Taylor. *Studies in Scottish History: Chiefly Ecclesiastical*. London: Hodder & Stoughton, 1893.
Innes, William. *The Christian Sabbath Vindicated*. Edinburgh: V. H. Nelson, 1841.
James, John Angell. *An Earnest Ministry: The Want of the Times*. Edinburgh: Banner of Truth, 1993.
Jeffrey, Kenneth S. *When the Lord Walked the Land: The 1858-62 Revival in the North East of Scotland*. Eugene, OR: Wipf & Stock, 2006.
Jeffrey, Peter. *Preachers Who Made a Difference*. Darlington, England: Evangelical Press, 2004.

Jones, Mark. *A Christian's Pocket Guide to Good Works and Rewards: In This Life and the Next*. Fearn, Scotland: Christian Focus, 2017.

Jones, Paul H. "Reformation Concepts: John Calvin." In *Christ's Eucharistic Presence: A History of the Doctrine*, 134–67. New York: Peter Lang, 1994.

Kaczmarek, Clair Puglisi. "Thomas Chalmers (1780–1847) and the 1843 Disruption: From Theological to Political Clash." *Scottish Bulletin of Evangelical Theology* 24 (2006) 19–35.

Kao, Chaoluan. *Reformation of Prayerbooks: The Humanist Transformation of Early Modern Piety in Germany and England*. Göttingen: Vandenhoeck & Ruprecht Academic, 2018.

Kay, Brian K. *Trinitarian Spirituality: John Owen and the Doctrine of God in Western Devotion*. Eugene, OR: Wipf & Stock, 2008.

Kea, Elizabeth Bonner. *Amazed by Grace*. Nashville: W Pub. Group, 2003.

Keller, Timothy. *Encounters with Jesus: Unexpected Answers to Life's Biggest Questions*. New York: Penguin, 2016.

———. *Walking with God through Pain and Suffering*. New York: Riverhead, 2015.

Kelly, Geffrey B. "Freedom and Discipline: Rhythms of a Christocentric Spirituality." In *Ethical Responsibility: Bonhoeffer's Legacy to The Churches*, edited by John D. Godsey, 307–36. New York: Edwin Mellen, 1981.

Kitto, John, Henry Burgess, and Benjamin Harris Cowper, eds. *The Journal of Sacred Literature and Biblical Record*. Edinburgh: W. Oliphant and Son, 1857.

Kyle, I. Francis. *An Uncommon Christian: James Brainerd Taylor: Forgotten Evangelist in America's Second Great Awakening*. Lanham, MD: University Press of America, 2008.

Lachman, D. C. *The Marrow Controversy*. Edinburgh: Rutherford House, 1988.

Lacunza, Manuel. *The Coming of Messiah in Glory and Majesty*. Translated by Edward Irving. London: L. B. Seeley and Son, 1827.

Lacy, John. *Introduction to the General Delusion of Christians Touching the Ways of God's Revealing Himself, to, and by the Prophets, Evinc'd from Scripture and Primitive Antiquity*. Edited by Edward Irving. 1715. Reprint, London: R. B. Seeley and W. Burnside, 1832.

Lamb, William. *M'Cheyne from the Pew: Being Extracts from the Diary of William Lamb*. Edited by Kirkwood Hewat. 1898. Reprint, Belfast: Ambassador, 1987.

Lane, Anthony N. S. *Calvin: Student of the Church Fathers*. Edinburgh: T. & T. Clark, 1999.

———. *Calvin and Bernard of Clairvaux*. Princeton: Princeton Theological Seminary, 1996.

Lee, Byung Sun. *"Christ's Sinful Flesh": Edward Irving's Christological Theology within the Context of His Life and Times*. Cambridge: Cambridge Scholars Publishing, 2013.

Letham, Robert. *The Westminster Assembly: Reading Its Theology in Historical Context*. Phillipsburg, NJ: P&R, 2009.

Lewis, Donald M., ed. *Dictionary of Evangelical Biography: 1730–1860*, vol. 2. Oxford: Blackwell, 1995.

———. ed. *The Future Shape of Anglican Ministry*. Vancouver: Regent College, 2004.

Lloyd-Jones, D. Martyn. *Preaching and Preachers*. London: Hodder & Stoughton, 1971.

———. *Preaching and Preachers*. 40th Anniversary ed. Grand Rapids: Zondervan, 2011.

Loane, Marcus L. *They Were Pilgrims*. 1970. Reprint, Edinburgh: Banner of Truth, 2006.

Long, Kimberly Bracken. *The Eucharistic Theology of the American Holy Fairs*. Louisville: Westminster John Knox, 2011.
Lopes, Augustus. "Calvin, Theologian of the Holy Spirit." *Scottish Bulletin of Evangelical Theology* 15 (1997) 38–49.
Love, Christopher. *The Works of Christopher Love*, vol. 1. Morgan, PA: Soli Deo Gloria, 1995.
Lovejoy, Arthur O. *Essays in the History of Ideas*. Baltimore: Johns Hopkins Press, 1948.
Lowber, James William. *Thought and Religion or The Mutual Contributions of Philosophy and Theology*. Boston: The Gorham Press, 1912.
Lyall, Francis. *Church and State in Scotland: Developing Law*. London: Routledge, 2016.
M'Cheyne, Robert Murray. *A Basket of Fragments*. 1848. Reprint, Inverness, Scotland: Christian Focus, 1975.
———. *The Believer's Joy*. 1858. Reprint, Glasgow: Free Presbyterian Publications, 1987.
———. *Comfort in Sorrow*. Fearn, Scotland: Christian Focus, 2002.
———. *Daily Bread: Being a Calendar for Reading through the Word of God in a Year*. Edinburgh: Banner of Truth Trust, 1842.
———. *Familiar Letters by the Rev. Robert Murray M'Cheyne: Containing an Account of His Travels as One of the Deputation Sent Out by the Church of Scotland on a Mission of Inquiry to the Jews in 1839*. Edited by Adam M'Cheyne. New York: Robert Carter, 1849.
———. *From the Preacher's Heart*. 1846. Reprint, Fearn, Scotland: Christian Focus, 1993.
———. *Helps to Devotion*. Glasgow: Free Presbyterian Publications, 1988.
———. *New Testament Sermons*. Edinburgh: Banner of Truth Trust, 2004.
———. *Old Testament Sermons*. Edinburgh: Banner of Truth Trust, 2004.
———. *The Passionate Preacher: Sermons of Robert Murray McCheyne*. Fearn, Scotland: Christian Focus Publications, 1999.
———. *Sermons of Robert Murray M'Cheyne*. London: Banner of Truth, 1961.
———. *Sermons on Hebrews*. Edinburgh: Banner of Truth Trust, 2004.
———. *The Seven Churches of Asia*. Fearn, Scotland: Christian Heritage, 2008.
———. *Songs of Zion to Cheer and Guide Pilgrims on Their Way to the New Jerusalem*. Dundee: William Middleton, 1843.
M'Crie, Thomas. *The Story of the Scottish Church: From the Reformation to the Disruption*. London: Blackie & Son, 1875.
M'Kerrow, J. *History of the Secession Church*. Glasgow: A. Fullerton and Co., 1841.
Macfarlan, Duncan. *A Treatise on the Authority, Ends, and Observance of the Christian Sabbath: With an Appendix, Containing a Variety of Documentary Evidence Respecting Prevalent Abuses, and Means for Their Supression*. Glasgow: William Collins, 1832.
Macgregor, Geddes. *Corpus Christi: The Nature of the Church According to the Reformed Tradition*. 1958. Reprint, Eugene, OR: Wipf & Stock, 2004.
Macgregor, Simon. *Proceedings of the General Assembly 1840*. Edinburgh: The Edinburgh Printing and Publishing Company, 1840.
MacIntosh, Mike, and Franklin Graham. *Falling in Love with Prayer*. Colorado Springs: Victor, 2004.
Mackintosh, H. R. *Types of Modern Theology*. London: Nisbet & Co., 1937.

Maclean, Donald John. "James Durham (1622–1658) and the Free Offer of the Gospel." *Puritan Reformed Journal* 2 (January 2010) 92–119.

Macleod, Donald. "The Doctrine of the Incarnation in Scottish Theology: Edward Irving." *Scottish Bulletin of Evangelical Theology* 9 (1991) 40–50.

MacLeod, John. *Scottish Theology in Relation to Church History*. 1943. Reprint, Edinburgh: Banner of Truth, 1974.

MacRae, Alexander. *Revivals in the Highlands and Islands in the 19th Century*. Stirling, Scotland: Eneas Mackay, 1906.

Marsden, George. *Jonathan Edwards: A Life*. New Haven, CT: Yale University Press, 2003.

Matter, E. Ann. *The Voice of My Beloved: The Song of Songs in Western Medieval Christianity*. Philadelphia: University of Pennsylvania Press, 1990.

Matthews, John W. *Anxious Souls Will Ask: The Christ-Centered Spirituality of Dietrich Bonhoeffer*. Grand Rapids: Eerdmans, 2005.

Maxwell, William D. *A History of Worship in the Church of Scotland*. London: Oxford University Press, 1955.

McCraw, Ian. *Victorian Dundee at Worship*. Dundee: Abertay Historical Society, 2002.

McClymond, Michael J., and Gerald R. McDermott. *The Theology of Jonathan Edwards*. Oxford: Oxford University Press, 2012.

McDonald, Suzanne. "Beholding the Glory of God in the Face of Jesus Christ: John Owen and the 'Reforming' of the Beatific Vision." In *The Ashgate Research Companion to John Owen's Theology*, edited by Kelly M. Kapic and Mark Jones, 141–58. Farnham, Surrey, England: Ashgate, 2012.

McFarlane, Graham W. P. *Christ and the Spirit: The Doctrine of the Incarnation according to Edward Irving*. Carlisle, England: Paternoster, 1996.

———. "Edward Irving and The Uniqueness of Christ." In *Mission and Meaning: Essays Presented to Peter Cotterell*, edited by Antony Billington and Max Turner, 217–29. Carlisle, England: Paternoster, 1995.

McGinn, Bernard, ed. *The Essential Writings of Christian Mysticism*. New York: Modern Library, 2006.

———. "*Unio Mystica*/Mystical Union." In *The Cambridge Companion to Christian Mysticism*, edited by Amy Hollywood and Patricia Z. Beckman, 200–10. Cambridge: Cambridge University Press, 2012.

McGrath, Alister E. *Christian Spirituality: An Introduction*. Oxford: Blackwell, 1999.

McGraw, Ryan M. *The Day of Worship: Reassessing the Christian Life in Light of the Sabbath*. Grand Rapids: Reformation Heritage, 2011.

———. *A Heavenly Directory: Trinitarian Piety, Public Worship and a Reassessment of John Owen's Theology*. Göttingen: Vandenhoeck & Ruprecht, 2014.

———. "Principles of Sabbath-Keeping: Jesus and Westminster." *Puritan Reformed Journal* 3 (January 2011) 316–27.

McKim, Donald K., and David F. Wright, eds. *Encyclopedia of the Reformed Faith*. Louisville: Westminster John Knox, 1992.

McLennan, Bruce. *McCheyne's Dundee*. Grand Rapids: Reformation Heritage, 2018.

McMullen, Michael. *God's Polished Arrow: William Chalmers Burns*. Fearn, Scotland: Christian Focus, 2000.

McMullen, Michael D. "McCheyne, Robert Murray." In *Oxford Dictionary of National Biography*, 122–23. Oxford: Oxford University Press, 2004.

McWilliams, David B. "The Covenant Theology of the Westminster Confession of Faith and Recent Criticism." *The Westminster Theological Journal* 53 (1991) 109-24.
Michael, Sally, ed. *Victorian Britain: An Encyclopedia*. New York: Routledge, 1988.
Miller, Basil. *Robert Murray M'Cheyne*. Pensacola, FL: Christian Life Books, 2003.
———. *Ten Famous Evangelists*. Grand Rapids: Zondervan, 1949.
Miller, Hugh. *The Two Parties in the Church of Scotland, Exhibited as Missionary and Anti-Missionary; Their Contendings in These Opposite Characters in the Past, and Their Statistics Now*. Edinburgh: John Johnstone, 1842.
Moncreiff, Henry Wellwood. *The Practice of the Free Church of Scotland in Her Several Courts*. Edinburgh: Maclaren and Macniven, 1877.
———. *The Vindication of the Free Church Claim of Right*. Edinburgh: Maclaren & Macniven, 1877.
Moody-Stuart, Alexander. *Recollections of the Late John Duncan, LL.D.: Professor of Hebrew and Oriental Languages, New College, Edinburgh*. Edinburgh: Edmonston and Douglas, 1872.
———. *The Song of Songs: An Exposition of the Song of Solomon*. London: James Nisbet and Co., 1860.
Moody Stuart, Kenneth. *Alexander Moody Stuart: A Memoir, Partly Autobiographical*. London: Hodder & Stoughton, 1899.
Morgan, Christopher W., and Robert A. Peterson. *Hell Under Fire: Modern Scholarship Reinvents Eternal Punishment*. Grand Rapids: Zondervan, 2004.
Morton, Thomas. *The Lord's Supper: Or, A Vindication of the Sacrament of the Blessed Body & Blood of Christ according to Its Primitive Institution*. London: R. M., 1652.
Mouw, Richard. *Calvinism in the Las Vegas Airport*. Grand Rapids: Zondervan, 2004.
Mullan, David George. *Scottish Puritanism, 1590-1638*. Oxford: Oxford University Press, 2000.
Muller, Richard A. *The Unaccommodated Calvin: Studies in the Foundation of a Theological Tradition*. Oxford: Oxford University Press, 2000.
Murison, Barbara. "'Old Favourites' or 'New Styles': Creating the Hymnal of the Presbyterian Church in Canada." In *Singing the Lord's Song in a Strange Land Hymnody in the History of North American Protestantism*, edited by Edith L. Blumhofer and Mark A. Noll, 64-91. Tuscaloosa: University of Alabama Press, 2014.
Murray, Douglas M. "The Sabbath Question in Victorian Scotland in Context." In *The Use and Abuse of Time in Christian History*, edited by Robert Norman Swanson, 319-30. Woodbridge, England: Boydell, 2002.
Murray, Iain H. *A Scottish Christian Heritage*. Edinburgh: Banner of Truth, 2006.
———. *The Puritan Hope: Revival and the Interpretation of Prophecy*. Edinburgh: Banner of Truth, 1971.
———. "Thomas Chalmers and The Revival of the Church." *Banner of Truth* 198 (March 1980) 1-32.
Nicole, Roger R. "Patrick Fairbairn and Biblical Hermeneutics as Related to the Quotations of the Old Testament in the New." In *Hermeneutics, Inerrancy, and the Bible*, edited by Earl D. Radmacher and Robert D. Preus, 767-76. Grand Rapids: Zondervan, 1984.
Noll, Mark A. "Jonathan Edwards, Edwardsian Theologies, and the Presbyterians." In *After Jonathan Edwards: The Courses of New England Theology*, edited by Oliver D. Crisp and Douglas A. Sweeney, 178-96. Oxford: Oxford University Press, 2012.

———. "Thomas Chalmers (1780–1847) in North America (ca. 1830–1917)." *Church History* 66 (December 1997) 762–77.
Old, Hughes Oliphant. *The Reading and Preaching of the Scriptures in the Worship of the Christian Church*, vol. 3. Grand Rapids: Eerdmans, 1999.
———. *The Reading and Preaching of the Scriptures in the Worship of the Christian Church*, vol. 6. Grand Rapids: Baker, 2007.
———. "Rescuing Spirituality from the Cloister." *Christianity Today* 38 (June 20, 1994) 27–29.
———. "What is Reformed Spirituality?" *Perspectives: A Journal of Reformed Thought* 9 (January 1994) 8–10.
Olford, S. F. and D. L. Olford. *Anointed Expository Preaching*. Nashville: B&H, 1998.
Oliphant, B. R. "Horatius Bonar (1808–1889), Hymn Writer, Theologian, Preacher, Churchman: A Study of His Religious Thought and Activity." PhD diss., University of Edinburgh, 1985.
Oliphant, Margaret Wilson. *Thomas Chalmers*. London: Metheun, 1905.
Owen, John. *Christologia: Or, a Declaration of the Glorious Mystery of the Person of Christ, God and Man*. Glasgow: Ebenezer Miller, 1790.
———. *An Exposition to the Epistle to the Hebrews*, vol. 2. Edinburgh: Banner of Truth, 1991.
———. *The Glorious Mystery of the Person of Christ, God and Man: To Which are Subjoined, Meditations and Discourses on the Glory of Christ*. New York: Robert Carter, 1839.
———. *Meditations and Discourses on the Glory of Christ in Two Parts*. Edinburgh: William Gray: 1750.
Oxford Dictionary of National Biography. Oxford: Oxford University Press, 2004.
Packer, J. I., and Carolyn Nystrom. *Praying: Finding Our Way through Duty to Delight*. Downers Grove, IL: InterVarsity, 2006.
Palau, Luis, Stephen Sorenson, and Amanda Sorenson. *Stop Pretending*. Colorado Springs: Victor, 2003.
Palmer, Robert E. "Andrew A. Bonar (1810–1892): A Study of His Life, Work, and Religious Thought." PhD diss., University of Edinburgh, 1955.
Parker, Kenneth. *The English Sabbath: A Study of Doctrine and Discipline from the Reformation to the Civil War*. Cambridge: Cambridge University Press, 1988.
Parsons, Gerald, and John Wolffe. *Religion in Victorian Britain*. 5 vols. Manchester: Manchester University Press, 1997.
Patterson, Mark. "Designing the Last Days: Edward Irving, The Albury Circle, and the Theology of *The Morning Watch*." PhD diss., King's College, London, 2001.
Perkins, Douglas Lloyd. "Thomas Chalmers: Urban Advocate of the Poor." *Urban Mission* 10 (1993) 25–36.
Peterson, Randall J. *Unity in Diversity: English Puritans and the Puritan Reformation, 1603–1689*. Leiden: Brill, 2014.
Philip, Adam. *The Devotional Literature of Scotland*. London: James Clarke, 1923.
Piggin, Stuart. "The Expanding Knowledge of God: Jonathan Edwards's Influence on Missionary Thinking and Promotion." In *Jonathan Edwards at Home and Abroad: Historical Memories, Cultural Movements, Global Horizons*, edited by David W. Kling and Douglas A. Sweeney, 266–96. Columbia, SC: University of South Carolina Press, 2003.
Pipa, Joseph A. *The Lord's Day*. Fearn, Scotland: Christian Focus, 1997.

Piper, John. "He Kissed the Rose and Felt the Thorn: Living and Dying in the Morning of Life." *Sermons* (blog), *desiringGod*, February 1, 2011, http://www.desiringgod.org/messages/he-kissed-the-rose-and-felt-the-thorn-living-and-dying-in-the-morning-of-life.
Pittock, Murray, ed. *The Edinburgh Companion to Scottish Romanticism*. Edinburgh: Edinburgh University Press, 2011.
Porter, Roy, and Mikulás Teich. *The Enlightenment in National Context*. Cambridge: Cambridge University Press, 1981.
Prime, Derek. *Robert Murray McCheyne: In the Footsteps of a Godly Scottish Pastor*. Leominster, UK: Day One, 2007.
Primrose, Gilbert. *The Table of the Lord*. London: Nicholas Bourne, 1626.
Primus, John H. "Calvin and the Puritan Sabbath: A Comparative Study." In *Exploring the Heritage of John Calvin*, edited by David E. Holwerda, 40–75. Grand Rapids: Baker, 1976.
———. *Holy Time: Moderate Puritanism and the Sabbath*. Macon, GA: Mercer University Press, 1989.
Quistrop, Heinrich. *Calvin's Doctrine of the Last Things*. Translated by Harold Knight. Eugene, OR: Wipf & Stock, 2009.
Raffe, Alasdair. "Presbyterians and Episcopalians: The Formation of Confessional Cultures in Scotland, 1660–1715." *The English Historical Review* 125 (2010) 570–98.
Rainy, Robert. *Three Lectures on the Church of Scotland, with Especial Reference to the Dean of Westminster's Recent Course on that Subject*. Edinburgh: John Maclaren, 1872.
Rainy, Robert, and James Mackenzie. *Life of William Cunningham*. London: T. Nelson and Sons, 1871.
Raith, Charles II. *After Merit: John Calvin's Theology of Good Works and Rewards*. Göttingen: Vandenhoeck & Ruprecht, 2016.
Reardon, Bernard. *Religion in the Age of Romanticism: Studies in Early Nineteenth-Century Thought*. Cambridge: Cambridge University Press, 1985.
Redekop, Benjamin W. "Reid's Influence in Britain, Germany, France, and America." In *The Cambridge Companion to Thomas Reid*, edited by Terence Cuneo and René van Woudenberg, 316. Cambridge: Cambridge University Press, 2004.
Reid, Alvin L. *Light the Fire: Raising Up a Generation to Live Radically for Jesus Christ*. Enumclaw, WA: WinePress, 2002.
Reid, Thomas. *An Inquiry into the Human Mind on the Principles of Common Sense*. Edited by Derek R. Brookes. 1764. Reprint, Edinburgh: Edinburgh University Press, 1997.
Reuver, Arie de. *Sweet Communion: Trajectories of Spirituality from the Middle Ages through the Further Reformation*. Translated by James A. De Jong. Grand Rapids: Baker Academic, 2007.
Richard, Guy M. *The Supremacy of God in the Theology of Samuel Rutherford*. Eugene, OR: Wipf & Stock, 2008.
Rittgers, Ronald K. *The Reformation of Suffering: Pastoral Theology and Lay Piety in Late Medieval and Early Modern Germany*. Oxford: Oxford University Press, 2012.
Robertson, C. J. A. "Early Scottish Railways and the Observance of the Sabbath." *The Scottish Historical Review* 57 (1978) 143–67.

Robertson, David. *Awakening: The Life and Ministry of Robert Murray McCheyne.* Fearn, Scotland: Christian Focus, 2004.

Rodger, Alan. *The Courts, The Church, and The Constitution: Aspects of the Disruption of 1843.* Edinburgh: Edinburgh University Press, 2008.

Rogers, Jack. *Presbyterian Creeds: A Guide to the Book of Confessions.* Louisville: Westminster John Knox, 1985.

Ross, John S. "Man about Town: Robert Murray M'Cheyne in London (1839)." *The Reformed Theological Review* 67 (2008) 29–40.

Roxborogh, John. "The Legacy of Thomas Chalmers." *International Bulletin of Missionary Research* 23 (October 1999) 173–76.

———. *Thomas Chalmers: Enthusiast for Mission: The Christian Good of Scotland and The Rise of the Missionary Movement.* Edinburgh: Rutherford House, 1999.

Sargent, Tony. *The Sacred Anointing.* Wheaton, IL: Crossway, 1994.

Sarkissian, Mike J. *Before God: The Biblical Doctrine of Prayer.* Longwood, FL: Xulon Press, 2009.

Schmidt, Leigh Eric. *Holy Fairs: Scotland and the Making of American Revolution.* Grand Rapids: Eerdmans, 2001.

Schwanda, Tom. *Soul Recreation: The Contemplative-Mystical Piety of Puritanism.* Eugene, OR: Pickwick, 2012.

Scott, Walter, ed. *The Evangelist: A Monthly Periodical Devoted to the True Gospel of Christ; and Designed to Discuss and Define the Facts, Principles, Duties, and Privileges of Christianity, and Show the Perfect Adaptation of the Gospel to the Nature and Wants of Man in His Present State,* vol. 8. Cincinnati: Hefley, Hubbell & Co., 1840.

Sefton, Henry. "Continuity and Discontinuity: The Lord's Supper in Historical Perspective." *Theology in Scotland* 20 (2008) 53–58.

Shaw, Ian J. "Thomas Chalmers, David Nasmith, and the Origins of the City Mission Movement." *The Evangelical Quarterly* 76 (January 2004) 31–46.

Sher, R. B. *Church and University in the Scottish Enlightenment: The Moderate Literati of Edinburgh.* Edinburgh: Edinburgh University Press, 1985.

Sibbes, Richard. *Works of Richard Sibbes,* vol. 4. Edinburgh: Banner of Truth, 1983.

Sloan, C. Joanne, and Cheryl Sloan Wray. *A Life That Matters: Spiritual Disciplines That Change the World.* Birmingham, AL: New Hope Publishers, 2002.

Smart, Robert Davis, Michael A.G. Haykin, and Ian Hugh Clary, eds. *Pentecostal Outpourings: Revival and the Reformed Tradition.* Grand Rapids: Reformation Heritage, 2016.

Smellie, Alexander. *Biography of R. M. McCheyne.* 1913. Reprint, Fearn: Scotland: Christian Focus, 1995.

Smith, George. *The Life of Alexander Duff.* London: Hodder & Stoughton, 1881.

———. *A Modern Apostle: Alexander Somerville.* London: John Murray, 1891.

Smith, J. C. *Robert Murray M'Cheyne: A Good Minister of Jesus Christ.* 1870. Reprint, Belfast: Ambassador Productions, 1998.

Smith, Mark A. "Religion." In *A Companion to Nineteenth-Century Britain,* edited by Chris Williams, 342–43. Oxford: Blackwell, 2004.

Smith, S. F., ed. *The Christian Review,* vol. 13. Boston: John Putnam, 1848.

Solberg, Winton U. *Redeem the Time: The Puritan Sabbath in Early America.* Cambridge, MA: Harvard University Press, 1977.

Somerville, Alexander. *Precious Seed Sown in Many Lands.* London: John Murray, 1890.

Spurgeon, C. H. *Commenting and Commentaries: Lectures Addresses to the Students of the Pastor's College, Metropolitan Tabernacle, with a List of the Best Biblical Commentaries and Expositions, Also a Lecture on Eccentric Preachers with a Complete List of All of Spurgeon's Sermons, with the Scripture Texts Used.* New York: Sheldon & Company, 1876.

———. *Lectures to My Students: A Selection from Addresses Delivered to the Students of the Pastors' College Metropolitan Tabernacle, London.* New York: Robert Carter & Brothers, 1890.

Stanford, Reid W. "Bernard of Clairvaux in the Thought of John Calvin." *Westminster Theological Journal* 41 (1978) 127–45.

Stanley, Arthur Penrhyn. *Lectures on the History of the Church of Scotland: Delivered in Edinburgh in 1872.* London: John Murray, 1879.

Steel, Robert. *The Achievements of Youth.* Edinburgh: T. Nelson and Sons, 1890.

———. *Burning and Shining Lights, Or, Memoirs of Eminent Ministers of Christ.* London: T. Nelson and Sons, 1864.

Stek, John H. "Biblical Typology Yesterday and Today." *Calvin Theological Journal* 5 (November 1970) 133–62.

Stewart, James Alexander. *Robert Murray McCheyne: Scholar, Saint, Seer, Soul Winner.* Philadelphia: Revival Literature, 1964.

———. *William Chalmers Burns: A Man with a Passion for Souls.* Alexandria, VA: Lamplighter, 1963.

Stewart, M. A., ed. *Studies in the Philosophy of the Scottish Enlightenment.* Oxford: Clarendon Press, 1990.

Stewart, William. *British and Irish Poets: A Biographical Dictionary, 449–2006.* Jefferson, NC: McFarland and Company, 2014.

Stubenrauch, Joseph. *The Evangelical Age of Ingenuity in Industrial Britain.* Oxford: Oxford University Press, 2016.

Sweeney, Douglas A. *Edwards the Exegete: Biblical Interpretation and Anglo-Protestant Culture on the Edge of the Enlightenment.* Oxford: Oxford University Press, 2016.

Tamburello, Dennis E. *Union with Christ: John Calvin and the Mysticism of St. Bernard.* Louisville: Westminster John Knox, 1994.

The Westminster Standards. Norcross, GA: Great Commission Publications, 1978.

Thomas, I. D. E., ed. *A Puritan Golden Treasury.* Edinburgh: Banner of Truth, 1977.

Thomson, Thomas. *A Biographical Dictionary of Eminent Scotsmen.* Glasgow: Blackie and Son, 1855.

Torrance, J. B. "Covenant or Contract? A Study of the Theological Background of Worship in Seventeenth-Century Scotland." *Scottish Journal of Theology* 23 (1970) 51–76.

———. "Strengths and Weaknesses of the Westminster Theology." In *The Westminster Confession*, edited by Alistair Heron, 40–53. Edinburgh: St. Andrews, 1982.

Tulloch, John. "Dean Stanley and the Moderates." *The Contemporary Review* 20 (1872) 698–717.

Turretin, Francis. *Institutes of Elenctic Theology*, vol. 3. Translated by George Musgrave Giger. Phillipsburg, NJ: P&R, 1997.

Tylenda, Joseph. "Calvin and Christ's Presence in the Supper—True or Real." *Scottish Journal of Theology* 27 (1974) 65–75.

Van Valen, L. J. *Constrained by His Love: A New Biography on Robert Murray McCheyne.* Fearn, Scotland: Christian Focus, 2002.

VanDoodewaard, William. "Marrow Theology and Secession Church History." *The Westminster Theological Journal* 71 (September 2009) 399–416.

Vasholz, Robert I. "Amusements on the Sabbath: A Puritan Response." *Presbyterion* 13 (1987) 24–28.

Venema, Cornelius P. *Christ & Covenant Theology: Essays on Election, Republication, and the Covenants*. Phillipsburg, NJ: P&R, 2017.

Voges, Friedhelm. "Moderate and Evangelical Thinking in the Later Eighteenth Century: Differences and Shared Attitudes." *Records of Scottish Church Historical Society* 22 (1986) 141–57.

Walker, Charles. "Thomas Chalmers: A Christian Strategist." *Banner of Truth* (May 1969) 29–36.

Warfield, B. B. "John Calvin the Theologian." In *Calvin and Augustine*, edited by Samuel G. Craig. Philadelphia: Presbyterian and Reformed, 1956.

Warfield, E. D., ed. *The Works of Benjamin B. Warfield*. 10 vols. 1931. Reprint, Grand Rapids: Baker, 1981.

Watson, Jean L. *Life of Robert Smith Candlish*. Edinburgh: James Gemmell, 1882.

Watson, Thomas. *The Saint's Spiritual Delight, and a Christian on the Mount*. London: The Religious Tract Society, 1657.

Watt, Hugh. *Thomas Chalmers and the Disruption*. Edinburgh: T. Nelson and Sons, 1943.

Weddle, David A. "The Melancholy Saint: Jonathan Edwards's Interpretation of David Brainerd as a Model of Evangelical Spirituality." *Harvard Theological Review* 81 (1988) 297–318.

Whedon, D. D., ed. *The Methodist Review*. New York: Nelson & Phillips, 1873.

Whytock, Jack. *An Educated Clergy: Scottish Theological Education and Training in the Kirk and Secession, 1560–1850*. Eugene, OR: Wipf & Stock, 2007.

Wiersbe, Warren W. *Be Equipped: Acquiring the Tools for Spiritual Success*. Colorado Springs: David C. Cook, 2010.

Wigley, J. *The Rise and Fall of the Victorian Sunday*. Manchester: Manchester University Press, 1980.

Wilkinson, Paul Richard. *For Zion's Sake: Christian Zionism and the Role of John Nelson Darby*. Eugene, OR: Wipf & Stock, 2008.

Wilks, Washington. *Edward Irving: An Ecclesiastical and Literary Biography*. London: W. Freeman, 1854.

Willard, Dallas. "Christ-Centered Piety." In *Where Shall My Wond'ring Soul Begin? The Landscape of Evangelical Piety and Thought*, edited by Mark A. Noll and Ronald F. Theimann, 27–35. Grand Rapids: Eerdmans, 2000.

Williams, Chris, ed. *A Companion to Nineteenth-Century Britain*. Oxford: Blackwell, 2004.

Wilson, William. *Free Church Principles*. Edinburgh: Macniven & Wallace, 1887.

———. *Memorials of Robert Smith Candlish*. Edinburgh: Adam and Charles Black, 1880.

Withrington, Donald J. "The Disruption: A Century and a Half of Historical Interpretation." *Record of the Scottish Church History Society* 25 (1993) 118–53.

Wolffe, John. *The Expansion of Evangelicalism: The Age of Wilberforce, More, Chalmers and Finney: A History of Evangelicalism. People, Movements and Ideas in the English-Speaking World*. Downers Grove, IL: InterVarsity, 2007.

Woolsey, Andrew. *Unity and Continuity in Covenantal Thought: A Study in the Reformed Tradition to the Westminster Assembly*. Grand Rapids: Reformation Heritage, 2012.

Yeaworth, David Victor. "Robert Murray M'Cheyne (1813–1843): A Study of an Early Nineteenth-Century Scottish Evangelical." PhD diss., University of Edinburgh, 1957.

Yuille, J. Stephen. *Looking unto Jesus: The Christ-Centered Piety of Seventeenth-Century Baptists*. Eugene, OR: Pickwick, 2013.

———. *Puritan Spirituality: The Fear of God in the Affective Theology of George Swinnock*. Eugene, OR: Wipf & Stock, 2008.

Index

Baxter, Richard, 69
Bebbington, David, 56
Brainerd, David, 70, 71–72, 94n138,
    109n55, 171n10
Bonar, Andrew, 12
    Appoint to the Mission of Inquiry,
        34n114
    Early Friendship with M'Cheyne,
        24–25
    Eschatology 212–214,
    Interaction with M'Cheyne on
        Preaching, 152
    Recommended to St. Peter's, 29
    Tract on Baptism 128n43
Bonar, John, 27, 28, 43, 65–66
Boston, Thomas, 69, 129n49, 201
Brunton, Alexander, 18, 22
Burns, William Chalmers, 36–37, 38, 79,
    116, 123n13, 170, 181, 184, 194
Calvin, John, 68–69, 91, 100–01n10,
    132n60, 195n30, 223n78
Candlish, Robert Smith, 3, 29, 30, 33,
    33n113, 43, 49, 66–67, 119,
    182n72
Chalmers, Thomas, 3
    Free Offer of the Gospel, 94–95
    Influence on M'Cheyne, 22–24, 43,
        63–64, 70–71, 94–95
    Hermeneutics, 147–48
    Philosophy, 54–55
    Use of Johnathan Edwards, 70–71
Chapel Act, 47
Claim of Right, 48
Common Sense Realism, 54–55
Duncan, Henry, 3, 43, 61–62

Duncan, John, 74
Edwards, Jonathan, 70–72, 94n138,
    102n13, 163
Enlightenment, 52, 57
Erastianism in the Church of Scotland,
    46–47
Flavel, John, 69
Great Disruption, 43, 47, 48
Hume, David, 53
Irving, Edward, 61, 209–12
Knox, John, 22, 68, 69,
Luther, Martin, 68
M'Cheyne, Adam, 13–15
M'Cheyne, David, 19–20
M'Cheyne, Robert Murray,
    Bible Reading, 122–26
    Biography, 13–42
    Call to St. Peter's, 29–31
    Church Extension, 184–87
    Consideration of Missionary Work,
        170–71n10
    Conversion, 18–21
    Covenant Theology, 76–80
    Death, 40–41
    Education, 15–18
    Eternal Perspective, 220–24
    Free Offer of the Gospel, 93–97
    Itinerant Ministry, 38–40, 169–70
    Millenarianism, 208–209, 215
    Ministry to Children, 33, 175–78
    Mission of Inquiry, 33–35
    Ordination, 32
    "Personal Reformation," 109–110,
        112–13, 119, 136, 137, 140, 142
    Prayer, 32–33, 135–143

M'Cheyne, Robert Murray(Continued),
   Preaching, 28–29, 65, 88–89, 146–67
   Presbytery Exams, 25–26
   Recently Reprinted Sermons, 6
   Role in the Ten Years' Conflict, 49–52
   Sabbatarianism, 194–206
   Sacraments, 126–35
   Struggles with Sin, 83–84
   Subscription to the Westminster Standards, 75–76
   Use of "Trysts" for the Means of Grace, 11, 105–06, 113, 122, 133, 134, 144, 190, 200, 203, 204, 227
   Typology, 148–49
   View of the Song of Songs, 100–04
   Visitation, 28, 32, 65, 65, 171–75
McMullen, Michael, 6–7
Moderatism in the Church of Scotland, 44–45
Moody-Stuart, Alexander, 74, 119
Muir, William, 18
Owen, John, 69, 102, 139n97, 220n58
Reid, Thomas, 53–54
Revival, 36–38, 178–84, 219
Romanticism, 56, 57–58
Rutherford, Samuel, 9, 69–70, 98, 101n13, 102
Sabbath Railroad Controversy, 191–194
Scottish Enlightenment, 52n42, 53,
Somerville, Alexander, 23, 24–25
Ten Years' Conflict, 43, 47–52
Veto Act, 47
Victorian Culture, 58–59
Welsh, David, 22, 29

www.ingramcontent.com/pod-product-compliance
Lightning Source LLC
Chambersburg PA
CBHW050843230426
43667CB00012B/2129